Blessed With Hope

DOREEN MURPHY

Copyrights © 2024 by Doreen Murphy
All Rights Reserved

No part of this publication may be reproduced, distributed, or transmitted in any form or by any means, including photocopying, recording, or other electronic or mechanical methods, without the prior written permission of the publisher, except as permitted by U.S. copyright law. For permission requests, contact the author.

First edition 2024

Some names have been changed to protect the privacy of the individuals.

This book is dedicated to Michael, my husband, my dearest friend, confidante, advisor and my strength, who encouraged me in the writing of this book. He sensed that it would be the greatest part of my healing and, hopefully, the healing of many others who find themselves in similar circumstances.

ACKNOWLEDGMENTS

I would like to thank the many family members and friends who supported me during the difficult years of my childhood and former marriage. Thanks also go to my church family, who prayed for me and gave me strength when I needed it most. Lastly, I want to thank my husband, Michael, without whose encouragement this book would not have been written.

ABOUT THE AUTHOR

Doreen Murphy was born in the midst of the bombing of London during World War II. Following her father's death, her mother remarried a physically abusive man, who, when Doreen was a teenager, took the family to South Africa. There, she met and married a man whom she would later discover was a psychopath. For her children's sake, she remained in the marriage until his death, after being shot. Her story is one of survival and how she was able to break the cycle of abuse and find happiness with a new life in America.

CONTENTS

PREFACE xiii
INTRODUCTION xv

PART ONE: UNWANTED

BLITZ BABY 1
WALES 7
BOARDING SCHOOL 11
LIVING WITH FEAR 16
DYMCHURCH 20
8, FARNABY ROAD 23
BROMLEY ROAD SCHOOL 29
RUDE AWAKENINGS 33
THE TOMBOY 38
STEPFATHER 44
A MINI WAR-ZONE 48
CHORES AND CHILDHOOD MEMORIES 51
CALAMITIES 59

VISITORS FROM SOUTH AFRICA 65
GRAMMAR SCHOOL 69
RUNAWAY 74
A BABY BROTHER 78
MONEY MATTERS 81
DEVON 86
ALMOST GROWN, WITH BUNIONS! 90
ST. NICHOLAS COLLEGE 94
BAD EXPERIENCES 105
MISS KERRISK 110
ANOTHER PAUL WELMAN 113
THE FINAL STRAW 117
MY ESCAPE 121
WORMWOOD SCRUBS 129
ONE LAST CHANCE 132
THE MOVIES 137
TEDDY 142
LEAVING ENGLAND 148

PART TWO: UNLOVED

THE CARNARVON CASTLE 155
PRETORIA 162
DESMOND 167
SETTLING IN 171

BREAKING TIES	177
THE ENGAGEMENT	183
CHANGES	190
THE WEDDING	195
THE HONEYMOON	201
MARRIED LIFE	203
A PIGEON PAIR	206
BETRAYAL	216
OUR NEW HOME	221
EMERGENCY	228
PAPPIE	231
A CLOSE CALL	234
A MAJOR DECISION	237
MOVING AGAIN AND AGAIN	240
THE PHONE CALL	247
ANOTHER BABY	250
LYTTELTON	255
A DEATH AND A BIRTH	266
LILY	274
CAMPING OUT	277
BRONBERRIK	287
TRYING AGAIN	297
GUN SHOTS	309
PROBLEMS	316
THE TUMBLEWEED TAVERN	320

NIGHT CALLS 337
DES' DREAM HOUSE 343
CULPRIT IDENTIFIED 352
ST. LUCIA 361
A SHOT IN THE NIGHT... 365
THE COURT CASE 380
LIFE AFTER JUDGMENT 386
WESKOPPIES.. 390
CONSTANTIA.. 400
HOME AGAIN 405
THE AUCTION 410
A DATE TO REMEMBER 418
REVENGE 426
A WIDOW 431
DREAMS DO COME TRUE................................... 441
DOWN THE AISLE TO HAPPINESS 446

PART THREE: BLESSED!

A NEW BEGINNING... 455
FAMILY MATTERS 466
HEALTHY SOLUTIONS.. 472
MAMA AND MICHAEL... 475
MY ULTIMATE HEALING..................................... 480

PREFACE

Until now, I was adamant that this was a story I couldn't write, because I felt that too many people might be hurt by it, but those people have long since passed away. I also hesitated because my story is so bizarre, I felt readers would be reluctant to believe it.

Throughout my lifetime, I have come across many victims of physical and mental abuse. This led me to believe that it would be helpful for them to know that someone else who was trapped in similar circumstances, was able to break the cycle of abuse.

Over the years, my husband, Michael, always a good listener, lovingly encouraged me to share my past with him. Knowing that he truly cared, I was able to share both the good and the bad.

The night before I began writing, I lay awake for part of the night thinking about my childhood and early life, recalling some of the events I had carefully hidden away, stored in a safe place where they could no longer cause me pain. When I awoke at four in the morning with the first paragraph of my story clearly fixed in my mind, I knew it was time to begin.

I wrote that day and carried on through the next. I found all the information I needed in old records, as well as in my Bible and old calendars. My roots, the very foundation of my life, were there before me, waiting to be written down, and the words tumbled onto the page at such a speed I could barely keep up with them. I marveled at my ability to write so effortlessly, having never written anything as challenging as this before. Memories were revealed that my brain had stored, some that I was not even aware of until I needed them for this, the story of my life.

INTRODUCTION

If my mother had had her way, I wouldn't be here to tell this story. World War II was declared in September of 1939, and I was born a year later. With her world falling apart, and my father soon to be sent to the battlefront, my impending birth must have been a terrifying prospect for her. I was thirteen years old before my mother felt compelled to tell me that she had attempted to end her pregnancy. Fortunately, her lack of surgical skill turned out to be the first of many narrow escapes, in what was to become an exciting, although not always joyful, life.

Life has changed in many ways since I was a child. Growing up in war-torn England was a time of uncertainty and terror. The difficult years following the war were not much better, but they provided a far simpler, and, in some ways, a happier world than we know today. In others, it was not. Basic nutrition was a constant concern. But with the bombing finally at an end, having scarcities of everything was hardly considered a hardship by comparison and I was always blessed with the hope that things would get better. In many ways, those years were an opportunity to be more creative and resourceful than had been necessary before the war.

Young girls always face a certain amount of risk. Finding safe passage through the dangers and hardships of life can be fraught with unpleasant experiences. Sometimes, they can take a lifetime to overcome, as they did for me. I was fortunate to find a path to safety, and have been blessed with a wonderful life lived out on three continents. I became a mother and grandmother with many steadfast and loyal friends, experiencing some of the best and sometimes the worst that life has to offer. Every woman who survives to become a grandmother has a story to tell. This is mine.

PART ONE: UNWANTED

BLITZ BABY

(England during the 1940s and 1950s)

Germany invaded Poland on September 1st, 1939. Great Britain entered the war on September 3rd, and World War II was declared. It changed everything. Food and clothing were rationed, bomb shelters were built in back yards, and black-outs and sirens became a way of life.

I was born in London on October 18th, 1940, during the heaviest bombardment of the Blitz. With bombs falling all around us, and aircraft dogfighting overhead, the nurse assisting my delivery looked up beseechingly and said, "Oh please stop. We have enough of a mess down here already," although, according to my mother, her language wasn't that polite.

As soon as my mother had delivered, I was literally thrown into her arms, and she was ordered to run to the hallway where, away from the windows, it was marginally safer. She must have been in greater terror than pain, because she did as she was told, and we both survived the attack.

At the time, I was thought to be in good health, and only when I was fifteen, did I discover from an X-ray, that I had suffered a broken collarbone. It knitted itself back together in a fashion, but left the bone slightly deformed. The doctor concluded that it must have happened during my birth, or shortly thereafter. My mother told me, that as a baby, I never stopped crying, which was possibly due to the pain caused by the broken collar bone, but there was no way she could have known about it. As a result, I was known affectionately as Grizzleguts, an unflattering name for crybaby. My mother must have been sorely tested, having a baby that cried all the time, while everything around her was in such turmoil.

And so, the scene was set for my life to begin, starting with World War II, and followed by many small private wars that were to be fought on the stage of my world during the first fifty years of my life.

My first six weeks were spent with my parents and older sister, Sheila, in our house in West Wickham, Kent, about ten miles outside London. We lived next door to my father's sister, Lillian and her husband, Jack.

When war broke out, my father and Uncle Jack built a bomb shelter between our adjoining yards. Lined with corrugated iron, and because it had to house both families, it was twice the size of a regular shelter. They covered it with earth, and to make it look more attractive, they built a rockery on top with weathered rocks and plants. The shelter became an unwelcome alternative to our two houses every time the siren sounded the warning of an impending attack, and just prior to my birth, it saved our lives on at least one occasion.

Three weeks before I was born, the siren sounded at mid-morning. My father and Uncle Jack were at work, so my mother, Sheila and Aunt Lillian quickly ran to the shelter. When Aunt Lillian discovered that she had forgotten her purse in the house, she ran back for it. On her return, just as she entered the shelter, a British Spitfire fighter plane, shot down during aerial combat, crashed into Aunt Lillian's house, totally demolishing it. The force of the blast caught Aunt Lillian in the walled entry to the bomb shelter, trapping her, and burying my pregnant mother and sister inside. When the Spitfire crashed, the engine separated from the fuselage and continued on its journey to the end of my mother's yard, crashed through the fence, and plowed the length of the neighbor's yard, before coming to rest against the wall of their house.

Doreen's aunt's house demolished by the Spitfire fighter plane

When the rescue crew arrived, Aunt Lillian was pulled from the entry with her face and arm full of shrapnel, and rushed to hospital by ambulance. My mother and sister were then dug out of the shelter, and since there was no other ambulance available, they were transported by fire engine to a different hospital. When my father arrived home from work, he was told that my mother and sister had been taken to hospital, and he searched frantically for hours before locating them.

Even though I was yet to be born, one thing that I inherited from the crash, was the nickname of *Spitfire*. Aunt Lillian bore the scars of her ordeal for the rest of her life. Her only son, my cousin Roy, told me that my father found a machine gun in the rubble left by the crash, and announced that he was going to shoot down all the Gerries – our name for the Germans – but the machine gun wasn't loaded, and the War Office had other plans for my father.

My father, Jack Wheble, was born in 1910 in the London suburb of Lewisham. I never learned much about him, since I grew up after he went to war and, ultimately, his early death. Never having known him, I didn't even have a name for him. My father was one of four children, a gentle soul who, for seven years, apprenticed to be a piano tuner and French polisher, before entering the trade.

My mother, Martha Jane Evans, known as Mattie by family and friends, was the sixth of eight children. She was born in 1913, and grew up in the small mining village of Merthyr Vale in Glamorgan, South Wales. Mummy was the youngest sister of the family, and beloved by all her siblings. Being a girl in Wales called for my mother to be domesticated at a young age, and she learned to cook for the family when she was just eight years old. Having responsibility thrust upon her from an early age, she grew up quickly, and as money was short at home, she left school and went to work at the age of fourteen. As there was no work for her in Merthyr, she traveled to London where, working as a maid, she received free board and lodging. A couple of years later, she moved in with her Auntie Sally and found employment in a chocolate factory.

While working in London, Mummy's cousin, Jackie Busby, took a photograph of Mummy to work and showed it to my father who was nineteen at the time. He asked to meet my mother, who was then almost sixteen. On their first date, my father took her to the movies, and of course, to be proper, cousin Jackie went along as their chaperone. My father could barely understand my mother's strong Welsh accent, so he had to constantly ask Jackie what my mother was saying. She was a pretty girl, and I am sure my father was smitten, even if he couldn't understand her. Two weeks later, no doubt sensing that my father was serious about the young lady, his parents asked to meet her. After dating for almost four years, they married, and a few years later were blessed with the birth of my sister Sheila, who was their only child, until I was born five years later.

During the early days of World War II, the German Luftwaffe mounted a sustained bombing attack on English cities. Beginning in September 1940, London was shattered by daily aerial bombings, which lasted for two months. During the Blitz, The Battle of Britain, as it was called, destroyed a million homes and killed 40,000 people.

To escape the Blitz, many women and children were sent to the countryside. I was six weeks old when my father was called into national service. During his physical examination, he was diagnosed with a duodenal ulcer, but the army accepted him anyway, and sent him to the British Military Barracks at Aldershot, near London. My mother was evacuated to Wales with Sheila and me. Mummy bundled up what belongings she could carry, and took us to our grandparents in South Wales.

At the railway station, chaos awaited us, with hundreds of people milling around saying their tearful farewells. Unlike my sister and myself, many less fortunate children were evacuated without their parents. Hysterical, some were being torn from the arms of their parents by volunteers who were organizing the evacuation. Each child had to wear an identification tag with their name on it. Children traveling without their parents were transported to families in other parts of the British Isles, who had kindly opened their hearts and homes, offering them a safe haven. Some mothers, who had made the decision to let their children go, changed their minds at the last minute and attempted to retrieve their little ones from the long lines of tearful children behind the barriers, only to be told they could not. Once the papers had been signed, the decision was final. The children would be relatively safe in the countryside, but being separated from their parents made for many heartbreaking farewells.

Waiting for our train to Wales to arrive, Mummy stood on one platform with me in her arms, holding Sheila's hand, while my father stood helplessly on the opposite platform in his army uniform. We were to part for our separate destinations on different trains. My parents were both crying, not knowing if they would ever see one another again.

The long journey to Wales was an arduous one. Mummy's heart was breaking, and fear of what the future held must have been overwhelming for her. I was told that I cried a lot and drank sorrow-filled milk at her breast, while the picturesque English countryside we traveled through offered no comfort on that sad journey.

Arriving in Cardiff, the train full of refugees then parted company to travel on different trains and buses to destinations all over Wales. I was to become fatherless, but I was fortunate to have a grandfather and uncles to take his place for a few years. I was also to discover what it was like to be a part of a caring community in a small mining village in Wales.

WALES

My grandparents' house in Merthyr Vale became home for Mummy, Sheila and me, and there I spent the next three years of my life, along with many other members of our family who sought refuge there during the war years. Regrettably, I have no recollection of those years surrounded by a close, loving family.

Meanwhile, my father trained hard in Aldershot for six months. During this time, he was granted one week's leave, and was able to visit us in Wales. My parents made the most of those seven precious days together. The family took over the care of Sheila and me, to allow them as much time together as possible. I am sure they must have felt the same desperation as many other young couples at that time, not knowing if there would be any tomorrows. My grandparents would tell of their long walks up in the mountains, just wanting to spend time alone together. All too soon, it was time for my father to return to camp.

Sheila and I received a lot of attention from the family. I was fed and nursed in the old Welsh family shawl, before being placed in my cradle. Since I cried all the time, my Granddad tied a string on his finger and attached it to the cradle. With this arrangement, he was able to rock me all through the night, without having to get out of bed.

Doreen's parents - taken the day her father went to war

Two or three months passed, while Mummy anxiously waited for the postman to bring news from my father. When he finally came home for the last time, he arrived in his army uniform, with a pack on his back and a rifle over his shoulder. The few days flew by until inevitably, the time came for our final farewells. This was the last time my father was able to hold me in his arms, and sadly, I cannot remember the warmth of his breath on my face, or the tender love he must have felt for me, knowing that he might never see me growing up. How I wish I could! My parents clung desperately to each other. Granny stood holding me in the shawl, while Granddad held Sheila's hand. My father kissed

Granny, Sheila and me and shook Granddad's hand. He then turned to my grandparents and said, "Please look after Mattie and my two girls."

"That Jack is a promise we will keep," my Granddad replied. I can only imagine the heartbreak of those final moments of parting for my parents.

My father had trained as a gunner in the Royal Artillery, before being shipped overseas to fight against the Japanese. There, along with his regiment, he was captured and became a Japanese prisoner of war. As prisoners of war, they were shipped to Thailand to build a railway through the jungle, stretching from Thailand to Burma. It became known as the Death Railway.

The heat and disease of the jungle made it almost impossible to work under the conditions of cruelty, sickness, and malnutrition they suffered. With no medical attention, it took the lives of 100,000 men during the railway's construction, and my father was one of them. Suffering from malaria and dysentery, he died at the age of thirty-three.

The next few years must have been difficult for Mummy, raising two children without a husband, not knowing if he would ever return from the war. I think she was wise to stay in Wales for as long as she did, even though the Blitz had long since ended. Eventually, perhaps because of the cramped living conditions in Wales, she probably felt the need for her own home, and so we returned to our house in West Wickham.

After living in hope for my father's safe return, my mother waited for more than a year after his death to receive an official notification from the war office. She also received a letter of condolence from King George, which, at the time, must have been of small consolation.

My father was buried in Thailand, but after the war, his remains were moved to Kranji War Cemetery north of the city of Singapore, overlooking the Straits of Johor. It was to take many years before I was in a position to visit his grave, and bring closure in my heart for the father I never knew.

Long after the war had ended, while watching a newsreel at our local movie theater, they showed prisoners of war from the concentration camps in Thailand. Those disturbing images will forever remain etched in my memory. The naked prisoners were lined up, waiting to receive their meager rations of food, and on seeing those walking skeletons, I realized with horror that one of them could well have been my father.

I was five years old when the war ended, and I now consider it a blessing that my only recollections of it are the smells and sounds associated with that terrible time. Sirens and the sound of planes diving still give me cold chills and make it difficult for me to breathe. I also find the smell of rubber nauseating, and I put it down to the memory of the claustrophobic sensation I felt while practicing wearing my gas mask. Memories of the war years that took so many innocent lives, are better forgotten, and I am grateful that I remember so little.

BOARDING SCHOOL

Towards the end of 1943, Mummy sold our house in West Wickham and rented a house in Shortlands, a small village in Kent. I don't know exactly why, but I suspect it had something to do with our finances. The house in Shortlands had a living room, dining room and kitchen downstairs and three small bedrooms and a bathroom upstairs.

Each time there was a bomb blast nearby, the front door landed on the stairs facing the entrance. It was in the closet beneath those same stairs where we took refuge during attacks, as we didn't have a bomb shelter in the yard. The blast shattered our windows, and after replacing them several times, Mummy made do with the compulsory black-out curtains.

My most vivid memory of that house was of the kitchen. I was a difficult child, and with Mummy under constant stress, she had limited tolerance for my disobedience. I spent much of my time sitting on a chair facing the corner of the kitchen, as an added punishment, after Mummy had given me a spanking for one of my many misdemeanors. An hour or more spent in the corner was an excruciating experience for a restless little girl, and I don't recall that it ever had the desired effect.

Someone offered us a cat, telling us it was half-Siamese, and Blackie entered our lives. In the house, he was quite tame, but outside, he became wild and impossible to catch. He was black, except for a small patch of white under his chin, and he looked nothing like a Siamese cat. I loved to stroke his soft, shiny fur and childishly, because we both had green eyes, I felt he was mostly mine.

Shortlands is situated between the towns of Bromley and Beckenham, and it was while we lived there that my formal education began. I was three and a half, and Sheila was nine when Mummy enrolled us at a local boarding school run by two elderly sisters, Miss Kendall and Miss Constance. They didn't usually take girls under the age of five, but somehow, Mummy persuaded them to take me, and I became the youngest pupil at the school. Sheila went first, and I followed a few days later. Because it was so traumatic, I can still remember the day Mummy walked me to school as if it were yesterday. I was frightened, and didn't want to go, forcing her to drag me all the way.

Because the school fees were more than Mummy could afford, she agreed that Sheila and I could help with the chores to offset the expenses. Sheila swept the rooms, while my job was to take the small dustpan and brush, sweep up the dirt and throw it in the trash can.

I also helped preparing the vegetables, and I vividly remember being awakened one night at midnight by Miss Constance. She discovered me in the kitchen when she went to lock up for the night. Left alone in the large kitchen, I had fallen asleep with my head resting on the mountain of fresh peas that I had been shelling. Miss Constance took me by the hand and led me upstairs, where she put me to bed. I wasn't used to having someone put me to bed and tuck me in, and it made me feel special.

The two spinsters were kindly ladies. Miss Kendall was tall and thin with a stern face and she wore mostly black or navy dresses almost down to her ankles. She grew to love Sheila dearly, and they corresponded for many years after we left the school. Miss Constance was short, stout and gentle, and wore long brown dresses. As our school uniform was a brown tunic over a white blouse worn with a brown blazer, life at boarding school was not very colorful.

Although it lacked color, the Raymont School for Girls was considered an excellent school for teaching girls to become young ladies. Sheila and I learned deportment and poise. We were taught to walk across the room with a few books stacked on our heads without letting them fall, which is not easy until you master the art of good posture. We also received elocution lessons, and reciting the words, "How now, brown cow, grazing in the green, green pastures," became a part of my daily tuition. We were also taught the usual lessons of reading, writing and arithmetic.

We ate good healthy food at the school. With the war still ongoing, I am sure it wasn't easy to find ample nutritious food, but Miss Kendall and Miss Constance were resourceful. They planted a large vegetable garden at the back of the school grounds, and we enjoyed fresh vegetables with our meals. At night, before going to bed, we were given a tablespoon of cod liver oil and malt as a supplement, and I grew to love this war-time tonic, which I am sure kept us healthy during the years when food was scarce.

Discipline was strict at the school, and I learned this early on through an unpleasant experience. As in most schools, there was a bully, a young girl much older than me, who used to tease me a lot. One day, she was teasing me while holding both my arms, rendering me helpless. I begged her to let me go to no avail, so in the anger and frustration of the moment, I bit her arm.

As punishment, I was locked in the library for a couple of hours with a bowl of bread soaked in hot milk for my dinner. I was not to be allowed out until I had eaten it all, but just the smell made me nauseous. After a while, Sheila was sent to check on me, and I persuaded her to throw it down the toilet.

The next day, I was made to wear a large placard on my back that read, KEEP AWAY, I BITE! Worse than the placard, were the smirks on the faces of the other children as they sniggered at me. That day, I learned the meaning of humiliation.

We slept in large dormitory rooms, and I was placed in an attic room with seven other girls. It was on the third floor, and we had to descend a narrow, rickety staircase to the toilet. I was scared of the dark but even more terrified of wetting the bed, so when the need was urgent, I braved the stairs. How I longed to go home and sleep in my own bed, and there were many nights when I cried myself to sleep.

Meanwhile, Mummy worked at a local pub in Shortlands called The Tavern, where she was the cook. She worked hard, and I am sure it made her life easier to know that Sheila and I were safe in boarding school. Mummy was, by this time, about thirty, and Sheila told me years later that our mother used to have regular parties at home.

On one of the few occasions when we were at home for the weekend, Sheila felt sick in the middle of the night, and went to Mummy's bedroom for help. Mummy had company at the time, and didn't appreciate the intrusion. She slapped Sheila through the face, knocking her down the stairs. Sheila didn't have much respect for my mother after that, and when she later shared her childhood memories with me, I understood why. Tragically, our mother felt the need for male company so much that she was prepared to jeopardize her relationship with us. But she was still young and beautiful, and I am sure she must have been lonely.

A merchant seaman, by the name of Paul Welman, frequented The Tavern, charming Mummy, who fell in love with him. He was a typical seaman, a heavy drinker and smoker, who swore a lot. Having run away from home at the age of fourteen, he lied about his age, claiming to be sixteen, in order to join the merchant navy. He sailed around the world for twenty years, during which time he met and married an English girl. He was mostly away at sea, and the marriage ended in divorce, when he came home on leave and discovered his wife was having an affair.

The romance between my mother and Paul Welman quickly blossomed and led to their marriage. He became my stepfather, who would make my life miserable, and rob me of what little sense of security I had in life.

LIVING WITH FEAR

Mummy married my stepfather in March of 1946, three days after his thirty-fifth birthday. He continued to add two years to his age, so that the marriage certificate stated that he was thirty-seven. Maybe having falsified his age for so long, he actually believed it himself, because he kept up the façade throughout his life.

Mummy and Daddy, as I called him, married on a Saturday morning at the Bromley Registrar's office. Mummy's older brother, Uncle Billy and his wife, Ethel, were their only witnesses, and after the ceremony, my stepfather and Uncle Billy went to watch a football match, while my mother and Auntie Ethel went shopping. It was not the most romantic of wedding days.

After their marriage, my stepfather moved in with Mummy. This caused quite a stir in the neighborhood, and the house quickly became the target of vandalism. Stones were thrown at the windows, and black ink was flung all over their white sheets and pillowcases, while they were drying on the wash line. Mummy put up with it for a while before she pasted her marriage certificate in the front window. But the pattern of disapproval had been set, and the sneers and jeers and looks of contempt continued, until they felt they had no option but to move.

I clearly remember the first time Sheila and I went home for a weekend after their marriage. Home visits didn't happen often because Mummy was busy. By this time, my parents had moved into the upstairs apartment of a semi-detached house in Shortlands.

Mummy fetched us at boarding school, and we walked home together. In the living room stood a tall, well-built man, and Mummy told us that he was our new Daddy. I was excited. Nearly all the other children in school had daddies, but we didn't. By that time, I was five and a half years old, and Sheila was eleven.

Later that day, my stepfather was sitting at his desk in the living room, and I walked over to him and tried to climb up on his knee. He helped me up, and I put my arms around him, and gave him a hug. He asked me, "Well now, what are you after?" I was puzzled by his response, and didn't know quite what to think of it. I should have told him I wanted a Daddy, but knowing what I know now, I realize that wouldn't have changed anything.

That evening, Mummy allowed my stepfather to bathe me, and I learned what it was to feel violated. At the time, I didn't understand my feelings. They were a mixture of confusion and hurt, as well as a kind of pleasure, that made me feel uncomfortable. I wanted my stepfather to love me, but what he did to me, didn't feel right. I called him Daddy, but was a daddy supposed to do what he did? I believe that there is more than one kind of rape. That day my stepfather raped me of my innocence, and stole my childhood.

One Sunday morning, soon after that, I went into their bedroom to ask Mummy something and found my stepfather alone in their bed. I heard Mummy clattering pots in the kitchen, but before I could turn around, Stepfather called me softly, reached out and put his arm around me, pulling me into the bed next to him. He stroked my body and told me I was his sweetheart, but that I mustn't tell Mummy, as it was to be our special secret.

This behavior is typical of a child molester, but how was I to know anything about that at such a young age? He was showing me what I perceived to be love and affection, and I was hungry for both. Mummy never cuddled me, so I felt she didn't love me. My need was great, and outward expressions of love had not been offered as part of the boarding school curriculum. From then on, my life changed dramatically.

Stepfather and Mummy opened a printing business in Shortlands. Now and again, Sheila and I helped out on the odd weekend when we were allowed home. Most weekends, we stayed at the school and helped with the cleaning. The factory smelled of paper and glue, and I was allowed to paste the glue on the envelopes, which were fanned out carefully on a large table. Mummy was good at fanning the envelopes, laying them neatly side by side with the exact amount of envelope exposed, where the glue should be applied. That way, with a wide brush, I could paint the glue on a couple of dozen envelopes at one time. Writing pads and envelopes were in short supply after the war, so the business prospered.

On another weekend, when Sheila and I were at home, a strange man came to our front door. He had been my biological father's best army buddy, who had been captured with him during the war. Just before my father died, knowing he didn't have long to live, he made his friend promise that if he survived the war, he would return home to England, marry my mother, and raise his two girls. Unfortunately, his friend was so starved and near death when the war ended, it took a year in hospital and a nursing home to restore his body to some semblance of normality.

By that time, Mummy had already married my stepfather. For me, this was sad news, because even though I was only six years old at the time, I felt that life could have been vastly different had Mummy married such a kind, gentle man.

In contrast to my father's friend, my stepfather smoked heavily, drank excessively and often turned violent. My mother had not made a good choice and consequently, we were all to learn what it was like to live with fear.

DYMCHURCH

In July of 1947, at the end of the school year, Sheila and I were taken out of Raymont School for Girls and placed in day schools. We then went home to begin our lives as a family with Mummy and Stepfather. The rare weekends at home were unpleasant, but I was to learn that living at home was a perpetual nightmare.

We had barely begun that life when, at the beginning of September, we all went to Dymchurch, a charming seaside village just south of Dover, for our first two-week holiday by the sea. I was excited, as I had never seen the sea, even though it was no more than thirty miles away.

My stepfather drove us to Dymchurch in the delivery van that he used for the printing business. Because it was a small van, only my parents could sit in front, while Sheila and I sat in the back on the boxes of food that we took with us. There were no side windows, so our view was limited to a small window that looked into the front cab, and a back window that showed us where we had already been.

That first year, we rented a travel trailer, which stood in a large camp ground full of trailers. It turned out to be even smaller than my parents had anticipated. Mummy and Stepfather slept at the far end on a double bed, which had to be folded away during the day to make place for us to eat at a dropdown table. Sheila and I slept on bunk beds in the tiny middle room. They were so close, one above the other, that I, sleeping on the bottom bunk, found it almost impossible to turn over during the night. We had hardly any privacy, and changing clothes in such a small space had to be timed just right to avoid Stepfather's prying eyes. We showered in the communal showers, which were too few for the number of people in the camp, and standing in queues became part of the daily holiday routine.

Doreen with her stepfather and sister, Sheila on holiday in Dymchurch

We had quite a long walk from the camp grounds to the village stores and the beach. The local amusement park close to the beach sported a roller-skating rink, which, at the cost of one shilling an hour, became one of my favorite pastimes. I never became an expert at skating, and the scars on my ankles were proof of my inability to turn corners gracefully, but I enjoyed it tremendously.

We only traveled to Dymchurch in the van once, as it was sold along with the printing business not long after our first trip. Stepfather never drove again, and years later, I learned from Mummy that he had an accident while driving, and had killed someone. He never spoke about it. On subsequent trips to Dymchurch, we traveled by steam train, or coach. The steam train was an exciting experience, as we chugged through the English countryside, leaving a trail of sooty smoke behind.

Every year, we went to the same trailer park, but we always stayed in different trailers. Sometimes, other family members went with us, staying in another trailer close by, which ensured that Stepfather was more careful about his 'manners.'

Our holidays were often marred by disagreements between my stepfather and Sheila. She loved to go dancing at the local dancehall. He hated her going, and took great delight in slapping her across her face if she was just a couple of minutes late getting back to the trailer. I'm sure the whole camp knew about it. The pitying looks we received from our neighbors said it all. Quite often my parents went dancing too, and then Stepfather made sure that Sheila returned to the trailer with them. I loved those evenings when I was left alone. For a brief period, peace reigned.

In spite of everything, those two weeks of holiday were a welcome change from the daily routine at home. There was less violence in the trailer, probably because there was not much space to allow for the usual fisticuff fights, but even so, Stepfather was usually able to manage at least one during the holiday.

8, FARNABY ROAD

By the end of the war, more than a million houses around London had been destroyed or damaged by the bombings. Because housing was in such short supply, we were fortunate to have found a place at all. It was at 8, Farnaby Road, a charming old two-story semi-detached house where so many early experiences shaped my life. It was there that I learned to take pride in housekeeping, as well as other unpleasant lessons I would have preferred not to learn.

The house was subdivided into two apartments; our upstairs apartment was fairly spacious, with a living/dining area, kitchen, three bedrooms, and, a rarity at that time, an indoor toilet and bathroom. The front porch was covered with a large wisteria vine that made for an inviting entry. The porch had a tiled floor with a brass threshold as well as a brass letterbox and doorknocker. One of my chores was to polish the brass until it gleamed, and I took great pride in it.

A bay window looked down onto the street from the front room, which served as a living room, dining room, as well as a study for my stepfather. He had an oak desk and chair in front of the window, but the only thing I ever saw him study was the football pools. Although we were constantly short of money, he always had enough to bet on the football teams, after which he listened to the results on the radio, when strict silence had to be observed. He also placed bets on the horses and greyhounds on Saturdays, always confident that he was going to win a fortune. If he ever did, we never heard of it. His gambling, cigarettes, and brandy would have taken it all anyway.

Mummy and Stepfather had a spacious bedroom in the middle of the apartment furnished with a beautiful dark oak bedroom suite. Mummy made a blue bedspread with matching drapes, which made a nice contrast to the dark wood. In one corner of the room stood a large china willow pattern coffee table with a matching vase that I dusted carefully every day, knowing that to break either one would be a calamity.

Sheila's bedroom was at the back of the apartment, overlooking the backyard. A large apple tree kept her room dark and dismal, and I was happy that my room, although it was much smaller, was sunny and bright; that is when the sun shone! Sunshine is usually rare in England.

Sheila spent much of her time in her room reading and working on the newspaper crossword puzzles. I guess the difference in our ages was the main reason for our not being close. She considered me a nuisance, often finding it necessary to put me in my place. Mummy left her in charge of me when she went out, a responsibility that Sheila did not take to kindly. She constantly teased me and gave me French burns on my arms, then holding my hand, she scrunched my bones together, neither of which I found to be pleasant.

One day, Sheila went too far. I am sure I must have done something really annoying to provoke her, because after punching me in the face, she then pushed me into the bathroom and closed the door, threatening to end my life, if I dared come out. With my nose bleeding profusely, I leaned over the washbasin, watching in fascination as my blood formed tiny red rivulets that ran down into the drain. In a strange way, I derived some satisfaction from the situation, thinking that when she discovered what had happened, she might feel sorry for what she'd done. When she eventually opened the door and discovered the basin streaked with blood, she got a terrible fright and made me swear not to tell Mummy. I never did, and Sheila treated me a little more kindly for a while.

Due to the constantly rainy weather with little sunshine, England could be incredibly damp, and as a result, my sister moved into my bedroom with me quite often while Mummy dried out her room with our small electric heater. My room also became damp now and again, but Sheila's bedroom was more prone, because the apple tree shaded her outside wall. The main reason for the dampness in the apartment was the decaying mortar between the bricks, but it would be many years before the landlord would replace it. Once Mummy had the room good and dry, she brushed off the mildew and stippled Sheila's wallpaper with a sponge dipped in green paint, which hid the stains. My room, with its pink rose wallpaper, was stippled in pink.

My south facing bedroom window looked down onto the street from above the front porch. Being old, the branches of the wisteria, which covered the porch, had become twisted and gnarled, intertwined in one another to form a perfect ladder to the ground below. This became my escape route when I needed time away from the toxic atmosphere that was my home. The sweet scent of the wisteria blossoms filled the air in the summer, and it was a welcome visitor to my bedroom.

The wisteria was not only my escape route. Leaving my window open a few inches also allowed entry for Blackie. Mummy smeared butter on Blackie's paws when she moved from the rent house. She said that after licking the butter off, he would feel at home. Amazingly, it worked, and Blackie became my cat, the one living thing I could love, that loved me in return. He slept in my bed every night, curled in the crook of my left arm, until we were awakened in the morning by my stepfather, whereupon, Blackie flew out of the window. There were many mornings when I wished that I could fly out with him.

Unfortunately for me, I didn't know at the time that I was allergic to cats. I developed eczema on my arms, neck and face. Eczema is hereditary and mostly aggravated by stress, but certain things, such as a cat's fur, can also irritate it, and worsen the condition. As time passed, the itching became unbearable, and the more I scratched, the worse it became. Mummy bound my arms with bandages in an effort to stop me scratching and many lotions and ointments were applied to the rash, only to be discarded when they didn't help. As a result, I became increasingly self-conscious about my appearance.

Mrs. Stoddard, the lady who lived in the apartment downstairs, told me I should call her Auntie Lily and her husband, Uncle David. This was an English convention, used mostly when addressing close friends of the parents. Uncle David had a great voice, and often sang *Jerusalem* or *Land of Hope and Glory*, at the top of his voice. The magnificence of Elgar's music was not lost on me even as a young child, and as it filtered up from downstairs, I felt my heart swell within me. I loved it when he sang. There was not much singing in our home, except when Sheila was in a good mood, and we sang along with her pop records.

Auntie Lily was fond of me, and since she had no children of her own, she often called me downstairs if she needed a hand with something. Helping her was always a pleasure. The small lawn in the backyard with the large apple tree was in their half of the yard. Once, when Auntie Lily's push lawnmower was broken, I cut her lawn with an old pair of scissors. It took me a whole weekend to complete the task, and my poor hand complained bitterly, but I was pleased to do it for her because she was generous with her praise, and I earned a little pocket money.

As time passed, the altercations grew louder and more violent in our home. The first few houses along Farnaby Road all looked alike, but the neighbors next door in the adjoining apartment owned both the upstairs and downstairs. Separated by a common wall, it wasn't thick enough to block out the sounds of our family feuds. We hardly ever saw them, but frequently heard them banging on the wall, when the sounds of discord at number 8 got out of hand. If it wasn't the neighbor banging on the wall, it was Uncle David downstairs knocking on the ceiling with a broom. Not that either one helped much. What an insane way to live!

Leaving Raymont School for Girls and living at home changed everything, and not for the better. My life outside our home was pleasant enough as I learned what it was to become part of a small village community.

Shortlands was a typical English village, with a butcher, baker, greengrocer, fishmonger, grocer, and a dairy, as well as candy stores and a ladies' clothing store on the main street. Round the corner, near the station, was a small store that sold newspapers, magazines, candy and tobacco.

I did most of the shopping for the family with a wicker basket in one hand and a money purse and shopping list in the other. I felt important and thrived on the responsibility of taking care of the household needs. Money was tight, so only small amounts of this and that could be purchased at a time. Also, we didn't have much storage space in our kitchen, and for many years, there was no refrigerator, so shopping, by necessity, was a daily event.

In the early days after the war, everything was in short supply in England, due to the destruction from the bombing. Most food, like sugar, butter, and bacon, were rationed and not always easy to find. For those, I had to give the grocer our ration book coupons, which remained in use for almost a decade after the war ended.

At the grocery store, the grocer took my basket and list, and gathered the requested items together, crossing them off as he went along. He wrote the price next to each item, and then rang it up on the cash register. Finally, the total amount was written at the bottom of the list. I handed the money and ration coupons over to the grocer and carefully tucked the change away in my purse. On my return home, Mummy added all the slips together and checked the change. It was not a good day for me if the change was short, so I quickly learned to check it after each purchase. This was good for both Mummy's budget and my bookkeeping skills.

As a child, I believed in luck, and I was sometimes lucky enough to pick up a penny in the street, which I spent in the candy store. Picking up a pin and sticking it in my collar was said to bring good luck, and I never walked under a ladder, as that was sure to bring bad luck. If an ambulance drove by, I held on to my collar until I saw a man on a bicycle, knowing full well if I didn't, something really bad would happen. Thankfully, I am no longer superstitious.

Superstition was something I learned from my mother. It was her habit every time there was a new moon, to run into the house and get her purse, shake it well and bow three times before the moon. She was convinced that this was why she never ran out of money. I found it embarrassing, especially if she did it in front of other people.

Every year, winter fog descended on our village, and when it was really bad, it was called smog, which was quite scary. There were no cars on the deserted streets, and the village turned into a ghostly, eerie-looking place. Shopping was not easy on those days. Crossing Farnaby Road, I turned right towards the village. There was a long row of billboards bordering the sidewalk, and I felt my way along it with my right hand; while holding the basket in my left. With my vivid imagination, I was always relieved to arrive safely in the brightly lit stores.

BROMLEY ROAD SCHOOL

When we returned from Dymchurch that first September, Sheila and I started day school in Beckenham. Sheila attended a technical school, where she learned domestic science and typing, while I was sent to Bromley Road Junior School. During the four years I spent there, I traveled to and from school on the number 227, a small single-decker bus.

In the classrooms, we shared double desks, which had seats affixed to the desktops with steel frames. The desks had lift-up lids which, when opened, provided a place for our books. An inkwell depression was built in on the right-hand side and we wrote with dip pens with replaceable nibs. They were awkward to write with, and sometimes the point of the nib would stick in the paper if pressed too hard, resulting in a spray of ink blobs across the page. Blotting paper took care of the worst of it, but the ink stain remained, so turning in neat work was always a challenge. Of course, with a good imagination, the ink blobs could quite easily be turned into insects or monsters. And the temptation to be creative was compelling. When fountain pens arrived, our lives became a lot easier.

In those days, we were strictly disciplined, and my bad behavior often earned me a rap on the knuckles or the palm of my hand with a ruler. Although those reprimands produced stinging pain, I always blinked away my tears, refusing to give the teacher the satisfaction of seeing me cry. Caning was usually reserved for the boys, although on occasion, I managed to tempt some of my teachers to make an exception. When I was kept in after school for detention, I got in trouble at home because I arrived late to do my chores. School hours were from nine in the morning until four in the afternoon, with an hour break for lunch, which consisted of a hot meal and dessert. The meals were not memorable, but since I was always hungry, I ate them with relish.

My best friend Marian, invited me to her home for a weekend now and again. I was sure that her family must be very rich, because their double-story house was filled with pretty things. They also had a car and a telephone. On my first weekend there, we spent half the night giggling, and were reprimanded by her parents several times before we eventually fell asleep. The next day, Marian taught me how to ride her bicycle. I had always wanted a bicycle, but I knew that dream was out of reach, but at least now I knew how to ride one.

Marian was a quiet, well-behaved girl, while I was naughty and often in trouble at school. I invited her to come and stay with me for a weekend, but her parents wouldn't allow it. I guess they came to the conclusion that our family was not the kind of influence they wanted for their daughter, and so it was better not to encourage our friendship. They were probably right, but we remained good friends at school.

One of the things I enjoyed most about school was our weekly trip to the municipality's heated, indoor swimming pool. I found the strong smell of chlorine trapped in the confines of the building overpowering, but after a few weeks, I learned to swim, which gave me great satisfaction. Sheila was an excellent swimmer and had received a certificate for swimming a mile. I tried my best, but only managed a certificate for one length of the pool, swimming dog paddle style. I didn't enjoy putting my face in the water and try as I might, I couldn't seem to lift my left arm out of the water to swim freestyle. This could have been due to my broken collarbone, a problem that remained with me into adulthood.

Because I now had a certificate proving that I could swim, my parents sometimes allowed me to go to the municipal pool on weekends. One of those occasions, I remember quite vividly. It was the day I almost drowned!

I could dive after a fashion, so that day, while showing off, I dove into the deep end and swam to the shallow end of the pool. For me, it was quite an achievement that I could dive in and hold my breath until I surfaced. I then swam in my usual dog-paddle style, a slow, strenuous stroke, which caused me to tire quickly.

When I was about halfway down the length of the pool, I attempted to stand and promptly disappeared beneath the water. My arms and legs went lame, partly due to fatigue and partly from the fear of knowing that I was out of my depth, and I found that trying to swim to the surface proved futile. My body ceased to function, and I only surfaced briefly, gulping in a mouth full of air, before going under several times. I knew that I wasn't going to make it, and unable to hold my breath any longer, I reluctantly inhaled the water. As my lungs filled with water, I was overcome with a strange, peaceful feeling; my mind was calm, and my body relaxed, and I felt as if I was floating in a dream.

Losing the ability to fight, I gave in, and had it not been for two teenage boys who saw me drowning and jumped in to save me, I would probably not be writing my story now. They lifted me out of the pool and laid me on my stomach. Coughing and spluttering, with water pouring out of my nose and mouth, I found myself encircled by inquisitive young faces. Horribly embarrassed, I wanted to run away, but it was quite a few minutes before I was able to move.

The boys sat with me until I had recovered, and then they insisted on taking me back into the pool, but this time at the shallow end. I protested and begged them to leave me alone, but wisely, they persuaded me that it was the right thing to do; otherwise, I might have been left with a fear of water. It was good advice, and I was grateful to them for having saved my life, and my courage.

    I didn't dare tell my parents what had happened, as I knew they would never let me go swimming alone again. Following my near-death experience, I have never been quite so keen to go swimming under any circumstances.

RUDE AWAKENINGS

The cold, wet English winters often left me sick with tonsillitis, and the day arrived when it became necessary for me to have my tonsils removed. Because we had no car, Mummy took me to hospital on the 227 bus. I was given ether to put me to sleep, which was unpleasant, and the smell of the black rubber mask placed over my nose and mouth reminded me of my wartime gas mask. I had to stay overnight in the hospital, and the kind nurses gave me lots of jello to eat, which almost made the surgery worthwhile. My brief stay didn't seem so bad at the time, but a couple of years later, I changed my mind about hospitals.

    I guess Mummy must have felt I deserved a reward for good behavior after having my tonsils removed, because soon afterward, she came home with the doll that I had been looking at longingly in the window of the book and toy store in Shortlands. I had told Mummy about her and how I wished that she was mine, but I was sure that my mother couldn't afford to buy me such an expensive doll, so she was added to my wish list. In this case, my wish came true, and it wasn't even Christmas! Since she was the only doll I ever owned, she was well-loved.

I only had a few toys as a child, but I never felt deprived. Each Christmas Eve, Sheila and I tucked pillowcases under the end of our beds before going to sleep, in the same way that American children hang stockings over the fireplace. After decorating the living room and Christmas tree, we usually went to bed late, but by five or six o'clock in the morning, I was wide awake, feverishly investigating the contents of my pillow case. That was okay when I was sleeping alone, but if I was sharing a bedroom with Sheila, she quickly expressed her displeasure at being awakened at such an early hour. My mother's sister, Auntie Violet and sister-in-law, Auntie Ethel, often gave me coloring books and crayons, or jigsaw puzzles for Christmas, and I sometimes received a book from my parents, since they knew I loved to read. Mostly, the contents consisted of an apple, orange and a banana, some dried fruit and nuts and maybe some handkerchiefs or socks. It was considered a big treat if there was some chocolate!

When I slept alone in my own bedroom, it was my stepfather who woke me for school, and I woke up every morning to find his hands inside my pajamas, exploring my body. By this time, I was acutely aware that what he was doing was wrong, and I fought him off, even as I was fighting off the remnants of my fitful sleep, wanting to scream at him, but stupidly holding the scream inside. He always laughed at me before walking out, leaving me feeling angry and humiliated. That was the beginning of my day, every day!

Only years later did I learn that Sheila experienced the same thing. I suspect that she was having an even worse time than I, since she was so much older, well-developed and pretty. Stepfather adored her, and spent hours talking to her or insisting that she play a card game called cribbage with him. I realize now that the weeks when Sheila and I had to share a room, due to the mildew, were a blessing for both of us. We were together, and Stepfather was more careful.

Both Sheila and I felt that his attentions were somehow our fault, something we had done to make him act that way, and feeling ashamed, we never confided in each other until after we were both grown. We then admitted that we both felt the need to protect Mummy by never telling her, although as an adult, I came to believe that she must have known, or at least suspected, what was going on. Perhaps her own insecurity prevented her from looking further.

To make matters even worse for me, because we didn't have enough blankets, Mummy insisted on placing my stepfather's black greatcoat on my bed during the winter months. It was thick, and unbearably heavy. I felt as if I was suffocating, and found it difficult to turn under the weight of it. He wore it every day, so it reeked of him, and so not only did I wake up to his groping hands every morning, but I felt almost as if I was sleeping with him. I begged Mummy not to put it on my bed, but she insisted. As a result, I became a light sleeper, waking at the slightest noise. I slept in fear of waking up, knowing what to expect, and nightmares became a regular unwelcome intruder to my sleep.

It took several years before I had the opportunity, as well as the courage, to tell an adult about what my stepfather was doing to me. In those days, adults were reluctant to discuss such matters, so I was never warned by my mother about the dangers of being molested. I felt guilty, unloved and helpless. Having no one to turn to, and not really understanding why my stepfather was doing those things to me, I learned to cope as best I could. I escaped to the park as often as possible, but my daily routine didn't allow me much leisure time, so even that was difficult.

I often wished I could go to Mummy and pour out my heart, tell her everything and get her to stop my stepfather from molesting me. That should have been the perfect solution, but Mummy and I weren't close. She never showed me any affection and I am sure that there were many good reasons for her being unable to do so, but as a child, I felt that it must be because I was undeserving of her love.

As an adult, in reflection on my mother's lack of affection, I came to believe that one of the main reasons was that she must have resented my coming along as an added burden at the worst possible time, a time of war, with no end in sight. Understandably, her precarious condition probably kept her in a constant state of stress. Also, because I had lived away at boarding school from such a young age, she didn't really know or understand me. My character was formed by Miss Kendall and Miss Constance, so I was probably not the little girl she expected me to be. At the boarding school, I was taught good manners, as well as how to speak, walk, and act like a young lady, and maybe that made Mummy feel uncomfortable, perhaps thinking I was putting on airs. I became both resentful and angry, and I cannot imagine that, under those circumstances, I could have been very lovable. Lastly, and most importantly, Mummy didn't receive love from my stepfather, and I believe if you don't receive love, eventually you have none to give. She was a victim of her circumstances as I was of mine, but as a child, I couldn't see that.

I dearly loved our trips to visit Auntie Violet and Auntie Ethel in the East End of London. My stepfather and Sheila never wanted to go, so it was usually just the two of us, and having Mummy all to myself was special to me. We traveled by train and then a bus to get there. We usually visited Uncle Billy and Auntie Ethel for tea first. Then we walked over the railway bridge and down Lynton Road, dwarfed by the tall gray brick wall that ran for blocks alongside the railway yards. We then spent the evening with Auntie Violet, Uncle Jim and their three daughters. Both aunts made special treats for us to eat, and as they were both excellent cooks, we always came away well-fed.

Traveling home was the best, especially in the winter when Mummy wore her fur coat over a smart suit. With an elegant hat framing her face, she looked beautiful. On the way home on the train, I snuggled up to her, enjoying the softness of the fur and the gentle fragrance of her Chanel No. 5. Gazing up at the face of the Madonna on her cameo broach and lulled by the rhythmic movement of the train, I inevitably fell into a peaceful sleep. Even though Mummy never cuddled me, I felt loved just being close to her, and I cherish those memories.

THE TOMBOY

Mummy had to budget carefully to make sure we managed to stretch our income from one Friday to the next. For doing the chores I was paid a shilling (a dime) a week, which enabled me to go to the Saturday morning movies. I lived for Saturdays. I had no chores, there was no school, and I got to go to the movies.

We queued up in the side alley of the Odeon Theater on Bromley High Street and entering by the side door, we paid sixpence (a nickel) for the privilege of seeing a cartoon, a short, which was usually a serial, and the main movie. Usherettes, (ladies with trays hanging from their necks,) sold candy and ice-creams, and as I only had a nickel left after purchasing my movie ticket, I had to choose carefully, which one to buy. I usually bought a packet of wine gums, as they lasted a couple of days.

The noise in the movie theater was deafening, while we waited for the cartoon to begin, and I didn't enjoy all the yelling and screaming. Kids sometimes threw things at each other, causing the odd fight. The manager walked up and down the aisles, attempting to keep us calm, which couldn't have been easy. The Disney characters brought shrieks of joy from the audience, and it was good to laugh at their antics. The short was usually an episode of some cowboy series starring Roy Rogers or Gene Autry. I wasn't mad about the cowboys, but the boys loved them. If the movie was one that we children liked, we cheered and clapped, but if it wasn't, or the film broke, there was a lot of yelling and stomping of feet. The main movie was my best thing because I could lose myself in the world of make-believe. Saturday mornings at the Odeon were three hours of sheer bliss.

The local park in Shortlands was called The Mead, and that was where I spent my spare time on Saturday afternoons. It had a large circular lawn in the middle, which was home to the traveling fair that visited our village once a year. There was a wide path around the perimeter, where small children could safely ride their bikes, and Mums could take their babies for walks. The Ravensbourne River flowed through the park, and there was a swing and a roundabout for the children to play on. There was also a small store selling candy and soda pop. A winding footpath led from The Mead, up through some rolling hills appropriately called The Hills to Bromley South. Along the top of The Hills was another footpath connecting Bromley South to Dead Man's Steps, so named, because of the bad things that had happened there.

When I was about eight, we were blessed with a heavy snowstorm. Buses were unable to run, so the schools were closed. When it stopped snowing and the sun came out, a winter wonderland beckoned, and I ran off to The Hills. I stopped on the way at our greengrocer, where I asked the owner, Mrs. Bishop, for a wooden tomato box. Mrs. Bishop, with her red rosy cheeks and round chubby body, was always cheerful, which made shopping in her store a pleasure. She gladly obliged, asking me what I wanted it for. "A toboggan," I replied. She smiled broadly and looked for the sturdiest box she could find. After warning me to be careful of splinters, she urged me to go and have some fun.

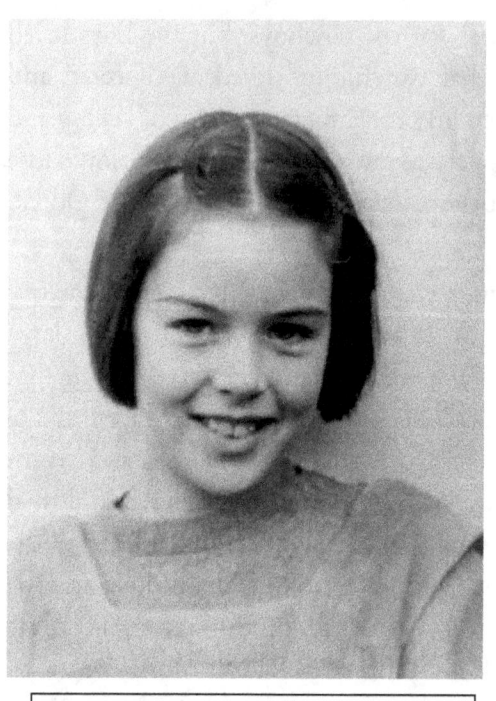

Doreen at school aged eight

I knew I would find other children with the same idea. Of course, they all had real toboggans, but none of them were as special as my tomato box, and I had the best time competing with the 'professionals.'

For some reason, Mummy decided that although she didn't attend church, I should go to Sunday school. Maybe the old Bible a friend of hers gave me prompted her with this decision. There was a Church of England in Bromley, which was not too far, so I was dressed up in my Sunday best and given sixpence for collection. I dutifully attended Sunday school for a few weeks but found it boring. I was sure that I could make better use of my time, as well as the sixpence, so the next Sunday, I stopped by the candy store, before heading for The Mead, where I whiled away the hour on the swing.

The swing had a long seat suspended between steel poles, large enough to hold about eight children sitting back-to-back. Two children stood on the ends of the seat and holding onto the poles, they worked the swing back and forth, soaring higher and higher, with the other children cheering them on. When swinging alone, I worked the swing until the seat where I was standing, crashed against the top cross bar, then I would see how many times I could make it crash before I got tired. Inevitably, this ended in disaster when one day, after crashing it several times I got tired, at which moment, both my feet slipped off the end of the seat and my hands slipped down the poles. I held on for dear life, but try as I might, I could not regain my footing. Hanging on by my arms with the end of the seat pummeling my stomach, I was soon compelled to let go. I fell to the ground and hit the back of my head on the concrete paving. I saw stars, but they were not beautiful!

I don't know how long I lay there before I was able to move. I do know that I watched the swing swaying back and forth above my head for quite some time before it came to a standstill, by which time I had recovered enough to roll out from under it and drag myself slowly to my feet.

I obviously couldn't tell Mummy what had happened because I was supposed to be in Sunday school. The huge lump on the back of my head was covered by my hair, so she couldn't see it, but it was quite a while before I could comfortably brush my hair without wincing. I am sure Mummy wondered why the back of my dress was so dirty when I got home that day, but she just gave me one of her looks and shook her head. I was a real tomboy, and she was used to me getting dirty.

My newfound freedom was short-lived, when a couple of weeks later, my secret was revealed. I was at the park eating candy, wondering what to do. The swing was becoming a bit boring, and I was no longer quite so eager to see how many times I could make it crash, with the lump on my head still there to remind me of my recent mishap.

Just then, a group of kids about my age arrived at the park and asked me to join them, and we all went to play down by the river. There were steppingstones positioned strategically across the water, to enable those brave enough to cross without using the footbridge. We had a grand time jumping back and forth, seeing who could cross to the other side the fastest. I was doing quite well until my dress hampered my stride, causing me to slip on one of the steppingstones. I fell into the murky river, which was not deep so I wasn't in any danger, but my dress was full of the slimy water, and my white socks were soaked through to a dingy shade of greenish-brown. I was in trouble. Nothing could save me, and nothing did! I walked home, where I confessed my sins, for which I was severely punished and never allowed to go to Sunday school again.

Typical of a tomboy, I always had a lot of energy, and one day, I was doing handstands on the armchair in the living room. This, as it turned out, was not a good idea. I got my legs up in the air just fine, but then my body twisted on the way down, and somehow, I managed to hit the corner of the dining room table with my shin. In the process, I knocked a tiny piece of wood off the corner of the oak table. Even worse, from my point of view, was that I could see my shinbone in the newly formed gap in my flesh. My screams brought my mother running in to see what had happened. It was not a pretty sight that greeted her, but I'm not sure what distressed her the most: my wound, the injury to the table, or the blood gushing out all over the dining room carpet.

My second trip to the hospital on the 227 bus was accompanied by many heartfelt comments from my fellow passengers, as well as lots of sympathy from the bus driver. Mummy had ripped up an old sheet and wrapped it around my leg, and by the size of the large red stain on the sheet, it seemed that I was rapidly depleting my body of its blood supply. By the time we got to the hospital, I was not feeling at all well, but I assumed the nurses would soon make everything better. After all, that's what they did when I had my tonsils taken out.

This time, things were very different, and there was no jello! A large man, who turned out to be the doctor, came into the room where I was lying on an examination table. He asked my mother what had caused the ugly wound on my leg, and she told him the sad story. He turned, and looked at me with a sadistic smile on his face, which reminded me of my stepfather when he touched me. My heart froze in an instant, and I felt quite sick. His next words confirmed my worst fears when he said, "Well, we will have to teach her a lesson, won't we?"

He instructed two nurses to hold me down, and I frantically fought them, while pleading with my mother to help me. Another nurse was called in, so now I was being held down by three nurses and my mother.

The doctor proceeded to stitch up my wound without the benefit of an anesthetic. Making contact with the corner of the table had hurt, but it was nothing in comparison to the pain of that needle being forced in and out of my protesting flesh. Mummy had the good grace to cry, but she didn't even attempt to stop the wretched man from satisfying his need to teach a small child a lesson. My screams were so loud, that in the middle of the procedure, the door was flung open, and several nurses ran in from other parts of the hospital to see what was happening.

I never quite understood my mother's lack of intervention that day. The ugly scar on my shin still reminds me how an adult should not behave, and despite the doctor's good intentions, the only lesson I learned that day was that there are more cruel and unfeeling people around who obviously do not like children. In my humble opinion, that doctor chose the wrong profession. He should rather have become a butcher. As a result of his treatment of me, my respect for adults diminished even more, and I determined not to rely on them for anything. From that day on, I was going to take care of myself.

STEPFATHER

Sheila was shy and self-conscious, and when we shared a room, she undressed behind the door in the dark. In spite of my childish jealousy about what I perceived to be her close relationship with my mother, I loved and admired her, and I tried to be just like her. I copied her in every way I could where my appearance was concerned. When Stepfather was around, Sheila could often be found sitting hunched over in the living room, reading. She sat holding herself, so that her breasts were totally covered by her arms, with the book resting on her lap. As my breasts developed, I followed suit, and all our lessons on deportment and posture at boarding school were wasted as we both became more and more round-shouldered.

Stepfather insisted that Sheila play cribbage with him in the evenings and on weekends. Cribbage is traditionally a game for two players, played with cards and a wooden pegboard to keep score. I knew she hated it, but she didn't dare refuse. Stepfather kept repeating things like, "Fifteen two, fifteen four, fifteen six and a pair makes eight."

I found it irritating, hearing it over and over again. Thankfully, he never asked me to play with him and when Sheila began winning, he was no longer so keen to play with her either. Playing cribbage was bad enough, but it wasn't the worst thing that Sheila had to put up with.

One Saturday afternoon, when Mummy was out, I walked into the living room to find Sheila lying on the floor with Stepfather on top of her. He sat astride her, pinning her arms down, and he was licking her just beneath her nose. She was struggling to free herself, while he was laughing at her. Without stopping to think, I pounced on him and screamed for him to let her go, and a quick punch from his fist sent me sprawling across the room.

Why, oh why, did Mummy marry this man? That day, I experienced hatred in a whole new way. Hating someone for what they did to somebody you loved was different somehow, and my hatred for Stepfather became far more intense. Fortunately, I eventually came to learn how futile it is to hate anybody, and I learned to channel the intensity of those negative feelings into a positive sense of independence, which helped me to withstand Stepfather's abuse and become a survivor.

Kissing Stepfather hello and goodbye was required on a daily basis. It was an ordeal, as he often grabbed hold of my face and forced his tongue into my mouth, with his breath smelling of brandy and cigarettes. Refusing to kiss him was not an option, as I soon learned that his fists were heavy and always at the ready if he wasn't greeted properly.

There were many things about my stepfather that I found repulsive. He smoked fifty cigarettes a day, which stained his teeth, as well as the fingers on his right hand. He had lost the middle finger of that hand while in the merchant navy, so he held his cigarettes with his index and third fingers. The nicotine turned them a dirty yellow color. When he ran out of cigarettes, he took all the butts that he had saved in an empty tobacco tin, tore off the papers and carefully gathered the smelly contents into a pile. He then held a cigarette paper in the palm of his left hand and, after placing the used tobacco along the length of it, licked the edge and rolled it into an evil-smelling cigarette.

I was supposed to be impressed when Stepfather came home with a small cigarette machine and proudly showed me how he could feed the cigarette paper into it, string the old tobacco along the length of the paper, lick it and turning the machine, produce a professional-looking cigarette. Much to my disgust, making his second-hand cigarettes became one of my regular chores. Stepfather had an equally smelly black pipe, and the smoke from his pipe or cigarettes regularly filled the house. My mother smoked thirty cigarettes a day, and later on, my sister started smoking too, so it was probably not a very healthy environment to grow up in.

Stepfather plastered hair oil so thickly on his hair, that when out in the rain, the droplets ran off the solid greasy mass. Mummy had to cover his pillow with a towel, and she also placed a towel on the back of the chair where he sometimes sat in the living room, to protect the fabric. He washed his hair once a week, and after drying it with a towel, he sat in the kitchen, scratching at the thick dandruff on his scalp, while simultaneously shaking it all over the floor. It was my job to scrub the kitchen floor, and under the circumstances, it was not a job that I relished.

Foul language came easily to Stepfather, partly because he had become accustomed to it in the merchant navy, and partly because he took great pleasure in shocking and irritating us. Some of the words were so foreign to me I never did quite understand what they meant, but the context in which he used them, told me they were disgusting. Vulgarity was a part of his make-up, which I found abhorrent. He obviously enjoyed embarrassing me, causing me to blush, which I did easily. I hated the feeling of humiliation brought on by his every look.

Knowledge was important to my stepfather, not so much because he thirsted for it, but because he liked to be able to prove his superiority over others. On the few occasions when we had visitors, inevitably, the conversation turned into an argument, requiring him to immediately fetch the encyclopedia to put an end to the dispute and prove himself right. The sarcasm with which he quoted the printed evidence was embarrassing. As a result, visitors came less and less often.

The thing I despised most about my stepfather was the way he teased Blackie. Blackie came to us with a gentle nature, but Stepfather teased him until he became quite a different cat. Holding his hand up as if he was going to grab Blackie's face, he jerked it viciously back and forth, until he provoked the cat into attacking him. Blackie's eyes blazed, his ears flattened, and he attacked Stepfather's hand like a wild cat. Growling and cringing, this went on until my stepfather grew tired of it. Blackie grew to be suspicious and aggressive, and as a result, I got bitten and scratched by him on many occasions when I attempted to pick him up. I gradually learned to allow him to come to me on his own terms.

I am sure that something dreadful must have happened to my stepfather when he was a boy, causing him to run away from home when he was fourteen and become the hard, cruel man that he was. It seems that often, abused children grow up, only to take out their sadness, anger, and frustration on their own families. I never once heard my stepfather speak of his childhood or his parents. It was as if they had never existed, and I am sure there must have been a good reason for that.

Mummy once told me about one of Stepfather's war experiences that must have been terribly traumatic for him. At Dunkirk, he was on one of the small boats that picked up the stranded soldiers from the beaches. Stepfather was compelled to hit the hands of those trying to get into their overcrowded boat. Had he not done so, they would have all drowned, but knowing he was likely sending some of those desperate men to their deaths must have been extremely difficult for him. Everyone has a cross to bear, as well as memories that are painful, and some people are unable to live with the pain without hurting others. Stepfather, it seems, was one of them, and it made him both hard and cynical.

A MINI WAR-ZONE

As time passed, the tension increased, and our home took on the appearance of an unsupervised boxing arena, with fights occurring almost nightly. When Stepfather sold the printing business, he found a job in a sawmill, which just happened to have a pub conveniently situated nearby. Apparently, the aroma drifting from the establishment proved to be irresistible, and he started coming home drunk nearly every night. When he didn't arrive in time for dinner, Mummy kept his plate of food warm on a pot of simmering hot water, and this did not make her happy.

My bedroom was next to the staircase, so I could hear him crawling up the stairs on his hands and knees late at night. Sighs and contented humming sounds accompanied his erratic ascent, and then the inevitable fight began.

Mummy always stood at the top of the stairs and asked him where the hell he had been? I was sure she knew and wondered why she bothered to ask. Then she went on and on about how his food was ruined, and she didn't know why she bothered to cook for him. He then responded in the friendly, sing-song voice of the happily inebriated, although the words were so slurred it was difficult to understand him.

He then tried to hug and kiss my mother, who inevitably pushed him away. That was it. Chaos ensued! He hit her, and Sheila and I would fly out of our bedrooms to try and stop him. By the time he was finished, we were lying all over the floor, battered and bruised. Going to school the next morning, when it was possible, was always embarrassing. I became increasingly resentful, and learned to give my stepfather 'the look.' which earned me many additional beatings.

Mummy grew bitter and irritable. She developed a short fuse, and was easily angered. She often lashed out with a slap across my face, or any other part of my body that was available, which became a regular occurrence. Much to my dismay, she even broke my pretty hairbrush on my legs, but Mummy's discipline was preferable to what I received from my stepfather, who only knew to use his fists or his leather belt.

Mostly, because the beatings happened so regularly, the memory of them seems to have merged into one long, miserable nightmare. But a few stand out as being especially bad, like the time when Stepfather hit Mummy with such force against the kitchen wall, that when she fell to the floor, she couldn't get up.

I dared to scream at him to stop, and he turned on me like a wild animal and hit me across my ear with his open hand, knocking me to the floor. As I got up, I received a blow to my other ear that left me dazed. Then he punched me viciously in the face with his fist, and my nose bled so badly I couldn't get it to stop. The next morning, when I got up, I fainted, and I wasn't able to go to school that day. Hitting me in the face was unusual, and I am sure he regretted doing so, as he didn't want any evidence of his brutality to escape the confines of our apartment.

Stepfather was clever, and usually beat us with his fists where it wouldn't show, like a blow to the head or our arms and backs. If we fell down, the blows continued wherever he found an opening, so I was never sure which part of my body to protect first. If he went to fetch his belt, I knew my bottom or my legs would suffer. This knowledge didn't help much with the pain, but at least I knew what to expect.

My days began with Stepfather waking me in his hateful fashion just before he left for work, and after getting dressed, I went through to the kitchen. Sheila usually came in a few minutes later while I was having breakfast. She was always in a foul mood in the mornings, which I might have understood had I known that she had received the same wake-up call as me. If I greeted her, she growled, "I've told you not to speak to me in the mornings!"

Eventually, I learned not to. After eating my cornflakes, I made a sandwich for school break, made my bed and got myself off to school.

CHORES AND CHILDHOOD MEMORIES

Mummy worked full-time at Woolworths on Bromley High Street, so most of the housework fell to Sheila and me. We were supposed to share the chores after school, but Sheila hated housework and always managed to wiggle out of most of her share. For one thing, I got home earlier than she did, and since she always had more homework than me, it was easy for her to say she didn't have time to help.

My days after school followed a routine. After changing out of my school clothes, I went down into the village with the shopping list for the day. Returning home, my first chore was to clean the ashes from the fire grate and shovel them into an old enamel bowl. Next, I cleaned the fireplace with a damp cloth, polished it if necessary, and laid the fire, first placing small pieces of paper and firewood, before piling the coal on top.

Cleaning the fireplace made lots of ash dust, so it was necessary to dust and mop the apartment every day. I had to make sure I didn't miss any ledges or rungs on the furniture because Mummy often ran her finger along out-of-the-way places, and if she found any dust, I was punished. The kitchen, bathroom and toilet floors were covered in linoleum and had to be scrubbed, but not every day. If I complained to Sheila that she wasn't doing her share of the housework and I was going to tell Mummy, she paid me a shilling for my silence. Standard rate to do her share of the dishes was a sixpence. Unwittingly, Sheila helped teach me the value and advantage of earning and saving money.

Preparation for dinner was next. After peeling and washing the vegetables, I set them on the gas stove to cook. I then took the vegetable peelings with the bowl of ashes from the fireplace, along with the kitchen trashcan, down the stairs and around the side of the house to the trash can. After throwing the vegetable peelings to Auntie Lily's chickens, I emptied the ashes and trash in the bin. That task was to lead to one of the most catastrophic days of my childhood!

With the bowl in my arms, and the trashcan dangling precariously from my right hand, I slowly descended the stairs. As they were both particularly heavy that day, I should probably have made two trips, but that isn't what I did. Without being able to hold on to the banister, the result was inevitable. There were fifteen steps in all and, as bad luck would have it, I miss-stepped on the top stair. The result was a topsy-turvy fall from top to bottom, with the ashes, trash and vegetable peelings flying in all directions, covering the stairs and me from head to toe. The only good thing about the fall was that I didn't break anything, which in itself was a small miracle. I surveyed the mess, knowing that I needed at least an hour to clean it up, and unhappily, I didn't have an hour.

A couple of minutes later, my mother arrived home from work. Her eyes narrowed as she looked at the chaotic scene, and with her face distorted with rage, she screamed at me, "Doreen, look at this mess. I'm going to spifflicate you! You make me sick. Don't you think I have enough to do without cleaning up after you? I have been working hard all day, and I'm tired!"

Her hand was raised, ready to slap me, but perhaps she saw that I was already hurt enough and thought better of it, because her hand fell to her side.

I had no idea what spifflicate meant, but it sounded serious enough to have the desired effect, and I was terrified. Between sobs, I told her over and over that I was sorry and would be more careful in the future. She replied, "You had better be, or God help you!"

But would He? I had become convinced that I was too bad for God to ever want to help me. I finally persuaded Mummy that I would clean up the mess, and she could go upstairs and finish preparing the dinner.

Our old vacuum cleaner was my best friend that day, but my bruises told the world that the turmoil continued in the Welman household, even though, for a change, my stepfather wasn't to blame. Mummy, in her constant state of distress, didn't seem to understand that accidents can happen, and that I really hadn't fallen down the stairs on purpose.

Two or three evenings a week, I ironed the clothes and linen for the family. Thinking back, I can scarcely believe that I could stand and iron until ten or eleven in the evening and still get up for school the next morning. I also had homework to do, and in my limited spare time, I loved to draw, write poetry, sew and knit. I was also an avid reader, and I read while riding to and from school on the bus. I also read while walking in the street from the bus stop to our home, crossing streets on the way, while hardly being aware of doing so. Mummy often fussed with me at night when she discovered me reading by the light from the window in summer, or with a flashlight, hidden under the bedclothes in winter.

We were all surprised when, out of the blue, my stepfather made contact with his relatives in South Africa. I never knew what prompted this, as he had never mentioned them before. He corresponded with someone called Aunt Annie, who I believe was his mother's sister. As he had never spoken about his parents, I assumed that he must have lived with his aunt as a boy. From then on, Aunt Annie sent us a food parcel every Christmas, full of assorted nuts and dried fruits. They were a wonderful addition to what my parents could afford out of their weekly salaries. Aunt Annie also sent us photographs, and looking at the picture of the old lady with white hair, I longed for grandparents of my own.

Shortly after this, Mummy announced that we were to go and visit my biological father's parents in Lewisham. As it was only a half-hour's bus ride from Bromley, I couldn't understand why she had never taken me before, or what made her take me then, but I was excited about meeting them.

My grandfather Wheble was fairly stout, and he wore a brown suit, with a waistcoat. He smoked a pipe, which I found to be quite smelly, but he had a kind manner, and I liked him instantly. My grandmother was small and thin, and she wore a floral dress. She smiled and asked me who I was, to which I replied, "I am Doreen, Granny."

She then asked me in the same crackly voice, "How old are you, dear?" to which I replied, "I am nine, Granny."

A few minutes later, she asked me the same two questions, to which I gave the same replies. Much to my distress, this conversation continued for the duration of our visit, and on our way home, Mummy explained to me that Granny was senile, which I only fully understood when I was much older. That was to be my only memory of my grandparents, since they both died when I was twelve, and I never saw them again after our one disastrous visit.

It appears that Mummy didn't have much contact with my grandparents after my father died. She didn't seem to want to talk about them, or my father for that matter, and I grew up knowing very little about them. Much later in life, I once mentioned my love of classical music, curious about its origin, since I had had no introduction to it at home. Mummy seemed surprised that I didn't know that my grandfather had played the violin and double bass, and even had his own orchestra at one time. The classics were to play an enormous healing role in my later years, and it felt good to discover a possible source.

Before stoppages, Stepfather earned £10.00 a week at the Sawmill. £1.10s went to pay the rent. Then, there was electricity, food and bus fares, not to mention coal, which I seem to remember cost £20.00 for a ton at that time. Mummy still worked at Woolworths, where she eventually became a supervisor. Even with their two salaries, there was not much left over for luxuries. I found it infuriating to see Stepfather squandering so much money on his brandy and gambling, while Mummy and I were being so frugal with the housekeeping money.

Often in the winter, we had to manage without a coal fire for a few weeks before Christmas, in order to save enough coal for the holidays. The small electric bar heater only gave out enough heat to warm the kitchen, so that was where we spent our evenings. If the money in the electricity meter was running short, then the gas oven was lit, turned down low, and the oven door was left open.

Because we couldn't always afford good quality coal, Mummy sometimes bought slag, which spat small pieces out of the fireplace, making burn marks on the carpet. Alternatively, we burned coke, which is a residue left over from the distillation of coal. It didn't burn well and made lots of smoke. But the worst was when reaching the bottom of the coal bin; I had to scrape up the fine coal dust to put on the fire. To my dismay, it often extinguished the fire that I had so carefully coaxed into life. On a few occasions, when we were totally out of coal as well as money, I had to walk about a quarter of a mile into the village to borrow a bucket of coal from a kind neighbor.

A real treat for me was when the coal truck drove too fast around the corner of Farnaby Road down into the village, and some pieces of coal fell off into the road. When that happened, I grabbed the coal bucket and raced down the stairs, trying to beat the neighbors to the prize. I loved to see the smile on Mummy's face when I came home with a few pieces of free coal.

Coal was delivered to our house. The friendly coalman's face, full of coal dust, was almost as black as the coal itself, and when he smiled, his white teeth dazzled in the middle of his blackened face. We had a large coal bin with a corrugated iron roof situated up the side alley of the house. The coalman had to first shovel the coal into hundredweight hessian sacks from the back of the truck, before carrying them up the alley to the bin. Holding the open end closed with his hand, he carried the sacks on his shoulder and emptied them into the bin. There were twenty hundredweight to the ton, and since our coal bin could only accommodate a half a ton, it took ten sacks to fill it.

After the roof was replaced on the coal bin, we placed bricks on it to keep it from blowing off in a strong wind. I could then open the small door in front, to fill the bucket with coal. Carrying it down the alley, through the front door, up the stairs and into the living room, I made up the fire and lit it during the winter months. The small door was kept locked with a padlock, which was rather silly, because I knew if someone wanted to steal the coal, all they had to do, was remove the roof. They did, too! When, or who it was, we didn't know, but when people are desperately cold, I guess they can be easily tempted to climb a fence, and help themselves to the neighbor's precious coal.

Some of my happiest childhood memories are of the delivery and tradesmen who visited Shortlands on a daily, weekly or annual basis. They were just everyday people doing everyday jobs, but they kept the wheels of the country turning, and were a vital part of life in England at that time.

The milkman made daily deliveries from a battery-powered electric truck that he pulled down the street. When I heard the chink of the bottles in the crate as he walked up the path to the porch, I usually ran down to fetch the milk. If I didn't, and the milk bottles stood outside for any length of time, birds would peck a hole in the tin foil caps and steal the cream, which didn't make Mummy happy. Despite the hardships of delivering milk in the unpredictable English weather, the milkman was always cheerful.

The postman trudged up and down Farnaby Road with a large canvas mailbag slung over his shoulder. When he pushed the letters through the mail slot in the front door, they landed with a plop on the doormat. It didn't make a lot of noise, but because fetching the mail was one of my favorite things, I seldom failed to hear it. I separated ours from Auntie Lily's, and then pushed hers under her door.

The street sweeper was stout and had the reddest, rosiest cheeks I ever saw. He cleaned our street every few weeks, pushing a cart with two large trash cans and a couple of large brooms in it. Sweeping the gutters, he deposited the trash in one bin and leaves in the other. He was always ready with a smile and friendly "hello." In the winter, he wore several layers of clothing that made him look even stouter than he actually was. His gray woolen gloves had no fingers to make it easier for him to work, but I am sure they didn't help much to keep his hands warm.

The chimney sweep was my favorite. He came at the end of each winter to clean the chimney. I loved his visits. Arriving on his bicycle, his grimy face was as black as the chimneys he swept, and when he wiped his brow with his handkerchief, I caught a glimpse of his pink skin beneath. He carried his brushes up the stairs in a canvas sack, then carefully threaded them up through the chimney in the living room.

I acted as his assistant, running outside and over to the other side of the road, where I had a good view of the chimney. When the brush's bushy head pushed through the top of the chimney, I yelled, "It's through, it's through!" at the top of my voice. After Mummy paid him, he went down our street, knocking on doors, and cleaning all the chimneys. Sometimes, a tiny bit of soot sneaked back down into the living room, and Mummy got upset, but mostly with his cleaning cloths and brushes; he worked his magic without messing, and we were ready for another winter.

About once a year, the Rag and Bone man drove by on his old wooden cart pulled by a skinny, dejected-looking horse. The man himself was so thin that I used to think a puff of wind would blow him right off his cart. He drove through the streets yelling, "Rags and bones, rags and bones," and people ran out into the street to see if he wanted to buy any of their old discarded furniture, scrap metal and the like. He looked so poor and sad; I don't think he made much of a living out of the rags and bones he bought.

My daily chores may have been boring and repetitive, but the delivery and tradesmen helped to make our lives a little more interesting and a whole lot easier.

CALAMITIES

When Sheila was sixteen, she found work at an office in London, and all of a sudden, she was a grownup young lady. I admired Sheila, despite the fact that I usually irritated her, and I constantly tried to imitate her. Although I resented having to wear her old cast-offs, I loved to wear them just so that I could look like her. When Sheila permed her hair, I permed mine, too. I tried to walk like her, talk like her and generally made myself miserable, trying to be someone I wasn't. Trying to be like Sheila became a habit, and pretty soon, I imitated other people as well. I did this for quite a few years, while not quite knowing who I was.

Sheila dated a few young men, until Dennis Buckley started dating her. He drove a Morgan three-wheeler sports car, which could seat two people, and in the evenings, they either went to the movies or ballroom dancing. How I envied her being able to get out of the house. Of course, Stepfather never approved of any of Sheila's boyfriends, and if she came home even a few minutes late, he expressed his displeasure with his fists. I could never understand why Dennis didn't intervene when Stepfather hit Sheila, and I came to the conclusion that he was a coward, afraid of my stepfather and basically, a similar type of man.

In the spring of 1951, I began my final year at Bromley Road School. I was due to write my eleven-plus exam, and I wasn't confident that I would pass. I never did like exams and, indeed, I didn't care much for school either. The next few months were to make me even more nervous, with one calamity following another in quick succession.

Around the end of May, two months before the end of the school year, Mummy announced that we were going to the London Zoo with Auntie Violet and my cousin, Valerie. I was beside myself with excitement. I had never been to the Zoo, and family outings were a rarity.

Sunday morning arrived, and I woke up with a sore throat. I was sleeping in my sister's bedroom, as my room was damp at the time. I complained to Sheila about my sore throat, and turning toward me, she burst out laughing. I couldn't understand what could possibly be so funny, until she gave me her hand mirror. Staring back at me, I saw a fat, round face on an equally fat neck that couldn't possibly be mine. But of course, it really was me, and Mummy confirmed my worst fears. I had the mumps! Instead of going to the Zoo, I was left with Stepfather for the day while Mummy and Sheila went off without me. The next day, the doctor confirmed Mummy's diagnosis, and I was quarantined at home for three weeks, which was usual for contagious childhood diseases in those days.

After I recovered from my initial disappointment, I came to the conclusion that three weeks at home might not be so bad, as it gave me time for reading and drawing. But a week later, I was feeling much better, and I found myself busy with my chores again. Mummy said that it was too close to my final exam so, on her afternoon off, she went to the school and returned with a pile of homework, so that I could prepare for it.

By the end of the three weeks, I was more than ready to be back at school. I was bored, and when I no longer looked contagious, Stepfather was up to his old tricks again. On the day I was due to return to school,

I awoke to find my stepfather's hands running up and down my body and, as usual, I fought him off, until he suddenly froze and pulled his hands away as if he'd burned them. He glared at me, shook his head, and told me to stay in bed. Mummy was summoned, and after a quick examination, she told me that now I had measles.

This hardly seemed fair. Dr. Dyson arrived, and confirmed that I did indeed have the measles. The dear old man said that he also didn't think it was fair, but that I would have to be quarantined for yet another three weeks. I was beside myself with frustration! Mummy always said, "When things like this happen, it's God's punishment." I felt sure that whatever I had done to deserve it, this seemed too much to bear. Then, as if our lives were not chaotic enough, another drama was about to unfold that was to put the whole house in a tailspin.

The next morning, I was lying in bed, feeling sorry for myself. The measles made me feel much worse than the mumps had. I had a fever and itched all over. Mummy, who was scurrying around getting ready to go to work, told me that I should stay in bed and she would bring me a bowl of cornflakes on a tray.

Stepfather and Sheila had both left for work, and I was alone in Sheila's bedroom, which was particularly gloomy that morning. It was dark, and the sound of distant thunder made me nervous. It got louder and louder, and then there was a huge flash of lightning, and Mummy screamed! I froze, but only for a moment. Jumping out of bed, I rushed to the kitchen. Mummy was hunched over, hanging on to the edge of the kitchen table. She was screaming at the top of her voice, obviously in terrible pain. My bowl of cornflakes lay strewn across the kitchen floor, and I knew that something was seriously wrong, as Mummy never messed.

I flew downstairs, and into Auntie Lily's apartment shouting, "Auntie Lily, come quick! Mummy's been struck by lightning!" She ran upstairs, with me close behind. Mummy was still hunched over, screaming in agony. Auntie Lily took hold of her, and to my astonishment, she threw my mother over her shoulder like a sack of potatoes, rushed through to Mummy's bedroom, and deposited her unceremoniously on the bed. Mummy's eyes looked as if they were about to pop out of her head. She screamed all the louder, and I wondered where the lightning had struck her, as I couldn't see any visible burn marks.

Dr. Dyson was summoned for the third time in as many weeks, and after a thorough examination, he concluded that Mummy had a slipped disc in her back. Because she was in too much pain to be moved, she was told to remain in bed for at least six weeks. Mummy had not been struck by lightning, but we decided that the fright of the lightning strike may have caused her to jerk, dislocating the disc.

The thunderstorm had been a bad one, and it was unusual to have such a severe storm so early in the morning. We were used to storms in our house, but of a different kind. I was left with no option but to set aside any feelings of self-pity, and assume the role of a young housewife again.

Another trip had to be made to school, this time by my stepfather. He came home with even more homework than before. The day I would finally be allowed to return to school just happened to be the day scheduled for the exam. I complained bitterly, and said that I couldn't possibly be expected to prepare for the exam under the circumstances. My stepfather then gave me something to think about, informing me that he would make sure I passed that exam, or I was going to be one sorry little girl.

Every evening, for the next three weeks, we sat at the dining room table where I normally did my homework. Stepfather taught me, and I learned. If I complained, I received a physical incentive not to. He drilled me late into the night, every night when he came home from work. If I dared to fall asleep, he shook me awake, slapped me, and informed me that it wasn't any fun for him either, and I am sure it wasn't. On weekends, I worked, and worked some more, with Stepfather yelling at me, telling me that I was stupid, lazy, and ignorant. I had to prove him wrong and miraculously, that is what I did.

At the end of the six weeks, I returned to school and wrote the exam. There were about thirty children in my class, and I was one of only fourteen who passed. My teacher read the results to the class, but when she read my name, the look on her face told me that she didn't believe it possible that Doreen Wheble, that naughty, lazy girl, had actually passed. She insisted that I re-write the exam, which I did, and once again, I passed. This time, with some reluctance, she gave me my certificate, and I was then in a position to attend the Beckenham Grammar School for Girls, with the opportunity for a college education, although I was unaware of that at the time. In England, students are divided into different types of education systems when they enter high school: for technical training, or for preparation for higher education, which I had just qualified for. Stepfather's tuition, along with his physical encouragement, had produced positive results.

With Mummy laid up in bed for six weeks, Stepfather was free to make my life unbearable, and he did. When tutoring me for my exam was over, he came home late every evening, but this time, it seemed he wasn't just visiting the pub.

When I returned to school, Auntie Lily was kind enough to make lunch for my mother. Mummy didn't have much tolerance for staying in bed, but as each movement caused her pain, she had little choice. I was trying my best to keep up with the housework, as well as the cooking and laundry, when I came home from school, but nothing I did was good enough. Mummy was like a pressure cooker ready to explode … and, with good reason, explode, she did!

It happened the night when Mummy accused Stepfather of having an affair. The other woman was a divorcee, who had worked for my parents in the printing business. She still came to visit us now and again. I couldn't imagine why Stepfather found the woman attractive. She wasn't particularly pretty, wore thick makeup, bright red lipstick and the black roots of her hair revealed that she was not a natural blonde. Mummy often said, with great contempt, that the woman was a bottle blonde. She wasn't even clean, and often had stains on her clothes. Mummy was much prettier, and besides that, she was always clean and tidy.

After Mummy recovered from the slipped disc, the atmosphere in the house became even more strained, with the fights occurring more frequently and with greater ferocity. I couldn't begin to imagine how it was all going to end.

VISITORS FROM SOUTH AFRICA

That summer, there was great excitement in the house when we received a letter from Aunt Annie in South Africa, telling us that her daughter and son-in-law were planning a holiday to the British Isles in August, and they wanted to visit us.

When they arrived, they booked into a local hotel, frequently visiting us during their two-week stay in Bromley. Aunt Joey wore elegant suits and jewelry, high-heeled shoes and hats. Uncle Percy was a kindly gentleman, who always dressed in a suit and tie and I thought that they were lovely people.

They were childless, and took great delight in taking me up to London, where they bought me a Hungarian-style blouse with puffed sleeves and a tunic to wear over it, by far the prettiest clothes I had ever owned, and they were brand new! Used to wearing Sheila's hand-me-downs, I felt special when they spoiled me. We enjoyed lunch in a Lyons Corner House, a popular restaurant in the West End. It was a memorable day, and with Uncle Percy holding my one hand and Aunt Joey the other, I felt as if I belonged to them, and I found it easy to be on my best behavior.

Not long after their visit, I experienced one of the happiest days of my life, a day I will never forget. Hearing a knock at the front door, I ran downstairs and found a man standing on the front porch holding a bicycle, and I wondered why he brought his bicycle right up onto our porch. He held a clipboard and pen in his hand, and, smiling broadly, enquired if I was Doreen Wheble. "Yes," I replied, "I am."

"Then, this is for you, young lady," he said, looking down at the bicycle.

I couldn't believe my ears, and terribly excited, I yelled, "For me? For me?" He nodded.

By this time, Mummy had come downstairs to see what all the fuss was about. Examining the invoice, she shook her head in disbelief and said, "Your Aunt Joey and Uncle Percy have sent you this bicycle for your birthday, Doreen. My word, I can't believe it! They must think a lot of you."

She said this with a great deal of surprise, as if she couldn't believe that they actually liked me. I can never explain the joy I felt at receiving this wonderful gift. And yes, they actually liked me! It was an exhilarating feeling.

Receiving such a special birthday present, even before my birthday had arrived, made me the happiest child in the neighborhood. The day when I had learned to ride Marian's bicycle a couple of years earlier came to mind, and I realized that dreams do sometimes come true. Elated, I rode up and down the street every chance I had. Apart from the sheer enjoyment of riding, I wanted everyone in the street to see me riding on my new bicycle.

The bicycle was a blessing, and it changed my life in many ways. I had a great deal more freedom than I ever had before and I knew that, with a bicycle, there was a good chance that I could get a job delivering newspapers. That would enable me to earn my own pocket money, while opening doors to even greater independence.

A few weeks later, something even more remarkable happened. My mother took me into the living room, sat me down and said she had something to tell me. The look on her face told me it was something serious. She said, "Doreen, I received this letter from Aunt Joey and Uncle Percy, asking me if they could adopt you."

Adopt me? I understood about adoption. I knew a girl at school who lived at the local orphanage. She had told me how some of the children got to be adopted and go to a permanent home. But why did they want to adopt me? I wasn't an orphan.

Mummy explained, "They don't have any children of their own, and can't expect to ever have any. After discussing the matter at length, they agreed that they really like you and want to adopt you."

Aunt Joey and Uncle Percy were so entirely different from my stepfather; it was hard to believe they were from the same family. It was even more difficult to believe that they wanted to adopt me. Here was my chance! The two people I would love to have for parents, wanted me to be their child.

Then I looked at Mummy, and she suddenly looked old and very tired. In some ways, I was already mature beyond my years, and I felt an overwhelming pity for her. I was almost eleven and old enough to feel compassion for this woman who had made a bad choice, and had to live with the consequences. Mummy continued, "If you agree to do this, you will go and live in South Africa on their farm. Uncle Percy said that you will have your very own pony; you will go to a good school and have pretty clothes and anything else your heart desires."

With a tremor in her voice, Mummy explained that it was truly the chance of a lifetime, and if I wanted to do this, she would not stand in my way.

My thoughts were racing at such a speed, I couldn't speak. The opportunity to get away from my stepfather was uppermost in my mind. Then I looked once more at my mother, and saw tears well up in her eyes.

How could I leave her? Who would protect her from my stepfather? Sheila was out with Dennis most evenings. Somebody had to take care of Mummy. So, I stayed.

GRAMMAR SCHOOL

At the start of the new school year, I found myself once again traveling on the 227 bus, but this time, I passed by Bromley Road School and traveled further along the main road to Beckenham Grammar School for Girls. I had passed the exam, and was now on my way to a first-class education. The only problem was, I didn't want it. All I wanted was to paint and draw, as my one ambition was to become a commercial artist. I had no idea how to go about doing this, and I didn't understand that I needed a college education to become one. It was only by chance that I wound up in the grammar school, not because of any intention to go to college. Understandably, Mummy needed me to get a job as soon as possible to assist with the finances, and since she had had little education herself, she never investigated what might be required for me to follow my dream.

The Grammar School was not a bad school, although it was a bit stuffy, but by now, I had become a full-blown rebel, determined to pursue my ambition to study art. We had two art classes back-to-back, once a week, and I got exceptionally high marks for every project, but it wasn't nearly enough to satisfy me. Time and time again, I found myself in trouble for drawing, while attending other classes. I was happiest while painting or drawing, and thrived on the compliments I received from my art teacher and fellow pupils. These admirers did not include Philippa, a tall girl with long plaits, who was exceptionally good at art and with whom I regularly found myself in fierce competition.

Science was interesting, with Bunsen burners and test tubes and the possibility of blowing up the laboratory. It was just not what I wanted to do. In fact, I had little interest in most of what the school had to offer. History, geography, arithmetic and all of what I considered the mundane subjects that contribute to a good education, didn't appeal to me, and I was constantly being told to pay attention. I had neither the insight nor the guidance from home to appreciate the opportunity set before me.

In October, my eleventh birthday came and went. I was almost a grown-up, and for my age and experience, that is exactly how I felt – grown up! The first thing I did the day after my birthday was to ride to the newspaper shop opposite the railway station, where I bought Stepfather's newspapers and cigarettes. I was just old enough to deliver newspapers, and amazingly, there was a vacancy for one of the morning newspaper rounds. When I landed the job, I was in heaven and couldn't wait to tell Mummy. She was happy for me, as she couldn't afford to increase my pocket money and now, that shilling that she gave me could remain in her housekeeping allowance.

Stepfather still woke me in his usual disgusting fashion in the mornings. Getting up, my cheeks burning with humiliation, I'd throw on some clothes, hurrying to be at the newspaper shop by six. The big canvas bag was so heavy, that when I first started work, the storekeeper had to help me to place it diagonally over my shoulder. I wobbled off precariously on my bicycle, trying my utmost to keep my balance. As I progressed along my route, the weight gradually decreased, and my balance improved. Riding up and down the steep hills every day, I soon became fit and strong and able to handle my heavy load with ease.

As winter slowly overtook fall, I discovered that riding in snow and ice was not nearly as easy as on a dry surface. The corner at the end of Farnaby Road was particularly sharp, and one day, while trying to make it around much faster than the corner allowed, I fell, and the bag full of newspapers lay strewn all over the road. My right knee was grazed, bleeding and stinging from the snow. Brushing the snow off my clothes, I straightened my bent handlebars and gathered up the wet newspapers, knowing that it was not going to be my best delivery day.

In those days, newspapers were not covered in plastic as they are today, so most of them were thoroughly soaked through. Delivering them through the mail slots proved out of the question, and I found myself trembling at the front door of one of the grand houses on Ravensbourne Avenue. Because the newspaper was wet, it tore slightly as I tried to push it through the slot in the door, and I needed to apologize.

The man who answered the doorbell was obviously not a morning person, and he made his own delivery to me in the form of a lecture on the virtues of being more careful with his newspaper. When I explained that I had had a fall, he was not at all understanding and called my employer to complain. I determined to be more careful in the future, as I couldn't afford to lose my job. The money was far too important.

There were some nice people along the route who made up for the grumpy man. One elderly lady gave me a cookie as a treat now and again. She owned a great dane, and at first, I was terrified to go through her big iron gate, until I discovered that his heart was the biggest thing about him. He regularly jumped up, nearly knocking me over, while licking my face, and we soon became fast friends. I wished that I could have a dog of my own, but living in an upstairs apartment made it impossible, so I had to be content with Blackie.

Delivering the newspapers took about an hour and on my way home, I had to pass the bus stop where my stepfather caught the bus to work just after seven o'clock. I tried to time it so that I was behind the bus, arriving after he was already gone. Inevitably, there were some mornings when he was still there, calling out for me to stop. I always yelled that I couldn't, as I would be late for school, but sometimes he stepped out into the street, and grabbed my handlebars, bringing me to an abrupt halt. He then kissed me viciously, and just as viciously, I wiped the kiss off with the back of my hand. With his mocking laugh ringing in my ears, and my eyes stinging with salty tears, I rode home feeling flushed and angry.

For the morning paper round, I received eleven shillings. There were quite a few people who only bought the Sunday papers, which were thick and heavy, and with the addition of those extras, my Sunday round took me about twice as long as on weekdays.

Now that I was 'rich' and tired of wearing Sheila's old hand-me-downs, I purchased some new clothes from the store in Shortlands. First, I bought a blouse, which I paid off a few shillings at a time, until it was mine. Next, I bought a skirt, then a dress, and I slowly built up a wardrobe of pretty clothes.

Although I didn't really enjoy the Grammar School, I enjoyed meal times. We had a short lunch break at midmorning, when we ate snacks that we brought from home. Our main meal was at one o'clock in the large dining room where we sat eight at a table. I had a good appetite, and it was as if I could never get enough to eat. I often ate the leftovers from the other children at my table, especially if they didn't eat their dessert. Always skinny as a child; Mummy used to say that she didn't know where I put all my food. I guess delivering newspapers and doing my chores gave me a good, healthy appetite.

In May of 1952, the year I turned twelve, they held a nationwide Handwriting Competition for all the schoolchildren in Great Britain. It was organized by the Children's Newspaper, and I was delighted when I received a certificate and a prize for good handwriting. I had carefully followed the rules and wrote in the exact manner required. Philippa, my art rival, who wrote beautifully, insisted on keeping to her usual slanted style. It angered her when I won, and at breaktime, she teased and bullied me unmercifully. Because she was the biggest girl in the class, there wasn't much that I could do about it, but I felt sure that if she had just followed the rules, she would probably have done even better than me.

I don't think Mummy understood how important winning a prize in the competition was for me, because her only response when I told her about it was, "That's nice, Doreen." I received the same reaction when I won a prize in the nationwide, 'Knit a Square' competition. Why could she never be proud of me? Mummy didn't seem interested in any of my school activities, and never attended the school for parents' open days. She did, however, go to the school when she was summoned to see the headmistress for one of my many misdemeanors, and another such day was fast approaching.

RUNAWAY

Sundays at home were gloomy, even when the sun shone. My parents always slept late and when I got home from delivering newspapers, I made their breakfast of toast, eggs and bacon, and took it in to them on trays. Stepfather spent the rest of the morning in the living room, reading the Sunday newspaper from cover to cover, and I had better keep quiet, or else! Somber music played on the radio. Sometimes, I was fortunate enough to find myself alone in the living room when my parents took an afternoon nap, in which case, I searched for AFN – American Forces Network. They played the top forty hits, which I enjoyed.

After breakfast, the kitchen had to be cleaned up, and then I helped Mummy prepare the vegetables for lunch. We ate frugally, knowing exactly what meal to expect on any given day. Standard meals were made with ground beef, sausages, canned bully beef or fish. Occasionally, Mummy made an egg and bacon pie. On Sundays, we had beef or lamb roast. The roast was usually small, because the meat was still rationed, and it tended to shrink in the oven, but somehow, after having one slice each, there was usually enough left over for Monday night's pie, which Mummy ground in her cast iron sausage grinder.

On one occasion, just after the war, when Mummy couldn't find any affordable meat, the butcher offered her some horse meat. It looked pretty good, but after cooking it slowly all morning, it was still too tough to chew. I think the poor horse must have been about fifty years old and worked hard all of its life. Mummy dutifully ran it through the grinder, and we ate it in a pie the next day.

One Sunday morning, I came home from delivering newspapers to find Mummy and Stepfather having a loud argument. This was not unusual, but because it was a Sunday and I disliked Sundays anyway, I wanted out. They didn't even notice me walk down the stairs and out of the front door. When they were fighting, they didn't seem to notice much of anything, and they certainly didn't care about the plight of our poor neighbors, who had to put up with the constant shouting and screaming that filtered through the walls of our adjoining apartments.

Outside the unpleasant atmosphere of our home, the sun was shining out of a clear blue sky, and it felt pleasant on my skin. There was a sweet scent of lavender growing on yard walls along the way, and lazy bees drifted from one flower to another. Birds chirping and singing added to the tranquility of the day.

I walked past the grand houses at the wealthy end of Farnaby Road, cutting through to the Ravensbourne River that ran through Shortlands. It was the same river where I had fallen in further downstream, but after a few weeks of drought, it had dried up, enabling me to walk along the riverbed and dream. Cob trees lined the riverbed, and I gathered some of the plentiful nuts and stuffed them into my pockets.

Somewhere along the way I met up with a girl I knew from Shortlands, and we ambled along together. I told her I had just run away from home, and she was suitably impressed. I felt quite elated, and exceptionally grown up.

Around lunchtime, we stopped along the riverbank and, sitting down, cracked open the cobnuts with our teeth, and ate our fill. By now, I was getting thirsty, and although my stomach was full of nuts, I couldn't help thinking longingly about the roast lamb I was missing, not to mention the apple pie and custard that I knew was for dessert. We only had dessert on Sundays, so maybe I should rather have planned to run away on a weekday.

My friend and I walked back along the riverbed, and as we neared Shortlands, we came across a wooded area, where a man was out walking his dog. While petting the dog, the man asked us where we lived and what we were doing in the woods. We told him we were just having fun, and he suggested a game of hide and seek. It sounded good, so my friend stayed in one place while I went to hide.

The man followed me with his dog, and soon, we were hiding behind some bushes together. Somehow, this didn't feel right, and I got the same feeling in the pit of my stomach that I got when my stepfather fondled me. My heart beat a warning, telling me that this was not a good situation and before he could stop me, I jumped up and ran towards my friend. The dog chased me, and so did the man. As I neared my friend, I told her to run, and sensing the urgency of my warning, she responded immediately, grabbing my hand as we ran off as fast as we could. I believe that was the first time I felt a woman's intuition, and I was grateful for it.

Panting and out of breath, we reached the road and, looking back, found that the man had given up the chase, so we parted and hurried home. Halfway there, I met Sheila, who had a face like a thundercloud, and I knew I was in deep trouble. She told me that Mummy had called the police, who informed her that if I was not home by sundown, they would send out a patrol to look for me. I was terrified! I offered Sheila some cobnuts, but she wouldn't even look at them, or me for that matter. She grabbed my hand and marched me home, scrunching my hand all the way. My hand hurt, and I dreaded to think what was waiting for me at home.

On reaching the house, I found my mother in hysterics. She screamed and swore at me, which was bad enough, but when my stepfather joined in, he hit me with such force that I almost toppled backwards down the stairs. I received a terrible beating with his belt before being sent to my room. I had only made matters worse by running away, and I would receive no Sunday roast or apple pie that day.

A BABY BROTHER

Sometimes, when Mummy was dressed up in one of her smart suits, wearing a hat with a feather, she was mistaken for the Duchess of Kent. She couldn't afford a lot of clothes, but what she bought was tasteful and of good quality. She loved Chanel No. 5 and somehow, even though it was expensive, she always managed to have a tiny bottle of the perfume reserved for special occasions. Mummy received a lot of attention when she was dressed up, and I felt really important, being with my mother, who looked just like the Duchess of Kent.

Mummy worked at Woolworths until she fell pregnant with my brother. She was thirty-nine at the time, and assuming that she had begun the change of life, she didn't realize that she had been pregnant for almost five months. Family and friends were shocked when they heard. To me, the news was quite wonderful, because a baby in the house meant having a real live doll to play with. Surely, Stepfather would now love and respect my mother, and maybe, just maybe, he would leave me alone.

When we discovered that Mummy was pregnant, with only four months before the birth, I spent every spare minute knitting for the baby, while Mummy made baby clothes on her sewing machine.

It was surprising that Mummy survived the pregnancy because the beatings continued just as before. She carried a lot of water, which made her legs and feet swell. She also developed ugly varicose veins on her legs, but she got no sympathy from my stepfather. Somehow, I don't think he was capable of feeling sympathy.

My baby brother was born in late September. Mummy was in the kitchen when her water broke, and I got a terrible fright, not comprehending what was happening. Once again, I witnessed my mother's cries of pain, this time caused by labor pains, as she gathered her things together to go to the hospital. Auntie Lily's sister, who lived nearby, now had a telephone in her house, so I was sent to ask her to call for an ambulance to take Mummy to the hospital.

Mummy gave birth to a bouncing baby boy weighing just over nine pounds. She stayed in the hospital for ten days, and knowing how my stepfather took advantage of the situation with me, I can just imagine how Sheila must have suffered during that time. While Mummy was in the hospital, she wrote me tiny notes on scraps of paper telling me that I was going to love my baby brother, and that she was sorry that I was too young to be allowed in the hospital to see him. I still have those pencil-written notes, even though they have faded with time. Every hint of love was precious to me, although, for the most part, the notes expressed her concerns about my behavior, and whether or not I was keeping up with my household chores.

I was overjoyed when Mummy brought Ross home. I was sure that I loved him more than anyone else. I bathed him, changed his diapers, took him for walks and fed him when Mummy added solid foods to his diet.

Ross escaped my stepfather's wrath for a while, until, as a toddler, he learned to say "no," which was not permissible. Gradually, he learned the meaning of Stepfather's harsh discipline, and my heart would break when he got a beating. If I tried to protect him, I would receive double his punishment. Secretly, I hoped that when Ross became a grown man, he would teach my stepfather a lesson, but Ross had a gentle nature and never retaliated.

MONEY MATTERS

After Ross was born, Mummy was no longer able to work at Woolworths, so she took in clothing alterations, and made drapes to supplement Stepfather's income. With Sheila now employed, she paid board and lodging, but money was still tight, so the income I earned from delivering newspapers helped me a lot.

By this time, I had an evening paper round as well, for which I was paid an extra nine shillings. Earning £1.00 a week enabled me to save for our annual holiday, and I always had a tidy sum of money put away by the time September came around. I was careful to ensure that it lasted the whole two weeks, but Mummy and Sheila were not as careful, and towards the end of the holiday, they often had to borrow from me, and it pleased me to be in a position to help out.

One Friday, my stepfather came straight home from work, which was highly unusual. He laid his brown pay envelope with his week's wages in it, on the dining room table. Mummy assumed it was empty and being excessively tidy, threw it into the fire. I was amazed he didn't kill her that night; he was that angry. He kept yelling at her, telling her how stupid and useless she was, and the next thing I knew, they were having a full-blown fight, with his fists flying in all directions. Mummy,

Sheila and I were ducking, diving and screaming, and the people next door were banging on the wall, while Uncle David downstairs was knocking on the ceiling. All we needed was an orchestra, and we would have our very own opera. A bad one, but an opera, nevertheless.

Friday was not only payday; it was also our weekly bath night. Because we had no running hot water, Mummy filled the big metal boiler with cold water and brought it to a boil on the gas stove in the kitchen. Mummy and Sheila then carried it by its handles down the hallway into the bathroom and tipped it into the bathtub. By the time it hit the cold bathtub and I had undressed, it was just the right temperature for me to bathe. Of course, there was barely enough water to allow me to rinse off properly, but I managed somehow. While I bathed, the boiler was refilled and placed back on the stove. This was then added to my bathwater, which by that time was almost cold, and Sheila took her bath. One more boiler full of water enabled Mummy to bathe, and last, but not least, with one last boiler full, my stepfather could bathe in the luxury of all the dirty water from the rest of the family. Ross was bathed in the sink in the kitchen until he was big enough to bathe ahead of me in the big bathtub. And then, there were five!

What a treat it was when Mummy bought a gas ring, which was a single burner stove, that she plugged into the gas outlet in the bathroom wall. We could then boil the water right next to the bathtub, which was much safer than carrying it from the kitchen. An added benefit of the gas ring was that while it was boiling the water, it also heated the bathroom, which, in the winter, was a luxury we hadn't known before.

The rest of the week, we all took it in turns to wash ourselves in the kitchen using a large enamel bowl. Terrified that my stepfather might come in, I always washed as quickly as I could. Should I hear the approach of his heavy step, I yelled at the top of my voice for everyone to hear, "You can't come in." That way, there was a chance that he wouldn't come barging in, but I always kept my towel handy, just in case. As a result of the unpleasant circumstances surrounding my childhood, I became painfully shy and protective of my body. I also developed an obsession about my personal hygiene. When Stepfather touched me, I felt dirty, and even though I scrubbed myself sore, I never felt clean enough. It would be many years before I was able to rid myself of that feeling, only to find myself reliving it again under different circumstances as an adult.

My stepfather continued to spend much of his salary on brandy and cigarettes, so Mummy was compelled to take in more and more sewing to supplement our income. She was a wonderful seamstress, and with the vintage Singer sewing machine inherited from my Welsh grandmother, she made enough money for us to get by. The old Singer had originally worked with a foot treadle, but my grandmother had it converted into a hand crank machine. I grew to love that machine and, over time, learned to sew and make clothes with it. Sometimes, Mummy even allowed me help her with the alterations. The wonderful clickety-clack sound it made as she worked far into the night on the dining room table was music to my ears. Sometimes, she sewed until one or two o'clock in the morning, to finish an alteration for a customer so that we could go to the movies.

Most of Mummy's customers were local folk who lived in Shortlands. The biggest order she ever received was to make drapes for Major Loch and his wife, who lived in a grand house on the other side of the village. They ordered heavy brocade drapes, which had to be fully lined, and as the windows were exceptionally large, I went with Mummy to help her measure up.

Their house was a mansion compared to ours, and walking through the pillars at the entrance made me feel about a quarter of my normal size. I wondered why anyone needed a front door as large as theirs, and I was grateful that I didn't have to clean all the brass that adorned it. Inside, the house resembled a museum, with large paintings of stern-looking elderly people, mostly dressed in black, hanging on the walls. The elaborate frames were an art form of their own. The floors were covered with exquisite Persian carpets, while porcelain and bronze ornaments, almost as tall as me, stood on pedestals in the entrance hall and living and dining rooms. I was completely overwhelmed by the grandeur of the house.

Once we had taken the measurements, Major Loch had the fabric delivered to our house. Several bolts of heavy brocade fabric arrived, along with a couple of rolls of lining. I was horrified at the enormity of the task that lay ahead, but Mummy was confident that she could handle it. Furniture was pushed aside, and the dining room table was cleared to allow for the cutting of the fabric. The table was not long enough, even when the extra leaves were added, so I helped by holding onto the fabric, preventing it from moving around, while Mummy cut it into lengths with her old sewing scissors. Her poor hands suffered, as she battled to cut through the heavy fabric.

For the first time, I questioned my mother's capability as a seamstress, but I should have known better. Mummy and her old Singer were a formidable pair, able to perform miracles. Cut, pin, then sew, sew, sew! Oh, how Mummy worked on her faithful old machine. It clickety-clacked on into the night, every night for weeks. Mrs. Loch wanted the drapes finished in time for the holidays. Christmas was coming, and we needed the money. There would be no luxuries if Mummy didn't finish them on time, but I feared that she would have a nervous breakdown, she was that anxious to finish them. Needle after needle broke, protesting the impossibility of forcing a path through four to six thicknesses of fabric on the seams and corners.

Mummy finally sewed the Rufflette tape onto the tops of the drapes, after which she pronounced them finished. My relief upon hearing this was short-lived, however, when she said that we still had to sew on the curtain rings. We, being Mummy and me! Sheila always insisted that she couldn't sew and I loved sewing, so why should it not be my privilege to help sew on the rings? It was a job I grew to dislike intensely in just a few days. The fabric was thick, and my small fingers objected to the many times I pricked my flesh, as I battled to force the needle through. Mummy used a thimble, but she didn't have one to fit my small finger.

A couple of days before Christmas, Mummy and I pushed Ross' pram piled high with neatly folded and pressed drapes through the lamplit streets to Major Loch's house. We had no option but to use the pram as a means of transport, as Mummy was far too proud to ask the Major to come and fetch them in his car, and he didn't offer to collect them. Fortunately, no snow had fallen so far that winter, which would have made our journey even more of a challenge. We made about six trips in all, and while walking past the gaily decorated stores, my excitement grew at the prospect of a Christmas with enough money to ensure that it was going to be a grand one.

The store windows in the village were full of Christmas lights, making it look like fairyland. There were no community decorations in the streets like we have nowadays, but the streetlights gave off a soft yellow glow in the misty darkness, adding to the festive atmosphere, while villagers greeted one another with a cheery, "Merry Christmas."

Sheila and I were decorating the tree on Christmas Eve, when we heard shouts of joy in the street. We went outside, and found neighbors dancing in celebration of a flurry of snow, heralding a white Christmas an hour or two before midnight. Only occasionally did we have an early snowfall, covering the village in a blanket of glistening white flakes. Bing Crosby's record, 'I'm Dreaming of a White Christmas,' took on a whole new meaning that year.

The Major and his wife were well pleased with the finished drapes, and Mummy was paid handsomely for her efforts. That year, we had a splendid Christmas.

DEVON

Uncle David, downstairs, had been in poor health for a long time, and I was saddened when he eventually died. Shortly after his death, Auntie Lily announced that her sister, Vera, who was also widowed, had moved down to Axminster in Devon, and that she was going to visit her for two weeks. She asked my mother if I could accompany her, and much to my delight, Mummy agreed. Two weeks away from Stepfather and the fighting sounded like a grand idea, and it turned out to be a bright spot in my otherwise troubled life. We traveled down on the steam train, and on our arrival, Auntie Lily's sister picked us up in her car and took us to lunch. While in the restaurant, Auntie Lily told me all about Axminster and how it was famous for making woolen carpets.

Then, the sisters took me to an auction, and I fell in love with auctions instantly. The auctioneer was barely understandable, and I was astounded that anyone could speak that fast. He rattled on and on, faster and faster, every now and then pausing to yell, "Sold!" I was totally captivated. People milled around the auctioneer, either holding up a hand or a card with a number on it. Some would just nod their heads, but he always seemed to know what they meant. Auntie Lily warned me to be careful not to wave or nod in the direction of the auctioneer, or I might end up buying something I didn't want. It was all very exciting.

While the auction was in progress, I wandered around and came upon a box of chinaware and trinkets. On top was a teapot, but it was not just any teapot. It was crafted in the form of a little thatch-roofed cottage, with a spout on one side and a handle on the other. The roof formed the lid.

Not having had the opportunity to plan ahead for the holiday, I only had ten shillings left from my paper round money, which had to last for the whole two weeks. I ran over to Auntie Lily and asked her to come and look at the treasure I had found. She dutifully admired the teapot, which I suspect was not to her taste, and I asked her if she thought I could bid for it and how much it would cost. She told me that it would be sold along with the contents of the box and thought the box might go for about ten shillings. As that was all the money I had, I knew that if I bought it, I'd have nothing left for ice cream or candy. But no matter, I was sure that Mummy would love it.

We watched while other items were bid for and sold, until eventually, the auctioneer came to 'my' box. I held my breath. He asked how much he was bid, and a lady bid five shillings. Hesitating for only a moment, I plucked up all my courage and bid six. The lady promptly bid seven shillings, and I countered with eight. She bid nine shillings, and after looking at her with the most mournful expression I could muster, I said in what I hoped was a loud, confident voice, "Ten shillings!" There was a moment's silence as I waited for the auctioneer to pound on the podium with his little hammer, yelling the magic word, "Sold!" Then, a male voice from the back shouted, "Eleven shillings!" I was terribly disappointed. My beautiful teapot was lost, but without realizing it at the time, I had become an auction fan for life.

After the auction, Auntie Vera drove us to her little cottage in the country. It was like looking at a picture in a book. The cottage was small, painted white with a thatch roof, and it immediately became my dream house, and would remain so for always. The front door led into a cozy living room, with a stone fireplace heavily adorned with copper and brass kettles and other bric-a-brac. A kitchen led off to the left, emitting a wonderful aroma from a large pot of stew. To my young, eager eyes, everything was just perfect. Straight ahead was a winding staircase leading upstairs. Halfway up, we had to duck to avoid bumping our heads on an enormous black wooden beam that stretched the length of the living room.

Upstairs, there were three bedrooms and a bathroom. I was to sleep in the smallest bedroom on an antique brass bed, covered with a pretty patchwork quilt. The window had a deep window seat just below it, where I could curl up with a book and look out onto a meadow full of cows. To add to my joy, little cottontail rabbits sometimes ran around in the garden. Those were two of the happiest weeks of my life, except for the day when the cows chased me.

Never having been around cows before, I knew nothing about them. The next day, on a walk in the backyard, I discovered an apple tree and picked a couple of apples. I then climbed over a stile and into the meadow, where I walked up to one of the cows and held out an apple. She didn't seem very interested, but the rest of the cows became curious, and started trundling over towards me at quite a speed. I was a good way from the stile, and seeing the stampede approaching, I panicked and ran back. They all ran after me, and I barely made it over the stile in time. Once we had the fence between us, they didn't look nearly as ferocious, and I felt quite silly. Turning around, I saw Auntie Lily and her sister standing at the kitchen window, enjoying a good chuckle. I felt a little sheepish at my lack of courage, but when I joined them, we all enjoyed a good laugh at my expense.

Another day, I went for a walk and found myself in the neighbor's farmyard, where I came upon an enormous sow. She had a litter of piglets, which were adorable. The sow turned to look at me and the menacing look in her eyes had me running for the fence once again.

Despite my two close encounters, I guess I must have been a country girl at heart because I was sad when the holiday ended, and I had to return to village life and home.

ALMOST GROWN, WITH BUNIONS!

After two years of reluctant attendance at the Grammar School, Miss Henshaw, the headmistress, called my mother up to the school and informed her that I was wasting their time, while depriving some other bright child's chance for a good education. I am sure that Mummy was embarrassed, but she was accustomed to me being a problem child. I was dutifully removed from the Grammar School, unknowingly squandering my chance for a university education. Miss Henshaw recommended that I attend St. Nicholas College for Girls, where she felt sure that I would be in a better position to have extra art classes.

Meanwhile, I had bunions! I think I was actually born with them, but they were not too noticeable until I reached the ripe old age of eight. By the age of twelve, I began to notice that when I stood with my feet together, my big toes formed a perfect "V" for victory. However, I didn't feel very victorious, particularly when my feet became the object of ridicule at school. The snide remarks I received from the other children were always countered with some brave retort, even though I didn't feel very brave, especially when hot tears threatened to escape from my eyes. Cheap shoes, and hand-me-downs from Sheila, didn't improve the situation. The bunions became red and painful, and to make matters worse, every winter, I also suffered from chilblains, inflammatory swellings caused by exposure to cold, damp conditions, which were painful as well as itchy.

My mother eventually took me to an Orthopedic specialist, who said he was sure that he could fix my bunions, and I was presented with what looked like two small metal walking sticks with straps attached to them. At night, the metal hooks were placed around my ankles, with one strap tied around my instep and another around my big toe, pulling it over, and forcing it into some semblance of straightness. The pain was unbearable, and with the braces gripping both feet, and the eczema creeping up the length of my arms, face and neck, I didn't get much sleep. Sometimes, I dared to take the braces off during the night, but a slap from my stepfather the next morning, encouraged me to leave them on and endure the pain.

Needless to say, the steel braces didn't help, and after six months, the specialist recommended surgery. He was to operate on one foot at a time, each foot requiring two surgeries. This would alleviate the necessity for a wheelchair, which was supposed to make me feel really happy! With the first surgery, he cut open the bunion on my left foot, removed part of the bone at the joint, and inserted a screw into the bone. The foot remained in a plaster cast for six weeks, followed by a recuperation period of another six weeks. With the second surgery, he removed the screw, followed by another six weeks in plaster. Both procedures required walking with crutches, to avoid putting weight on my foot.

The first surgery was performed at the beginning of the summer, ruining my entire school holiday. Mummy and I traveled on the bus to the Children's Hospital in Sydenham. From the bus stop, we took a shortcut through a wooded park, where, to my delight, we encountered a gentleman walking his horse, which he allowed me to stroke. With my mother's permission, he set me up on the mare, and I rode her to the other side of the park, where he gently lifted me off, pointing to the gate leading to the hospital.

Having just experienced the thrill of my life, riding on a horse for the very first time, I was in no mood to go to hospital, but after my mother signed some papers, I was led into the ward and shown to my bed. Remembering my last experience when I cut my leg open, I was nervous, but this time, I found myself in good hands.

After the initial shock and pain of the surgery, I enjoyed being spoiled at the hands of Nurse Lennox and Nurse Barker. After all these years, it is a testament to their kindness that I so clearly remember their names as well as their appearance. Nurse Lennox had short black hair, and Nurse Barker, long auburn hair. I admired them in their starched white uniforms, thinking that if their belted waistlines were any smaller, they would surely break in two. They were both highly dedicated young women, and for a while after leaving the hospital, I fantasized about becoming a nurse.

Mummy wasn't able to visit me often in the hospital, since she had her hands full with Ross, so I soon became anxious to go home. It was not easy crossing the park on crutches to catch the bus home, and the next six weeks were to be a test of my endurance. But I was young and strong, and the possibility of having pretty feet that didn't hurt anymore, made it all seem worthwhile. By the time I had my second surgery, I was in my new school, and that was to be more of a challenge.

With my foot in plaster, our annual family holiday in Dymchurch wasn't much fun. The crutches made me sore under my arms, especially on the long walk from the trailer park to the sea, and worse than anything, I wasn't able to roller-skate.

Once we were back home, I returned to the doctor to have the plaster removed. For a while, because the foot was swollen, I had to borrow a left shoe from Mummy or Sheila. Limping along in odd shoes, I acquired a new nickname from the children in Shortlands. I became known as Hop-a-long.

With the onset of womanhood, my mother felt that it was time to tell me the facts of life. Mummy obviously found it awkward to talk to me about such intimate things, and I found it terribly embarrassing as she explained why my body was changing, and how babies were made. Thinking about the things Stepfather was doing to me, I felt apprehensive, and wondered what it meant and why he was doing those things? It all felt so wrong.

That was also the day when Mummy found it necessary to tell me in graphic detail how she had tried to terminate her pregnancy with me. I believe she wanted to unburden herself of the feelings of guilt she was no doubt experiencing, but to hear her describing how she had done it made me feel sick! Knowing that my mother had never wanted me, even before I was born, was too much for me to bear. I now understood the full meaning of her lack of affection, and pregnancy and childbirth took on a foreboding sense of darkness in my young mind.

With the changes in my body, my stepfather became even more aggressive, groping at my tiny breasts and the more I tried to push him away, the more he hurt me. I squirmed and fought him off, but my strength was no match for his. On one of those occasions, I told him that I hated him, whereupon he punched me viciously. Then he grinned and walked out of the room. Such was his ego; I don't think he ever really believed that I hated him, no matter how many times I told him.

While walking down the hallway one day, I glanced into my parents' bedroom and caught a glimpse of Stepfather standing naked in front of the mirror. I am sure it was no accident that the door was standing wide open, and I wished I was anywhere but in the same apartment as Paul Welman.

ST. NICHOLAS COLLEGE

In September of 1953, I boarded the 227 bus, but this time I traveled in the opposite direction, towards Chistlehurst. I was to attend St. Nicholas College for Girls. It sounded rather grand, but it was actually the same technical school that Sheila had attended. Only the name had changed. I was dubious as to whether this was going to afford me the chance to become a commercial artist, but at least now, I had hope.

The campus consisted of three stately old houses set in thickly wooded grounds. The largest of the three, Bullerswood, was the most beautiful. The rooms were spacious and made for comfortable classrooms, as well as a dining room, where we ate our midday meal. Inglewood, the second largest, boasted an extensive lawn in front where we spent our breaks, while Hydeswood was the smallest of the three and rather plain in design.

My first day didn't go well. Mummy couldn't afford the school uniform, which, in summer, was either a blue or pink check dress, and she insisted that I wear a red and white check taffeta dress with a white boat-style neck, which Sheila had outgrown. It was a pretty dress, but with its full-circle skirt, it was far more appropriate as a party dress. The whisperings and giggles from my peers were almost more than I could bear, and my limp didn't help much either. I looked and felt pretty pathetic, and as a result, I became angry, which I found to be a satisfying substitute for self-pity.

The first class I attended was English, and Miss Pethybridge commenced by calling out our names to confirm attendance. When she came to my name, I raised my hand, and she smiled at me and said, "Oh yes, you must be Sheila Wheble's sister. She was a good student."

Her comment was like a red flag, and I bristled. So, I was to be compared to my sister, who was always considered by everyone to be smarter than me. I determined to show the teacher who was better, and I earned many detentions while in her class.

Unlike the syllabus at the Grammar School, we were taught practical skills to prepare us for a trade. I was placed in the shorthand/typing class, and I hated it. At the end of the first term, we were given a test, and because I hadn't taken the slightest interest in shorthand, I was left with no alternative other than to turn in a blank paper. The teacher was not amused! I was promptly dismissed and transferred to the domestic science class.

Before I even had time to settle into my new class, I returned to the Children's Hospital for my second surgery. The screw was removed, and I was back in plaster and on crutches, which made the mile-and-a-half walk from the bus stop to school slow going. The surgeon kindly gave me the screw to take home as a souvenir. It looked like an ordinary screw, but it had four tiny metal wings protruding from the point. It gained me a lot of attention at school with many "oohs" and "aahs" from the other girls.

When I returned to the surgeon three months later, he examined my foot and shook his head. He told my mother that he regretted that the surgery had not been successful, and that my feet were so badly deformed by the bunions that I would probably end up in a wheelchair by age forty. Now, that was something to look forward to! To make matters worse, I now not only had bunions, but the skin was so thin where he had operated, that for the next few years, the chilblains I developed during winter became ulcerated. I limped for over a year after the surgeries, ensuring that I kept my nickname of Hop-a-long.

On my return to school, I was told that I was to take needlework instead of art classes and so ended my ambition to become a commercial artist. My disappointment was great, but I knew that it wouldn't help to complain. I had to work fast to catch up with the rest of the needlework class, having missed the whole first term while attending the shorthand and typing classes, as well as my time in the hospital. The needlework teacher, Miss O'Hanessian was a short, stout woman with a strong Eastern European accent and an abrupt manner, and I had the feeling that she didn't much like me.

For her class, I embroidered a tray cloth for my mother. It had baskets of flowers in the corners, and because I was good at needlework, having learned in boarding school, I felt that I had done an excellent job and Mummy would be both pleased and proud. The only problem was that because I missed the first term, I wasn't present on the first day of class, when Miss O'Hanessian gave out the tray cloths and the embroidery silks. Along with the materials, she also announced the rules for her embroidery class. **No knots allowed** happened to be rule number one, and my absence during this important announcement was to lead to a devastating result.

On the last day of term, we all handed in our tray cloths, and I expected high marks. Miss O'Hanessian had inspected my work regularly during the term and never said a word, so I was convinced that my work had to be perfect. I was wrong! She took my tray cloth in her hands, looked at it carefully, and then turned it over. An unpleasant smile hovered on her lips as she picked up her large pair of scissors. Looking straight at me, she tilted her head to one side, and said quietly and precisely, just two words, "No knots!" Very slowly, and with apparent satisfaction, she cut off every knot.

I tried to protest, but no words were forthcoming. How could this woman be so cruel? This was to have been a present for my mother, and now it was ruined. I knew that with each snip of her scissors, the baskets of flowers were sure to unravel, and of course, that's exactly what happened. War was once again declared, and I knew I had found a formidable enemy. This woman obviously disliked me as much as I disliked her. Because she also taught Scripture and History, she had a profoundly negative effect on my education. On my school report, Miss O'Hanessian gave me extremely low grades or no grades at all for the three subjects that she taught.

All the other grades on my report were either a B or B+, with favorable comments from the respective teachers. The Headmistress, Mrs. Gibson, must have noted the grades from Miss O'Hanessian, or the absence of them, because her concluding comment at the bottom of my report was: "I am very pleased with this improvement." She was astute and also fair in her judgment.

The school grounds were heavily wooded, with many large horse chestnut trees and masses of rhododendrons. When the rhododendrons bloomed, the woods were covered in a wonderful array of white, pink and purple flowers. My friends and I spent most of our break times in the woods, where we built a clubhouse under the bushes. When I played truant from Miss O'Hanessian's classes, I passed the time there with a library book, and if I didn't have one, I dreamed of a happier life which, at that time, seemed unattainable. But maybe one day ...

Each week of that first year I was awarded a detention, the punishment for which, was to stay in for half an hour after school, writing lines or something equally unpleasant. I'm sure I deserved all of them, as I was forever talking in class or drawing, when I should have been paying attention. In music class, I sat on the back row singing like an opera star at the top of my voice. The singing teacher was the same one who had told me that Sheila was so wonderful, and she regularly called me to the front, and, with a sigh, told me that I was nothing like my sister. She then either sent me out into the hallway for the remainder of the class, or gave me another detention. A detention was usually preferable, since her classroom door was opposite the headmistress' office and should she see me standing in the hall, a frown from Mrs. Gibson made me want to evaporate.

Miss Penwill taught us dancing. She was the most old-fashioned lady I had come across since leaving the sisters at boarding school. Her gray hair was pulled back in a bun, which gave her a stern appearance, and she wore spectacles that were forever sliding down her nose, giving her much cause for irritation. She wore long black or brown dresses with thick black stockings and high-laced pointed shoes. When she twirled, while giving us a demonstration of the polka, we could see her long pantaloons, causing us to stifle our giggles. Miss Penwill had a preoccupation about clean hands and fingernails, so at the beginning of class, she held an inspection and should our nails be dirty, we had to pay her a one-penny fine.

I had enough detentions left over from my first year at the school to last for the whole first term of my second year. Naturally, this didn't deter me from adding to my collection, which I did with great regularity. One of the consequences of my rebellion was a string of bad reports, which I didn't dare take home to my parents for fear of reprisals. Mummy rarely asked for my reports, so I convinced her that we only received one at the end of each school year. I actually got three a year which had to be signed by one of my parents, so I quickly learned how to copy my mother's signature, which was fairly easy, adding forgery to my lengthening list of crimes. I nearly always found an excuse at the end of the year as to why I didn't have a report for her to sign, and Mummy never seemed too concerned about it.

In spite of her lack of interest in anything I did, I still wanted to impress my mother. I made pretty cards for her birthdays and wrote special poems inside, but she usually just glanced at them, saying, "That's nice, Doreen," before tossing them aside.

At the end of the summer, I started my second year at the technical school, and, like so many others, it was a total disaster.

We were given a choice of foreign languages, and a few of us decided to take German rather than French. We were instructed to meet in a classroom on the second floor of Hydeswood, during the first week of term, but the German teacher never arrived. The second week, the same thing happened. We were a small group of seven students, and I exercised my limited leadership skills by persuading the others that we could take advantage of this perceived lack of coordination between staff and curriculum. This went on for many weeks without discovery. Had we simply continued in this fashion, all would have been well, at least until the end of the term. But I got bored, and, feeling the need for some excitement, went looking for it, persuading my fellow students to go along with me.

Mrs. Strickland was teaching her French class at the other end of the building. We tiptoed down the passage until we were standing outside her classroom. Next door, we discovered a small room, which contained a single table and chair. I beckoned for the girls to follow me inside and quietly closed the door behind us. Looking up at the ceiling, I noticed a square entry to the loft above. I placed the chair on the table and climbed up on it. This enabled me to push the cover to one side and pull myself up into the attic. Once there, I encouraged the others to join me, and soon we were all in the attic, trying not to giggle as we moved from one rafter to another. We could hear Mrs. Strickland giving instructions below, and I couldn't resist mimicking her as she taught her students the basics of French. *"Ouvre la porte"* and *"fermé la fenetre"* and so on.

Whispering the phrases after her, we found it almost impossible not to laugh out loud.

Suddenly, there was an ominous silence. Mrs. Strickland was quiet. The students were quiet. We held our breath, trying to keep as quiet as possible, until a head popped through the opening in the ceiling. It was Mrs. Strickland. Quietly but firmly, she instructed us to come down, – right now! We immediately obeyed!

Sheepishly, we marched into her classroom. Her students were all looking at us with wide eyes. Mrs. Strickland asked what we were doing, and why we were doing it. Precisely, what were we doing in the attic? I, on the other hand, wanted to know how she knew we were there. Admittedly, we had been giggling, but very quietly! It turned out that the ceiling was old, and the plaster had deteriorated, causing tiny pieces to rain down on the student's heads as we moved around on the rafters. This led Mrs. Strickland to the conclusion that something was amiss aloft!

Another visit to the Headmistress' office led to yet another detention and the immediate transfer of all of us to Mrs. Strickland's French lessons, where I quickly learned to enjoy French.

The other girls were not impressed with my leadership skills, or the results thereof, and I was 'sent to Coventry.' To send someone to Coventry is British slang, meaning to ostracize someone, usually by not speaking to them, and for several weeks, no one spoke to me, which I found to be an even worse punishment than a detention.

Eventually, I was forgiven by the girls, and four of us became fast friends. I envied them all. I never heard any of my three friends talk about being beaten, nor did they ever come to school covered in bruises. Ann had five brothers and five sisters, and visiting their home was great fun, because it was filled with laughter. Maureen was quiet and gentle and called me Do-Do like the extinct bird. She went along with almost everything I suggested, which was not always something we should have been getting up to. Maisie called me Dot. She was cute and blonde and almost as naughty as me. She was game for anything. And then there was me!

One day, while the four of us were exploring the grounds during break, we discovered a gate almost hidden by undergrowth in the fence between the school grounds and the adjoining property. On the other side of the fence was an apple orchard and in the middle of it, a stable. Unable to resist the temptation, we entered the stable, where we discovered a ladder attached to the wall, which led up to a loft, the perfect place for a clubhouse and far superior to the one we had built under the rhododendron bushes. From then on, we met there regularly during break times.

A stroke of genius on my part produced a marvelous idea. We could spend the night up there. My three friends looked dubious, and after a lengthy discussion, only adventurous Maisie was prepared to join me. We told our parents that each of us was to sleep at the other's house, and the next day, we smuggled some doll blankets to school. I was able to get hold of some candles and matches while Maisie brought a flashlight. After lunch, we hurried down to the orchard, intending to store some apples in the clubhouse for our dinner. Climbing one of the trees, we soon had a good supply of apples in our pockets. Suddenly, we heard a stern voice ordering us out of the tree. "Come down! At once!" The commanding voice left no room for hesitation.

Horrified, I recognized the voice of our headmistress. Shaking with fear and burning with humiliation, we climbed down. Mrs. Gibson was some way off, so we took the opportunity to dispose of some of the apples, before coming face to face with her. She was furious! The owner of the orchard had heard our laughter and called the school. Why had we been so careless? Another trip to Mrs. Gibson's office left us both shamefaced and miserable. Our plan to sleep in the stable was not going to happen, and Maisie and I were accused of being thieves as well as trespassers, and another detention was added to my ample collection.

My next crime was a really big one, and I am not proud of it. I'm not proud of any of my crimes, but this one was particularly bad. I no longer took the bus to school, preferring to travel by train. The walk from the station to the school was almost the same distance, but the bus was often crowded, and I had to stand. Sometimes, this was quite uncomfortable, especially when we had an enthusiastic driver.

Going home, I was nearly always late for the train, forcing me to run through the gate, stopping just long enough for the ticket collector to clip my daily return ticket. One day as I ran into the train station, I saw a weekly season ticket lying discarded on the floor and picked it up. It had expired, which is why it had been thrown away. I had noticed that the people who had season tickets simply showed it to the ticket collector and walked on through. The temptation was great, allowing me to save my train fare for candy or ice-cream, and sadly, I couldn't resist.

For about a week, I carefully timed it so that I ran through the gate at the last minute, with the train already on the platform. Flashing the season ticket, I yelled a cheery hello to the ticket collector, and he waved me on. Then came the day when he didn't wave me on and instead told me to stop. Now! He took the expired season ticket out of my hand, looked at it, and, shaking his head, asked me what I was up to. I couldn't tell him that I was up to no good, and with no reasonable explanation forthcoming, I burst into tears. Of course, that didn't help, and I was escorted to the stationmaster's office and the police were called. I knew that this time, I was in serious trouble.

The policeman was stern, and asked me for my name, address and telephone number. I had no telephone number at home, so he called the headmistress at school. Mrs. Gibson drove down to the station and conferred with the stationmaster and policeman. I was told to inform my parents of exactly what had happened, and make sure that one of them came to school the next day, when a decision was to be made with regard to my future.

Mummy looked shocked and asked me how could I do this to her? Why was I so bad? She always related whatever I did wrong to the way it affected her. Stepfather was told when he came home from work, and I received a terrible beating with his belt.

The following day, at the pre-arranged time, I was called to Mrs. Gibson's office. Mummy was there, as well as the policeman. I was asked what I had to say for myself, and I stammered and stuttered, knowing full well that what I had done was unforgivable and amounted to stealing. There was no excuse good enough. I was just plain bad, and that was all there was to it. I was threatened with expulsion, and I knew I deserved it. What was to become of me?

Mrs. Gibson must have seen some good in me, or maybe it was in her, because she suggested that I be put on probation and given one last chance. That kind lady should have become a Supreme Court Justice; she was that just.

I had to report to my probation officer on a weekly basis, and found her to be a kindly lady who I felt I could talk to. Slowly, I poured out my heart, and told her what my stepfather was doing to me. All the years of molestation and beatings, as well the shame that accompanied them, tumbled out, amid sobs. The relief was enormous! Here was someone who was willing to listen, and could surely help me.

She listened, but did nothing, and I experienced my first taste of a justice system that was to let me and those dear to me down, time and again throughout my life.

I finished my probation visitations feeling even worse about myself than before. Surely, if the probation officer couldn't help me, it simply meant that she either didn't believe me, or she was convinced that I deserved everything that had happened to me. It never occurred to me that she might not have been in a position to help. My already heavily burdened conscience gave me much cause for self-recrimination, and I didn't much like myself.

BAD EXPERIENCES

I was now fourteen, and at the beginning of the school holidays, I found a good-paying job potting plants at a nursery in Bromley. After planting the seedlings in terracotta pots, it was exciting to see them perk up after being watered. In those few weeks, I accumulated a tidy sum of money for our annual holiday in September. And although our time at Dymchurch turned out to be no more pleasant than any of the previous times, it was good to get away, and we survived another two weeks in the trailer.

Following our holiday, it was time to begin my final year at school. Tired of delivering newspapers and anticipating another cold, wet winter, I applied for a Saturday morning job at Boots the Chemist, a pharmacy on Bromley High Street. There, I earned the same amount of money for one morning's work as I had made delivering newspapers twice daily for the whole week.

The manager of the chemist lived at the wealthy end of Farnaby Road, and one day, while walking home, a car stopped next to me, and a young man offered me a lift. I hesitated, until I recognized him as the manager's son, whom I had seen in the store, so I accepted his kind offer. When I told my mother, she was delighted and enquired as to whether the young man had asked me out. He had, but much to Mummy's dismay, I had declined the invitation.

I was soon to learn that Harry was much nicer than some of the other young men I would meet. In a short period of time, I experienced three unpleasant encounters that were to leave me highly disillusioned.

The first occurred one evening after a friend and I had been to see a movie at the Odeon. It was still light when we came out of the theater, and as it was early, I offered to walk with her to the station at the other end of town. Chatting as we walked along, we looked longingly at the latest fashions in the smart stores on Bromley High Street. I then accompanied her across the high street, so we could walk by the coffee shop, savoring the heavenly aroma as we passed by.

Bromley High Street in 1957

Saying goodbye at the station, I passed a group of boys standing on the sidewalk outside the Gaumont movie theater, and one whistled at me. I pretended not to notice and, ignoring them, walked on. Suddenly

I was surrounded, and they pulled me into a side street towards the alley at the back of the movie theater. I screamed! An elderly couple walked by, and I begged them to help me, but not wanting to get involved, they ignored my pleas and hurried on. The boys dragged me into the alley among the trash cans, and one of them told the others, "I'll have her first."

The others jeered and whistled, egging him on, but then he insisted that they leave us alone, while he had his turn. I knew whatever he was intending was not going to be pleasant.

Reluctantly, the other boys shuffled away, and his grip on my arm tightened as he tried to pull up my skirt. I cried hysterically and begged him to let me go. I closed my eyes and sobbed. Time stood still! Why did no one come to help me? Suddenly, he pushed me roughly away and told me to go home and grow up. I couldn't believe it. He was actually letting me go! I ran as fast as my legs would carry me, but as I reached the corner of the high street, the other boys saw me and yelled at me to stop. I ran on, and just managed to jump onto the number 47 bus as it pulled away from the bus stop. The people on the bus all stared at my tear-stained face, but I didn't care. I was safe!

I didn't dare tell my parents, as I knew my stepfather would say that I had done something to encourage the boys and I would probably never be allowed out again.

Not long after that terrifying evening, I was again walking home from the movies, when a boy from Shortlands, whom I had known most of my life, joined me and offered to walk me home. With the previous experience still fresh in my memory, I appreciated his offer. This old friend would surely take care of me.

He suggested that we take a shortcut through The Hills, the top part of The Mead, where I had tobogganed when I was small. It was a shortcut I never took alone after dark as it led down Dead Man's steps, a long, dark concrete stairway with only one street light halfway down.

I loved to run down there in the daytime, but at night, it was a different story. I was confident that I would be safe with this boy. We had played together in the park many times, and he was always great fun to be with. Unfortunately, my trust turned out to be misplaced.

We ambled along the path that led across the top of The Hills, laughing and talking as we went. Halfway down Dead Man's steps, he stopped, grabbed hold of me and tried to kiss me. I might have forgiven him for that, but he made the mistake of trying to force his tongue in my mouth, and being reminded of Stepfather, I pushed him away, while telling him to stop being ridiculous. The jovial expression on his face changed to one of anger as he grabbed me again, his hands groping at my breasts. I struggled to get free, but he was much stronger than me, and soon, in the forceful grip of his arms, I simply couldn't breathe. Panic swept through my body until somewhere in the back of my mind, I heard my mother's voice, and I did what she had told me to do if I ever found myself in a difficult situation. With all my strength, I raised my right knee and hit him in the groin as hard as I could.

He doubled over in pain and abruptly let me go. I turned and stumbled down the remaining stairs while he yelled after me, "I'll get you for this, you bitch. I'll get you!" He sounded just like my stepfather. I ran home, vowing that I would never trust another boy again, as long as I lived. Just like the previous time, I didn't dare tell my parents.

I guess I must have been at an age when bad things happen, because shortly afterwards, two boys followed me down Swan Hill when I was on my way home. They kept their distance most of the way, making catcalls and whistling at me. I ignored them and walked on as fast as I could. Just before I reached the corner of Farnaby Road, they grabbed me from behind. I hit one over the head with my purse, breaking the strap, as I fought my way to the corner. Once there, I shouted, "Daddy! Daddy!" at the top of my voice.

Stepfather was at the gate almost immediately and one look at the large, menacing man and the boys fled. It was one of the few occasions that I ever asked my stepfather for help, but it was one time when I would be eternally grateful that he was there for me. Of course, I received a long lecture. It had to be my fault! I had probably flirted with the boys, and the more I protested my innocence, the angrier Stepfather became until I finally gave in and said, "Yes, it was probably my fault." He always knew how to make me feel guilty.

Considering my stepfather's reaction to my plight, and his accusations, it was just as well that I hadn't mentioned my two previous experiences, and I became convinced that keeping quiet was my best option.

MISS KERRISK

I was now left with just one year of school, and I had no interest in staying in the domestic science class, pursuing cookery or sewing as a career. It was now obvious to me that I was never going to be a commercial artist. My parents and the school system, not to mention my own rebellious attitude, had made sure of that. I asked to be transferred to the copy-typing class. It was not the most appealing career, but without shorthand, it might prove useful, and it didn't seem quite as daunting to me.

It was this decision that led me to Miss Kerrisk's class. Having her as a teacher was a blessing. If there was one person who was to make a difference in my life and save me from disaster, it was Miss Kerrisk, and I grew to love and respect her more than any other adult.

I will never forget my first day in her class. I made a beeline for the back row, always my preference, so that I was free to draw and daydream. Miss Kerrisk, who was also our class teacher, proceeded to call our names to ensure that we were all present. When she called my name, I put up my hand and answered, "Present."

She smiled kindly at me and gently, but firmly, told me to gather up my things and move to the front row, where there was an empty desk.

This did not appeal to me at all! I hesitated until she repeated her request, and reluctantly, I walked to the front amid giggles from my new classmates. My reputation had obviously preceded me.

Blushing, I sat down and unpacked my things into the desk. I looked to my left and saw a petite blonde girl sitting next to me. I was to learn that her name was June Jupp, and she was to become one of my dearest friends.

Miss Kerrisk took a special interest in me, and in her kind, gentle way, taught me much more than copy typing and geography. Her example of a devoted, dedicated teacher was something I would appreciate for many years. While in her class, I wondered why she had never married, judging her to be in her late forties at that time. She was pretty, with long hair tied in a feminine French knot at the nape of her neck. Her hair was silver gray, which only added to her gentle demeanor. I later learned that Miss Kerrisk had never married because, as well as teaching, she took care of her mother, who was confined to a wheelchair.

I tried my best to please Miss Kerrisk, but I was a hopeless typist and she struggled to teach me to type the basic letters on the typewriter. Constantly admonishing me for looking down at the keys, she instructed me to either look at the written letter I was copying or straight ahead at the letter I was typing. Slowly, I learned to type on the old Royal typewriter, but when the time came for us to do the speed test, I failed miserably, and had to start over and over again. I fear that with all the paper I wasted, I may have been responsible for the destruction of a good many trees.

In Miss Kerrisk's Geography class, I did well. I loved the subject, especially drawing maps, which I was good at. The praise I received from her made me want to do even better. All I had ever needed was some encouragement, and I longed for that kind of encouragement at home, but it was never forthcoming.

My new friend June was amazing. She was an excellent typist, and turned out to be the best in the class by the end of the year. We became fast friends, and she tried her utmost to keep me out of trouble. She was constantly pleading with me to behave. I still occasionally skipped Miss O'Hanessian's classes and hid beneath the rhododendron bushes, but June never went with me, and I suspect that she covered for me if Miss O'Hanessian asked where I was. I teased June and called her a goody-goody, but deep down, I envied her. Gentle, kind and hardworking, she was everything I wanted to be. I visited her home a few times and found it to be calm and comfortable, totally unlike anything that I was used to. How fortunate some people are to live normal, happy lives, totally unaware that for many, life is anything but normal.

ANOTHER PAUL WELMAN

In October of 1955, about a month after school began, there was a knock on our front door. When I opened it, there stood a tall young man in army uniform with a kit bag over his shoulder. He had black hair and a ruddy complexion. Something about him was vaguely familiar, and when he introduced himself as Paul Welman, I was shocked to realize that he must have been my stepfather's son from his previous marriage.

Naturally, I invited him in and took him upstairs, knowing that this was going to be quite a surprise for my unsuspecting parents. When we entered the living room, Stepfather looked as if he was going to have a heart attack, and Mummy looked ready to faint.

Paul explained that he had been made exempt from his two years of compulsory National Service because of his acute asthma attacks. His mother had turned him out of the house, and his Granny didn't have room for him, so he was in need of a place to stay. Paul said he didn't get on with his stepfather, which was a good enough reason for him to have an ally in me. How he tracked his father down was a mystery, but here he was!

This was, as the British say, a fine kettle of fish! Once he got over his initial shock, my stepfather seemed to relish the idea of having a grown-up son. He had never mentioned young Paul to us, but he must have known about him, as he had only been married to Mummy since 1946, when Paul would have been about seven years old. How could Stepfather not have shown any interest in his own flesh and blood, and why had he not kept up with his son? The resemblance between them was striking. Mummy was in shock and obviously either didn't know of Paul's existence, or didn't want to know. She didn't seem at all keen to welcome Paul into our family circle, but she knew better than to argue with my stepfather.

Paul moved into Sheila's bedroom, and Sheila moved in with me. Ross was two years old by this time, and he slept on a small divan bed in a corner of the living room. The apartment that had once been so spacious was becoming pretty crowded. Paul was looking for work, and I managed to get him a job at the nursery where I had worked during the previous summer. He enjoyed it, and for a while, all went well.

Of course, that couldn't possibly last in our house, and it didn't. Ironically, following a terrible row, Sheila and Dennis had broken up, so she didn't have a boyfriend at the time. Paul and Sheila sat and talked for hours, and it soon became obvious to me that they were becoming much more than sister and stepbrother. Sheila was pretty, and I could easily understand why Paul found her attractive.

Paul hadn't been living with us for long when the military police came knocking on the door. Contrary to what he had told us, Paul was AWOL from the Catterick Garrison in North Yorkshire, the British Army training base. He had barely begun his military service when he ran away. He was arrested, and accompanied back to Catterick by the two MPs and placed in military jail, where he spent the next few weeks.

Sheila was devastated when Paul was taken away. By now, she was sure that she was in love with him, and I felt sorry for her. Life returned to our version of normal but only for a very short time.

The Army eventually accepted the fact that Paul's severe asthma attacks wouldn't allow him to complete his military service, and he was finally dismissed. He then returned to 8, Farnaby Road, this time causing a terrible uproar. He moved back into Sheila's room, and Sheila moved back in with me, but it was only to be a temporary arrangement.

After a couple of weeks, Paul and Sheila told Stepfather that they needed to speak to him and Mummy, and they all went into the living room and shut the door. It didn't take more than a few minutes before screams and shouts erupted, and I knew there would not be a good outcome for anyone. Paul told my stepfather that he wanted to marry Sheila, whereupon Stepfather hit Paul, and a fight erupted. Sheila was screaming. Mummy was screaming, and Ross was crying. I dared to enter the room, and was told to, "Get the hell out!"

Paul became so upset that he had a severe asthma attack and couldn't breathe. I wasn't witness to the end of the fight, but after a while, Paul recovered somewhat and was ordered out of the apartment. He hurriedly grabbed his things and left.

Sheila withdrew and retreated into her room. I tried everything to get her to talk to me, but she was angry, frustrated and sick of the whole situation. She was twenty by then, and I wondered why she didn't just pack up and leave.

Late the following night, when a pebble hit my bedroom window, I guessed immediately that it was Paul. I opened the window and saw him standing below. He quietly beckoned me to come down, so I climbed down the wisteria vine. He told me that he was sleeping at the nursery, and he wanted Sheila to meet him there. I'm not sure if it was because of her fear of Stepfather or if marrying Paul didn't seem quite so appealing after all, but for whatever reason, she refused.

From then on, Paul pestered me for money or cigarettes, and I gave him what I could. He often came after dark and summoned me to climb down so we could talk. He was all alone with nowhere to go, and somehow, even though I was younger than he was, I felt responsible for him. After he was kicked out of the apartment, we were no longer even allowed to mention his name. It was as if he had never existed.

Sheila stayed in a bad mood for weeks, until she happened to bump into Dennis' mother, who told her that Dennis was in the hospital, and he wanted to offer Sheila an apology and resume their courtship. Dennis's mother was fond of Sheila and begged her to visit him until she relented, went to see him, and they made up. They were to continue with their stormy relationship, followed by an even stormier marriage.

Paul continued to work at the nursery and I went to visit him from time to time. I was shocked to learn that he was sleeping on a bed of straw in the barn. During one of our many conversations, he told me about a family he knew in Llanelli, near Cardiff in South Wales. They sounded like a nice family and I kept this information somewhere in the back of my mind, not knowing that I would be in need of it in the very near future.

The father of one of my school friends owned a paint store in Beckenham, and he needed someone to work in the store, so I told Paul about the vacancy, and he got the job. Charming the family, he not only got the job, but even moved into their home, so I thought I could stop worrying about him as it seemed as if they had accepted him as part of their family. Sadly, it didn't last.

THE FINAL STRAW

Stepfather was furious about Sheila's relationship with Paul, and even though it was over, he stayed angry for weeks. The atmosphere in the house grew more intense, until the day our world exploded in total chaos. It started with something trivial, but quickly got out of hand. Stepfather punched Mummy so hard she fell against the wall, hit her head and didn't get up. She was unconscious! Sheila was hitting Stepfather, and he was punching her. I dared to get in the way, and his punches were then aimed at both of us.

The screams were so loud that Auntie Lily came running up from downstairs. She was a strong woman and tackled Stepfather with the force of a man, but with one blow, she landed on the floor next to my mother. Bodies were lying everywhere, and with my stepfather raving like a madman, I feared that he was going to kill us all. It was terrifying to see him lose that last bit of control he had over his unbridled emotions. As I was the only one still on my feet, I knew that I had to do something.

I could hardly breathe as I ran down the stairs and out into the darkness. I attempted to run across the street and down into the village to the public telephone box, but my legs felt like lead and refused to cooperate. The feeling of helplessness only intensified my sense of terror. In order to move, I literally had to take each leg with my hands and place it in front of the other. I felt as if I would never be able to reach the phone box, but finally, I made it, and dialed the emergency number. A male voice answered, saying, "Police, fire and ambulance," and I managed to stammer that my stepfather was killing my mother, sister and the lady downstairs. The voice on the other end calmly asked me where I lived, and I gave him our address.

With my legs still feeling numb and my whole body shaking with fear, I slowly walked back home. By the time I got there, the police had arrived. They stayed for quite a while, asking questions and taking notes. I felt great relief knowing that, at last, my stepfather would be arrested and taken off to jail, and we would be safe.

After answering some questions, Auntie Lily went back downstairs. She never interfered again.

Then suddenly, the police were gone. Gone! How could they be gone? Why had they not arrested my stepfather? I couldn't understand it. Being a child, I didn't know that the police couldn't interfere in acts of domestic violence unless someone was dead. Somehow, I don't think that they would be of much use under those circumstances.

The police had no sooner left than my stepfather grabbed my arm, and between clenched teeth, he said, "I'll get you for this, you little bitch!"

I was sure he meant what he said, and I didn't get much sleep that night. Was there no justice in the world? Several times during the night, I got up to tend to Ross when I heard him whimpering. He was terrified by all that had happened, and I felt sorry for my little brother, who had done nothing to deserve such an unhappy life. He was born into it, and consequently didn't know, or expect, any better.

That night, I reached the decision that I could no longer live in the same house with my stepfather. I had no idea what he meant when he said he was going to get me, and I didn't want to stay around to find out. I was determined to run away and make a life for myself elsewhere. I was prepared to go anywhere, as long as it was far away from him. Slowly, a plan formed in my mind, one I was sure could work.

I went to see Paul, remembering the family he had told me about in South Wales. He flirted with me, and I told him I was not Sheila and he should stop acting like a fool, because, to me, he was my older brother. He just grinned and shrugged. He had a big ego, and I am sure lots of girls found him attractive, but he looked a lot like his father and as a consequence, he held no attraction for me.

Paul gave me the address and directions for the family in Wales. He told me that it was about 170 miles from London to Llanelli, and I would have to take a train from London to Cardiff in Wales, and then catch another train to Llanelli. In addition to that, it was twelve miles from Shortlands to London, so I would be traveling almost two hundred miles altogether. Hopefully, that would be far enough away that I would never be found. I was ready to plan my escape.

Llanelli was difficult to pronounce, so I practiced it in my mind. I knew it was going to cost a lot of money for the train tickets. I also needed money to live on for a few days until I could find a job, and since I wasn't yet qualified as a typist, that might prove a challenge. So, I devised a plan to add to my meagre savings.

The following Monday morning, I left the house at the usual time, pretending to go to school, but I didn't get on either the bus or the train. Instead, I went down to the phone box, placed a handkerchief over the mouthpiece just like they did in the movies, and placed a call to my school. In my most grown-up voice, I told the lady in the office that I was Mrs. Welman, Doreen Wheble's mother, and asked to be put through to Miss Kerrisk.

When Miss Kerrisk answered, I was so nervous that I almost dropped the telephone. I managed to maintain enough composure to say, "Miss Kerrisk, this is Mrs. Welman, Doreen's mother. I wish to inform you that Doreen is not well, and the doctor has advised me to keep her in bed for at least a week."

There was a moment's silence before Miss Kerrisk said she was sorry to hear I wasn't well, and hoped that I would feel better soon. I felt bad about lying to her, and, once again, I didn't like myself very much. I knew I would be letting her down, but I couldn't even begin to think of an alternative solution, other than the plan I had so carefully worked out.

I caught the bus to the nursery, where I worked every day for the whole week. The owner never once questioned why I was in school uniform, or why I was not at school. I think he knew from what Paul had told him that things were not good at home, and assumed it was better not to ask. I wore an apron to keep my school clothes clean, and because I always wore garden gloves at the nursery, my hands stayed clean, ensuring that my secret was safe.

By the end of the week, I felt that I had enough money saved, and I was confident I was doing the right thing. I carefully packed my suitcase, and as I had no intention of returning, everything had to go with me, even the pictures of my favorite movie stars that were pinned on the wall above the fireplace in my room. Those, I carefully removed and placed them in a folder. I didn't have a lot of clothes, but by the time I had packed them all in, along with a few special keepsakes, the suitcase could barely close. A paper shopping bag had to hold the rest. The suitcase and shopping bag were then carefully hidden beneath my bed.

I didn't write a goodbye note to Mummy. What could I say? Having spent all those years hiding the truth from her, I felt I couldn't possibly tell her now. I had no idea if she would even believe me, or if she did, whether or not she would care. I was ready to make my escape.

MY ESCAPE

It was a cold Friday evening, so I wore my fashionable green coat, which had a black collar and cuffs. A lady that lived further down Farnaby Road, where I sometimes baby-sat, had given it to me, and it made me feel quite grown-up. I knew there was a possibility that my absence might be discovered before getting far enough away from home, so a disguise was deemed necessary. I wore a hat with a net-nose veil that covered my eyes, and I managed to get my hands on an old pair of eyeglasses that Sheila no longer wore. They made everything slightly blurry, but no matter. With a dab of lipstick, I was convinced that I would look like a confident, grown-up young lady, and nothing like Doreen Wheble.

Before dinnertime, while the family was in the kitchen, I carried my suitcase and shopping bag down the stairs and around the side of the house, where I hid them behind the side door so they were not visible from the street. My only fear was that if Auntie Lily were to go out to the side alley for some reason, she might see them from her kitchen door, but as it was already getting dark and cold, I was prepared to take the risk.

A short while later, Mummy went to the landing window at the top of the stairs and shook out the dustmop, and had she looked down, she would have seen my suitcase. She must have spilled something, because I had already shaken it out when I finished mopping the house that afternoon. Thankfully, Mummy didn't look down, and I breathed a little easier.

After dinner, Mummy, Stepfather, Ross and I were all sitting in the living room with the door closed to keep the heat in. Sheila had gone out with Dennis for the evening, so I wouldn't see her again. Looking at the three of them, I suddenly felt my resolve falter. Could I really go through with my plan? Could I run away, knowing that I would never see them again? One last look at my stepfather, sitting at the dining room table checking his football pools, with his smelly pipe stuck in one side of his mouth, was enough to convince me that I could. I played with Ross for a few minutes, gave him a hug, and then, as casually as I could, I left the living room and went to my bedroom, where I put on my hat and coat. I placed the reading glasses and money in my purse, and with my heart pounding wildly, I closed my bedroom door for the last time and crept down the stairs. The second step from the bottom always creaked loudly, so I carefully stepped over it.

I said a mental goodbye to Mummy, Sheila and Ross and felt Ross tugging at my heart. I loved my little brother dearly, and he loved me back, unconditionally. I knew I would miss him dreadfully. Mummy might miss all the help I gave her with the housework and Ross, but it never occurred to me that she might miss me for myself. Sheila had always said that I was a nuisance, so she would probably be glad that I was gone. As for my stepfather, I *never* wanted to see him again, ever!

It was early evening, but because the sun sets in England by four or five o'clock during the winter months, it was already dark. The streetlights shed a friendly orange glow throughout the village, and as I passed by the stores in Shortlands, my emotions were in turmoil. All the familiar faces of the folks that owned, or worked in the stores, flitted through my mind, and I knew that I would probably never see them again. It was a daunting thought, and for a brief moment, I hesitated, but I knew there was no going back, not only because I couldn't go on living in the same house with my stepfather, but now there was no way I could chance trying to get back in the house unseen. Maybe my absence had already been discovered. There was simply no turning back! I was on my way to a new, and I hoped for a happier life, because surely nothing could be any worse than my life at 8, Farnaby Road.

At the station, I purchased a single ticket to Victoria Station in London. As I struggled up the steps to the platform with my suitcase, I was sure that each step I took echoed loudly enough to be heard throughout the village. Waiting for the train took forever, and when I heard footsteps echoing in the subway or on the stairs leading up to the platform, I half expected to be grabbed by my stepfather.

At last, the train drew into the station, and I carefully chose a "ladies only" compartment and opened the door. At that moment - a catastrophe! The string handle on my paper shopping bag, protesting under its excessive load, tore loose, spilling the contents onto the platform. Almost in tears, I heaved my suitcase into the compartment and gathered up my things, throwing them onto the seat next to the door. Fortunately, the conductor was close by and he helped me, a look of genuine concern on his face. But judging by the looks on the faces of the ladies sitting in the compartment, they found my assortment of treasures amusing, and no doubt to anyone else they were, but to me, they were my whole world. The train took off for London, and I spent the entire trip forcing the contents of the broken shopping bag into my already bulging suitcase.

At Victoria, I purchased a ticket for the underground train to Paddington Station. By this time, it was getting late, and I was nervous, being out alone in London, so I was careful to avoid starting up a conversation with anyone. At Paddington, I bought a one-way ticket to Cardiff and learned that the Express train only left the station at midnight. I still had a couple of hours to wait, so I bought a newspaper and settled down on a bench to await my train to freedom.

A couple of policemen were standing off to one side of the station entrance, and I wondered if they were already looking for me. My heart pounded in my chest. I whispered softly, "Be still, heart; someone might hear you."

Wearing Sheila's old eyeglasses, I pretended to read the newspaper. The words were blurred, but under the circumstances, I wouldn't have been able to absorb a word of it anyway. I was, however, able to use the newspaper as a shield, protecting me from the sharp eyes of the policemen.

I couldn't believe that no one stopped me. Did the police not suspect that I was a runaway, even with my pathetic disguise? I was fifteen years old, trying to look eighteen, and with my confidence rapidly waning, I was sure they could tell.

The minute hand slowly dragged around the face of the large station clock, frustrating my desperate need for time to fly. It was the longest two hours of my life! Finally, the voice over the loudspeaker announced the arrival of the train that was to take me to Cardiff, and I walked down the platform doing my best to look calm and self-confident. In my anxiety, I forgot to look for a 'ladies only' compartment, but finding an empty one, and hoping that I wouldn't have to talk to anyone, I climbed in and tried to make myself comfortable for the night. My limited savings didn't allow me the luxury of a sleeping compartment, as they were much more expensive. The station clock boomed out twelve chimes, the conductor blew his whistle, and I was on my way.

The express train clattered along the tracks, gathering speed between the few stations where it stopped in the larger towns. There, people either climbed aboard or disembarked, followed by the clatter of doors being slammed, echoing down the length of the train. The conductor then blew his whistle, yelling, "All aboard!" and our journey continued. The smaller stations received a long blast of the train's whistle as we sped through them. I couldn't get comfortable on the hard seat, and a few fitful moments of sleep were all I could manage during what was to be a short night. I found myself recalling the events of the day, and wondering what the future might hold for me.

At five o'clock in the morning, the train stopped at a station, and a tall black gentleman entered the compartment. Until then, the only black people I had ever seen were in Brixton, a suburb of London where Mummy did most of her Christmas shopping. Before the 1950s, there were almost no black people in England. At that time, there was a mass migration of workers from the English-speaking Caribbean, particularly Jamaica, who entered Great Britain and many of them settled in and around Brixton, choosing to start their own community. I had never before spoken to a black person, and although I would have been nervous in the company of any man, a black man was completely foreign to me. So here I was, alone with a strange man, and I became acutely aware of the fact that I had not chosen a 'ladies only' compartment.

He had every right to be in my compartment, so what now? I sat up straight, swallowing hard. Maybe if I closed my eyes, he would disappear, or at the very least, not speak to me. Not so! He greeted me with a cheery, "Good morning," and I returned the greeting. He asked me where I was off to, and I told him I was going to spend a holiday with some friends of the family. He was very pleasant, and, for the next hour, kept up a lighthearted conversation, telling me all about his family and informing me that he worked for the railways as a ticket collector. He probably felt my apprehension, and knew that light conversation might ease my fears. He got off at the next station, where he was to work that day, and I relaxed for the first time since leaving home. My fears had been unfounded, and I discovered that black people were no different from whites. And maybe, in my limited experience, they were a lot kinder.

From Cardiff, I took another train to Llanelli, and, following Paul's directions, arrived on the front doorstep of the family I was hoping to stay with. I don't even remember their names, but I do remember that they were kind, and I must have given them a convincing story as to why I had left home and traveled to Wales, because they took me in without question. I told them I wanted to look for work, and asked if they could please put me up for a few days until I had found a job and a place to stay. I would then happily reimburse them.

It was a joy to spend the whole of Saturday and Sunday in their home. They were a close-knit family, and I felt intoxicated as I joined in their laughter. They showed me around the coastal town, and I knew instinctively that I was there to stay.

My joy was short-lived when, late on Sunday afternoon, there was a knock on the door and there stood Sheila with two policemen. My heart sank, and I knew that my brief taste of freedom was over before it had hardly begun. The family was horribly embarrassed when they learned that I had run away from home, and I was sternly admonished for deceiving them. I apologized, and I felt bad for having taken advantage of such a kindhearted and generous family. Sheila was invited to stay the night, and it was an uncomfortable evening for all of us. Needless to say, I didn't sleep much that night either.

Early the next morning found us standing on the station platform, waiting for the train to take us back home. Two gentlemen stood watching us until we got on the train. They were obviously plain-clothes detectives, making sure that the wayward runaway was safely on her way home.

My plan had failed, and I dreaded the consequences. Sheila lectured me all the way home about how ungrateful I was! What a nuisance I was! She said that she was heartily sick to death of having a terrible pest of a sister like me. I dared to enquire as to how they knew where I was, but it was obvious, even before Sheila told me, that Paul must have told her. He had, and I vowed never to speak to him again.

As I had visualized, my homecoming was utterly dreadful. Stepfather and Mummy were standing at the top of the stairs as we ascended. Mummy was, as usual, completely hysterical. "How could you do this to me?" she kept asking in a horribly distorted voice. "You are a disgusting, hateful girl!"

I couldn't feel sorry for her. She didn't seem able to see what was going on under her nose. And if she did, then she obviously didn't care.

Mummy never even asked me why I ran away. Two hundred miles in England took me to the other side of the country. By comparison, it would be like a thousand miles here in America. Mummy either knew what was going on and didn't dare ask, fearing my answer, or she suspected the truth and simply didn't want to admit it, especially not to herself. I later found it completely understandable. Mummy stood to lose the only security she had, and even though it was quite awful, she couldn't risk losing it.

It seems that most people who are trapped in difficult circumstances are prepared to cling to the known, no matter how bad it is, to avoid facing the unknown. In post-war England, husbands represented security for a family, and the number of men of a certain age had been greatly reduced by the war. And I'm sure my mother was terrified of being without the financial support Stepfather offered, such as it was.

One look at Stepfather's face told me what to expect. He grabbed my arm, and I felt his nails pierce my flesh as he pushed me into my room, where he proceeded to give me the beating of my life. Expecting it didn't make it any easier. Blow after blow seemed to go on forever. His fists were like steel, and the more I tried to protect myself, the angrier he became. I couldn't imagine how anyone could be so vicious. Had he no heart? When I felt as if I had no more fight left in me, I gave up. I simply didn't care anymore. Let him beat me. He had ruined my life and couldn't hurt me any more than he already had. My mother obviously didn't care; she didn't even protest his vicious beating, and I had lost my best chance to escape.

Defeated, I went back to school the next day, covered in bruises. Fortunately, it was winter, and my school uniform covered most of them. Miss Kerrisk took me to one side and gently asked me if I was feeling better. The look of concern on her kind face said a thousand words. She never mentioned the phone call, even though I felt sure she must have known it was me. I longed to tell her everything, but I was too ashamed, and besides, adults had never been able to help me before, so why should I expect one to help me now. However, Miss Kerrisk treated me even more kindly after that, and thanks to her, I was afforded a secure future.

As a consequence of my recent adventure, and the trauma that followed, my eczema worsened, and another trip to our doctor resulted in six weeks of radiation treatment. This entailed my going to the hospital a couple of times a week for exposures. I was thrilled when my eczema disappeared, and my skin was clear for the first time in years. It was, however, destined to return again much later in my life, under extremely stressful circumstances.

My escape hadn't been successful, but having tried, and almost gotten away with it, boosted my self-confidence, and I felt that much stronger. It also strengthened my resolve not to let my stepfather break my spirit, knowing that one day, I would be in a position to leave home and be free of him.

WORMWOOD SCRUBS

Shortly after my return to school, the girl whose father owned the paint store, took me aside, and told me that Paul had been caught stealing from the cash register. Her father had called the police, and Paul had been arrested. She was devastated and professed to be in love with him, which didn't surprise me, as most girls found him irresistible. I, on the other hand, felt an overwhelming pity for him, because trouble followed him even more closely than it did me.

The distraught girl told me that Paul had been sent to Wormwood Scrubs, a maximum-security prison in West London, as a category B prisoner. This meant that he didn't need maximum security, as was required for the more violent category A criminals. I was not surprised by the news, but I couldn't bear the thought of Paul being in prison, especially with him having such terrible asthma attacks. Who would even care about him being there? I knew his mother and Stepfather wouldn't. The girl was afraid to go to Wormwood Scrubs, so despite my vow never to speak to him again, I agreed to visit him myself.

I'm not sure how I found out where to go, or even whether or not I would be allowed into the prison, since I was under eighteen. I guess my detective skills must have been up to the task because one Saturday, I found myself outside the entrance to Wormwood Scrubs. It was a formidable entrance, and with my heart in my mouth, I swallowed hard before requesting entry. I don't remember what story I gave to my parents to allow me to spend the whole day it took traveling up to London and back but it must have been a good one, because there I was, lying to the prison guard about my age. "Yes," I said. "I am eighteen. Paul is my step-brother, and please, may I visit him?"

I passed the age test. I don't know how, since I certainly didn't look eighteen. Once inside the prison, I was met with the dank, musty aroma of a building holding too many people, but lacking any sense of human warmth. The prison doors were enormous, as were the keys used to open them, and the echoes of their rattling reverberating from the stone surfaces amplified the atmosphere of misery and hopelessness. The clanging of the doors and jangle of keys produced a surreal effect, making me feel as though I was playing a part in some dark movie. When the doors slammed shut behind me, I imagined being one of the prisoners and was overwhelmed by the awful sense of being locked up and shut off from life outside those high, intimidating walls.

I followed the guard down several long hallways, through many doors, and then I was thoroughly searched before being allowed to see Paul. He was seated on the other side of a wire mesh partition, in a room with armed guards. He looked lost and forlorn, but brightened up when he saw me, and my heart went out to him. We talked for a while, and then he asked me to visit his grandmother, who lived in London. She had no idea that he was in prison and would be worried, not having heard from him in a while.

Paul also asked me to visit him again and bring him some magazines and cigarettes. I promised to do what I could, and we said our goodbyes. We never discussed his betrayal of me when I ran away. I didn't think it would be fair to make him feel any worse than he already did in his present situation.

Following his directions, I left the prison and went to see his grandmother, who turned out to be a kind old lady who obviously loved Paul dearly. Her health wasn't good, and she said that she couldn't bear to see him in prison, so she gave me money to buy him some magazines, and I promised that I would go and visit him again for her sake, which I did.

ONE LAST CHANCE

The 1956 school year came to a close before I was ready. I was almost sixteen, at the end of my school career, and I had only managed to attain a typing speed of 25 words per minute. I was the worst typist in the class, and I knew it. A minimum speed of 35 wpm was required to qualify for the typing certificate that was necessary to get a job. June was typing 65 wpm, and while I admired her tremendously, I felt pretty pathetic as a copy typist.

The last day of term arrived, and my classmates were out exchanging autographs with their friends and teachers, saying their last-minute goodbyes. Miss Kerrisk called me aside, and told me that she wanted to give me one last chance. She took me to the typing room, where we stayed nearly all day, while I typed one speed test after another. I managed to pass the 30-wpm test, but the 35 remained elusive. By the middle of the afternoon, I finally managed to type the whole speed test without a single mistake, and Miss Kerrisk was able to give me a legitimate certificate for 35 wpm. That was all I needed, and with a satisfactory report from school, I was in a position to apply for a job as a copy typist. I applied to the Aviation Department of Lumley of Lloyds in London.

As my last school report was a good one, I was able to safely take it home to show my parents. Miss Kerrisk gave me good marks for both typing and geography and said in her progress report:

'Doreen has improved very much. She is a capable girl and always ready to help. Her work is much better, and if she perseveres with it, she will develop confidence and thus reach a higher standard.'

I was overwhelmed with a feeling of gratitude for what dear Miss Kerrisk had done for me. After giving her a hug of thanks, I said goodbye and graduated from St. Nicholas College for Girls. Before leaving, Miss Kerrisk gave me her home address and asked that I write to her. We corresponded faithfully for over thirty years, until I was finally in a position to visit and thank her personally for believing in me enough to spend a year helping me to become a copy typist, and so much more.

My job application to Lumley of Lloyds led to an interview, which was followed by a letter saying that they were pleased to offer me a position as a junior typist on their staff, starting on August 13th 1956. I gratefully accepted and started work, earning £4.15s a week. I was elated! I was not yet sixteen and already I had a job with an important firm in St. Mary Axe, in the East End of London. I could scarcely wait to start, but my feeling of elation was brief when I remembered that I was still not much of a copy-typist. Getting the job was one thing, but keeping it might prove to be quite another.

In the aviation department, Miss Higgins, a stern, middle-aged lady, was in charge of our office. We were four copy typists in all. Miss Higgins, Mrs. Marshall, a plump older lady, Iris, who was about a year older than I, and then there was me. Miss Higgins and Mrs. Marshall were amazing. Their fingers flew over the keys, and they hardly ever made a mistake. Iris was also pretty good. But I, – I was a disaster!

Upon our arrival at the office in the mornings, we were each given a stack of letters to be typed, and as they were written by different men in the department, no two were alike. Their handwriting was, for the most part, appalling, almost as bad as my typing, and by the end of the first day, I was close to tears. Iris tried to console me, but it was hopeless. I was not a natural-born typist. Miss Higgins sighed, and told me that it was no doubt just first-day jitters, and she was sure it would be easier tomorrow, but I knew better.

Surprisingly, Sheila sympathized with me. She was a good typist, and had been working for about six years by that time. She gave me some tips, as well as an eraser, a piece of white chalk and a razor blade. She then taught me the art of fixing my typing errors, as there was no such thing as correction fluid in those days.

The typewriters we used in the office clattered away noisily, a bell signaling the end of each line, when we returned the carriage with the lever. Letters required two carbon copies, and quite often, I placed the carbon paper in the wrong way, ending up with either just one copy or no copies at all. I was definitely not cut out for this line of work, but left with no other choice; I determined to become the most talented fixer-upper of typing errors.

The men in our department were typical London office gentlemen, arriving at the office precisely on time each morning in their dark pin-striped suits complete with waistcoats, conservative shirts and ties. Black shoes, bowler hats, and a black umbrella completed their somber ensemble.

Like me, after arriving at London Bridge railway station, they joined the throngs of the pin-stripe brigade crossing the bridge. Some gentlemen were short, some tall, some thin and some stout, but all were dressed almost identically. Heads bobbed up and down as they strode along, some using their umbrellas as canes, in order to look even more distinguished. On the street, you could scarcely tell them apart.

More often than not, I arrived at the station late for work, and being left with no other alternative, I had to leave the side path and run in the gutter alongside all those distinguished-looking gentlemen. As I ran, I often found myself the target of many a frown or the shaking of a head, at such unladylike behavior.

I was careful with my salary. After deductions, I received a weekly salary of about £4.00. I gave half to Mummy for my board and lodging. The balance was spent on train fare, clothes, toiletries and cigarettes. Yes, foolishly, I had started to smoke! It seemed so sophisticated at the time, and with Stepfather smoking fifty cigarettes a day, as well as Mummy and Sheila both smoking thirty, I guess it was inevitable that I would follow suit. No one tried to discourage me, and I began by smoking a couple of cigarettes on the train when traveling to and from work, but eventually found myself smoking between ten and twenty a day. When I think back on my childhood, remembering the thick haze of smoke in the apartment, I now realize it was not just from the coal fire. We all contributed to making our very own smog right there at home!

Working in London was exciting. The walk over London Bridge, when I was not late, was an unforgettable experience. Over to my right, I could see the magnificent Tower Bridge spanning the River Thames. Built between 1886 and 1894, it is a stunning example of Victorian engineering, and a popular tourist attraction in London. On mornings when it was foggy and gray, I loved hearing the muffled sound of the deep-throated foghorns of barges moving up and down the river. For me, the River Thames was an amazing sight in any kind of weather. On clear, sunny mornings, the water shimmered and sparkled like thousands of tiny diamonds, their brilliance adding to the joy of my day. Best of all, was the penetrating sound of Big Ben chiming the hour as I walked over the bridge.

Out of necessity, my first purchase after starting work was an umbrella. Very often, if it didn't rain in the morning, it was bound to rain in the afternoon. I chose what I considered to be the nicest umbrella in the store, and it accompanied me to work each day for almost a week.

When traveling on the train, I placed it in the overhead rack so that it was out of the way of the other passengers.

On Friday, as I was on my way home at the end of my second week at work, a dear old lady sitting opposite me struck up a conversation. We chatted amiably until we reached the station before mine, when she stood up, saying that this was her stop. We said our goodbyes, and just before she opened the carriage door, she reached above my head, and then she was out of the door, slamming it behind her.

It took me only a couple of seconds to realize that she hadn't put anything in the rack, and glancing up, I saw that my brand-new umbrella had vanished. I pulled down the window of the carriage door, and saw her walking up the platform towards the exit, triumphantly swinging *my umbrella*! I was in the last compartment of the train, next to the conductor's van, and he was about to blow his whistle as a signal to the driver that the train could now depart. Pointing at the fast departing, *dear* old lady, I cried out, "That woman stole my new umbrella!" The conductor looked at me and said, "Well, go after her then." I burst into tears, saying, "I dare not, or I will be late home, and my stepfather will kill me."

The conductor shook his head sadly and said, "Sorry, my girl, but you can't trust anyone these days." I learned yet another of life's lessons about fairness, or the lack thereof, and with my next week's wages, I bought a plain black umbrella.

After I began working, my life took on a fairly pleasant routine. I did my own laundry, cleaned my bedroom and still spent a couple of evenings a week ironing for the family. For pleasure, I took up ballroom dancing at a dance studio above the Regal movie theater in Beckenham on Wednesday and Friday evenings. I still had to be home by ten o'clock as my stepfather hadn't changed his house rules just because I was now a working girl. He also didn't change his behavior towards me, and if anything, his unwanted attention only increased.

THE MOVIES

Sheila and Dennis were going steady again. They regularly broke up and then, got back together. Dennis had, by this time, sold his Morgan, and he now owned a motorbike with a sidecar for Sheila to ride in. How I envied the freedom that Sheila now enjoyed.

In those days, the movie house program consisted of two movies, a cartoon and the news. These ran continuously from mid-morning until late at night. Because I had to be home by ten, I usually watched the second half of the main feature first, the remainder of the program and lastly, the beginning of the main film. This meant that I always knew the end of the movie before seeing the beginning, which I thought was terribly unfair.

John Wayne was starring in the movie, *The High and The Mighty*, at the Regal in Beckenham, and I was eager to see it. I arranged to meet a friend at the theater and asked Stepfather if I could please stay out a bit later, so that I could watch the main movie from start to finish. Stepfather automatically said no. I say automatically, because that's how it always was. Whatever I asked him, he said, "No," sometimes even before I had finished my sentence.

That night, I made up my mind that I was going to see the movie from beginning to end, even though I knew I would be about an hour late getting home. I decided that it would be worth the inevitable punishment. The movie kept us on the edge of our seats, but as it neared the end, I started to feel panicky. I knew what to expect when I got home, and it wasn't going to be pleasant. I whispered to my friend that I was going to stand at the back of the theater, so that I could run out quickly, before they played God Save the Queen. Playing the National Anthem was standard procedure in all the movie theaters at the end of each evening. The audience stood reverently until the anthem was finished, then everyone made a rush for the exit.

The final scene of the movie played out, and I ran outside to the bus stop ahead of the crowd. While we were in the theater, it had turned freezing cold, and to my dismay, the queue for the bus was several blocks long. One of the people in the queue told me that a cold front had blown in, and because it had rained earlier in the day, the roads were completely iced over. The sand trucks were out in full force, but down in the Shortlands valley, the roads were slick, and several of the fleet of 227 buses were stuck there, unable to climb the steep hills to either Beckenham or Bromley. It took hours for the sand trucks to distribute enough sand for the buses to get traction up the hills, after which they still had to drive through Beckenham to the Penge Depot, turn around and make their way back, picking up stranded passengers along the way.

I stood in the queue with my teeth chattering and my body shaking, partly from the cold and partly from the fear of arriving home at least two hours late. While standing there, a motorbike with a sidecar drove slowly around the circle and approached the queue. It was Sheila and Dennis. I was saved! I yelled out for them to stop and begged Dennis to give me a lift, but he refused since I wasn't dressed appropriately to ride on the back of a motorbike. Sheila just fit into the small sidecar, so riding with her was not an option. Utterly defeated, I asked Sheila to please tell

Stepfather what had happened, so I wouldn't get a beating when I got home.

It then occurred to me that just maybe the icy conditions could be my alibi, and Stepfather would never know that I had willfully arrived late at the theater. That was wishful thinking! It was unfortunate that, by being so strict, and refusing to say yes to even my most reasonable requests, my stepfather had taught me to be devious. I simply wanted to be treated fairly, and allowed to grow up in an open and honest way, but that was not possible in our house.

Sheila explained the situation to Stepfather, but when I got home, I was greeted with his fists, and pushing and shoving me all the way into my room; he told me in no uncertain terms that I was grounded for two weeks. He was going to show me who was boss! As if I didn't already know. No amount of explanations or begging for forgiveness got me anywhere. He pushed me onto my bed, and I lay there while he pounded me blow after blow. I was determined not to give him the satisfaction of seeing me cry, and I yelled at him over and over again, "I hate you! I hate you!" That made him even madder, and he kept yelling obscenities at me, while hitting me all the harder.

I drew my body into a fetal position, and clasped my knees with my hands to protect myself from the blows. My head spun as I received blows to my head and ears. My resolve weakened, and when I eventually started to cry, he abruptly stopped hitting me, smiled with satisfaction and walked out of the room, slamming the door behind him. The pain was unbearable, and my frustration was enormous as I lay there sobbing, determined that next time, I would be stronger and wouldn't cry.

I am sure that Stepfather felt that he had won, but having seen the movie from beginning to end, I felt that, in some small way, I had won a small victory. Losing myself in the world of fantasy gave me the chance to escape my real world for a couple of hours, and it was a delicious feeling.

A few weeks later, Sheila and Dennis went to see a movie at the new Pullman theater in Bromley called *A Streetcar Named Desire*. They said it was a great movie, so naturally, I also wanted to see it. It had an 'X' rating, which meant that you had to be eighteen to be admitted. Well, I had fooled the prison authorities, hadn't I? I reasoned that if I could fool them, I could fool anyone. So, I dressed up in my most grown-up clothes, put on some lipstick and soon I was watching the worst movie I had ever seen. It was dreadful! I didn't need to go to the movies to see that side of life; I experienced enough of that at home.

Mummy had always warned me that when I was disobedient, God would punish me, and I believed her, because when I did something bad, I nearly always ended up hurting myself or losing something precious. In my young mind, God became unpleasant and vengeful. As if my experience with the 'X' rated movie wasn't punishment enough for lying about my age, I received what I considered to be my real punishment while walking home from work a couple of nights later.

My route home from Bromley North Station required me to cut through an alley, cross the High Street, and then walk down Swan Hill to Shortlands, and home. I had almost reached the High Street when a young man grabbed me from behind and pushed me into a tiny side alley. His intentions were clear, and I tried my best to fight him off. What happened next remains forever etched in my memory. He swore at me, told me I was a useless bitch and punched me in my stomach. The pain was indescribable, and I was unable to catch my breath. He had winded me, and I learned what it felt like to be rendered totally helpless. He could have done anything to me at that moment, and I would have been unable to defend myself. He kicked me as I lay on the ground, and then miraculously, he walked away. I lay there in a daze until the pain subsided, and I was able to make my way home. I kept the attack to myself and determined to have nothing more to do with boys. In my experience, most of them were just mean bullies, forcing themselves on any girl who was unable to defend herself.

TEDDY

I learned from one of the men at Lumley's that Sir John Cass Art College was near our office, and they offered evening classes. Excited, I felt a glimmer of hope. Maybe I could make my dream come true after all. I went to the college during my lunch hour and signed up for a semester of figure drawing. I attended classes two nights a week and gradually improved so that by the end of the semester, I was one of six students chosen to go to Paris on a sketching tour. This was my big chance, but despite my best intentions, spring in Paris was not to be in my future.

Instead, in the next few weeks, our lives were to undergo a dramatic upheaval. My stepfather had developed a bad cough and went to see our doctor, who ordered X-rays to be taken. A lung condition was diagnosed, and because my mother's best friend, who visited us regularly, had tuberculosis, it was considered a serious matter, and our whole family was summoned to have X-rays. That was when my chest X-ray revealed my broken collarbone.

The doctor told my stepfather that it would be beneficial for him to move to a warm, dry climate. At least, that is what he told us. Out of the blue, he calmly informed us that we were all moving to South Africa. He might just as well have said that we were moving to the moon. I couldn't believe my ears! I was supposed to give up my job, my friends and move to Africa, a jungle full of lions and tigers? He had to be kidding, but of course, he wasn't. Mummy was astounded! For her, leaving Wales to go to London when she was a teenager, had been to do the unthinkable. But Africa? This was just too much, even for her to grasp.

Within a couple of weeks, my stepfather had written to Aunt Joey and Uncle Percy. They agreed to lend us the money for Stepfather's air fare and our fares on one of the Union Castle mail ships, which traveled weekly from Southampton Docks in England to Cape Town and other ports in South Africa. I couldn't believe this was happening to me. I, Doreen Wheble, who planned to become a commercial artist and, later on, marry, have children and live happily ever after in a thatched-roofed cottage like the one I had stayed in as a child on that unforgettable holiday in Devon.

Ignoring our lack of enthusiasm, my stepfather went ahead with his plans, and soon, all the arrangements had been made. My stepfather was to fly to South Africa ahead of us and stay with his cousin, Sannie, and her husband. There was a job waiting for him at Iscor, the national steelworks in Pretoria, which was the capital city of the country. We were to follow three months later by sea, and begin our new lives in South Africa with him. My mind screamed, "No, I *can't* do this and I *won't* do it!" But, knowing it wouldn't help, I said nothing.

Stepfather left in early April of 1957, taking Ross' birth certificate with him. Before leaving, he threatened Mummy, telling her that if she even considered staying in England, she would lose her only son. He also had Ross' name put on Mummy's passport as a minor to accompany her to South Africa, and left the necessary legal documents to enable him to enter the country with her.

After Stepfather left, life was wonderful. I was able to go to sleep and wake up in the morning feeling clean and unmolested. He was gone, and the relief was overwhelming. I felt free to be me. But who was I? I really didn't know.

The week that Stepfather left, I met a young man at the ballroom dancing classes. He was the kindest and most gentle young man I had ever met. After all my bad experiences with boys and men, he proved to be completely different, and my resolve never to have a boyfriend was quickly forgotten.

Teddy was unlike any of the other boys I knew. He even dressed differently. Edwardian suits were in fashion in the fifties, and most young boys dressed in black suits with velvet collars and stovepipe pants. With their long hair, they looked pretty ridiculous to me, much like Daddy Long-legged spiders, so I found it refreshing to see Teddy dressed in slacks and sports jackets. Where all the other boys wore their hair unkempt and greasy, Teddy's brown hair was clean and shiny, combed to the side in a soft wave. He didn't have to prove himself to anyone. He was just plain nice, and it showed.

Teddy put me on a pedestal and treated me like the young lady I had always dreamed of being. He was busy with an apprenticeship in a printing business and didn't earn much money, but he spoiled me with flowers and chocolates, and took me to the movies. He made me feel special and good about myself, something I had never felt before. Best of all, he didn't try to take advantage of me the way other boys had. I was pleased to have the attentions of someone who I could like and respect, even though the move to South Africa was uppermost in my mind. How unfair that I should meet Teddy now.

Then, Sheila dropped her bombshell! She was not going with us to South Africa. After seven stormy years of dating, she was going to marry Dennis. Mummy was heartbroken. Sheila was twenty-two, and didn't have to ask permission to get married or be told where she should live, so eventually Mummy relented, and accepted that Sheila was going to stay behind.

Stepfather told us that we would be leaving England at the beginning of July on the Carnarvon Castle, one of the larger mail ships of the Union Castle line. That left us just three months to plan Sheila's wedding and make all the arrangements for our emigration. My mind was a whirl of rebellious thoughts. Why did I *have* to go to South Africa? I had had the perfect opportunity to be adopted by Aunt Joey and Uncle Percy when I was eleven, and I had thrown it away to stay with my mother because she needed me. Now, I didn't want to go, but I wasn't given a choice.

We could only afford to take a few of our household things on the ship, so Sheila and Dennis offered to stay on in the apartment that was filled with Mummy's furniture, linen and other household goods. Mummy only found out much later, that because she was a war widow, the government would have paid for us to emigrate along with all our belongings. But as she didn't know it at the time, she had to make some tough choices, as did I.

Teddy and I had dated for two months, by which time we had fallen in love. But affairs of the heart were of little consequence, with Sheila's wedding plans occupying most of our spare time.

Sheila had a grand church wedding in Bromley on June 1st. In her white lace wedding gown, holding her bouquet of red roses, she looked completely serene as she walked down the aisle. How I envied her! She would never again have to live with Stepfather, even though her life with Dennis was not destined to be much better. I was Sheila's bridesmaid, and her best friend Maureen was maid of honor. The wedding reception was held in our apartment, and as the living room could not accommodate all the guests, many of them spilled out into the hallway, finding a place to stand wherever they could.

Teddy was marvelous! After the guests had gone, he stayed and helped wash the dishes and vacuum the carpet, which was a mess. I will never forget seeing him running across the street a few minutes before midnight to catch the last bus home to Penge. The bus stop was in the middle of the village, and he could never have made it there in time, but the kindly bus driver saw him running, stopped to pick him up, and I gave a huge sigh of relief.

The next morning, Teddy was back at eight o'clock, looking at me with his gentle eyes full of love. They crinkled up when he smiled, and my heart melted. I knew then that I couldn't give him up to go to South Africa. I didn't even want to go to South Africa, so I secretly looked for, and found, board and lodgings at a price I could afford in a house close to Bromley North Station, where I caught the train to work.

A couple of days later, I plucked up courage, and told Mummy that I wasn't going with her to South Africa. I was going to stay in England, and Teddy and I were going to save up to get married. I should have known, even as I told her, it was not going to happen. My mother got that hurt look on her face, and then she started to cry. Unlike when Aunt Joey wanted to adopt me, this time Mummy didn't give me an option, but begged me to go with her, insisting that she couldn't go without both of her daughters. I looked at this woman who I felt didn't love me, but who needed me. I needed to be needed, so I gave in to Mummy's pleadings. I couldn't possibly have known what lay ahead of me. It was beyond anyone's wildest imagination.

Teddy was heartbroken when I told him I had to go with Mummy. He couldn't believe that I would even want to, since I had told him about my stepfather, and he wanted me to have a better life. He told me that he loved me and wanted to protect me. He begged and pleaded with me, and I felt as if I was drowning in a sea of conflicting emotions. I was torn between love and responsibility. Responsibility prevailed.

After the wedding, we had just one month before we were to board the Carnarvon Castle. I worked up until a couple of days before we sailed because I needed the money. While saying goodbye to my colleagues at the office, I was constantly reminded how fortunate I was to be going to the land of sunshine and opportunity. I couldn't agree, but I put on a brave face, knowing all the while that I was not going to stay in South Africa. I intended to return to England and Teddy at the earliest opportunity.

LEAVING ENGLAND

Before leaving England, we had to have vaccinations for yellow fever and smallpox, as well as malaria, which only added to my fears. I was convinced that we were going to live in the jungle, despite what Aunt Joey and Uncle Percy had told us, and I was nervous at the prospect.

I went to Wormwood Scrubs one last time to say goodbye to Paul. He didn't want to believe we were going to South Africa, or that Sheila had actually married Dennis. He begged me to write to him, and as he had no one else who cared about him except his grandmother, I consented and made a note of his prison address.

Mummy packed her most precious chinaware in two tea chests, large plywood boxes originally used to ship tea from Asia to the British Isles. She was able to take very few pieces, carefully wrapping them in clothes and towels to protect them during the long voyage. Everything else was left behind for Sheila and Dennis. I was devastated to learn later that Sheila, considering Mummy's furniture and ornaments to be old-fashioned, gave everything away when she and Dennis left England to live in Zambia.

With a heavy heart, I sold my bicycle. It had served me well for almost six years, and it was in excellent condition. With the proceeds, I bought a set of three pasteboard suitcases at a small luggage store down Petticoat Lane in the east end of London. Petticoat Lane was famous for its variety of cheap goods, and even more famous for its highly professional pickpockets. I had spent countless lunch hours down the lane, so I was well aware of the dangers of shopping there. The suitcases were not good quality, but they were affordable and fitting one inside the other; they saved space when not in use, once we arrived in South Africa.

After purchasing the suitcases and a few other necessities, I was left with £1.10s in my purse. It was not much to start a new life. But then, I didn't want that life, so I wasn't too concerned about my poor financial status.

Saying goodbye to our friends and family was heartbreaking for Mummy and me, but leaving Teddy was to be the hardest farewell of all. My cousin Betty, Auntie Violet's eldest daughter, who was much older than me, loved Teddy. She promised that if I saved half of my return fare, she would save the other half. Teddy promised to save for an engagement ring, and I was to return to England as soon as I had repaid the £96.00 loan to Aunt Joey and Uncle Percy for my boat fare.

My last Sunday in England arrived all too soon, and I boarded the 227 bus for the last time, headed for Penge to meet Teddy. He was waiting at the bus stop, and when I saw him, my stomach literally turned over, and it felt as if it was full of butterflies. Young love is incredibly intense, and I felt as if I would die if I had to leave him. We both tried to put on a brave face and enjoy our last day together, but it wasn't easy.

We first went to visit his parents, a dear elderly couple, who obviously adored Teddy. They had made me feel welcome in their home and obviously approved of our courtship. I said goodbye to them, and Teddy and I then went for a long walk. He asked me what I wanted to do on my last Sunday in England. I said I wanted fish and chips and a pickled onion, so he took me to the local fish and chip shop and bought me my heart's desire. In those days, fish and chips were first wrapped in greaseproof paper and then in newspaper. I don't know why, but newspaper always made the fish and chips taste extra good, and it was the best pickled onion I'd ever eaten. Despite it being my heart's desire, swallowing was hard. The day was bittersweet, knowing that it was our last day together.

Thursday, July 4, 1957, the day of sailing, arrived sooner than anyone wanted it to. We left 8, Farnaby Road for the last time, and I was relieved to say goodbye to the house that held so many unhappy memories for Mummy, Ross and me. Sheila and Dennis would continue living there for the next year or so, adding a few more unhappy memories of their own.

Southampton Docks was enormous, and looking up at the huge ocean liner, I wondered how anything so big could possibly stay afloat. And if it didn't sink, what was waiting for me in Africa? Mummy held on to Ross' hand. He was almost five, could run fast, and losing him in the crowds at the dockside would have been a calamity. A porter took our luggage on board for us. We had quite a few suitcases, and Mummy had been given an old tin trunk in which she packed her Singer sewing machine. It was stored carefully beneath Mummy's bunk in our cabin, being much too precious to be stored in the hold along with all the other cargo.

A band was playing all the wonderful rousing music that you expected to hear when a ship leaves port. When they played "Land of Hope and Glory," it made me think of our neighbor, Uncle David, who had died some years earlier. The atmosphere amongst the crowd was electric with excitement, fear, and heartbreak. People were laughing and crying, some both at the same time, and relatives of the departing passengers were clinging to them as if their lives depended on it.

The ship's whistle blew a few times, and we knew it was time to board. The whole family was there to see us off, and tears were flowing freely. I kept blinking my eyes, but I couldn't prevent the tears from running down my cheeks.

After saying goodbye to my aunts, uncles, and cousins, I turned to Teddy and was shocked to see he was also crying. He held me tenderly in his arms, whispering over and over again, "Doreen, dearest Doreen, please come back to me."

I felt as if my heart would break. Would I ever see my Teddy again?

PART TWO: UNLOVED

THE CARNARVON CASTLE

The Carnarvon Castle mail ship that took Doreen to South Africa in 1957

The band continued to play while we stood at the rail, waving goodbye to our family and friends on the dockside. I sobbed as Teddy melted away into the sea of faces around him. For three short months, he had made me feel worthy and loved, and it would be many years before someone was able to make me feel that special again.

As the coastline of England faded into the distance, Mummy suggested that we go down to our cabin and unpack. Because we were traveling tourist class, our tiny cabin was situated on one of the ship's lower decks. To the right of the cabin door were two bunk beds. Mummy chose the bottom bunk, since it was easier for me to climb the ladder. Ross slept at the other end of the cabin on a single bunk. The cabin had a couple of closets and a tiny washbasin, and further down the passageway, were communal toilets and showers. Fresh water was available for washing and showering while we were in port, but not while we were at sea. I quickly discovered that no matter how much soap I used with the seawater, it produced no lather, and it left my skin feeling dry with a salty residue.

That first evening on board ship, there was a party to welcome the passengers, and a stewardess looked after Ross, while Mummy and I joined in the festivities. We met many of our fellow passengers, and I reached the conclusion that our voyage might be quite pleasant. A variety of activities were offered, such as swimming, bingo, and dancing, to keep us busy during the trip.

Keeping up with Ross was a fulltime job, since he was hyperactive and never sat still for more than a few minutes. Not long after our departure, he caused great consternation when, while Mummy and I were sitting on deck, he suddenly disappeared. Mummy quickly became hysterical, and I couldn't get her to calm down. Many of the crew members ran around looking for my elusive little brother. Messages were passed from one to another, and I was sick with worry and quite mortified by all the fuss. How could this have happened, and where was Ross?

About an hour later, although at the time it felt much longer, a kindly stewardess approached, holding Ross by the hand. Mummy went to pieces; her relief was so great. When she regained her composure, she asked where Ross had been found. "In the first-class playroom," was the reply. How he was able to find the playroom on the other side of the ship was unclear but he had managed somehow.

We enjoyed a few days of relative calm before the next drama unfolded. This time we were in our cabin, when suddenly Ross screamed at the top of his voice. I asked him what was wrong, but I couldn't understand his garbled reply. His eyes looked as if they were about to pop out of his head at any moment, and his face became bright scarlet. Then, I noticed a small bulge near the bridge of his nose. He was holding a packet of sugar-coated licorice candy, so I quickly came to the conclusion that he had pushed one of them up his nose. Children do the strangest things!

Mummy was by now in no position to help, so when, at that moment, our kind stewardess knocked on the cabin door, obviously alarmed by the screams, I welcomed her in. I told her what had happened, and she held Ross in her arms while gently massaging the offending candy downwards until it popped out into her lap. My darling baby brother certainly kept life interesting, and continued to ensure that our days were not lacking in drama, while we were out of touch with his father.

I was sixteen years old, and trying my best to portray myself as a sophisticated young lady, but Ross was determined to thwart my best efforts. I was mortified, when, a few days later, we were having lunch in the dining room when I heard a shrill voice yell, "Mummy, Mummy, I want to wee, wee!"

Everyone in the dining room stopped eating, and all eyes turned towards my wide-eyed little brother, standing at the entrance to the dining room, holding himself, while dancing around in circles. He was quick, and had somehow escaped the cabin where the stewardess was reading to him. I have to admit, that apart from those three episodes, Ross was no trouble at all.

Seated at our dining table was a girl of about my own age and we quickly became friends. The two stewards who served at our table offered to escort the two of us ashore when we docked at the island of Madeira, a Portuguese territory in the Atlantic Ocean. Women in colorful traditional costumes greeted us as we disembarked, and the four of us went on a short tour of the island. A memorable day ashore revealed an island paradise covered in exotic tropical shrubs, amid lush greenery. We also enjoyed browsing in the stores. Had I not been in such a poor financial position, I would have loved to have purchased one of the many exquisitely embroidered table cloths for my mother.

Mummy stayed onboard the ship that day. She had become friends with a man named Braam, who also sat at our table. He was on his way home to Zambia by way of South Africa. They became inseparable and it was good to see her so relaxed, but I felt uncomfortable watching her holding hands and giggling with him.

One night, I went down to our cabin at about ten o'clock and upon gently opening the door so as not to wake Mummy or Ross, the light from the passageway revealed her lying in her bunk with Braam. I didn't want to believe what I was seeing, and quickly slammed the door shut. I ran up the passageway, barely reaching the toilet, before I threw up. After I had recovered somewhat, I went back on deck and stood at the rail for a long time, trying to convince myself that I had imagined what I had just seen.

Not even the cool sea breeze could obliterate the image of what I had witnessed, and after a while, I returned to the cabin, where I found Mummy alone in her bunk. Without a word, I undressed in the dark and climbed up into my bunk. Mummy never said anything, and the matter was never discussed. Although I understood that she also needed to be loved and was grasping at what could only have been a temporary chance of happiness, a part of me died when I saw them lying together. I lost what little respect I had for her in that moment, and resented the fact that she didn't seem to care about my feelings at all.

From then on, the trip was no longer a pleasure for me. I avoided Mummy as much as possible, spending most of my time with my new friend and the other young people on board. We hit some rough seas as we approached the Cape of Good Hope, and Mummy spent most of the time below deck, fighting off seasickness.

After two weeks at sea, we arrived at Cape Town. Anxious to see what it looked like, everyone went up on deck at about 6.30 that morning. In front of us was a gray, dingy-looking dock, which, despite the early hour, was a hive of activity. Table Mountain was obliterated by heavy clouds, and my heart sank as I surveyed the dismal scene. Was this the sunny South Africa where I was to spend the next couple of years of my life?

Disappointed, we all went below to have breakfast and get ourselves ready for a day ashore. The steward at our table offered to show me around the city, while Mummy was to spend the day ashore with Braam. Ross stayed in the playroom in the care of the stewardess.

When we went back up on deck, the transformation was unbelievable. The sun was shining brightly out of a clear blue sky, and Table Mountain appeared in all its glory, overlooking the city. The scene was truly magnificent and it was hard to believe what a difference a couple of hours had made. Mummy and I stood at the rail watching the cargo being off-loaded on to the dockside, from where it was to be transported inland either by road or rail. I pointed out what looked like Mummy's two tea chests being lowered by a crane in a huge net. We could only stand and gasp as we saw them being dropped the last couple of feet onto the concrete dockside, and we hoped we had been mistaken in identifying them.

Stepping ashore, my legs felt as though they were made of rubber, while my body felt like it was still on-board ship, and I experienced a peculiar swaying sensation. After finding my land legs again, the steward and I spent a pleasant day in Cape Town. I was amazed at the size of the city, with its skyscrapers, gracious old houses and parks. It was nothing like what I had imagined. I saw no jungle full of lions and tigers, but I found myself wondering what it would look like inland.

I also went ashore when we docked in at the cities of Port Elizabeth and East London, where the ship stayed for a day in each port on its way to Durban, our final destination. Fresh fruit and vegetables were taken on board in Cape Town, as well as at the other ports, and our meals improved greatly with the fresh produce. We were also delighted to find that we had fresh water showers for the rest of the voyage.

Mummy and Braam said their goodbyes before the ship docked in Durban. He was a confirmed bachelor, and although I think he was quite attracted to her, it was obviously just a shipboard romance for him. I believe the fear of Daddy taking Ross away may have stopped Mummy from pursuing the romance any further. She had a little weep, and then resigned herself to the inevitable.

I still missed Teddy dreadfully, and I wondered if I would ever be able to fully enjoy anything without him. I had experienced many interesting and exotic things since leaving Southampton, but I still felt disconsolate. I missed the feeling of being loved for who I was, and closing my eyes, I pictured his kind face with those eyes that crinkled up when he smiled, and imagined hearing his gentle voice. Was he missing me as much as I missed him? I knew that I would have to pay back the money I had borrowed from Uncle Percy as quickly as possible, so that I could save to go home to Teddy.

Our ship reached Durban on July 23rd, 1957, and Aunt Joey and Uncle Percy were there waiting to welcome us. It was wonderful to see them again. They drove us to a friend's cottage at Umhlanga Rocks, a few miles up the coast from Durban. Umhlanga is a Zulu word meaning, place of reeds. The cottage had a lovely view of the ocean, and the setting was spectacular. Beautiful evening sunsets slipped below billowing clouds that rolled up from the warm waters of the Indian Ocean, so common to tropical waters, but completely foreign to me. We spent a few tranquil days there resting up after the voyage.

On the beach, we discovered where Umhlanga Rocks acquired the second part of its name. The weathered rock outcrops were magnificent, and I spent many contented hours exploring the beach and rocks for shells and other treasures relinquished by the sea.

All too soon, those few peaceful days came to an abrupt end, and it was time for us to drive inland to Pretoria. Knowing that I would soon be seeing Stepfather again was almost more than I could bear. We traveled all day, and I became increasingly anxious. How could a country be so big? The open countryside looked nothing like England, even though the KwaZulu-Natal Province was green and lush, due to its winter rainfall. The scale of the mountains and valleys was enormous compared to what I was used to. Driving west, we traversed the Free State Province, where there were miles and miles of nothing except level grassland, devoid of trees, stretching as far as the eye could see. The tall grass was the color of straw, having been starved of rain for several months now. We traveled on and on, and I wondered how anyone could live so far from the sea and not die!

PRETORIA

By the time we reached Gauteng Province, it was almost dark. I leaned my head back on the seat of Uncle Percy's car and looked up through the rear window, where I saw millions of stars shining brightly in the clear Highveld sky. In the countryside, there was no pollution; the air was clean and pure, and the vastness of the sky was overwhelming. Having never seen anything like it before, I could barely grasp the immense scale of the open South African landscape, so totally different from anything I had ever known in England.

Arriving in Pretoria, we drove to Aunt Joey's house in the gracious old suburb of Brooklyn. The streets were lined with tropical Jacaranda trees whose branches met high above to form a glorious shady tunnel, that, during the day, filtered out the harsh African sun. Aunt Joey and Uncle Percy welcomed us into their home, and we were introduced to their elegant lifestyle.

Upon our arrival, a tall black gentleman dressed in a white uniform greeted us and carried our luggage inside. His name was Laxton, and he was what Aunt Joey described as her houseboy. I found it strange that a grown man could be referred to as a boy, but I soon learned that there were many strange South African customs that I would have to get used to.

Laxton was from Malawi, and I am not sure how Aunt Joey found him, since it was considered unusual to employ servants imported from other countries. He was well-mannered, spoke fluent English, and ran Aunt Joey's household like clockwork. He cleaned, cooked, and even baked cakes. When she had company, Laxton made tea, and, wearing white gloves, served it elegantly on a tray with dainty sandwiches that he had prepared. Once a year, Laxton went home for his annual holiday to see his wife and family and renew his visa. I thought it was a most unsatisfactory way to live, but apparently, there was no work for him in Malawi. He lived in a tiny room with an adjoining bathroom in Uncle Percy's backyard.

Uncle Percy also employed a gardener, who worked for him on weekdays, but he returned home each evening to one of the black townships on the outskirts of the city.

I found Pretoria, with its population at that time of 370,000, to be a charming and delightful city. Situated at an elevation of a mile above sea level, it had an almost perfect climate, so the houses were neither air-conditioned nor heated. It is located in the broad Apies River valley between the Magaliesburg Mountains to the north and a range of smaller hills to the south. Famously known as the Jacaranda City, the streets and yards of the city display thousands of Jacaranda trees that are quite spectacular in all seasons, but particularly so in spring when they are adorned with sprays of exquisite purple bells.

A wonderful variety of flowering shrubs compete with each other, and an abundance of bird life provides a wide variety of songs and colors to the manicured yards. Outdoor living was popular, and most families held many of their meals outside on a verandah or around a swimming pool.

The stately homes in Pretoria's wealthy suburbs complimented their surroundings, with architectural styles ranging from gabled Cape Dutch houses with thatch roofs to Mediterranean, British Tudor, contemporary moderns and many others. These were all in sharp contrast to the small government houses and tin-roofed shacks belonging to the black people in their townships, which can only be described as grimly utilitarian.

I was pleasantly surprised to note that nowhere did I see the jungle that I had been so fearful of living in. I discovered that jungle conditions are only prevalent in central Africa, and Africa is an exceptionally large and diverse continent. The wild animals I had anticipated roaming around, with the exception of tigers, which I was to learn do not occur in Africa, were confined to the Kruger National Park, and the many other smaller nature preserves dotted around the country.

When we arrived in Pretoria, Stepfather was still living with his cousin, Sannie and her husband, Peter. He stayed in their small guest cottage, and as they lived close to the Iscor steel mill where he worked, it was convenient for him. Aunt Joey's small spare room was just large enough for Mummy and Ross, so I slept on a couch in Uncle Percy's study. I was relieved to learn that Stepfather would not be living with us for a while. I think Aunt Joey was, too, although she was much too polite to have said so.

The day after we arrived, Aunt Sannie drove Stepfather over to see us. He looked exceptionally healthy. He had a marvelous tan from swimming in their pool every day, and playing tennis with Aunt Sannie on their private court. I could hardly believe that this was the same man who sat around at home in England, and whose only exercise, apart from going to work, was to play cards and gamble.

Being with Stepfather again made it hard for me to breathe, although being surrounded by family, he was unable to greet me in his usual offensive manner. Even so, it was all I could do not to shudder when he kissed me. His breath smelled of brandy and cigarettes, and all the old, unwelcome memories flooded back.

Shortly after his arrival, my parents went into the spare room, and soon, we heard their voices raised in anger. Mummy shouted, "No, I haven't got any money! What have you been doing with your salary, Paul?"

We could hear every word loud and clear. Obviously, Stepfather had been squandering his salary, and it didn't take much imagination to guess what they were arguing about. We had just traveled from the other side of the world, and he, after working for four months, had no money. Poor Mummy sounded beside herself with frustration. We had just arrived, and they were already fighting. Life was back to normal! Normal should have made me feel good, but it didn't, because our normal was anything but.

An uncomfortable silence followed the departure of Aunt Sannie and Stepfather. Our financial situation was obviously known to everyone, and Uncle Percy kindly offered to lend Mummy some money. We were both embarrassed because Uncle Percy was not our relative, and only by marriage was he related to Stepfather, but she had no option but to accept his offer.

By this time, my fortune had dwindled from £1.10s to a single sixpence, a three-penny bit, and a penny. This is about ten American cents, so I also had to borrow from Uncle Percy to get through the month. The 1955 brass three-penny bit, portraying the young Queen Elizabeth had an unusual shape with twelve sides, and I later had it made into a pendant to remind me of my humble beginnings in South Africa.

Before we arrived, Uncle Percy had arranged a job interview for me at the Standard Bank, situated on Church Square in the center of Pretoria. Thanks to a good letter of reference from Lumley of Lloyds, I was immediately employed as a copy typist, and I started work the following Monday. I made friends with Brenda, who shared an office with me, and I worked for the Bank for more than a year, until I found a better paying job.

The tea chests arrived from Cape Town sooner than we anticipated. Mummy and I looked at them and seeing the long cracks down the sides, it was obvious that they were indeed the ones we had seen dropped onto the dockside. Uncle Percy opened them with a small crowbar, and our worst fears were realized. Not only had they been dropped, but someone had pried open the cracks and pulled out the clothes and towels used to wrap the breakables, destroying almost all of Mummy's dainty chinaware. I cried with her. She certainly didn't deserve that. Now, she had almost nothing to start her new home.

DESMOND

We stayed with Aunt Joey and Uncle Percy for six weeks, and just a week after our arrival, they offered to take me to their niece's twenty-first birthday party, where I could meet some people of my own age.

Uncle Percy owned a shoe repair store just off Church Square. The woman who worked in the store had a nephew by the name of Desmond Jacobs, and Uncle Percy suggested that he might be a suitable escort to accompany me to the party. Not being used to blind dates, I was uncomfortable with the arrangement, but nevertheless, to be polite, I agreed to it.

The shoe repair store was close to the bank where I worked, so Uncle Percy arranged for me to meet my escort during my lunch hour. When I arrived, I was introduced to Desmond's aunt, and we chatted for some time before he arrived. Not pleased with his tardiness, I was on the point of leaving, when Desmond walked in. He was twenty years old, six feet tall, tanned and handsome in his safari shorts with knee-length socks, and I decided that maybe I could be persuaded to allow him to escort me to the party after all.

I learned later that Desmond was dating another girl at the time, so he also wasn't keen on the idea of a blind date. He had told his cousin that he had been asked to act as my escort, but that he wasn't really interested. His cousin, Nimrod, suggested that they just go and have a look at me, so they came to the store together. The cousin peeped at me through the store window and told Desmond that I looked okay, so he came in to meet me, and I guess he liked what he saw.

I owned one party dress, so there was no decision to be made about what I was to wear. It was a pretty dress made of white lace, and when Aunt Joey pinned an orchid corsage on my shoulder, I was more than satisfied with the result. I went to great lengths to set my hair in soft waves and curls, and when Desmond arrived on his bicycle dressed in a white tuxedo, I could tell by the way he looked at me that he approved. We sat in the back of Uncle Percy's car, making small talk on the way to the party, and he told me to call him Des.

The party was a grand affair, with a formal dinner and speeches made by the girl's father, uncle, and friends of the family. The band was great, and I discovered that Des was a good dancer. He was so good in fact, that when we danced to a Rock and Roll song, everyone else stopped dancing to watch us. We had a good time that evening, and I felt my first pangs of genuine excitement at being in this strange country so far from home. The party ended at midnight, and Uncle Percy and Aunt Joey drove us home to Brooklyn. Des said a formal goodnight and, shaking my hand, promised to call me in a week's time.

Des didn't wait a week. In fact, the very next day, a Sunday, he came to visit me in the afternoon, and we talked for a couple of hours. From then on, lunchtimes found him waiting outside the bank, and although I found his attentions flattering, I also felt guilty when I thought of Teddy waiting for me back home in England.

In the evenings, Des rode over to Aunt Joey's house on his bicycle, and we sometimes went for walks, or took the bus into town to see a movie. I found him both attractive and interesting. He didn't try to hold my hand or kiss me during the few weeks while we were staying with

Aunt Joey, and I found that strange, but refreshing. Stepfather's constant molestation had made me fearful of being touched. As a result, I felt safe with Des.

Then, one evening, just before we were to move into our own home, we were sitting on the couch in the living room, and Des kissed me. It wasn't a passionate kiss, not even a warm kiss, but a kiss I might have expected from my brother. I thought it was very sweet, until he accusingly asked me why I had allowed him to kiss me. I was stunned! I had not expected the kiss and he had kissed me, not the other way round. Why did he ask me that question, and why in that tone of voice? It was almost as if it was a test, and I had failed miserably. Warning bells sounded but there was nothing in my experience to enable me to understand the meaning of them, and unfortunately, I didn't listen.

Des was the eldest of seven children. He had four sisters and two brothers. They were a large, close-knit family who, except for Des, all lived in Witbank, a town about seventy miles from the Pretoria. At the age of twenty, Des had moved from the town of Amsterdam, where he had attended school, to Pretoria, and he was now living in a boarding house near the Pretoria Railway Station. He worked at the Bureau of Standards in the textiles department testing fabrics, which, if they passed the various tests, acquired the stamp of approval from the Bureau.

In the evenings, Des was studying medicine part-time at the University of Pretoria, and he had borrowed the money for his fees from a wealthy uncle. He bought his study books on an account at the University bookstore, and when I met him, he had many debts. He was exceptionally proud and ambitious, and wanted to prove to his family that he could make something of his life by studying to be a doctor. His whole life was molded by this ambition, and because he was never able to live up to his expectations, he eventually became bitter and angry, resenting everyone and everything that he perceived to come in the way of his becoming the great doctor he was sure he could be.

It should have been obvious to Des that due to his poor financial situation, it wasn't a good idea for him to have a steady girlfriend, and I believe he only wanted me because, being British, I was different, like a prized trophy that he could show off to his friends. Unfortunately, I was young, naïve, and vulnerable and, consequently, unable to see what this might mean for the future. I allowed myself to become involved with a young man who would ensure that my life would turn out to be a continuation of my unhappy childhood.

SETTLING IN

Shortly after we arrived in Pretoria, Uncle Percy went to the Pretoria City Council in search of a rental house for us. We were offered an old condemned house not far from Uncle Percy. The house was indeed condemned, but not because it was falling apart. It was a solid old brick and plaster house with a wonderful shady verandah stretching the full length of the façade. The verandah was enclosed by a low wall with pillars that gave the house a stately appearance. Standing on an acre of land, it had been purchased by the city to be demolished to make way for the widening of the street. This was planned for some time within the next two years, and despite the possibility that we might have only been able to live there for a few months, we rented it anyway. We painted the house a fresh shade of cream, and Mum and I scrubbed and waxed the dark wooden floors until they gleamed. It was about the time we moved into the house, that I stopped calling Mum by my childhood name for her. Sadly, she had forfeited the name Mummy, along with much of my respect, that dreadful night onboard ship.

The house was nice and larger than anywhere we had lived before. I had a spacious bedroom with a window looking out onto the verandah, while my parents had an equally large bedroom opposite mine. A hallway led from the front door through to a large living/dining room, with Ross's small bedroom leading off one side and the kitchen off to the other. It was not grand, but it was more than adequate for our needs. There was a small stoop at the back of the house, with a door leading into the bathroom, which had probably been added to the house at a later date. Unhappily, there was no hot water in the kitchen or bathroom, but Uncle Percy soon had the city council install a hot water heater. After that, I enjoyed the luxury of a hot bath every evening.

Because we had no furniture, Aunt Sannie lent us a dining room table and chairs. Uncle Percy took Mum to an estate sale and loaned her the money to purchase three beds, two wardrobes, two dressing tables, a couple of armchairs and a coffee table. Aunt Joey gave Mum an old wicker table for the kitchen and we sat on wooden boxes that Uncle Percy found in his garage. Aunt Joey also provided us with dishes, pots and pans, blankets and pillows. And so, we settled into our first home in South Africa.

Because the house was near the street, most of the land was behind the house. There was a barren terrace outside the kitchen. A large fig tree full of fruit made up for the lack of grass, but my ignorance showed, when I saw Des picking some of the green figs off the tree. I protested they were not nearly ripe and that he should wait until they were brown. He frowned at me and then laughed when it occurred to him that I only knew dried figs, which, of course, was true. We ate them once a year at Christmas time in England as a special treat. I had no way of knowing that figs were green or purple before they were dried. Feeling foolish and being overly sensitive, I blushed and blinked back my tears.

Below the upper terrace, the backyard was densely overgrown with shrubs and trees. There grew a large quince tree as well as a mulberry tree, both laden with fruit. There was also an abundance of prickly pears. Stepfather was familiar with them, although we had never seen them before. Wearing thick gloves to protect his hands from the hundreds of tiny thorns, he picked a bowl full, cut off the two ends with a knife and fork, sliced open the remaining skin and peeled them. After being chilled in the refrigerator, we found them to be quite delicious.

Not knowing about the dangers of crawling insects and snakes found in Africa, I took to sitting on a blanket in the lower part of the yard with a good book. I noticed several tiny black spiders jumping around on the blanket, and later told Des about them and how cute they were. He told me they were poisonous button spiders, and so, needless to say, I sat on a chair on the verandah from then on. That didn't help much, as a few days later, something on the verandah wall caught my eye. Looking up from my book, I saw the largest spider I had ever seen. It was brown with thick, hairy legs and a huge body. I ran in and called Stepfather, who informed me that it was a baboon spider, which he managed to catch in a jar. Des arrived shortly afterward, and to my amazement, he took the spider home to show to his roommates.

As if the spiders were not bad enough, I was in my bedroom getting ready for bed one night, when I saw something large moving around between my skirt and petticoat. Thinking it was another spider, I grabbed it with both hands and held it tightly while wrenching off my skirt. Taking it outside, I discovered an enormous grasshopper. Why was everything so big? Even the moths were about five times the size of English moths.

Ever mindful of being attacked by another oversized insect, I was reading in bed one evening, when I became aware of a loud flapping noise on top of my wardrobe. I assumed it was a large moth, and stood up on my bed armed with my pillow, ready to whack it if it attacked me. Suddenly, a huge bat flew straight at me, and I dived beneath my bedcovers, while screaming for my stepfather. For the second time in my life, he was there to save me. I stayed beneath the covers until he assured me that he had captured my attacker and disposed of it outside. I had been told if a bat gets entangled in your hair, you have to have it cut out, which did not appeal to me at all. I quickly learned from all these unpleasant experiences that Africa was very different from England, and not being used to these oversized bugs, I was not impressed.

For the first few months, we struggled financially, until the end of the year. As always, I gave Mum half my monthly salary, and Stepfather gave her an allowance. Ginsberg's, our local grocery store, was within walking distance, and Mum was frugal, saving as much as she could out of her allowance to purchase a few household necessities. This was a challenge since, in addition to the rent, utilities and food, our debt to Uncle Percy also had to be paid. However, as we didn't have a car, telephone or any other modern luxuries, we managed.

Aunt Joey insisted we have an ironing girl since, according to her, white women did not do their own housework, and definitely not the ironing. Besides, if the black women weren't employed as domestics, they had few other options for making a living. She brought her ironing girl, (as she was called) to Mum, and Betty became our first servant. Communication was difficult, since Betty spoke only Afrikaans, as well as her native tongue, but they managed somehow. I was shocked at how little money she asked to do the whole week's ironing. Having been the one to do the ironing for all those years in England, I knew what a chore it was.

Having a servant meant that we had to learn about apartheid, because the relations between black and white people were strictly determined by law. I found it strange that black people were considered inferior, so much so, that they were totally segregated from the whites. They lived in satellite townships, far outside the white cities and because of this, they were compelled to get up as early as four in the morning, just to be at work in the city by seven or eight. Most white families employed servants. A woman was referred to as 'the girl,' no matter her age, and a man who worked in the yard, was referred to as 'the boy.' Seldom did the whites enquire about their servant's surname, their families, or where they lived. They were just there, almost invisible, as they went about their daily tasks.

The women servants mostly stayed at the back of the property in a small room with a bathroom or shower and toilet. Wealthier families had two rooms enabling the gardener to sleep on the property as well. At that time, servants usually went home for a weekend once a month to visit their families. It seemed a completely unnatural way of living to me, and I also found it strange that black people were not allowed to own a home in a white suburb, and yet they were allowed to live at the back of the white people's property.

I was to discover many peculiar aspects of life living under the apartheid government during my first few weeks in South Africa, which made me even more determined to return to England. Many of these things took a while to understand and come to terms with, in order to fit in and live in harmony with the people around me. Some things I was never able to accept.

Salaries for the black people were meager, but most whites gave their servants a 25lb bag of cornmeal and an allowance of chuck beef in addition to their monthly salary and believed they were treating them well. Discarded clothing was either given, or sold cheaply to the black people by their employers. I regularly heard white women commenting about how well they treated their servants, and wondered, if the roles were reversed, if they themselves would feel well treated.

The Group Areas act, a housing segregation law used in the apartheid era, required that all black people carry a passbook, much like an identity document, which had to be signed monthly by their white employer. These passbooks allowed the owner's employees to live and work in a certain area. White police and their guard dogs could be seen regularly patrolling the white suburbs. Any black person brave enough to be outside his allotted area, ran the risk of being picked up and thrown into the wire mesh cage at the back of the truck and then hauled off to jail.

Blacks were not allowed to eat in the same restaurants as whites, nor were they allowed to use the same toilets or buses. They had to address their white employers as Boss and Missus and were encouraged to be so subservient that some of them even crouched down, while speaking to their employers. For me, the whole idea of apartheid was unacceptable, and I was horrified at the treatment the blacks received at the hands of the whites. Having grown up in England, I had no way of knowing about apartheid, or its ramifications, until I landed in South Africa.

Such was the land I found myself living in, and I was sad to discover that in this country of such great wealth and beauty, with its abundance of sunshine, fauna and flora, lived many people without the values and morals that I knew in my heart to be fair and right in the eyes of God.

BREAKING TIES

I received several heart-wrenching letters from Teddy. I wrote back and told him about Des, trying to explain the situation, but not really knowing how. All the promises Teddy and I had made to each other before I left England now seemed distant and unobtainable. I missed Teddy, but at the same time, I felt trapped in the present with Des, and I didn't know how to handle the situation. Des eventually handled it for me.

One evening, Des disappeared after dinner and stayed away for a good while, so I went to look for him. I found him in my bedroom, rifling through the drawers of my dressing table, where I kept my letters from Teddy. He had my bundle of letters as well as photographs of Teddy in his hand. Triumphantly, he held them up and asked me who Teddy was, and I confessed that Teddy was my boyfriend in England. He was furious, and we had the most awful argument, after which I asked him to leave. He grabbed my arms and told me that I belonged to him, and nobody else. I told him to get out, and never come back. He then called me a whore and a slut, and before I could stop myself, I slapped his face. He slapped me right back, almost knocking me off my feet. The blow stunned me for a moment, and then the realization of what had happened hit me, and I burst into tears. I was back in the same old routine, a horrible continuation of my childhood.

Des realized immediately that he had gone too far. He held me in his arms, begging me to forgive him. He promised it would never happen again. He hadn't meant to hurt me. "Please, Doreen, forgive me," he begged, over and over again.

My mind was in turmoil. What should I do? What was to become of me? Was I never to be free of violence? My parents must have heard us arguing, but neither of them even tried to intervene. They obviously didn't care what happened to me.

Following the row, Des wrote me several letters telling me how much he loved me and begging my forgiveness. It was as if another person had written them. I was confused. They were so completely out of character with the young man I was dating.

The letters and photographs of Teddy were never returned to me. Des took them home, read and destroyed them, saying I was to write to Teddy and tell him that it was over between us. Des was slowly taking over my life, draining me of what little self-confidence I had. He had a power over me that I cannot explain, and I felt helpless to resist him.

Although I never admitted it to myself at the time, I was just a teenager, vulnerable and lacking any dependable sense of self-worth. I desperately needed to be loved, and so I gave in to Des and did as he told me. I received a couple more heartbreaking letters from Teddy before I was able to convince him that it was over between us.

When Des felt sure of himself, and was satisfied that I had broken off with Teddy, he lay down his ground rules. I was never to talk about England as back home, and never to mention the Royal family, who he considered to be nothing more than a bunch of parasites. Not knowing the history of the Boer War, I had no idea the English were so hated in South Africa.

Only now do I understand the power Des had over my mind. At the time, it was scary, as I didn't seem to be able to resist him. He said we were going to be married and have four children. His wife would not drink, smoke, or swear. He refused to listen when I said I was not ready for any of that, promising to take such good care of me, that he would make me so happy that I would soon forget all about Teddy and my precious England. It was obvious that his idea of happiness wasn't anything like mine.

Des constantly criticized everything about me. My hair was never quite right. My figure wasn't good enough. He didn't like the way I walked. Why did I have to take such large steps? Ladies are supposed to take dainty steps. Meanwhile, I was always running to keep up with him as he strode ahead. One day, I asked him if there was anything about me that he liked. After some hesitation, he admitted I had pretty good legs and a nice back. As a result of his constant criticism, my poor self-image was being made even worse.

Afrikaans, a language derived from the Dutch who had immigrated to South Africa from the Netherlands, was Des' home language. I had no idea that there was such a language before I arrived in the country, but I soon learned from Des and his friends about the Boer War and the animosity between the Afrikaners and the English.

Des' friends refused to speak English when I was present, so I was completely excluded from the conversations. They laughed at my attempts to speak Afrikaans, so I eventually stopped trying. I experienced the same situation when in the company of other Afrikaans people. They also refused to speak English, even though they knew I had only recently arrived in the country. If I complained to Des that I felt left out of the conversation, he always replied in Afrikaans, *"leer of loop!"* which meant "learn or leave." Although I didn't grasp, or initially understand the depth of animosity that existed between the two cultures, I was soon to find out through an encounter with Des' grandmother.

Ouma (Grandmother) Jacobs, lived in a retirement home next door to our house. Des took me to visit her early on in our courtship, and I was delighted, anticipating a close relationship with her. Her room was tiny, with just enough space for a bed, chest of drawers and a chair. My heart went out to this dear old lady and I determined to visit her regularly.

As we were leaving, Ouma called Des back, and I learned that she told him that, as long as he was involved with that English girl, he wasn't welcome, and she never wanted to see him again. When he told me, I was shocked. What had I done? What had I said? It turned out that I had done or said nothing wrong. The problem was that I was British, and she was a proud Afrikaner, who had lived through the Boer War in the early part of the century. Tragically, she had lost nearly all of her children in the concentration camp, something I was completely unaware of, and when Des told me about it, I felt positively dreadful.

Having learned nothing of the Boer War in school, since it had been completely overshadowed by the First and Second World Wars in the intervening years, I was horrified when I read what the English had done to the Afrikaans women and children. Thousands of farm families were rounded up, and held in concentration camps, after their farms and homes had been burned to deny the Boer soldiers access to resources during the war. Boer is the Afrikaans word for farmer, and most of the men were farmers at that time in the country's history. Since the Boers were irregular volunteers, they went back to their farms after battle to replenish their provisions and restore their health, before returning to fight again.

Thousands of the elderly and children died from neglect and lack of nutrition and hygiene in the camps, over five times as many as those who fell in battle. I felt thoroughly ashamed of their treatment at the hands of my countrymen, and as a result, I understood Ouma Jacobs' reaction. I was disappointed that she didn't want to see me, and sad that she was prepared to write Des off, but it took several years before I was in a position to do anything about it.

Des' twenty-first birthday was in October, and although we had only been in the house for a couple of months, Mum and I wanted to help him celebrate. Money was tight, but we made a brave effort at a party, complete with a cake and candles. By this time, Des was visiting me in the evenings, as well as every weekend. Having all his meals with us, he soon became a part of the family, such as it was. Des and I followed the sad example set by my parents. Young Ross, by this time, received regular beatings from his father, so life was the same as it always had been, but now, Des was a part of it.

One day, Des arrived early at the Standard Bank, and he walked up to my office to fetch me after work. He discovered that I was still smoking, which he had strictly forbidden, even though he smoked himself. When we got home, we had a terrible argument about it. He hit me again and then, as before, begged my forgiveness. Thus, a pattern had been established. I smoked secretly for another year without him suspecting, until eventually, I made up my mind to stop as it didn't make me feel good, and I really couldn't afford it. I threw the pack away, and never felt the desire to smoke again.

My finances were not improving. I still gave Mum half my salary, and I had to give Uncle Percy £3.00 a month to pay off the three-year loan for my boat fare. Bus fares, clothes, and toiletries were part of my budget, and I was also helping Des to pay off his many debts.

Helping Des reminded me of Paul in prison, back in England, so I wrote him a letter with no return address, telling him that I felt it would be better if we didn't continue to write. I knew that if my stepfather found out we were corresponding, he would be furious, and I felt that being so far away, I simply couldn't help Paul anymore. Besides, I had more than enough problems of my own to deal with, so I wished him well, and said my final goodbye. My plan to return to England was now no more than a rapidly-fading dream, and cutting ties with Paul and Teddy seemed the only sensible thing to do.

THE ENGAGEMENT

In January, we had been dating for six months, and Des bought me an engagement ring. He took me to a jeweler who was having a sale, picked out a ring and placed it on my finger. There was no romantic proposal, which I found disappointing but, by this time, I had no illusions that things would be any better than I was used to. Des put down the deposit, but I was the one who made the monthly payments.

The ring was on my finger for barely a month, when we had another argument. Des was jealous, not only of other boys, but of my friends, and even my thoughts. He constantly asked me what I was thinking, and then got mad at me if I wasn't thinking what he thought I should be thinking. I had to be careful of every word I uttered, which I found incredibly stressful. One evening, we were sitting on the back porch, and he again asked me what I was thinking. When I told him, he became upset, and when I said I was sorry, he asked me what I was sorry for, and became verbally abusive.

He ended up calling me a whore again, and I took the ring off my finger and pushed it into his hand, saying I didn't want it, and I was not going to marry him. Des lost his temper completely, and looking at me with utter contempt, he threw the ring far down into the yard and stormed off on his bicycle.

That night, I couldn't sleep. By this time, I was deeply in love with Des, and despite his behavior, and my sense of foreboding, I felt I couldn't live without him. But, could I live with him? I lay awake for hours until, at about one o'clock, I heard a soft tapping on my window, and I knew it had to be Des. He whispered for me to meet him at the back door. I put on my dressing gown, quietly opened my bedroom door and stole through the house to the back door. The whisperings on the back porch continued for what felt like hours, and I despaired of ever convincing Des that I was not prepared to continue with our engagement. Eventually, when he saw that I was serious, he lost his temper once again, and left.

The next day, I searched for hours in the yard, before eventually finding the ring, which I placed in my jewelry box. At work, I was asked why I wasn't wearing it, and I told my co-workers that the engagement was off. The only person who didn't believe me was Des. He called the office three or four times a day and waited outside at lunchtimes, and after work. To avoid him, I sneaked out the back way, or I walked past him, while trying to ignore his pleadings. He also kept coming to the house, and I told my parents to tell him I wasn't at home.

This continued for three weeks, until my supervisor called me in and reminded me that I was not permitted to receive private calls at the office, and they had to stop. She was annoyed, and rightly so. After work that day, I told Des he must please stop pestering me. Once again, he showered me with his usual promises, continuing on, until eventually he wore me down, and I allowed him back into my life. The ring was back on my finger, and he was on his best behavior for about three months, during which time I lost my engagement ring.

It happened at work, when I hooked my ring onto the button of my cardigan while I washed my hands. I was chatting to a girl from another department, and while engrossed in conversation, I bent down to pick up my purse, forgetting about the ring. I met Des outside, and we walked over to Church square, where we sat on the grass, and while eating our sandwiches, I noticed with horror that my ring was missing from my finger. I jumped up, mumbled something to Des, and ran back to the restroom. I was sure that the ring must have fallen off my button when I bent down to pick up my purse, but with my heart racing, I kept my eyes on the ground all the way to the bank, making sure it hadn't fallen off on our way to the square. I checked the elevator. It wasn't there, and it wasn't in the restroom either. It was gone, and it wasn't even fully paid for.

I learned another hard lesson that day. Des was not in the mood to forgive me, and I received a long, angry lecture on how careless I was, and did I not know how much that ring cost? At that moment, it was convenient for him to forget that I was the one paying the monthly installments. He begrudgingly bought me an eternity ring with tiny marcasite stones as a replacement. He accused me of losing the ring on purpose, so that other young men wouldn't know I was engaged. I felt as if I were suffocating under his jealous possessiveness, while at the same time, I wanted to believe they were signs of his love for me.

Des could be charming, especially when we were out, and time and again, I was told how lucky I was to find him. Why could he not treat me decently when we were alone? It was becoming obvious to me that we were falling into the same pattern as my parents, and Sheila and Dennis. If I told Des he shouldn't speak to me in that tone of voice, or that he shouldn't swear at me, he said that it was the only language I could understand, and he may have been right. At home, it was all I had ever been used to. I didn't realize at the time, that allowing someone to treat you badly is the quickest way to lose their respect, and so I became a part of the problem.

It occurred to me that perhaps if I told Des about my stepfather, and what he had been subjecting me to since I was a child, he might be understanding and treat me more kindly. It turned out to be a big mistake. He asked me many questions in such a sympathetic manner that, bit by bit I told him the sad tale of my childhood. It felt good to be able to talk to someone who I was sure would support me. Once he understood, he would surely help me out of the terrible situation I found myself in. Stupidly, I also unburdened myself about my mother's indiscretion onboard the ship. I was to discover that, in my foolishness, all I had done was to give him enough ammunition to use against me for the rest of my life. He was good at throwing stones, and he remembered every single detail.

Des never said one word to either my stepfather or my mother. He may even have been more charming to them. I couldn't understand it. Did he not comprehend what I had told him, or did he simply not believe me?

Thankfully, it was no longer necessary for my stepfather to wake me in the mornings because I now had an alarm clock and what a blessing that was. He still grabbed at my breasts whenever he could, and his unwelcome kisses still made me feel sick to my stomach, so I avoided him as much as possible and made sure we were never alone together. He and Mum still argued, but I didn't interfere nearly as much as I had in the past. Stepfather's drinking problem got progressively worse, and he was now drinking neat brandy, eventually consuming a bottle a day, which he hid in every conceivable place, including his filing cabinet at work. He continued to chain-smoke, and his use of profanity never diminished.

January was the beginning of the school year in South Africa, and since Ross was now old enough, he attended an English primary school. This enabled Mum to take a job at Ginsberg's, a comprehensive grocery and department store complex, where she worked in the ladies' clothing department. She earned a good salary and soon had everything she needed to make our home comfortable.

Stepfather rode to work on a moped, since he had vowed never to drive a car again. No longer having a pub close at hand, he drank at home, and Mum was forever screaming at him for wasting money on brandy, which led to the usual confrontations.

Ross often bore the brunt of Stepfather's wrath at the receiving end of his *sjambok*. Replacing his leather belt, this was a short whip made of plaited rhinoceros hide with the strands tapering off at the end. It hung by a handle behind the kitchen door. The sjambok made lash marks, which left Ross's legs bruised for weeks on end. I couldn't believe that nobody at the school noticed, or if they did, why they didn't intervene.

Occasionally, when Des wanted to take me to the drive-in theater, he borrowed a friend's MG, an open sports car. It was then that I learned of Des' fanatical love of speed. He drove extremely fast, and since I was not used to cars, it was terrifying for me. One night, while driving home from the movies, he suddenly drew the steering wheel towards him, and it came right off the steering column. I gasped, realizing that he had no control over the car, but he simply grinned and slipped it back into place just in time to avoid crashing into a culvert. He roared with laughter at my obvious distress, and told me that he knew how to handle a car, and I should learn to trust him.

Des was proud, and borrowing his friend's car soon became an embarrassment for him, so he bought a small second-hand car. The pale blue Renault was cute in spite of being in terrible shape. It stood in our backyard, since he had no place to keep it at his boardinghouse, and he spent every weekend working on it until he got it up and running. This was to be the first of many cars that Des bought and sold over the years, but it would always remain one of my favorites.

Not long after becoming engaged, Des felt it was time to introduce me to his parents. He never spoke about them so I was curious, but also nervous to meet them. One Saturday afternoon, we drove to Witbank, and it took us quite a while to locate their house. When we eventually found it, Des stiffened as he looked around the dry, dusty yard. Nero, the dog, was tied to a tree, and chickens pecked around the yard. Des' sisters were playing outside, and they looked up at us with enquiring eyes.

Suddenly, the back door opened, and a tall woman came running out. She hugged Des, who stood stiffly without putting his arms around her. With tears in her eyes, she turned to me, and enquired who I was. Des introduced me to his mother, and I liked her instantly. She had a kind face and a homey appearance. Des' father followed her out, and they shook hands. Des then introduced me to his two brothers and four sisters. I felt quite overwhelmed, never having been part of a large family.

We all went inside and sat at the kitchen table for a while, talking. Des was angry, and even though I couldn't understand all of the words as everyone was speaking mostly in Afrikaans, judging by the hurt look on his mother's face, I knew he was saying things she didn't want to hear.

After a while, Des took me roughly by the arm, and steered me into the living room. He attempted to close the door, and it fell askew as one of the hinges was missing. He struggled to get it closed, and then he sat down next to me on the couch. He had a face like a thundercloud, and I asked him what was wrong. He exploded, saying, "This! All this, is what's wrong!"

He gestured around us with his hands, and I knew he was ashamed. I tried to comfort him by saying, "Yes, but they haven't long moved in here. They need time to get settled."

He replied bitterly, "Your mother has not long moved in either. There's no excuse." That was one of the few times I saw Des cry. The humiliation was too much for him to bear, and my heart broke for him.

Des' mother was an amazing cook. She cooked Boere style, which is completely different from English cooking, with several kinds of meats and vegetables. She made us a fabulous meal that night, and with ten of us to feed, four being grown men, I was amazed by the amount of food on the table. The family made me feel welcome, but I was unable to understand much of the conversation. They were all able to speak English, but being used to speaking only Afrikaans, I guessed that it was difficult for them to remember to speak English just for my benefit. I was shy, and as I didn't feel encouraged to speak much, I was relieved when Des said we were going home. We had originally intended to stay the night but it was clear to see that there was no place for us, so we drove back to Pretoria in awkward silence. This was the first of many strained visits to the Jacobs family.

Des made it plain that he was ashamed of his family, and didn't want to spend time with them. On many occasions, he told them how to behave or how they should live, and our visits were never pleasant. Should I dare defend his family or say something positive about them, I found myself the brunt of his anger, and I learned to keep quiet. He criticized their attempts to better themselves, saying he would show them by example how they should live. He was determined to make something of his life, to be somebody, and in his efforts to do so, he alienated himself as the black sheep of the family.

CHANGES

Without realizing it, I was following the typical path of an abused child as I turned to another abuser. In my heart, I knew that Des had a problem, but I sincerely believed that by loving him, I could help him to change.

Instead, the physical abuse increased, but worse than that, was the mental abuse. Des played mind games with me, and some of the time I didn't know who he was and even worse, most of the time, I didn't know who I was either. He could be kind and charming one moment, and then suddenly turn into a monster, screaming and hitting me. Just as suddenly he calmed down, and acted as if nothing had happened. I continued to live in hope that things would eventually improve when our life was more settled.

When Des told me he was going to buy a motorbike, I begged him not to make another debt, but brushing my protests aside, he bought it anyway. One night, returning from Witbank on one of the few occasions when he visited his parents alone, he hit a pothole, and the next thing he knew, he found himself on top of the motorbike, which was on its side, spinning around in circles. The bike was pretty banged up, but miraculously, Des only suffered minor cuts and bruises. He was stranded beside the road for some time, while attempting to stop a passerby. Several cars drove by ignoring him, until eventually, a black man stopped and offered to help him.

Des was proud, but not too proud to accept this good Samaritan's help, even if he was black. The man had no tools, so he drove into the next town and left his wristwatch with the owner of the garage as security for the loan of a screwdriver and a pair of pliers. He then helped Des repair the bike well enough for him to make it home. In payment, Des gave him all his loose change. Hearing Des relate the story, I hoped he might change his attitude towards black people, and treat them with more understanding, but he didn't. And now we not only had to pay for the bike, but the repair bill as well.

One night, returning home from the movies, we had another heated argument. Des shouted and swore at me, until I could take it no longer. I told him to stop the car; I preferred to walk home. He told me to get out, using really strong language, but he didn't even slow down. In frustration, I reached for the door handle and wrenched it open; I almost fell out. He leaned over and grabbed me by my hair, and we swerved all over the road. When he eventually managed to bring the car to a standstill, I received a beating that I will never forget.

After working a year at the Standard Bank, I heard about a vacancy at United Dominions Bank. By that time, I had been trained as a Dictaphone typist. I found it to be no easier than copy-typing, because instead of having to decipher the men's handwriting, we had to decipher what they were saying, but at least I was now better qualified. United Dominions was a new bank, and the salary was better. I was one of several typists who shared one big office with the young bankers.

We had lived in the house for two years before the city council finally notified us that they were ready to widen the street, and we had to move out. My parents were offered the opportunity to purchase a small council house just around the corner from Ginsberg's, not far from our old house. It had two tiny bedrooms, a small living room/dining room, a kitchen and a bathroom. It provided my parents the opportunity to own their own home instead of renting.

With only two bedrooms, Ross and I had to share the front bedroom for the next fifteen months. It was barely large enough for the bunk beds, a wardrobe and my dressing table, but we managed somehow.

Mum made the house look pretty, and Stepfather surprised us all by working in the yard. He pruned the peach trees that grew on half of the lot, and produced some of the best peaches I had ever eaten. He bought pipes and built a pergola over the large paved terrace to accommodate the neglected grape vines. We also had a couple of fig trees and a large mulberry tree. Stepfather took great care of his peach trees, spraying and pruning them regularly against pests, and painting what he called white 'spats' on their trunks annually. He took great pride in his small orchard, and friends and neighbors all benefited from his sumptuous crop.

Mum loved her job at Ginsberg's, and thrived on the compliments she received. A few of the Afrikaans customers gave her a hard time, telling her she should learn *die taal* (the language). Mostly, she stood her ground, and told them that she had emigrated as a grown woman, which made it difficult for her to learn the language and pronounce the guttural sounds that were a common part of it. There were a few occasions when she arrived home in tears, having been sneered at, or made fun of by a particularly unpleasant customer. But the majority of the customers liked her and her employer, Mr. Ginsberg, recognizing her worth, made her a supervisor.

Des and I had been engaged for almost two years at that time, and I was still without a ring, when one of the women in our office told me that she had recently married a young man who owned a jewelry store, and they were about to have a sale. She knew that I had lost my engagement ring, and thought that this might be a good opportunity to replace it. I mentioned it to Des, and we went to the store during our lunch hour and he picked out a ring that was even prettier than my first one. He put down the deposit, but as before, I was left to pay off the debt. I didn't mind because it was important to me that everyone knew that I was engaged to Des. We made several dates for our wedding, but each time, as the day drew near, he had another excuse as to why we couldn't get married, and usually, it had to do with our finances. We battled to get out of debt and save for the wedding.

At the end of the year, we drove down to Zululand to visit Alfred, an old friend of Des' whose parents were sugar cane farmers. The dirt roads were full of potholes, and it was surprising that the Renault survived the trip. We got a terrible fright, when we hit one extra large pot hole, and the hood flew open, completely obscuring our view of the road. Des was able to safely pull off the road, but the hood was dented so badly that it wouldn't close. Fortunately, he found some string in the trunk and was able to tie it down.

While on the farm, Des borrowed a rifle from Alfred, and shot an enormous crocodile down by the river. Just prior to the shooting, we had walked through the reeds near the river, and I was horrified when I realized that we could have been eaten alive. I was to learn many times over that Des was completely fearless. He was proud to have his photograph taken, with a rifle in hand, crouching next to his trophy.

A couple of months later, Alfred flew up to Pretoria in his private plane, and offered to take us for a short flight over Pretoria. I was not too happy when Alfred turned the plane sideways and flew in circles, until I convinced him I would be needing a paper sack if he didn't stop. Des obviously found it exhilarating and scoffed at my fears.

After we had finally paid off Des' debts, we were at last able to set a definite date for our wedding. Just prior to that date, we were fortunate enough to learn that a small three-bedroomed house just around the corner from Mum, was for sale. Rather than taking out a twenty-year mortgage, we arranged to put down a small deposit and pay the balance over five years. The rooms were small, the living room being the largest room in the house, measuring a mere nine by thirteen feet. We cleaned and painted the house, and bought some furniture, which we paid off over the next two years. We considered ourselves fortunate to own our own home, but it was not destined to be a happy one.

THE WEDDING

Our final wedding date, was October 15th, 1960, and this time, it actually happened. The ceremony took place in the Methodist church in Pretoria, and Mum and Stepfather suggested that we hold the reception under the grape arbor in their backyard, which could accommodate about seventy people. We agreed that would be lovely, although we would have to rely on the weather co-operating with us.

We rented trestle tables and folding chairs. Mum and I made savories as well as tiny sandwiches and cookies. Mum intended to make the wedding cake, but she didn't have enough time, so we ordered one from a local bakery. Des' mother offered to supply chickens for the meal. We gratefully accepted the offer, but they were received with some consternation when they arrived a couple of days before the wedding – alive! Mum was beside herself at the prospect of all the extra work, and it was as much as I could do to keep her calm. Surprisingly, Stepfather helped by wringing their necks, something he appeared to relish. No surprise there! We then dunked them in boiling water and plucked them. It wasn't the most pleasant task, but at least we knew they were fresh.

Des asked two friends from his boardinghouse to serve as his best man and groomsman, and Brenda, my friend from the Standard Bank, was to be my maid of honor. A girl who worked with me at UDC Bank asked if she could be my bridesmaid, and although I had intended to ask another friend, I felt obliged to say yes. Des' photographer friend agreed to take the photographs, and at last, everything was in place.

A week before the wedding, we were driving home from town, when Des stopped the car in a small roadside park, and said he had something to tell me. I was intrigued. He looked serious, and told me he couldn't marry me after all. I was shocked! This was one week before our wedding, and I couldn't help thinking of all the times I had tried to break up with him over the past three years. He would never let me go, and now *he* wanted to break off our engagement. Puzzled, I begged him to tell me what was wrong. What had I done? He became angry, and told me it was nothing I had done. It had something to do with his family, but he couldn't tell me what it was.

Des rarely spoke about his childhood, and I found this strange since I felt we should be able to share our past with one another, and he had insisted on knowing all about mine. On the few occasions when he did speak of his past, I caught a rare glimpse into his troubled world.

He once told me that his family had lived in Swaziland when he was a young boy. For some reason, his father visited the Swazi King, and he took Des with him. Following the Swazi tradition, they sat in a circle with the King and other tribal dignitaries. A cup was passed around the circle from which they all drank, but when it came to Des' turn, he refused. His father told him to drink, but Des again refused. Only when his father gripped Des' arm firmly, telling him a third time, in an unmistakably threatening way, to drink, did Des obey.

I was shocked to learn that Des had refused to drink from the same cup as the king, until I discovered that he never shared a cup or glass with anyone, including me. He avoided risking contact with another person's germs, even if they were family. This was confirmed when he told me that his father had once forced him, as a form of punishment, to chew his sister's chewing gum after she spat it out. It was obviously not easy for him to tell me about it, and I didn't have the heart to ask him why his father would do such a thing. I knew instinctively, that for Des, it must have been extremely humiliating.

The only other time he spoke of his past concerned, what I now believe, was a life-changing experience for him. Des' mother breast fed him until he was a toddler, and it seems they had a close relationship until one day, a friend of his mother and her little girl came to visit, and the two women sat and chatted together. The girl climbed up on her mother's lap and snuggled close to her. Des attempted to do the same with his mother, and she pushed him away, telling him to go outside and play. He says she used profanity when telling him to go outside. I felt sure she was just irritated and told Des so. To me, it sounded trivial, but in his young mind, it was a significant event, and he saw it as an act of complete rejection by his mother. He never recovered, and years later, it caused him to reject his mother, when he should have needed her support most.

What happened to cause Des to say he couldn't marry me remains a mystery. He kept me in limbo until the day before the ceremony, when he finally agreed to go through with it. Because he never told me the reason for his earlier refusal, I could only speculate as to what it was.

We had attended the Methodist church for three weeks before the marriage in order to have our banns read. The practice of reading the banns of marriage ensured that anyone who objected had ample opportunity to say so before the wedding. The minister informed the congregation of our impending marriage saying, "This is the first time of asking. If any of you know the cause or just impediment why these two persons should not be joined together in holy Matrimony, ye are to declare it now." This was repeated for three consecutive weeks. We also published the announcement of our forthcoming marriage in the Pretoria News. No one objected.

The day of the wedding arrived, and I was terribly nervous. What if Des didn't turn up at the church? After professing that he couldn't marry me just the week before, I couldn't be sure.

Brenda's father offered to drive my stepfather and me to the church in his Chevrolet. Sitting next to the man who had made my life utterly miserable for so many years, I found I couldn't even look at him. For once, he didn't attempt to touch me. I wanted Uncle Percy to give me away, but I didn't dare suggest it. What would Mum say, and what would everyone else think? We arrived at the church exactly on time, but Brenda's father insisted on driving around the block in order for us to be fashionably late. I was worried that arriving five minutes late might make Des angry, and, on this occasion, I would have preferred to be out of fashion.

Holding onto Stepfather's arm as he walked me down the aisle, I felt as if I was in a dream. In my beautiful white lace wedding dress, I felt like a princess, but was my prince waiting for me, and was I doing the right thing? I felt as if all the fears of the past three years were stuck in my throat, making it hard for me to swallow. Then suddenly, I was standing in front of Des. and he was looking down at me with such wonder and admiration that my fears evaporated. At that moment, I felt sure that finally, everything would be just perfect.

How naïve I was. Did I really believe Des was going to change? Did I honestly think that he meant all the words he repeated so clearly after the minister? I wanted so much to believe that he did. He slipped the wedding band on my left hand and kissed me when the minister told him he could. It wasn't a passionate kiss, but then there were all those people in the church – maybe later! When we left the church, he allowed me to hold on to his arm, and I walked out into the sunshine, smiling.

Miraculously, the service went off without a hitch. Up until that time, we had never attended church, and I chose the Methodist Church simply because it was next to the bank, where I had previously worked.

It was an elegant old church, but it had no place suitable as a backdrop for the photographs, so the photographer took us to a beautiful park, where he took dozens of photographs. In each one, Des stood to attention with his hands behind his back, carefully avoiding any physical contact with his new bride. Only at the reception, when we were photographed cutting the wedding cake, could he be seen with his hand on top of mine.

Des and Doreen on their wedding day in 1960

Our two families got on well, and the only hitch occurred when we wanted a family group picture taken. Stepfather had already removed his tie and he refused to put it back on. He had been drinking steadily, so I knew not to press the issue. The only concession he made was to stand slightly sideways to try and hide the fact that he wasn't wearing a tie, which, of course, didn't work. Since he had refused to wear his dark suit to please Mum and me, I was not surprised. All through my young life, he had ruined every birthday and Christmas, so why should I expect him to change now? In a few hours, I would be out of his house for ever, but was it going to make my life any easier?

THE HONEYMOON

After the last guests had left and we had cleaned up, Des and I walked over to our house, carrying our wedding gifts. Des lay down on our new bed and fell asleep immediately, but I couldn't. The alarm was set for 2 a.m., and by three o'clock, we were in our Renault, on our way to spend a few days honeymoon at La Crete Hotel, in KwaZulu-Natal.

The first night in the hotel was not the romantic night I had dreamed about, and I suspected then that romance was not going to play a big part in our lives. Not only that, but it was marred by Des having a nightmare, and violently shaking me awake, while yelling that there was a snake under my pillow. I got a terrible fright, and he became angry and said that I had overreacted. I think he felt embarrassed and this was the only way he knew to deal with it.

We made friends with another honeymoon couple in the hotel, and the four of us had a good time together, and as we were with them most of the time, Des was on his best behavior. He was proud of his physique and loved to show it off, which made me feel uncomfortable. He and the other young man competed all the time, showing off their muscles, while standing on each other's shoulders on the beach. I was just the opposite, preferring not to be noticed, which probably had a lot to do with my stepfather's unwanted attention.

Des wasn't able to show me love and affection while we were dating, but I always assumed that things would change once we were married. It didn't, not even on our honeymoon, and slowly it dawned on me that he was never going to allow me to love him the way I wanted to, and sadly, I was not going to be loved by him in return. He hated kissing and always pursed his lips tightly, and I often found myself kissing the air. He disliked being touched and became highly irritated if I tried to hug him or stroke his face. I longed for what I perceived to be a healthy relationship, and seeing the other honeymoon couple holding hands made it even harder for me.

The four of us joined a bus tour to Oribi Gorge. The group was great fun, and we took turns taking photographs of one another. A large rock protruded out over the gorge, and Des insisted that we have our photograph taken sitting on the rock. I was terrified, but as our friends were brave enough to sit on it, I felt obliged to do the same. Because I have a fear of heights, it felt as if my stomach had already fallen over the ledge ahead of me, and I was soon to follow. And if that wasn't bad enough, Des then had us pose on a tall, narrow rock shaped like a chimney, which I found even more frightening. He thrived on danger, while what I wanted most of all was to feel safe.

Des and Doreen on their honeymoon

MARRIED LIFE

Back in Pretoria, we settled into married life. Just as my childhood had been one long, continual battle, my marriage to Des quickly became the same. Soon after our return from the honeymoon, I said something that made him angry, and I was asking his forgiveness, when he screamed at me to shut up. I tried, but I couldn't stop sobbing. Des had no tolerance for tears, and the pair of scissors that he held in his hand suddenly became a weapon, which he threw at me with such force that when it hit the wall of the living room, it left a perfect imprint of the scissors on the plastered wall. Fortunately, I was able to duck in time to avoid being injured, and we were about to wallpaper the living room. The indentation of the scissors is likely still hidden beneath the wallpaper.

Des quickly became bored with married life, and joined the Pretoria Motor Club, where he spent most evenings drinking and socializing with his friends. I discovered now that we were married; he was really a man's man. I was still working during the day, but my evenings were lonely. I begged him not to go out and drink so much, but it didn't help. He was then, and would always remain, a married bachelor.

I was twenty years old and still enjoyed going out, but that didn't happen often. I spent a lot of time sewing and making our home as comfortable as possible. I avoided going to my parents' house, but Mum usually invited us for Sunday lunch, and then I had to resume the cat and mouse game with Stepfather. Inevitably, he would be sitting on the verandah when we arrived, and if Des happened to look away, he grabbed at my breasts as I leaned over to kiss him hello. My face burned with humiliation, and the temptation to slap his face was almost impossible to resist.

Determined to make my marriage work, I bought a marriage counseling book and read it when I was alone, trying to understand why Des was so cold and aloof, and what I might do to make things better. There was a lot of practical advice in the book and one Saturday evening, I put it to what I thought would be good use. I wore a pretty dress and made Des a really special meal complete with candles and flowers. He ate, and, without a word, left for the club. I was devastated, but I wasn't ready to give up. I bathed and put on my new shorty pajamas, and waited up until midnight for him to come home. I was sitting in bed reading when he arrived. He looked at me and, with great contempt, said, "What the hell is going on with you? You look like a slut!"

I stammered that I had bought the pajamas to please him. He told me to go and put on something decent. To me, they looked perfectly decent, but Des obviously didn't agree.

We had been married for just a few months, when Des called me while he was taking a bath in the late afternoon. I went to the door of the bathroom just in time to see him slip under the water with a book in his hand. Thinking he was ill, maybe even dying, I screamed, "Dessie, Dessie," as I reached down and tried to lift him bodily out of the water.

He was a dead weight, and as much as I struggled, I couldn't lift him. After what felt like an eternity, he burst up out of the water, laughing at me. It was his idea of a joke and he had totally fooled me. For Des, it was funny, but for me, it wasn't. We obviously didn't share the same sense of humor.

Des' sense of humor mostly came to the fore when he was with other men, and this sometimes got him into trouble. One of his favorite tricks was to ask a friend if he had a clean handkerchief and, in those days, every man carried one. Once they handed over their handkerchief, Des opened it up, took the middle between his fingers, shook it to form a tail and then took out his lighter. He then proceeded to set fire to the center of the handkerchief, allowing it to burn for just a few seconds before blowing out the flames. He then brushed off the burned part and held the handkerchief in his hands, while saying some magic words.

Mesmerized, the victim watched while he held up the handkerchief, revealing a large burned hole in the middle. With a grin, he declared with mock regret, that the trick hadn't worked. Not everyone appreciated his sense of humor, and on one occasion, he came up short at a party when the owner of a handkerchief became so angry, that during the ensuing fight, he actually bit Des on the ear. We went home early that night.

Topsy came into our lives with a smile, and a body that wiggled from one end to the other. She was an adorable golden spaniel who filled the void in my life for someone to love. When she was nine months old, she somehow managed to get out of the yard, and it soon became obvious that she was pregnant. She gave birth to six cute puppies, which we kept for six weeks until they were old enough to give away.

It was soon to be my turn to have babies.

A PIGEON PAIR

South Africa became a republic on May 31st, 1961. The country also went metric and changed their currency from the English pound to the South African rand. My ties with England were dwindling, and it was a bittersweet change for me. I was beginning to feel like a South African, but I wasn't quite there yet. My separation from England, the country of my birth, had not been by choice, so my transition was slow.

We had been married just six months when Des announced that it was time for us to start a family. I was still working at the time, and wanted to wait a while longer, until our finances were in better shape. Des had sold the Renault and purchased a 1961 German Goggomobil sports car. It was his pride and joy, and he turned heads wherever we went. He was proud of it, but along with the motorbike, it was one more thing to be paid off. Ignoring my protests, Des was adamant that we should start a family in spite of the additional debts and within a month, I found myself pregnant with our first child.

I continued to work until I was five months pregnant, and I will never forget the first time I experienced our baby moving within me. I was at the office when I felt a fluttering, almost like a tiny butterfly. I was excited to share the news with the girls in the office, but when I told Des, he didn't seem to share my enthusiasm. Because my doctor had not cautioned me to keep my weight down and my mother said that I was now eating for two, I quickly put on a lot of weight. I thought that being pregnant was special, something a couple shared with joy, but because Des repeatedly told me how fat and ugly I was becoming, he turned it into something distasteful.

As my tummy increased in size, my navel protruded through my dress. Des found it quite disgusting and told me so. I first tried using tape to flatten it with minimal effect, and when it became even more prominent, I bought a pregnancy girdle. It was made of elastic with laces up each side. It hid the problem, but the discomfort of wearing it through the hottest months of the year was unbearable. Des continued to criticize the way I looked, and the more he criticized, the more I ate. I turned to food for comfort, and it showed.

Like my mother when she was pregnant with Ross, I retained water. I looked and felt miserable, and I longed for some pretty clothes. My maternity wear consisted of hand-me-downs from a friend, which were well-worn and a size too big. My feet were so swollen; the only shoes I could wear were rubber beach flip-flops, which didn't improve my appearance, or my morale.

About two weeks before the baby was due, following a disagreement, Des threatened to walk out. He packed some of his clothes into a suitcase, and I clung to him, begging him not to leave me. He pushed me flying onto the bed, where I lay sobbing. He then stormed out of the house but as he didn't take his suitcase, I knew he had only gone to the club. When he came home smelling of alcohol, I didn't find his clumsy advances appealing.

Nine months came and went, and I was still carrying our child. It was an active baby who kicked a lot. Sometimes, it pushed a tiny fist or foot under my ribs, protesting its confinement. It was amazing to feel all this activity within me, and I felt sure the baby was ready to be born.

It was a week past the baby's due date and incredibly hot, when Des announced that his family was coming to Pretoria to visit his Ouma in the retirement home. About twenty family members arrived in the middle of a heavy rainstorm. I had cleaned the house the previous day in preparation for their visit, but within a couple of minutes, the floors were covered in mud. They brought a picnic lunch with them, but with so many people, there was no way we could eat in an orderly fashion, and I watched as my neat, tidy little house was turned into complete chaos. They didn't seem to notice the mud or the food dropped on the floor.

When they left, I sat down and wept. Des was annoyed by the mess, but I got no sympathy from him, and I found myself down on my hands and knees, scrubbing and cleaning for the remainder of the afternoon and the whole of the next day. I hoped that all the exertion might at least encourage the birth of my baby, but it was in no hurry, and it stayed right where it was for yet another week. Because I was now two weeks overdue, my doctor told me to drink orange juice and castor oil and go for a bumpy car ride, which only made me sick.

The next day, I packed my suitcase and went to the maternity hospital, where I was given an induction. Nine hours later, our son Larry was born, and as I pushed myself up on my elbows and watched him being born, I was filled with both wonder and astonishment. I had felt this tiny person kicking and moving around inside me for the last four months of my pregnancy, but he only became real for me when they placed him in my arms, a perfectly formed baby boy weighing 9lbs 9ozs. When they later brought him to me in the ward, I held him up against my shoulder, and he looked around as if he could see everything. The nun hurriedly told me that I needed to support his neck, but he was so strong he hardly seemed to need it. My gentle Larry was to bring me much joy.

Ironically, Larry was born on March 6th, 1962, my stepfather's birthday. I presented him with a grandson for his birthday, when the last thing I wanted was to please him. Des told me that his middle name should be Paul, after my stepfather, and although I didn't agree, that was the way it was to be.

Des arrived at the hospital carrying an arrangement of flowers with a tiny pair of leather boxing gloves affixed to the card. In his distinctive handwriting, he wrote:

> *"Thanks for our lovely son, my sweet.*
> *I am very proud of you!*
> *All my love, Des."*

He looked at both of us adoringly, and I was sure that Larry would be the seal on our marriage, and that now, all would be well.

For Des, however, the birth of our son was simply cause for a lengthy celebration, and I am sure all his friends thought so, too. When I returned home, he continued to go to the club every evening, staying out later and later, while I was left at home with Larry.

I loved being a mother, and having had so much experience helping to raise Ross; it came naturally to me. I was completely absorbed in taking care of the baby, in addition to my other household chores. We had no washing machine, so everything had to be washed by hand in the bathtub, but I didn't mind. I was a wife and mother and felt completely fulfilled for the first time in my life.

When Larry was three months old, I told Des that I felt like going out, and asked him if we could go and see a movie. He looked at me in shocked surprise and said, "What about Larry? We can't both go out, and we are not leaving him with anyone else." I couldn't believe what I was hearing, and frustrated, I burst into tears, which prompted Des to say, "Oh, there you go again, turning on the faucet."

Looking at me with complete distain, he told me I was hysterical, and left for the club, returning home drunk in the small hours of the morning. The more I complained, the more he went to the club, and the later he came home. I learned that complaining didn't help, but keeping quiet didn't help either. In fact, nothing helped!

Thankfully, when Larry was a little older, Des took me to the drive-in theater now and again, and occasionally we went to visit friends, taking Larry in his carrycot, so that he could sleep on the friends' bed.

My parents bought Larry a high chair, which made it a lot easier to feed him at meal times, but one day, he wiggled around so much that he loosened the latches that held the top and base together. When he leaned forward, the top of the chair tipped over with him in it, and he landed on his face, biting through his lower lip with his two front baby teeth. His lip bled profusely, and Des screamed at me, blaming me for what had happened. I received quite a beating that day, and I was to learn that this was to be a regular occurrence whenever one of our children got hurt.

Des applied for a job with an American pharmaceutical company, as a medical representative. This was perfect timing as he was now to earn a good salary, and was given a company car, with all expenses paid. He loved the job, and after training at their head office in Johannesburg, he visited all the Pretoria doctors, introducing them to the company's products and giving them samples to pass on to their patients. His territory included many of the small towns around Pretoria, some being quite a distance away. This required Des to go off once a month on a week-long country trip, leaving on Monday morning and returning on Friday afternoon.

It was about this time that Des told me that we should have another baby. I protested that it was much too soon. Larry was only five months old and still a baby himself, but my protests fell on deaf ears. I fell pregnant within a month, and, once again, had to endure all the insults of my previous pregnancy.

Des gave me an allowance to run the house, and I had to budget carefully to get through the month. He opened a checking account with a new bank in South Africa and was one of Trust Bank's first clients. It wasn't a joint account, and as he alone had control of the finances, I was completely dependent on him for all my needs.

I grew up being a light sleeper, but now that I had a baby, I woke at the slightest sound. One night, when Larry was six months old, I woke up in the middle of the night. It was a blustery night, and I lay awake listening, wondering what had disturbed me. Larry was fast asleep in his baby bed in the corner of our room, and Des was snoring softly beside me.

A noise at the window caught my attention, and I saw the drapes moving. The moon and streetlights were bright enough to outline the silhouette of a man with his hand reaching in through the small top window, which we had left open for ventilation. He was in the process of opening the larger side window, which would grant him easy access to the house. I shook Des and whispered that someone was breaking in. He woke instantly, jumped out of bed, quietly opened the closet and took out his revolver. In the meantime, the silhouette vanished, leaving the drapes blowing wildly now that both windows were open. Des then crept through the living room to the dining room, searching for the intruder.

I could scarcely breathe as I got out of bed and went to stand next to Larry's baby bed. Horrified, I saw the silhouette of the man move back past the open window and around the side of the house, only to reappear at our other bedroom window. We had left it open just a crack with the fastener tightened, but as he gently wiggled it, it slowly opened wider. I was trapped! Frozen, I was unable to move, and even if it were possible, I couldn't leave my baby. At that moment, Des returned to the bedroom, realizing that the intruder was not going to enter by the dining room window. The intruder obviously wanted as many windows open as possible, to ensure a quick exit once he was inside.

With the street light shining brightly behind the man, he was in plain view, and Des shot through the window, just above his head. Then, flinging open the window, he was just in time to see the man jumping across the flower bed. He fired at the man's feet, only to see him jump the fence and disappear down the street.

The next morning, we discovered one footprint and a few drops of blood in the freshly dug earth of the flower bed. The intruder had covered a span of about nine feet, leaving behind one footprint before clearing the fence. If he wasn't an athlete before that night, it seemed that he had quickly become one. Des went to the police station to report the incident, and was told by the police that they had picked up a man with a bullet in his foot. I expected there would be a court case, but surprisingly, we never heard about the incident again. No doubt the man was just thrown in jail along with all the other people who were picked up for passbook violations that night.

This attempted break-in inspired Des to purchase a gas pistol in addition to his revolver. Guns were to become an important part of his life and would remain so, ultimately with devastating consequences.

Meanwhile, pregnant with my second baby, and with Larry in the pram, I felt that it was time to visit Des' grandmother in the Princess Christian Home. By this time, I felt confident that my Afrikaans was good enough to converse with her. It bothered me that Des had no contact with her, and I felt I should try and make things right between them.

It was a gorgeous summer's day, making the walk to the home pleasant. Larry was a bonnie little boy and well-behaved, and I was excited to show Ouma Jacobs her great-grandson. We went straight to her room but found it empty, and the resident in the next room told me that Ouma was in the communal living room.

I remembered Ouma as a large woman with a big voice, which was probably due in part to my nervousness at confronting her. At first, I couldn't find her. The living room appeared to be completely deserted, but as I was about to leave, I noticed an old lady almost hidden in a wingback chair, and I pushed Larry over to her. While gently touching her on her arm so as not to startle her, I quietly asked her in Afrikaans, "Ouma Jacobs?" She looked up at me with a puzzled look on her face and said, *"Ja, wie is jy?"* "Yes, who are you?"

I told her I was Doreen, Des' wife, and that the baby boy in the pram was Larry, her great-grandson. She gasped, and, with surprising strength, grasped my hand and said, *"En jy praat Afrikaans? Sit kind!"* "And you speak Afrikaans? Sit, child!"

Ouma kept me with her for two hours and I knew that learning her language had opened a door, never to be closed again. We visited her often after that and, although Des never said so, I believe he appreciated my having made the effort. He learned from his mother that Ouma Jacobs told anyone who was willing to listen, that Des had the best wife, *and* she could speak Afrikaans. For an English girl to be able to speak her language seemed, in some small way, to help heal some of the deep wounds the concentration camp had inflicted on her, and I learned to love her dearly.

We were quite surprised when Mrs. Lovitt, who worked with my mother at Ginsberg's, asked us if we would be interested in swopping our house for half of her lot, one block away. Des and I discussed it, and with a second baby on the way, we felt that we should consider building a bigger house, so we agreed to the swop.

The lot served as collateral on a mortgage loan. We then found a builder, who told us that it would take about four months to build the house, so that if he began construction in early May, the house should be ready by the end of September. In April of 1963, I signed the agreement. Des put the house in my name to ensure that whatever businesses he might own in the future, our home would be safe should there ever be any form of bankruptcy.

Des' visits to the club continued, and I felt increasingly lonely. He treated me like a doormat, and I suppose I acted like one. Despite the circumstances, my pregnancy went well, and I loved my second baby even before it was born. Now that I knew what to expect, I could anticipate the birth of our second child, and when I felt it move for the first time, I wept, visualizing the tiny life that was soon to be a part of our family. Larry's eyes grew large when I placed his hand on my stomach, and told him that he was feeling his baby brother or sister in Mama's tummy. By the time the baby was born, he was ready to welcome the new addition to our family.

By this time, I had been in the country for almost six years, and I applied for South African citizenship. I was ready! Up until the time when I had Larry, I wasn't sure, but it was obvious now that I was never going to return to England. I was now a mother, and I knew that no matter how bad things were between us, I had to make the marriage work for the children's sake. I took my marriage vows seriously, and I loved Des in spite of the way he treated me. The tiniest things he did that were kind gave me hope, and I clung to them with fierce determination.

I received a notice to say that I was to attend the citizen induction ceremony on June 4th, 1963. That happened to be the day after my baby was due. If I didn't attend that day, I would have to wait months for another opportunity. I took a chance, and said yes, and my baby obliged. With mixed feelings of guilt at giving up my English citizenship and pride at becoming a South African, I became a citizen on the 4th and our baby daughter, Anne, was born a week later, on June 10th, 1963.

It was just fifteen months after delivering Larry, that I found myself back in the maternity hospital giving birth. Because Anne was a week overdue, I went through the same induction procedure that I had had with Larry, and she was born in the late afternoon.

Anne was born with jaundice, and since the hospital didn't have enough blood of her type, Des was sent around to various hospitals to collect blood for her transfusion. The thought of her having a blood transfusion was frightening, but the procedure went well, and she gradually turned pink. She was the smallest of my babies, weighing 8lbs 5ozs. Anne was altogether adorable, and I was delighted that she was a little girl. Des gave me another beautiful arrangement of flowers with an alabaster statuette of a lady standing on one side. The accompanying card read simply, "Love, Des."

The next day, Des left on a business trip, so although I felt well and strong after a few days, I had to stay a maximum of ten days in the hospital. On my mother's first visit, she told me that because I now had a boy and a girl, a pigeon pair, I didn't need to have any more children. I assured her that Des had told me we were going to have four children, and his decision was, of course, final.

BETRAYAL

On my mother's next visit, she said she had something to tell me. I had no idea what it could be, and I was shattered when she told me that she had been to our house to collect Des' laundry, and while washing it, she came to the conclusion that he was having an affair. After going into some detail, I was convinced that she was right. I had been trying to ignore what I had long suspected; that Des had a girlfriend. I was devastated! On one hand, I was grateful to my mother, but on the other hand, I wished she had waited a while to tell me. I was alone. My husband was away for more than a week; who knows where he was or who he was with? I had a new baby, who I was desperate to breastfeed, and now I had to contend with this.

When Des arrived to take us home, it was difficult for me to act normally. I tried my best, but I was hurting. And Des immediately sensed that something was wrong. I couldn't bring myself to confront him about his affair, so I just said I was tired and needed to rest. We picked Larry up from my mother's house and drove home. Larry was thrilled with his baby sister, and without any prompting, he immediately kissed her on the forehead. He was incredible with her, touching her gently and calling me whenever she awoke or cried. When Anne grew older, they became good friends, bringing me much pleasure. The joy and affection I received from the children became a substitute for the love that Des refused, or was unable to give me. In turn, I was able to lavish my love and affection on them.

Now that I was looking for it, I constantly found evidence of Des' affairs. I had often seen makeup and lipstick on his collar as well as on his handkerchief. It was almost as if he wanted me to see it. I was heartbroken. What I had quietly suspected for so long, was now staring me in the face. Our marriage was a mess in many ways, but faithfulness, the one thing that was good about it, was now spoiled.

The day I confronted Des with some evidence, he laughed at me and told me that I was crazy. He said that one of the women at work had a birthday, and he had kissed her and wiped the lipstick off on his handkerchief. I wanted to believe him, but how could I? I begged him to be honest with me. Des denied my allegations several times, then got mad at me and threatened to leave. After that, I continually punished myself, looking for evidence. Somehow, I couldn't stop myself. I always found it and made myself miserable in the process.

Des became like Jekyll and Hyde. He could be nice one minute and mean the next, and I never knew what to expect. One month after Anne was born, Des told me that he wanted to make a mask of my face. I was flattered and pleased to think he wanted to do that, until I learned what the procedure entailed, and I told him I couldn't do it. I had to lie perfectly still on the carpet in the living room while he molded the wet plaster of Paris over my face, then wait until it set. The thought of having my face covered for half an hour terrified me. I tended to be claustrophobic, but when Des pulled his face into his "You are just so pathetic" look, I knew I had disappointed him, so I relented, and told him to go ahead.

While Des mixed the plaster of Paris with water in a bowl, Larry stood by watching him, totally fascinated, and Des took his hand and stuck it in the mixture to make a cast of it, while waiting for my cast to dry. For a few minutes, Larry sat quietly, but then he began to wiggle, and said he wanted to go outside to play. Des smacked him and shouted at him to stand still and after a while, the form dried, and Des was able to remove the cast. Hearing Larry whimpering, while I was unable to see or move only added to my stress.

I endured mixed feelings that day. Des left two tiny holes for my nose, so that I could breathe, but I have always had a tendency to breathe through my mouth when lying down, so I had to constantly fight the desire to scream. Ironically, I couldn't have screamed even if I had wanted to. I couldn't see anything, and the black was blacker than anything I had ever experienced, and I wanted it off. I raised my right hand in an effort to plead with Des, but it didn't help. He simply ignored me. The relief I felt when he removed the plaster was indescribable. The life mask remains in my closet, a constant reminder of that frustrating day so long ago.

For the next few months, I had no time to think about anything other than feeding my family. I was either making a meal or breastfeeding Anne. In between, I had to bathe and dress the children, clean house, do the shopping, wash and iron, and smile. Des wanted to know what I did all day. I wanted to know what he did all day, and, even more importantly, what he did in the evenings. We still didn't have a telephone, so I wasn't able to call him at the club, should I need him. Maybe it was just as well, because I am sure he wasn't spending all his evenings at the club anyway. It was becoming clear to me that Des was now also a ladies' man.

Washing our clothes by hand in the bathtub was becoming increasingly difficult, especially now, with another baby, so I was grateful when Des bought a small drum-type washing machine from a friend to wash the diapers. By turning the handle, I could wash a few at a time, which helped a lot. Not long afterwards, he bought a small second-hand

Hoover washing machine. It could handle four shirts at a time, but I had to be careful not to let it run for more than five minutes, or it destroyed the clothes; it was that rambunctious. I then rinsed the clothes in the bathtub and ran them through the wringer situated on top of the washer. It took the whole morning to do the laundry, but at least I no longer had to wash by hand. Because laundry powder was expensive, for many years, I grated bars of laundry soap and dissolved it in the machine before adding the laundry. It was a time-consuming chore, but it saved us quite a bit of money.

Anne was a placid, gentle baby for the first few months; until the day when we were visiting my parents and I was changing her diaper. I was shocked when she screamed at me, and made it plain that she didn't want to be changed. She was only five months old by this time, but quite strong. I gently told her to lie still, whereupon she made her body incredibly stiff, and I couldn't get her to relax. Taking a deep breath, she held it, while rapidly becoming blue in the face. Then her eyes rolled back in her head, and she went limp. I held her in my arms and tried to calm her, to no avail.

My mother came running in to see what all the fuss was about and attempted to snatch Anne from my arms, which further frustrated me. I shook Anne gently, while calling her name, but it took a few minutes before she breathed normally and regained her natural pink complexion. This was to be the first of many such temper tantrums, although that first time, I had no idea what was happening.

Meanwhile, work on the new house progressed slowly, taking much longer than originally promised. By the end of September, it still wasn't complete and we asked Mrs. Lovitt if we could stay in our house a while longer, and she obliged us for another month. She was still living in her small house next door to where we were building, so she was well aware of the delay. September turned into October and I borrowed Mum's old singer sewing machine and busied myself making drapes for the house. I started packing well before the moving date and by the time we were supposed to move, we were ready, but the house was not. By the end of October, Mrs. Lovitt ran out of patience, and so we stored our furniture, and went to stay in a hotel until the house was finished.

Anne picked up a stomach bug while we were in the hotel. It was not as clean as our home, so I wasn't surprised. She quickly became ill, with constant diarrhea that caused her to become dehydrated and lose weight. The doctor prescribed some medicine, but she couldn't keep it down. He then put her on a drip and told Des we should feed her mashed overripe bananas for a few days. Miraculously, they worked, and the diarrhea stopped.

When Des mentioned to a friend that we were living in a hotel and that Anne was ill, he asked us to look after his house for a month, while he and his family were away on holiday. Our house still wasn't finished, so Des accepted his kind offer. Looking after their house and dog was helpful for them, but even more so for us.

OUR NEW HOME

We finally moved into our new home in January of 1964. A modest three-bedroomed house with two bathrooms, a study and laundry, it met all our needs, and I was hopeful that Des would spend more time at home, and for a while he did. On Saturdays and Sundays, he worked in the yard. I employed a young woman who came once a week to help me with the floors. At first, I was uncomfortable having a servant, but gradually, I learned to accept this as a natural part of life in South Africa.

A couple of months after we moved in the house, Des met an American heavyweight boxer, by the name of Buddy Turman. He was a big, well-built man with a heavy Texas drawl. Des was impressed with Buddy, who had fought against many top boxers, including Archie Moore. He was also friends with some of the other boxing greats, such as Jack Dempsey, Joe Louis, and Rocky Marciano. Buddy was in South Africa for a fight against a South African, by the name of Billy Lotter.

Des was a big boxing fan, and he invited Buddy to visit our home several times to share a meal. Buddy was always polite and well-mannered, and I enjoyed his visits. He and Des went out a few times together before Buddy insisted on taking both of us to a smart restaurant in town, to show his appreciation for our hospitality. The evening was pleasant enough, until I noticed that Des was drinking heavily, and his mood was rapidly changing to one of barely concealed anger.

After we dropped Buddy off at his hotel, Des wound himself up into a terrible rage. I had no idea what I had done until he suddenly pulled into a side street and screamed at me, "You cheap little bitch. I saw how you were flirting with Buddy. You like him, don't you? What do you take me for, a fool? What is going on behind my back? Have you been seeing him?"

I pleaded with Des to be reasonable. I said, "Don't be ridiculous, Dessie. I didn't flirt with him. Nothing is going on, I promise. I love you. Why would I flirt with another man?"

I didn't find Buddy attractive, and besides, I was a married woman. I had no desire to flirt with other men. In fact, I wouldn't dare flirt with any man. I was afraid of Des, and he had been sitting right there beside me. Being friendly to our guest; was that flirting? I didn't know what to say to convince Des that he was mistaken. I knew that nothing I said would help while he was so drunk. Nothing did, and I felt a stinging blow across the side of my face. I covered my face with my hands to protect it as his fists pounded me. He eventually calmed down, but the drive home was a nightmare. The car veered all over the road. There were no safety belts in those days, so I was flung from side to side as I clung to the window handle. It was a miracle that we arrived home safely, but then Des continued with his verbal attack until the small hours of the morning. I was grateful that the children were spending the night with my parents.

Buddy wasn't invited to our house again, but Des went away with him for a few days. I only learned about it later, when Des showed me some photographs. Buddy was friends with the movie star, Cornel Wilde, who was in Zimbabwe to make a movie called *The Naked Prey*. The last part of the movie was filmed in Northern Gauteng in South Africa, so Des and Buddy drove up with the movie crew, staying with them at a safari bush camp. Des was to play a soldier at the fort in a scene at the end of the movie. He craved attention, and although it wasn't a speaking part, he was elated at being in the movie. He proudly showed me a photograph of himself taken with Cornel Wilde, his wife, and Buddy.

We went to see the movie when it arrived in South Africa in 1966, and I waited in great anticipation until the last scene, when I had to look quickly to catch a glimpse of Des. It was a tiny part, but no matter; he was a movie star in a Hollywood movie released by Paramount Pictures! Before returning to Texas, Buddy gave Des a photograph signed, "Keep in touch, Buddy," and he and Des corresponded for a few years. After that, we lost touch with him, and it was the end of Des' movie career.

Following the month's stay in the hotel, Anne was more than a year old when she cut her first tooth, and became sick with tonsillitis. When we took her to the doctor, I also asked his advice about the tantrums. He suggested that we splash cold water on her face. That helped for a few weeks, but then the tantrums became even worse. This time, the doctor told me to either put her in a bath of cold water or give her a spanking. The bath sounded preferable, and it worked for a while, until the day she clashed with her father.

Anne was holding Des' comb, and when he asked her to give it to him, she refused. He was kind and gentle with our children until they developed a will of their own, then, things changed rapidly. Des again asked Anne to give him the comb, and Anne said, "uh, uh," which was her version of, "No!" Des then ordered her to give him the comb, and she promptly threw it down on the carpet. He gave her a smack, and the inevitable happened. Her eyes got big, and she promptly threw a tantrum and held her breath. She then passed out on the floor, and Des smacked her again and yelled at her to stop it. Shocked, she obeyed him immediately, and I hoped that the problem was solved.

This latest episode convinced Des that it was time for the children to be taught the meaning of discipline. He disappeared into the carport, where he had a workbench. He was there for quite some time before reappearing with *seelkunde*, which, translated, means "psychology." He took the handle of an old broken hammer to which he attached a thick strip of leather, about a foot long and two inches wide. On the back of it, he wrote in large letters, the word SEELKUNDE. He told our two children, aged almost three and eighteen months, that if they were naughty and didn't do exactly what Daddy told them, sielkunde would teach them how to be good.

I cringed, and that evening, after the children were in bed, I tried to have a talk with Des about it. I say tried to, because I wasn't allowed to say much before he exploded. The children's discipline was his department, and I was to raise them exactly as he ordered. Knowing it was no use protesting, I remained silent. My heart was heavy, and I determined to discipline our children as much as possible myself to avoid their having to face Des' wrath and the pain of seelkunde. This decision forced me to be far stricter than I wanted to be, but at least it saved them from a more severe punishment from their father.

A couple of weeks later, when Anne didn't get her way, she lost her temper again. This time, I resolved to end her tantrums once and for all. I spoke sternly to Anne, telling her to stop it. She screamed at the top of her voice and went red in the face. The red quickly turned to blue, her eyes rolled back, and she passed out on the floor. I knew it was now or never. I turned her on her side and spanked her bottom, and continued to do so until she finally caught her breath, and regained consciousness. She started crying normally, and I cried with her. While holding her in my arms, I told her that I loved her and she must stop doing this, because it was hurting both of us. Thankfully, Anne never held her breath again.

When not riding their plastic motorbikes around the house on the paving, the two children played in their sandpit. They never tired of playing together. Des made Larry responsible for Anne at a young age, promising him a good hiding if anything should happen to his sister. A gentle child, Larry took the threat seriously, and became overly protective of her. Anne adored him and copied everything he did. Because of this, she even toilet trained herself. When he sat on his potty, she sat on one too, pulling faces along with him, until one day, I discovered that she was actually doing something, and not just mimicking him. I was delighted.

Our house was just a block from the Austin Roberts Bird Sanctuary. Overlooking a small lake was a blind, where we could watch the wonderful variety of birds without disturbing them. We often walked to the sanctuary on Sunday afternoons to feed the ducks and watch the birds. From our house, we could hear the echoing sound of the peacock's call in the evenings. Des occasionally found small tortoises and chameleons on the road while traveling in Northern Gauteng, and he brought them home for the children to play with. After a few days, we put them under the fence of the bird sanctuary, and years later, we had the satisfaction of seeing the tortoises fully grown, while living safe and free. Later on, the city added small antelope and rabbits to the sanctuary, and it became a popular local attraction.

Des often brought home tiny bars of chocolate for the children. They always ran out, eager to greet him, hopeful for a treat. Small things like that meant a lot to the children and to me.

When Mr. Ginsberg asked me to help out at the cash registers in the supermarket on Saturday mornings, I asked Des if he would mind the children, and since he was usually at home during the day on Saturdays, he reluctantly agreed. I only worked for four hours, so I was always home by lunchtime. I found working with people satisfying, and it was good to have some money of my own. Mr. Ginsberg was kind enough to give me the staff discount, so I was able to buy a few luxuries for the house and clothes for the children, but sadly, it didn't last long. Des hated being tied down, so after just a few months, I wasn't surprised when he told me to give in my notice.

Around this time, Des' cousin and his wife invited us to go to see a movie with them. Des suggested that we leave the children with my parents, so we dropped them off, and the four of us went to a movie theater in downtown Pretoria.

Des had given me a topaz dress ring for my birthday, and I was anxious to wear it, but because it only fit the ring finger of my left hand, I wore it instead of my engagement ring, which I placed in my evening bag for safekeeping. The movie was a sad one, and I took out a tissue to wipe my eyes. On returning home, I went to replace the dress ring with my engagement ring, and it was gone. Panicking, I emptied the contents of my evening bag onto the bed but it simply wasn't there, and instinctively, I knew that I must have pulled it out of my purse when I took out the tissue. I felt all the blood drain from my face. For a second time, I had lost my engagement ring.

Telling Des was not something I wanted to do, but I had no choice because I had to ask him to take me to the cinema the next morning to search for the ring. He lost his temper, and I had to wear a long-sleeved blouse to hide my bruises. At the cinema, we searched under the seats where we had been sitting, but it was nowhere to be found. The cinema had already been cleaned, and the cleaners swore they had not seen a ring. Always careful when it came to looking after my possessions; I was devastated that this could have happened a second time.

I longed for greater independence and believed that if I learned to drive, it would be a big help. Des was my instructor for a short while, but because he had no patience, I had to find someone else, and I chose the wife of one of his friends. She was kind and patient, and with her help, I quickly gained confidence and felt enormous pride as I realized, for the second time in my life, the independence to be gained from mobility. Des' cousin taught me to reverse park in one afternoon, and the next day, I passed my driver's test on my first attempt. I didn't have my own car, so I wasn't completely independent, but I was well on my way.

EMERGENCY

A young couple bought the house next door where Mrs. Lovitt had once lived. They added a front porch and made the yard pretty with flower beds and a lawn. The wife was particularly kind to me after Des and I had one of our disagreements. No matter how much I begged Des to keep his voice down, it never helped. He simply didn't care who heard. She never questioned me, and I never told her how bad things were. I was too ashamed.

One evening, while we were having dinner, the telephone rang, and Des went to answer it. At the same moment I saw my neighbor waving me over to the fence dividing our two properties, so I ran outside to see what she wanted. Five minutes must have passed while we spoke, but I wasn't concerned, since I knew Larry and Anne were safe. Larry was three, and Anne, who was almost two, was strapped safely in her high chair. Tragically, what I didn't know, was that Larry was convinced that Des was eating M&Ms with his meal. The tiny bottle on the table next to the salt and pepper contained Valium, which Des was taking for anxiety. He took his job seriously and was always concerned about making his sales quota. He and the other medical reps frequently exchanged some of the free samples they were supposed to give to the doctors, and Des kept a good supply of Valium at the house.

In those five minutes, Larry generously shared the 'M&Ms' with his sister and when Des and I arrived back at the table at the same moment, we found Larry holding the empty bottle. He looked up at us, and seeing Des' expression, he shrank to half his size. Des screamed at Larry, "What have you done?" He then turned his fury on me. "You stupid useless bitch! Why did you leave the children alone? If they die, it will be all your fault."

No words could ever describe my feelings at that moment. Fear, guilt, and helplessness enveloped my entire mind and body. Des grabbed Larry and told me to take Anne to the car. Hardly able to breathe, I automatically obeyed. Driving at high speed to the hospital, Des ignored red lights and stop signs as cars swerved around us, almost colliding with us on several occasions. On our arrival, we rushed in through the emergency doors. Things moved quickly and just moments later, Larry and Anne were having their stomachs pumped. Sitting in the hall, I could hear the awful sounds filtering through the door. The choking, screaming and vomiting. It was dreadful!

Dr. Davie, the doctor on duty, was marvelous, and as a result of that hospital visit, he became our general practitioner and remained our family physician from then on. He was almost finished with his internship, so we became some of the first patients in his private practice.

We had to stay at the hospital for several hours before we were allowed to take the children home. The staff had to make sure they were going to be okay. Dr. Davie told us that we should wake them every hour through the night to make sure they didn't go into a coma. He was exceptionally knowledgeable, and he explained the implications of what had happened and what to expect in great detail. Des was very impressed.

We drove home in silence, and I feared what Des might do to me on our return. Surprisingly, he simply told me to go to bed and sleep. He said he would take the first shift and would wake me in a couple of hours. I was still in a state of shock, and it took me a good while before I was able to fall asleep, only to wake up to find it was daybreak and yet Des had not called me. I ran into Anne's room and found Des sitting at her bedside, wide awake. He had stayed awake all night. He looked exhausted, and in spite of his refusal to speak to me, I felt a great love and respect for him at that moment.

I was to be reminded of this terrible event often in the future, because, of course, it was all my fault.

PAPPIE

One Saturday, there was a knock on the door, and there stood Des' parents, along with a great many of his relatives. We learned that Des' maternal grandmother, who was known as *Moeder* (Mother) by the family, was in the general hospital in Pretoria, having suffered a massive stroke. The family had brought her from their farm, and after her condition was stabilized, they came to visit us.

Pappie, Des' grandfather, was a kindly old gentleman with only one leg, having lost the other in an accident. He always spoke to me in Afrikaans, until the day I was able to reply in Afrikaans. After that, he only spoke to me in English. It was as if he was rewarding me for learning his language, calling me an *Engels Boer*, (English Afrikaner), which was meant, and taken as a great compliment.

Later in the day, he took me aside and asked me if he could stay with us while Moeder was in the hospital. He adored her, and didn't want to be far from her side. I told him that he was more than welcome, and so Pappie came to stay with us for the next four months, and I grew to love him dearly. He had driven to Pretoria in his car, which he drove with the aid of hand controls.

After the family left, Pappie moved into Larry's bedroom, and we put Larry in with Anne. With Pappie in the house, Des was on his best behavior most of the time, which brought temporary peace to our war-torn home.

Pappie taught me what it means to have courage and endurance. Because he was nervous about driving in Pretoria, I became his chauffeur. I drove him to the hospital every day, which was good practice for me, and my driving skills improved rapidly. Pappie walked with crutches, always in obvious pain and discomfort, and my heart ached for him.

Moeder's stroke was severe, and she was confined to bed for quite some time, before being allowed to sit in a wheelchair. With her eyes open wide, unable to speak with her mouth drooping on one side, she stared beseechingly at Pappie. He held her hand, looking at her lovingly, willing her to come back to the life they had known. They were truly one flesh, and I envied them for their closeness and the love that was so obviously theirs. It was what I longed for more than anything.

During those four months, the family drove up from Witbank and Nelspruit and spent every weekend with us. We borrowed mattresses from friends and neighbors for the grownups and sleeping bags for the children. There were usually about forty relatives altogether, and I quickly learned what it meant to be a part of a large family. They usually brought food for a picnic, and between hospital visits, we spent the time at the Fountains Valley Park. The Jacobs family was close-knit and Moeder was much beloved by us all.

Pappie was a dear old man, and we spent many enjoyable hours together. We didn't talk a lot, but we developed a special bond. He was grateful to be in our home, close to Moeder, and he appreciated my being able to drive him to and from the hospital. I felt relaxed in his quiet presence. Sitting on his chair, smoking his pipe, I sometimes noticed the stump of the leg that he had lost, lift slightly. He winced, and I knew he was in pain. Occasionally, he looked irritated, and I learned that the missing leg itched, and he was unable to scratch it. In spite of his frustration, which was great, he never complained.

When Moeder was discharged from the hospital, Pappie's eyes sparkled. He wanted to be at home with his beloved wife, but I knew that I was going to miss him dreadfully.

Once they left, Des' affairs were uppermost in my mind again and seeing the evidence made me feel sick. As a result, I became sullen and irritable, which only added to the tension. I couldn't understand why Des felt the need to spend time with other women, when he didn't even want to spend time with his own wife and children. He hated being touched and kissed and yet the lipstick and perfume on his clothes proved just the opposite. It simply didn't make any sense.

A CLOSE CALL

One Saturday afternoon, Des went outside to trim the hedge between our yard and the neighbor's. He was about half way through, when he accidently disturbed a wasp nest and angered, they attacked him. Because he liked to get a tan while working in the yard, he only wore a pair of shorts so he had little protection and was stung several times. He came into the house in a foul mood, and I could do nothing right.

The children were visiting their grandparents, so we were alone. Des was in pain, angry and humiliated, and I said how sorry I was, which turned out to be a recipe for disaster. Des started screaming at me but, as usual, I had no idea what I had done wrong, and I kept saying that I was sorry. Sorry for his pain, sorry for the wasp stings, sorry for whatever I had done wrong. Saying sorry was a habit that I had picked up from my mother, and sometimes I didn't even realize that I was saying it. It turned out that it was one of the things that irritated Des most about me.

I was putting some of Larry's clothes away in his room, and the next thing I knew, Des was hitting and punching me. I cried out to him, "Please, Dessie, stop, I'm sorry. Please, Dessie, don't hit me." But he was completely out of control and didn't appear to hear me. He then grabbed me by my arms and started shaking me until I felt as if my head would fall off.

His grip on my arms slipped for a brief moment, and seizing the opportunity, I ran into the children's bathroom and locked the door. I was safe! Panting for breath, I realized that while I was safe, I was also trapped, because there were burglar bars on the window. No matter, I would just wait until Des calmed down.

But he didn't calm down, and he proceeded to kick the door down. After two kicks, the key fell to the floor, and I knelt down to retrieve it. At that moment, Des kicked the door again, and it split apart, flying open over my right hand, bursting all the cuticles of my nails open with the force. Blood spurted in all directions. He stood there looking down at me, and then realizing I was hurt, he took my hand in his and said he was sorry. I pushed him away and told him to leave me alone. That made him even more furious. Des could dish out rejection, but he couldn't handle it himself.

He dragged me back into Larry's room and threw me on the bed. His hands were around my throat, and I couldn't breathe. I gasped, and then I couldn't even gasp. Everything went gray, then became darker and darker. I knew I was dying from lack of oxygen, and for the second time in my life, I gave up the fight to live. I lost consciousness and woke to find Des shaking me again, yelling at me to wake up. Seeing me slipping away must have brought him to his senses.

It took me a while to recover, with Des whispering over and over again how sorry he was. He promised never to hurt me again, but because I had heard it all so many times before, I couldn't believe him. He bandaged my bleeding fingers, then told me to rest on Larry's bed until I felt better.

When I was sure that he had gone back outside, I slipped out of the house. I reached the other side of the road, and found a neighbor standing at her gate. She stopped me and asked what was going on, and what were those terrible marks on my neck? I burst into tears and begged her not to say anything to anyone. Even though I told her nothing, the way she looked at me and shook her head, I knew she guessed. I went to my parents' house and my mother looked at me and also shook her head. Stepfather just looked at me and didn't say a word. I hugged my children, and a few minutes later, Des came to take us home. He was smiling as if nothing had happened.

I couldn't discuss my problems with my parents, and since there was no one else I could trust, I kept them to myself. As a result, I became a bit stronger each day, and sadly, a little harder. I became a walking contradiction; on the one hand, sometimes feeling that I could handle anything and always living in the hope that things would get better, and on the other, feeling hopeless and ready to burst into tears. The two sides of me were in constant conflict, and I found the tension exhausting.

A MAJOR DECISION

When Moeder got sick again, she returned to the hospital, and Pappie stayed with us for another three months. We fell back into the old routine with many of the family members camping in our house. As before, we all met for a picnic lunch at the park on Sundays.

With Pappie in the house, a truce was declared once again. Pappie and I became even closer and remained so until his death a couple of years later. Moeder never fully recovered from the stroke, so unable to return to their farm, they lived with Des' parents until she died. Not surprisingly, six weeks later, Pappie died of a broken heart.

Uncle Percy also died about this time, and I knew I was going to miss him. He had come to mean a lot to me as a father figure, someone I could both love and respect. Aunt Joey was left alone, and I felt sorry for her. Never having had children, Uncle Percy was her whole world. The reception following the funeral was a gracious affair, held in Aunt Joey's house. Colorful dahlias from her yard, tastefully arranged by Aunt Joey herself, adorned the living room and verandah, where the guests gathered to partake of food prepared and served by Laxton.

Following Uncle Percy's death, Aunt Joey continued to live in the house and I visited her often with the children. Knowing that she had wanted to adopt me as a young girl, I always felt a special affection for her.

We had been in our house for just over two years, when I said or did something that annoyed Des, and he lost his temper, but that day was different. In his attack, he blamed me for his inability to become a doctor. He told me that he was highly intelligent and would have made a fantastic doctor had he not met me. I protested that he didn't have to marry me, and that I had never encouraged him to give up his part-time studies, but that only made him angrier. He went on about how he worked like a slave to provide for us and had sacrificed so much on our behalf, and I ended up feeling dreadful.

Then I had, what I thought, was a brilliant idea, and I put it to Des.

I said, "Dessie, what if we sell the house and put the money in the bank for emergencies. You could resume your medical studies, and I could get a job and put the children in nursery school. We could rent an apartment and because I know how to live frugally, I am sure we could manage."

He looked surprised; then, a hopeful expression came over his face. "Yes, Jakes, maybe you're right. I could get a part-time job, and we might just be able to make it." Des only ever called me Jakes when he was being particularly nice, so I felt encouraged.

Perhaps we were both being naïve, but he wanted the chance to study, and I wanted him to be happy, so the next day, we put the house on the market. The house looked nice, and by this time, the yard was well established, so it sold immediately and the people who bought it were extremely anxious to move in. They had only one week to move out of the house they were renting, and they said they were prepared to accept our price on condition that we would be out by the end of the month. This meant that we also had only one week to pack and find somewhere else to live.

I went to Ginsberg's looking for cardboard boxes, and started packing furiously. With seven days to pack and nowhere to go, I was feeling slightly frantic. Des went hunting for an apartment while I packed. By Saturday, Des had still not found an apartment that allowed pets, and I was not prepared to give Topsy, our spaniel away. She was a part of the family, and the children adored her. We had to be out of the house on the Monday. With only two days left, and still nowhere to go, Des again went off and, a few hours later, returned, announcing that he had found us a small upstairs apartment with only two bedrooms and one bathroom, but the landlord allowed pets. How we finished packing by Monday morning I will never know, but when the moving van arrived, we were ready, and the house was clean and awaiting its new owners.

MOVING AGAIN AND AGAIN

After the freedom of a house and yard, life in the small upstairs apartment was not easy. The children and Topsy had to be kept inside most of the time. At the back of the apartments was a communal yard with a large sandpit for the children. As there was no security fence around it, I had to sit and watch the children while they played. After a couple of months, I felt that I could let them play in the sandpit without me. There were plenty of other children for them to play with, and I was able to step out onto the balcony to check on them regularly while I did my housework.

I looked out a few times, waved and reassured them that Mama was close by. But the next time I checked, they were gone. I called their names – no answer. I flew down the steps two at a time and called again. Still no answer. A woman came out of her downstairs apartment and complained to me that the children had been making so much noise that they had woken her baby. She confessed that she had scolded them, but she didn't mean to chase them away. I said, "How could you? Where are they supposed to play? The sandpit is there for them to play in, and they are little children. Children make noise. Where are they now?"

I left her and raced right around the block of apartments, but they were nowhere to be seen. I then ran up the street calling their names, and far in the distance, I saw two tiny figures on the sidewalk. As I neared, I saw Larry standing still, holding Anne's hand. He looked up at me with pleading eyes. *"Jammer Mama. Jammer Mama,"* he stammered in Afrikaans. "Sorry, Mama." I held them close and cried with relief.

"Where did you think you were going?" I asked.

Larry told me that another lady had chased them away, and they were looking for a place to play. I couldn't be angry, and I didn't blame them. They were reprimanded enough as it was. But from then on, their freedom was even more restricted.

Des had still done nothing about making arrangements for his studies, and it slowly dawned on me that it wasn't ever going to happen. It was Des' dream, and it had more to do with his being able to say that he was going to be a doctor, with all the prestige attached to the position, than his actually wanting to be one.

When he came home that evening, I confronted him. With a great deal of sarcasm in his voice, he said he couldn't possibly study with a wife like me, that I had tied a noose around his neck, and it was just not possible. Frustrated, I told him in that case, he had better look for a new home for us because I didn't want my children run over in the street, and I confessed what had happened that day. That was a big mistake! All three of us got a beating.

A few months later, Des reluctantly agreed that we should look for a new home. He never once invited anyone to the apartment in the six months that we had lived there. It was not very grand, and I think he was ashamed for anyone to see that he couldn't provide better for us. Our next home would have to be big and grand to make up for the apartment, and it was. We moved to a spacious house in the country next door to some friends of ours.

It was an elegant Cape Dutch style house, which had once belonged to a Major General, a South African WWII military commander. When Des heard that the house belonged to a Major General, always impressed with position and wealth, he was determined to buy it. He approached the current owner and asked him if we could rent the house for six months, with the option to purchase and as the house had been standing vacant for quite some time, the owner agreed to Des' terms.

The house was expensive and far beyond our means, but for the next six months, Des went to every bank and building society in Pretoria, attempting to obtain a loan. Because his income wasn't high enough, not one of them was willing to grant us finance. By this time, Des had changed jobs and was working for a German Pharmaceutical company, which conducted much of its business in Namibia, where a large number of the people were German immigrants. Des now traveled more and earned a better salary, but it was still not enough to pay such a high mortgage. He became frustrated and angry. He desperately wanted the house and couldn't accept that it was not to be his. By the time the six-month rental lease was up, the owner had found another buyer, and we had to move out. And so, we found ourselves without a home again, and this time with a highly disgruntled Desmond Jacobs.

Sometime during the six months that we lived in the house, Des bought a German Shepherd puppy for the children, and we named him Wolfie. He was adorable, and the children were thrilled. Wolfie grew fast, but his ears never did stand up, and Des was furious, knowing that he had been deceived. Wolfie was supposed to be a pedigreed dog, but the floppy ears made him undesirable. It didn't matter to the rest of us, but it mattered a great deal to my husband, who was only satisfied with the best of everything.

Des was now a professional businessman and studying to become a doctor was no longer mentioned, except when he was throwing it back at me, blaming me for his inability to study. As we no longer needed the money from the sale of the house to pay his university fees, Des purchased two adjoining pieces of land in the Bronberrik subdivision on the other side of the new highway that was being built between Pretoria and Johannesburg. His plan was to build two houses, one on speculation that we could sell, and the other for us to live in. The land was a good investment, but we still had nowhere to live, no money to build a house, and no time to make a plan.

Two years earlier, there had been a bombing at the Johannesburg train station. One person was killed, and the bomber, a member of the African Resistance Movement, was charged with murder, and subsequently sentenced to death. Des heard that the bomber's house in Pretoria was for rent. Under the circumstances, no one else wanted to rent it, and so it had been standing empty for a long time. I was not comfortable moving into the rambling old house, but we were desperate for a place to live, and it was affordable. The house was thick with dust and full of sand fleas and spiders. We were all badly bitten, and the poor dogs also suffered.

The swimming pool next to the house had just enough green, slimy water for frogs and mosquitos to breed, adding to our misery. The eerie atmosphere of the house made me feel uncomfortable, and I couldn't wait to move out, so I was relieved when Des found us a small rent house in Silverton, a suburb of Pretoria. After only six weeks, we were on the move again and back to living in a house that was not up to Des' high standards.

When we moved to Silverton, the fleas moved with us, and it was a good while before I managed to get the situation under control. Because the rented house was so tiny, the children had to share a bedroom since Des couldn't manage without his study.

Frances, our new neighbor, and I became close friends. We often went shopping together and drank coffee at the kitchen table in the mornings, while our children listened to their program on the radio. My

Afrikaans improved considerably since we rarely spoke English. Frances told me that many Afrikaners were shy to speak English, for fear of making mistakes, which I could understand since I had felt the same way. I realized that maybe that was why Des' friends didn't want to speak English and perhaps they hadn't intended to be rude.

Frances was quick to sense that things were not wonderful in the Jacobs household, but when she asked me about it, I made excuses for Des and pretended things were fine.

Moving to Silverton, meant that we were quite far from my parents and the stores in the city center, so Des bought me a second-hand Renault R8. I now had a car, and at last, I was fully independent. How I loved that car. I cleaned and polished it, and looked after it really well since I wanted it to last for many years. How silly of me! Des bought and sold my cars whenever he came across a bargain, never once asking me what I wanted. Like everything else in our lives, nothing was ever really mine. My car was just another investment for him to make more money.

Because I now had a car, I was able to visit my mother and the few friends I had managed to keep. Friends didn't usually last long, since Des was insanely jealous of anyone who took up my time, and he regularly managed to be rude enough to drive them away, but Frances was the exception. Des liked her husband and besides, they were our neighbors. It suited him to allow her to share a small part of my life.

Des had been navigating for a couple of the well-known rally drivers at the motor club on weekends. One day he told me that he needed to borrow my car on the following Saturday. I asked him what for, and he told me that he was going on a rally. It then dawned on me why he had been generous enough to buy me the car. It was not just transport for myself and the children; it was to be his rally car. The Renault was a fast car and ideal for rallies, so he participated in many of them until he had an accident and had to replace the front corner section. It didn't seem to bother him at all, but I was devastated when I saw my car badly smashed up.

We didn't have a fence around the entire property, but the backyard was enclosed, so it was safe for the children and dogs to play there. The only problem was that the fence was fairly low, and Wolfie quickly discovered that he could easily jump over it and tour the neighborhood. Fortunately, we lived on a quiet street far from the main road that ran through Silverton, so I wasn't too worried about him. He was faithful and always returned home at dinnertime, where his meals were supplemented with table scraps, and he enjoyed my cooking.

One Saturday afternoon, Wolfie wandered off and still hadn't returned, when there was a knock on our front door. Des went to the door and found an extremely angry German woman standing there. Before Des could say a word, she asked him accusingly, "You ave ze dog wiz ze floppy ears, ja?"

I was standing just behind my husband, and I watched as Des, rendered speechless for a moment by the woman's angry accusation, nodded his head. The woman continued, "Vell, he az mein hond gespoilt."

In her anger, she was mixing English, German and Afrikaans together. She maintained that Wolfie had ruined her dog, a pedigreed bitch of some sort. At that moment, the four-legged culprit pushed past her and ran into the house, tongue hanging out of a smiling mouth, with his tail wagging. He looked so pleased with himself that for a moment, I forgot to feel embarrassed, and nervous as I was; it was as much as I could do not to smile. "Ja, ja," yelled the woman, triumphantly pointing at Wolfie. "Zat is ze dog, zat is ze dog! He az mein hond gespoilt."

Des couldn't deny that Wolfie was indeed the culprit, and for once in his life, he had to eat humble pie and apologize to the woman, but she was not to be consoled and stormed off in a huff, leaving Des looking highly uncomfortable. Determined not to let it happen again, he drove to town and bought some wire to raise the fence higher, but Wolfie was just as determined, and still managed to get out on occasion.

Living in Silverton certainly had its problems, but something exciting happened while we were there, something that made me very happy.

Frances wrote short Afrikaans stories for a children's monthly magazine. She invented a tiny fairy who went on a different adventure each month. One morning, as I was hanging the laundry on the wash line, Frances came to the fence looking quite gloomy. As she was usually very upbeat, I asked her what was wrong, and she confessed that she couldn't think of an idea for the fairy's next adventure for the magazine. I made a suggestion and rambled on and on until she suddenly stopped me mid-sentence. "Go in the house and write." She ordered!

I looked at her and laughed, but she wasn't joking and repeated herself until she finally convinced me that I could do it, and I went into the house and wrote a story. In fact, the story practically wrote itself. When finished, I took it to a local publisher who told me it was very good, but that I should send it overseas to England as it called for large colorful illustrations. At that time, in South Africa, they could only offer me small black-and-white illustrations.

Foolishly, I put it in the draw and forgot about it.

THE PHONE CALL

After nine years, my mother, accompanied by a friend, was able to visit our family in England and Wales. How I envied her. I badly wanted to see my family again, but with two young children, it just wasn't possible. I wasn't sure it ever would be, considering Des' attitude to anything British. Strangely, he never objected to me writing to my schoolteacher, Miss Kerrisk and my school friend, June, whose letters helped to keep me connected to my British roots.

Before Mum left, she asked me to keep an eye on Stepfather and Ross, and to be sure to go and visit them. She had to be kidding! She wasn't, but then, maybe she really didn't know about all the years of humiliation and hurt he had caused me, and was still causing me. Each time he touched me, I cringed and felt a burning anger rise up within me.

I didn't want to visit him, so I didn't!

During the last week that Mum was away, the telephone rang. Des was on a business trip, and I was enjoying a few days of peace and quiet with the children. When I answered the telephone, the voice on the other end made me catch my breath. It was my stepfather calling me from his workplace. Had something happened to my mother? Why was he calling? Was it Ross? It had to be bad news! It was, but not the kind I expected. His next words made me stiffen with revulsion. "Doreen, how are you? Please, will you come over and see me this evening?"

I asked, "What for? What do you want?" My tone of voice should have warned him to be careful, but obviously, it didn't.

He continued, "You know how I feel about you, girl. I have to see you. Please come."

That day, I again experienced the depth of hatred that I had felt as a child. Repressed, it had festered and grown within me, and all the years of pent-up hatred, bitterness and resentment exploded in my reply. "I hate you! I hate you! I have always hated you! You ruined my life! I will not set foot in your house again until Mum comes back from overseas. Now, just leave me alone!"

I couldn't stop shaking as I slammed the phone down and ran to my bedroom, where I cried bitterly until I could cry no more. I longed to be able to erase the conversation from my mind, but even after all these years, I can still hear every word, and I still feel the same revulsion that I felt back then.

I hoped that at least the telephone conversation would put an end to my stepfather touching me and kissing me inappropriately, but it didn't. He was what the British call thick-skinned, and nothing I said made the slightest difference to him. However, I may have touched a nerve, because his attitude became quite hostile, and his advances towards me were vicious. I didn't bother to tell Des about the call. In fact, I didn't tell anyone. Who was there that I could tell? Since leaving their neighborhood, we didn't see nearly as much of my parents, so at least, my days were easier.

That was not the case with my nights. I had bad dreams, mostly about Des or my stepfather. Gradually, over the years, the two of them changed places in my dreams so that I was never sure which one was which. They became one big monster, hiding in my subconscious, and my inability to sleep through the night became a regular occurrence. I often woke up shaking and perspiring from a terrible nightmare after which, I tossed and turned for hours. When I eventually got back to sleep, the nightmare sometimes continued where it had left off. As a result, I was constantly sleep-deprived and extremely tired.

Mum returned from overseas, covered in psoriasis. The disease would remain with her worsening over the years, and I felt genuinely sorry for her. I bought her many different ointments and creams, but none of them worked and living under constant stress didn't help her situation.

Stepfather's drinking was by now out of control, which was partly due to Mum being away overseas, when he had nothing else to do. I often caught him downing a glass of neat brandy in the kitchen before pouring himself another glass to drink on the verandah. He grinned at me conspiratorially, while putting his finger to his lips as a warning not to tell Mum. As it was when I was a child, the brandy always made him mellow and over-friendly until provoked to anger, and then he became violent. Mum and Ross lived in constant fear, with no end in sight.

ANOTHER BABY

When Anne was two, Des said that it was time for us to have a third child, but I couldn't fall pregnant. I was simply too stressed. Stressed with Des' angry attacks. Stressed from trying to be who and what he wanted me to be. Stressed from the many moves. Stressed from having all the responsibility of the children, because Des was either on a country trip, at the club, or wherever else he went. Stressed from never having enough money to cover expenses. Stressed from being sleep-deprived. How could we bring another child into this world when ours was such a mess?

About a year and a half later, it happened anyway. I finally fell pregnant. My immediate response was one of joy, but I was more excited to tell Frances than Des. Frances was due to come over for coffee the following day, so I bought some chocolate éclairs. I bought one extra, and she asked who it was for. I announced that it was for my baby, but I was happy to share it with her. Frances helped me through my pregnancy with words of encouragement, and plans for the new arrival. As with my previous pregnancies, I ate for two, and when Des made his usual cruel comments, I just longed for it to be over.

The annual Pretoria Show was a big attraction, and one particularly hot summer day in October, Des suggested that we spend the day there. I was eight months pregnant and uncomfortable, but grateful that Des wanted to do something as a family, so I got the children ready and put on my prettiest maternity dress. Des looked me up and down with great contempt and asked, "Are you going in that thing?"

I sighed and changed into another dress. He snarled, "That's worse than the other one."

I asked him what I should wear since my other two dresses were old and only good enough to wear around the house. "What about the black and white check dress you bought?" he asked.

"But Dessie," I protested, "It's a thick winter dress, and it is already too small for me."

"Well, it's that one, or you can stay at home," he snapped.

I told him that I would rather stay at home, but when the children cried and begged me to go with them, I changed into the winter dress. At the showgrounds, I lasted about an hour, by which time I was red in the face and perspiring, and because my legs and feet were so swollen, I couldn't walk, so I sat on a bench and waited for my family while they toured the show grounds.

Larry and Anne repeatedly suffered from tonsillitis and since they were often sick, antibiotics became the order of the day. Because we lived outside the municipality's sewerage system, the rent house had a French drain and a septic tank. The drain regularly overflowed in the driveway, and this most likely contributed to the children getting sick. Repeated complaints to the owner of the house, who lived in the Cape Province, fell on deaf ears. I became fanatical about disinfecting everything but with the dogs walking through the driveway and in and out of the house, it was a losing battle.

Eventually, the landlord agreed to have the French drain opened up and enlarged. It just so happened that the crew were to arrive on the day our baby was due but I told myself that as my babies were always late, I needn't worry about that. The crew dutifully arrived early the next morning and dug open the drain. The odor was dreadful, which was bad enough, but even worse, we couldn't use the toilet or the bathtub while the drain was open, so we made use of a bucket, and I took the children next door to Frances for a bath.

The next morning, the crew was back working, when something felt strange. Having had inductions with my other two children, I was unfamiliar with the preliminary signs of impending birth, but I quickly suspected that my baby was on its way! Having no idea what to expect, I was shocked when the contractions started almost immediately. It was 7:45 in the morning, and Des was getting ready to go to work. He was also unprepared for the news and looked quite startled when I told him that the baby was coming. I needed a bath, but using ours was out of the question, so I sent Larry over to ask Frances if I could please have a quick bath in her tub. She was happy to help out, but she spent the next ten minutes standing outside the bathroom door, asking me to tell her when I felt a contraction. They kept coming fast and furious, and Frances became quite frantic. "Hurry, hurry!" she kept repeating. She didn't want the baby born in her bathtub and neither did I! It was the quickest bath I have ever had before or since.

My bag was packed, and I was in the car and on my way to the maternity hospital in record time, and within minutes of my arrival, Justine was born at 8.30 a.m. on November 10th, 1967, weighing 9lbs 5ozs. There was no time for the usual preparations, and it was all over in forty-five minutes.

Des sent me flowers. His card read:

> 'Thanks very much for our new baby daughter and sister.
> With all our love,
> Des, Larry and Anne'

At just six weeks, Justine had her first bout of tonsillitis, and her temperature rose to a dangerous level. She held her breath just like Anne used to do, and my heart sank. On the doctor's instructions, Des placed her in a bath of cold water to bring her temperature down, before giving her the prescribed medication.

Frustrated, I told Des that we needed to move because our children were constantly getting sick, even with the French drain fixed. Acknowledging that I was right, he said we weren't in a position to build a house just yet, and not knowing the status of our financial situation, I had to rely on his judgment and wait.

Larry started school in Silverton. Des said that the children should be enrolled in Afrikaans schools because, at that time, the standard of education was higher than in the English schools, where there was a shortage of teachers. Raising the children in Afrikaans schools gave me the opportunity to improve my Afrikaans, as I was then in a position to help them with their homework and learn along with them. This pleased Des, and as the children heard us speaking English to each other, we all became fully bilingual. By this time, my Afrikaans was so good that few Afrikaners suspected that I had originally come from England. I was grateful, because I wanted to be fully accepted in my adopted country.

Des adored Justine, and sadly, our other two children were older and past the cute stage. They were dismissed as all his attention was devoted to our youngest. I made her floral dresses with matching bonnets, and Des took her with him on Saturday mornings when he went to the Trust Bank. The Bank had only young women for tellers, and as a result, they had mostly male clients. It was well known around Pretoria, that Trust Bank was the place to go to if you wanted attractive female service. I knew Des was still having affairs, but I didn't know that one of his girlfriends was a teller. But merely suspecting it made me miserable every time he went to town, and I longed to be able to confide in somebody.

I still visited Aunt Joey fairly regularly, and I was sorely tempted to confide in her but hesitated to do so as she had recently remarried and Uncle Joe was always present. I liked him, but he wasn't Uncle Percy, who I felt could never be replaced. He was rather stuffy and pompous, and shortly after their marriage, when Aunt Joey misplaced her diamond rings, Uncle Joe immediately accused Laxton, their servant, of stealing them. By that time, Laxton had worked for Aunt Joey for many years, but after being accused of theft, he left immediately. He had served her faithfully, and being accused of stealing was more than he could bear.

The rings turned up not long after he left, just where Aunt Joey had put them for safekeeping. Accusing their servants was common practice in South Africa when something of value went missing, and it was often true. But this time, it wasn't, and I know Aunt Joey deeply regretted the unfortunate outcome.

LYTTELTON

The owner of our rent house wrote to us, giving us a month's notice; I groaned inwardly, knowing this meant yet another move. Des then decided that we were throwing money away paying rent and we should rather buy a house. I couldn't understand how we could afford to do that, since we had put all our savings into the two pieces of land in Bronberrik. But he insisted he was going to find a way. He did, and I was to learn the real meaning of frugality.

In January of 1969, Des found us an old house in Lyttelton, a suburb of a newly developed town near Pretoria. A dirty, three-bedroom house with one bathroom on an acre of land, it had been a rent house for many years and was in terrible shape. Des bought it cheaply, but as we had no spare cash for a deposit, we had to take out two loans: a long-term mortgage loan from the building society and a three-year bank loan for the deposit from the Trust bank. Sick with worry, I wondered how on earth we could possibly manage to pay back both loans?

We moved in, and I spent the first few weeks scrubbing and cleaning. The kitchen was so filthy that it needed scraping before scrubbing, but I threw my heart into the job of making the house livable.

It was a well-built house without any structural cracks, so it seemed that we had made a pretty good purchase.

The inside had suffered from years of abuse from the various tenants, and the plaster cracks and holes could not be covered up with a simple coat of paint. Des' brother-in-law came over from Witbank with his crew and they plastered the walls, which made it look brand new again. Living in a construction site with three children wasn't easy but we had no other choice. Once the plaster was dry, the crew painted the walls, and they looked great. The floors were thick Rhodesian Teak, and after cleaning them with paraffin, I polished them until they gleamed. When we were finished, the house was almost unrecognizable.

The yard was another story, and it took me a whole year to get it in good shape. I brought the lawn back and built a large rockery along one side of the yard with the many old, weathered rocks that were lying around the property, planting succulents between the rocks.

While working in the lower part of the yard, I was puzzled when I discovered a couple of large holes in the ground. I learned from the neighbors that they were sink holes caused by the weathering of the dolomite rock, a type of limestone, which was prevalent in the area. While we were living in the house, one of the neighbors across the street lost their driveway when it disappeared down a large sinkhole. It took three truckloads of rocks and earth to fill it, which did nothing for my sense of security, and I was glad that it was only to be a temporary home.

When we moved in, Anne was only five and a half, but we felt she was ready for school, so we enrolled her along with Larry in the local primary school. The school uniform was expensive, but the fabric was available at a local store and somehow, I found the time to make her one school dress in time for the first day of class. I now owned a second-hand sewing machine and spent most of my evenings mending and making clothes. I also bought a small single-bed knitting machine on which I made sweaters for the children. Des was out most evenings, so it was a good way to keep busy.

When Des came home late at night, he always went in to say goodnight to the children. He inevitably woke them up, while kissing them and telling them how wonderful they were. We were all wonderful when he was under the influence, unless I dared complain about his inebriated state. When I begged Des not to wake the children, he always pushed me away, insisting that they were *his* children and he would do as he damn well pleased. Larry and Anne went straight back to sleep, but Justine couldn't. Sometimes I heard her tell her father to go away; that his breath stank, which inevitably made him angry. As a result of being awakened so often, she became a very light sleeper. Often, when Des was away and she called me in the night, I stroked her hair, while singing softly to her, and after a couple of nights, she slept through. It never lasted long, though, because when Des returned, he started the cycle all over again.

One night, Des came home around five in the morning, reeking of perfume and very drunk. He tried to hold me, and I pushed him away. It was obvious that he had been with another woman, and I was not going to allow him to force himself on me. I heard him go to the bathroom and run his bath water. Because I was afraid of what he might say or do when he eventually came to bed, I couldn't get back to sleep. I lay listening for about an hour and hearing nothing, I crept to the bathroom. He lay there fast asleep, in water that was almost cold. I pulled the plug out and allowed the water to drain away. I went back to bed only to hear Des swearing, then the sound of water filling the tub again.

Des continued taking Justine to the Trust bank on Saturday mornings until one day, when they returned home, she told me about the nice auntie at the bank. That was the last time he took her with him.

Soon after that, we were invited to a party and I was excited for the chance to get out of the house. Des still didn't take me out much, and I had a pretty dress a friend had given me that I was eager to wear. At the party, they played popular records, and Des danced with me quite a few times. In a good mood, he even flirted with me, and I hoped that, for once, we would have a good time until he suddenly disappeared. He was gone for a long time, and curious, I went to look for him. I found him in the kitchen, kissing the hostess who was giving the party. He was obviously not intimidated by my appearance and merely looked at me and grinned.

I was livid and decided that two could play at that game. I went back to the living room, and when another man asked me to dance, I did. We danced one dance, then another and another, until suddenly, I felt a vicelike grip on my arm. Through clenched teeth, Des told me that we were going home. I should have felt good, but somehow, I felt awful. Playing the same game as my husband was not the answer. But then, what was?

The woman in the kitchen just happened to be Des' latest girlfriend. She didn't look like his type, but obviously, I had no idea what type of women appealed to him. Knowing that he was spending time with other women, I simply couldn't trust him. He couldn't seem to love me, but yet he could make love to other women. I felt that I was losing my identity, or maybe I had never had one.

While we lived in Lyttelton, one of Anne's teachers told me about a young woman from England who lived a few houses down the street. She suggested that we meet, so I went to her house and introduced myself. Sarah was also from England, and she and I became good friends. Patrick, her husband, was a good father and I could tell that with their two boys, they were my idea of the perfect happy family.

I so badly wanted for us to be a happy family, and I made a real effort to be extra loving to Des. That only seemed to annoy him! If I made us a candlelight dinner, he wanted to know what was going on with me, and the evening inevitably ended up a disaster, after which, he badgered me far into the night. He never knew when to stop, and reminding him that I had to get up early to get the children off to school didn't help. Digging up the past, he threw things back at me until two or three in the morning. As he usually slept until nine or ten, for him it was never a problem.

I treasured the few good times we had! One of these happened while I still had my Renault R8. Des borrowed it to take part in a mud plug, racing the car around pylons on a mud track, and he offered to take me with him. I seized the opportunity, and we drove to an open piece of land near the Kyalami Race Track. Most of the guys from the motor club and their wives were gathered there when we arrived. The mud was thick, and a water tanker stood by to ensure that it stayed that way. The timekeeper kept score to see who made it around the muddy track the fastest, and then he announced the winners. I watched excitedly as, one after the other, they sped around the track. They slid and slithered all over the place, and I held my breath as some of them almost skidded into the spectators, causing them to jump out of the way. Des did well in my Renault, and I was sure he was going to win, but one of his friends beat his time. He was disappointed, as was I.

The meeting broke up, and with just a few people left standing around, chatting, Des asked me if I would like to drive around the track, and I jumped at the chance. I had driven the Renault for a few years by that time, and I knew what it was capable of. Des had taught me how to handle a car when it went into a skid, so I was able to control it well, even though, by this time, the mud was really sloppy. I felt like a real pro, and I was overjoyed when I discovered that Des had timed me with the stopwatch. He announced that I had beaten the winner's time. The look on Des' face was worth everything to me. He was proud of me, and it showed. Des bragged to his friends that I had beaten them all. They were duly impressed, and although I found it difficult to believe, I was ecstatic.

Shortly afterwards, to my dismay, Des sold my beloved Renault and bought me a Fiat, then he sold my Fiat and bought me another Renault, this time an R16 which was slightly bigger. Each time I got fond of a car, he sold it, and this he did with regularity throughout our marriage.

One afternoon Des called me from the motor club and told me to dress up and fix my hair. He was coming to pick me up and take me to model for Motor Magazine. I was flabbergasted. He could never give me a compliment and after telling me I never looked decent and didn't know how to walk properly, he was now telling me that I was to be a model. I asked him why he wanted me to do such a thing, and he explained that the magazine photographer was at the club complaining that his two models had been double booked, so they couldn't attend the photo shoot. The deadline had to be met, and the photographs needed to be submitted along with the article. The photographer asked the various members of the club if they knew anyone who might be able to substitute and Des volunteered me, his wife. I had never modelled in my life, but I knew better than to refuse.

Des seemed to be proud that I was featured in Motor Magazine, but I had the feeling that he just wanted to show me off to his friends, and not because he thought I did a good job as a model.

I was surprised when I discovered I was pregnant again. During the two years since Justine was born, I had been unable to fall pregnant, which was probably a good thing, considering our poor financial situation and many moves. Feeding Des, myself, three children and two dogs was a challenge on the small allowance I received. We were living on the staple South African corn meal porridge called pap, farmer's sausage, ground meat, fruit and vegetables. Fresh milk was unaffordable, so I bought 25lb bags of powdered milk. The children complained, but having no choice, they got used to it. However, they all threatened to throw up when presented with a soy meat substitute. It was nutritious and cheap, but I had to admit they were probably right when they said it tasted like dog food. Needless to say, the dogs enjoyed it!

Their school sandwiches also became a cause for complaint. All I could afford to put on their bread was fish paste, cheese and jam, or Marmite, a yeast extract spread with a beefy taste. I ate the same thing at home, so I could sympathize. Des conveniently ate at a restaurant in town, since he said that he didn't have time to come home for lunch and he didn't care for sandwiches.

One of Des' friends opened a butcher shop, and now and again, we were able to buy some meat at a reasonable price. Once, for a rare treat, we bought a leg of lamb, and after roasting it in the oven, I put it on top of the stove, while I carried the vegetables into the dining room for our Sunday lunch. I guess the wonderful aroma must have wafted out of the kitchen door because when I went back to the kitchen to fetch the roast, it was gone. The platter was still there, balanced precariously on the edge of the stovetop, looking horribly empty. Stunned, I called Des, and he came to the kitchen, followed by our three hungry children.

Des ran outside just in time to see the neighbor's dog pushing his way through a hole in the fence with our leg of lamb in his mouth. He was furious! Furious with me, of course, for allowing it to happen. Furious with our two dogs for sleeping through the intrusion, and furious with the neighbor for allowing his dog to steal our precious roast. He stormed next door, and a terrible argument ensued, which I am sure the whole neighborhood could hear. Des had met his match, and he discovered that the neighbor was just like him, not prepared to back down or apologize. Des came home and gave me the piece of his mind he was reluctant to give to our neighbor. With no roast, I had no option but to open a can of corned beef, and we ate our less-than-wonderful Sunday lunch in stony silence.

Des needed to make some extra money, so he and three of his friends went into a real estate speculation. Des arranged a bank loan at an exorbitant interest rate to buy another house a few blocks from ours that was going 'dirt cheap,' as he described it. I ventured to say that we couldn't afford to take chances while we were in such a poor financial situation. Des told me that I was too stupid to understand what he was doing, and since he was the provider, I should keep my nose out of his business.

Shortly after the papers were signed, a neighbor told us that the previous owners of the house they had purchased had almost fallen into a massive sink hole, which suddenly appeared in the center of their living room floor. Not being interested in turning it into an indoor swimming pool, they had it filled in, and then they sold the house to my husband and his friends for a bargain! Another sinkhole in the back yard had swallowed up their chicken coop, complete with a dozen chickens, and a few fresh eggs, no doubt. Needless to say, it took a good while for Des and his friends to sell the house to some other unsuspecting buyers, but sell it they did, and they made a profit!

Undaunted by the difficulties surrounding the real estate speculation, Des then went into business with a friend from the motor club, making sets of yard furniture, although I am not sure what part Des played, apart from ordering the steel and selling the sets. After a while, because Des was not forthcoming with information regarding the orders, the partner, who was providing all the manual labor, became frustrated, and the partnership broke up.

Determined to show everyone that he was a successful business man, Des then decided to go into the paint business. He bought a franchise and rented a small store near the train station in Pretoria, but that also didn't last long. Where he got the money to invest in the various businesses was beyond me. Whenever I asked him for extra housekeeping money, he always maintained that we were broke.

Des' arrogance made people angry, and sometimes his temper got him into trouble. One night, he went off to the club and after putting the children to bed, I settled down to my sewing. About an hour later, Des came home, almost unrecognizable. His face was covered in blood, and was beaten to a pulp. I helped him to the bathroom and he undressed. His body, which he was so proud of, was covered with cuts and bruises. He said he had driven up our street, where he came across a car parked on the rise. He stopped and told the four young men in the car that they couldn't park there as it was a blind rise and dangerous. They obviously didn't like being told what to do, and they made their feelings known by attacking Des and leaving him lying unconscious by the side of the road. It took him a good while to recover enough to drive home. Des didn't learn a lesson from the experience. If anything, he became even more arrogant.

It was about this time that Sheila and Dennis moved to South Africa from Zambia and Dennis got a job with the post office as a telephone technician. They borrowed a travel trailer from one of Des' friends, and parked it on our vacant piece of land in Bronberrik, where they camped for several months along with their two dogs, a few chickens and two geese.

One evening, Sheila and Dennis came for dinner at our house, and because their dogs didn't get along with ours, they left them locked up in the travel trailer. Obviously bored, their dogs chewed up a plastic bottle of dishwashing liquid as well as a sheepskin duster. The resulting mess was pretty awful, and it took Sheila a whole day to clean it up. The more she wiped, the more suds materialized, but she told me that the trailer was much cleaner when they eventually returned it to the owners. They then moved around the corner into a rent house for about a year, and because Dennis was not keen on mowing the lawn, a sheep was added to their collection of animals.

Dennis was not a patient man and he didn't get along with the black staff, and after losing his temper a few times, he was asked to leave the post office. He then applied for a job as a technician with the Post Office in Zimbabwe, and they moved there at the end of 1969.

Before they left, we offered to take George and Charlie, their two geese, so Dennis came over, and with the encouragement of many cups of tea, he built a wire mesh pen for them in our back yard. They were even better than watchdogs, screeching a warning whenever someone came on the property. With all the break-ins in South Africa, having two dogs and two geese, made me feel a lot safer when Des was away on a business trip.

Sadly, the dog next door decided that, as another roast was not forthcoming, the geese would make a good substitute for his dinner. He broke through the fence again and killed both geese. The trail of feathers led Des to the culprit, and another heated argument with the neighbor.

In December, we drove down to Nature's Valley, a small resort at the mouth of the Great River on the southernmost coast of South Africa. Aunt Joey's brother Ross and his wife, Stella, had a charming holiday cottage close to the lagoon, and they invited us to make use of it for our much-needed vacation. We drove down in my Austin, Des' latest bargain. It proved to be less of a bargain when, not far from our destination, the engine began overheating. The next day, Des drove the car to the nearest town, where he learned that the engine needed to be replaced. Since December in South Africa is when everyone goes on holiday for a month, they were not sure when they could expect the new engine to arrive. We had planned on a three-week vacation, but ended up staying for five, while waiting for the car to be repaired.

This meant that Des would be a week late in getting back to work and Uncle Ross and Aunt Stella were due to arrive the day we were supposed to leave. They were gracious and told us we were welcome to stay on, so we moved out of their bedroom and into a room in the large upstairs loft, where the children were sleeping. I was embarrassed about intruding on their holiday, but they were kindness itself, and made me feel at ease.

The children loved Nature's Valley. The lagoon water was shallow enough for them to paddle and play safely. Des was relaxed, and everything went well until the day Justine went missing. She was just two years old at the time. Des said he was going for a walk down to the sea with the children and I assumed he meant all three. I was sweeping the sand out of the cottage, when, about an hour later, Des came back with Larry and Anne. Looking around, he asked me where Justine was, and I replied, "But she went with you."

With his face distorted with rage, he gripped my shoulders and, shaking me violently, screamed at me. Where is she? If anything has happened to her, I'll kill you!"

At that moment, Uncle Ross and Aunt Stella returned from a drive, and Uncle Ross took charge of the situation. He told Des to check the street that ran alongside the lagoon. I should go down to the lagoon where the children always played, while he searched the forest behind the cottage. At the time, I couldn't decide which was worse: the thought of Justine being lost in the forest full of baboons and other wild life or being lost near the lagoon or the sea.

We went our separate ways and spent about an hour searching for her. Then I heard Des' loud whistle. He had found her! Justine discovered that Des and the children had gone off without her, and so she wandered up the street to the café where someone bought her an ice cream cone. Dressed in her pink polka dot bikini and matching hat, she was a picture of innocence, completely unaware that she was the cause of such panic. I will never forget seeing Des collapse on the grass. His face was white, and it was obvious he was completely distraught, and I tremble to think what might have happened had he not found her safe.

A DEATH AND A BIRTH

Des' company sent him on a three-week business trip to Namibia, where he was to visit the doctors in many of the smaller country towns. We arranged for him to send me a telegram when he arrived, and I was to write to him care of the post office in the various towns where he stayed.

Just before Des left, Stepfather became ill, and his condition rapidly deteriorated while Des was away. Mum had a problem with a small tumor in her throat that had to be removed. At the same time, Dennis' mother was dying, and Sheila flew to England to be with her and sort out her will and personal affairs. When Dennis heard that Stepfather was dying, he flew down from Zimbabwe to be with Mum. It was a challenging time for all of us, and I wrote to Des and told him what was happening. He wrote back, addressing his letter to 'My sweet,' and ended it, 'all my love.' Once again, he was able to write the words I wanted to hear, but was unable to say them.

I was pregnant with our fourth child, when my stepfather died in June of 1970. His death marked the end of his domineering influence on my life. He was sick for just six weeks, but they were six weeks of agony, and in spite of the years of abuse and molestation, I could not help but feel desperately sorry for him. I went with Mum to visit him almost every day, and watched him slowly swell out of proportion as his bodily functions began to break down. He had no relief, and he begged Mum and me to help ease his discomfort. It was winter in Pretoria, and poor circulation caused him to suffer bitterly from the cold. I cut a woolen scarf in half and made bed socks for his horribly swollen feet. Gradually, one by one, his organs succumbed to the years of abuse. Alcohol, cigarettes, and lack of exercise all combined to bring him to a terrible end.

As hateful as he had been, I would never have wished him such suffering. His eyes pleaded with me to forgive him, while the words eluded him. He couldn't say them, and I couldn't tell him that he was forgiven if he didn't ask, so he left the world without hearing the words that could have released both of us from a lifetime of misery. His death brought me no satisfaction. There was no closure, and it took me many years to forgive him for stealing my childhood, and for his failure to be the father I had so desperately needed.

The funeral was utterly dreadful. Just before Stepfather became ill, Mum had been to a lawyer to file for divorce. She said she couldn't live with him anymore. The beatings and constant fights had taken their toll, and she was exhausted. Mum refused to go to the funeral until I told her she should go because it was the right thing to do. How I wished that I hadn't! She was fine until we arrived at the service, where she went to pieces, making strange noises like a wild animal, with the family looking on in horror. You would have thought they had been the happiest couple on earth, and she was devastated by the loss of him.

My stepfather's brother and his wife attended the funeral. We had had very little contact with them up until Stepfather's death, but at a small family gathering at Mum's house, they couldn't wait to tell her that they wanted to buy her house. Mum was furious, and told them that she had no intention of selling it. She didn't, and she and Ross stayed on in the house.

That night, I had a terrible nightmare. I dreamed that the nurses pushed me into the hospital bed with Stepfather. To Des' dismay, I woke up screaming. I couldn't share my dream with him, and I was grateful that he didn't ask me what it was about. The relief I felt knowing it was only a bad dream and that my stepfather could never touch me again was overwhelming. He continues to visit me in my dreams until this present day, but they have slowly diminished in intensity over time. Twenty-five years of hatred, fear, and frustration were over. Life with Stepfather taught me to be a survivor, and I had skills I was going to need. Now, I only had Des to contend with, and it was just as well that I couldn't see into the future.

After Stepfather died, Mum gave me enough money out of his life insurance money to buy a sewing machine, but something prevented me from doing so, and I opened a savings account and hid the book in a shoebox. It was my secret and I told no one about it. It was not much, but it was mine.

One morning, while in my seventh month of pregnancy, I was in the kitchen washing the dishes, when I looked out of the window and noticed a thin column of smoke rising into the air at the far end of the yard. Curious, I went to investigate and discovered that our compost heap was on fire. Spontaneous combustion was not something I was familiar with, so I couldn't imagine how the fire had started. The neighbor's tree branches were dangling over the fire, and I knew that should they catch fire, their thatched roof house would be the next casualty. Running back to the house, I grabbed the hose outside the kitchen door and turned on the water, only to discover that the hose wasn't long enough to reach the fire. I ran back and forth with buckets of water, and in the process, I burned the soles of my shoes and quickly ran out of energy.

Realizing that I couldn't douse the flames, I called the fire department and explained that our compost was on fire and precariously close to the neighbor's house, adding that I was pregnant and needed their help. Within minutes, I heard sirens screaming up the street as two fire engines and an ambulance arrived simultaneously, along with all our neighbors who had rushed out into the street to see what was going on. The firemen quickly doused the flames and brought the fire under control. Des was on a business trip at the time, but even when he wasn't around, my life was always filled with some kind of drama, and a trip to visit my sister, Sheila, was to be no exception.

In my eighth month of pregnancy, I thought I should take the opportunity to visit Sheila and Dennis before the birth of the baby. They had moved to Rutenga in Zimbabwe, which at that time consisted of a few railway houses and a small community of mud huts. It was situated eighty-five miles beyond Beitbridge, the border crossing town between South Africa and Zimbabwe.

At the time, I had an Austin Mini station wagon. As usual, Des had bought it for a bargain, but it wasn't in good shape, so before I left, he had the engine replaced, and I was instructed to drive slowly for the first thousand miles in order to run it in safely, which was a necessity for new car engines at that time.

My mother went with us, so the Mini was packed to capacity. Mum sat in front with me, Larry and Anne occupied the back seat, and Justine sat in the rear with the luggage. December is the height of summer in South Africa, and incredibly hot, and without the luxury of air conditioning, it made for a long, uncomfortable trip. As we had made a late start, driving slowly, it took us the rest of the day to reach the border.

The trip went fairly well until we crossed the border into Zimbabwe. Once there, we discovered that the roads were in terrible shape, consisting of a dirt track with two narrow, poorly maintained strips of concrete full of pot holes. The track was barely wide enough for one car, and once on it, the Mini shook so badly that all four windows fell in on us. Before we knew it, with the windows missing, we were covered in thick dust, and I had to slow down even more. The children had dust in their eyes and complained bitterly, while my mother was dusty, tired and fed up. Being highly pregnant, I was feeling tired and irritable, when suddenly, as it was getting dusk, a Kudu buck, a large African antelope, ran across the road in front of us. I swerved and slammed on brakes, and we barely missed him. Shaken by the experience, I was thankful when, at last, we arrived at Sheila's house and were able to bathe, eat, and go to bed.

Staying with Sheila and Dennis wasn't easy. Dennis didn't have the slightest idea how to interact with the children, and he teased them incessantly. There were many tears shed while we were there, and I had words with Dennis, which didn't endear either one of us to the other. Their house stood close to the railway track, and the vibration of the trains passing through at night, blowing their whistles loud and long, prevented us from getting much sleep. Their cockerel was confused and crowed every night at midnight, with repeat performances every hour or so through the night. Mum complained about the cockerel, the heat, and the mosquitos the whole time we were there. As for me, by the end of the two weeks, I was covered in mosquito bites, swollen with water retention, and fervently wishing that we had never made the trip.

The Mini was still full of sand from the trip up, so the day before we left, Sheila's gardener cleaned it. He put the windows back in, fastening them temporarily with masking tape to prevent them from falling out again. Everyone was relieved when it was time to go home, and early in the morning, we piled into the Mini, hoping that this time, we could expect a pleasant, uneventful journey home.

We weren't many miles down the road when I smelled something burning and glancing down, I saw smoke drifting from beneath Mum's seat. I pulled off to the side of the road and ordered her out of the car - quickly! Larry and Anne jumped out, but Justine was trapped in the back with the luggage. I had locked the back door to prevent her from accidentally opening it, and now she was trapped. With Larry and Anne screaming and Mum in a state of panic, I grabbed the key and ran to the back, unlocked the door and dragged her out.

We stood waiting for the car to explode in flames, but thankfully nothing happened. When I was confident that it was safe to do so, I carefully investigated the source of the smoke and discovered that the gardener had placed the seat's metal support down on the battery terminal, which was under Mum's seat. I fixed the problem, and we resumed our journey.

Once over the border, it was a relief to be back on good roads again, and I relaxed and enjoyed the drive, but not for long! As we were attempting to pass a donkey cart traveling along the verge of the road, the driver suddenly pulled out in front of us, and I had to swerve around him. At that same moment, a large truck came careening over the rise towards us. With no time to get behind the cart, I put my foot down on the gas, but the Mini, being overloaded, didn't have enough power, and it struggled to get us to safety. We barely made it, and Mum complained bitterly about the stupid little car I had to drive, while Des drove a luxurious company car. I tried to defend him, but she was bitter, and not prepared to hear one good word about him.

A little further down the road, smoke started billowing from beneath the hood, and when I checked the gauge, I found that the car was overheating. It must have been contagious, as I also became extremely hot and bothered. We were not far from Messina, a fairly large town, so I slowly drove into the first garage I could find. The mechanic who examined the Mini shook his head. "Sorry, Madam," he said, "your engine has blown up!" The brand-new engine needed to be replaced! I was nearing my wit's end, and I felt as if I could blow a gasket myself. How could so many things go wrong on one trip? The mechanic was hopeful that he could get hold of a reconditioned engine and put it in for me, but that meant an overnight stay in a hotel.

I called Des from the hotel and told him what had happened. He was, of course, furious, and said that it had to be my fault, that I must have driven too fast and blown up the engine. I explained that the mechanic said he was sure that the new engine was faulty, but Des didn't want to hear that. Later the next day, with the new engine installed, we resumed our journey home. The remainder of the trip was slow, but mercifully, uneventful.

The birth of our fourth child was not easy. After Justine's quick birth, I was not prepared for a lengthy labor, but this one was different. With each contraction, it appeared as if the baby was ready to be born, only to turn around and go back again. It was almost as if the child knew what kind of chaotic world it was about to enter, and thought it better to stay where it was. I was shaking so much with exhaustion that I could no longer push, so my doctor gave me an injection to calm me down and went off to see a movie.

I was afraid he wouldn't be there for the birth, but the injection worked, and my body co-operated once more. When Dr. Davie returned, I pushed. The baby turned! This pattern repeated itself several times until he told me to relax, while he went to check on another patient. Completely exhausted; I just wanted this to be over. The nursing sister, a gentle nun who had assisted with the births of my other three children, said, "Come on dear, let's show the doctor. You can do it. Just one big push!"

It worked, and on January 2nd 1971, my youngest son, Craig, was born. The nun placed him on the scale and declared, with some astonishment, that he weighed exactly 10 pounds, making him my heaviest baby.

When she placed Craig in my arms, I was startled to see that he looked exactly like his father. A perfect miniature, I have always thought of him as my happy Des, and that is exactly what he turned out to be.

He would grow up to be a gentle child, seemingly immune to the constant turmoil that surrounded him.

Des sent me flowers with a card that read:

> *'My sweet,*
> *Thanks for a lovely baby boy –*
> *May he be as sweet as his Mummy.*
> *My love, Des'*

The next day, Des went off on a week's country trip. The flowers were beautiful, but I would have preferred my husband's presence and love. He was able to write the word *love*, but he was still completely incapable of saying or showing it.

Craig was a good baby and looking so much like his father, I often held him after Des had gone to work, and buried my face in his tiny neck. I could smell Des' aftershave that lingered after he had kissed Craig goodbye, and breathing deeply, I found myself dreaming of happier days.

LILY

With four children to care for, I was kept busy, but I longed for adult company. With Des gone most of the time, I was lonely. When I confronted him about his affairs, he denied that he had ever had one, or he said he would admit it when I could prove it. As far as I was concerned, I already had, but obviously, he didn't seem to think so. Many evenings when he was out found me lying on the carpet in the living room playing a Chopin record someone had given me. It was the only classical record I had and because it helped me to relax, I played it often.

Four pregnancies had left me with badly stretched skin. My babies were all quite big, and carrying so much water hadn't helped. Des made it very clear that he found my body repulsive, and out of desperation, I decided to see a plastic surgeon. I asked my mother to take care of the children while I was in the hospital, and I felt confident that after the surgery, Des would find me attractive.

Hope dissipated quickly when Des picked me up from the hospital. As I got into the car, he said with great contempt, "Well, I suppose you will have your breasts fixed next." His actual words were not that kind, and the sarcasm accompanying his vulgar remark cut into me like a knife. Choking back my tears, I realized that no matter how hard I tried, I could never please him.

On the way home from the hospital, I was feeling pretty weak, but I knew we needed bread and a few groceries, so I suggested that we stop at a small grocery store, before collecting the children from my parents. Once inside, I asked Des to get a loaf of bread, while I gathered the rest of the groceries. He disappeared down one of the aisles and when he stayed away, I wondered what was taking him so long. As I rounded the corner at the end of the aisle, I came across Des embracing a woman, while whispering in her ear. I felt all the blood drain out of my face, and I was grateful for the support of the shopping cart.

Of course, being caught in the act didn't faze Des, and he turned to me with a triumphant grin on his face as he introduced me to the woman. "Doreen, you remember Lily, don't you? Lily is a teller at the Trust Bank, and we went to her party a while ago. Lily, my wife, Doreen."

It took a great effort on my part to shake her hand, while attempting to smile. I recognized her as the woman in the kitchen at the party, but in my weakened state following the surgery, this was not a good time for me to have to confront my fears. She stood there smiling as if her behavior was perfectly acceptable. I could hardly believe that Des would find such a woman attractive. Her blonde hair revealed black roots that were in need of a touch-up. She wore thick make-up with lots of mascara and bright red lipstick. Her overly tight dress was full of stains. In short, she was everything Des said he detested in a woman. My mind flashed back to my childhood and the other woman in my stepfather's life. The two women looked eerily similar.

We drove home in silence, and I knew I couldn't go on like this. I resolved to confront the woman and have it out with her, but I felt the need to wait a couple of weeks until I was stronger.

The day I drove into town and entered the bank, I almost lost my nerve. What was I going to say to the woman, and how would she respond? Looking around, I didn't see her working as a teller, so I walked over to the enquiries desk and asked to speak to Lily. I realized at that moment that I didn't even know her surname. I was told she had been promoted and now had a private office upstairs on the second floor. When I found her, the words simply tumbled out, "Lily, we met the other day at the grocery store."

She nodded and smiled, and I continued, "Well, I want you to know that it seems I can't make Des happy, and if you want him, I am prepared to give him up."

Lily shook her head, and with a quizzical look on her face, she grinned and said, "I don't want him; I have my own husband, thank you very much."

Obviously, I had made a complete fool of myself. Their affair was just a game, and although they were both married, neither of them appeared to feel any shame about what they were doing. With my face burning with embarrassment, I turned around and went home. If anything, I had made myself even more miserable by confronting Lily.

From then on, I lived one day at a time, always wishing it was this time next year and hoping that by then, things might be better. I didn't realize that in the process, I was throwing my life away, one day at a time.

The three years we lived in Lyttelton passed by quickly, and the deposit we borrowed from the Trust Bank was finally paid off. After selling the house, Des went back to the contractor we had used previously, and asked him to build two houses on the lots we had bought in Bronberrik. It was time to move on.

CAMPING OUT

Once again, we found ourselves without a home. By this time, you would think I was used to being 'homeless,' but unfortunately, I am one of those people who is known as a worrywart, and having the responsibility of four children, it never became any easier.

One of Des's friends from the motor club said that we were welcome to stay on their farm and offered us the use of a small one-roomed cottage and we were delighted to accept his kind offer. We purchased a travel trailer for the children to sleep in and used the cottage as a bedroom for Des and me. It was spacious enough for us to build a bathroom in one corner, which also served as a laundry. Des also bought and assembled a large steel storage shed, which he mounted on a concrete slab. This served as both living room and dining room. It wasn't an ideal arrangement, but I am sure that the children enjoyed the year we spent camping out. They also had four friends to play with on several acres of land, bicycles to ride, games to play and the use of a swimming pool, so for them, it must have been like a long camping holiday.

The remainder of our furniture and household goods were stored in an old garage on the farm, which was quite far from the house. That was when I learned about the power of African witchcraft. The garage had no doors, and I protested that we could expect everything to be stolen. I assumed that Des would at least put doors on, but instead, he took an old human skull he had kept since his university days and hung it over the entrance. He then had me make two small muslin sacks, one of which he filled with grass and the other with herbs. The tiny sacks he called *muti* (medicine) were hung along with the skull, and just as he predicted, no one attempted to remove either the boxes or the furniture. Africans are superstitious and fear witchcraft. I had no knowledge of such things and was quite shocked to think that a human skull and a couple of bags of grass and herbs could be found to be so threatening.

Staying with Gerald and his wife Mary was not easy and we had our regular dramas while we were there. Des and Gerald spent most evenings and weekends either drinking on the verandah or at the motor club.

At the time, I was driving Des' latest bargain, a Jaguar that guzzled gas at an alarming rate. I spent much of my time taxiing the children, since we were now a good distance from their schools. With four children and two dogs, I had my hands full, especially when it rained continuously for six weeks. The area between our three dwellings turned into a sea of muddy red clay, and I despaired of ever getting the stains out of the children's clothes. Poor Topsy's ears were caked in mud and full of burrs, and both dogs were infested with ticks. The children were covered in mosquito and tick bites, and I was losing weight daily, and I had no idea why.

Des came home one morning at 5 am with his breath smelling of brandy and his body reeking of cheap perfume. The smell sickened me, and when he tried to force himself on me, I found the courage to say "No."

He froze next to me, and then hit me with such force that I could hardly get out of bed. He told me through clenched teeth that I was his wife, that it was his right, and I couldn't refuse. He grabbed hold of me and threw me back on the bed, where he taught me the meaning of the common use of the word rape. Yes, he was my husband, but he had just come from another woman. I felt violated! Somehow, I managed to push him away, and I scrambled out of the bed. He followed me and attacked me with such force, I lost my balance and fell to the floor.

Des lay on the bed for a while, then his whole demeaner changed, and he asked me to join him, calling me Jakes and saying he was sorry. I needed to get away from him, and instead of returning to bed, I ran to the door in a frantic bid to escape. Just as I reached it, he grabbed me and, snatching the key out of the lock, grinned while placing it in his pocket. I lunged towards the chest of drawers and tried to grab the gun out of the top draw. I was so desperate at that moment; I wasn't even able to think of the children. I wasn't able to think of anything, other than getting away from Des. Anticipating my intention, he pushed me aside, slammed the draw closed, locked it, and placed the drawer key in his pocket along with the other one. Then he snarled, "Don't you ever try that again."

The terror and desperation of the moment passed, and I never contemplated suicide again.

When Gerald and Mary went on vacation, they asked us to keep an eye on their house as well as their dog, Rebel, a big, ferocious dog with mean eyes. I never trusted him, especially since he had recently attacked and killed some sheep belonging to the neighbors. Mary's elderly mother remained in the house, but we didn't see much of her as she mostly stayed in her room with her little dog, Suzanna.

Larry loved both dogs, and one Saturday afternoon, he was playing with Suzanna, when Rebel came dashing around the corner. Jealous of Suzanna, he attacked Larry, ripping open his ear lobe and the right side of his face. Mary's mother heard the commotion and, between the two of us, we managed to drag Rebel off Larry. The blood was pouring from the wound, and I had no idea where Des was, so I ran into the house and called Dr. Davie. There was no reply, so I wrapped a towel around Larry's face, bundled the children in the Jaguar and turned the key. The gas tank showed almost empty and when I looked in my purse, I discovered I only had fifty cents. It was the end of the month, and Des had not yet given me my allowance.

I didn't dare drive fast, since I knew the fuel would then be consumed even faster. I drove to Dr. Davie's house, which was about ten miles away, hoping to find him there by the time we arrived, but he still wasn't home. The hospital was another twelve miles further on, so at the nearest gas station, I put in fifty cents worth of gas, and miraculously, it was enough to get us safely there.

By the time we arrived, Larry was as white as the towel I had wrapped around his face, and I had to half-carry him into the hospital. Leaving him with the nurse, I went back to the car to get the other children, and we all sat in the waiting room while the young doctor on duty stitched up Larry's face and ear. He did an excellent job, but I was nervous, knowing that I still had to face Des, who always blamed me for whatever happened to the children.

With no money to put in more gas, it was incredible that we made it home. Thinking back, I realize now that the Jaguar must have had a substantial reserve tank.

After getting the children cleaned up, fed and into bed, I was about to go to bed myself when Des arrived home. He had been drinking as usual, and smirking at me, he went to kiss the children goodnight. I followed him into the travel trailer and when he saw Larry's face, he sobered up quickly and demanded to know what had happened.

When I had finished telling him the whole sad story, I said that in the future, he should tell me where he was going, so that I could get hold of him in an emergency. I also told him I had no money to put gas in the car, which could have caused an even worse situation. He didn't apologize, but at least, for a change, he didn't blame me for what had happened.

The next morning, he took his revolver, went outside, and shot and killed Rebel.

A few days later, while sorting the laundry, I found a photograph in Des' shirt pocket. He was pictured wearing white karate clothes. As far as I knew, he had never taken up karate, so that night, I asked him about it. He grabbed the photograph out of my hand and put it in his pocket and said he didn't know what I was talking about. When I reminded him of the photograph, he asked innocently, "What photograph?" Psychological games are, in some ways, worse than physical violence, and I learned there was yet another kind of rape – that of the mind! Not prepared to admit anything, he told me I was completely crazy and needed to be committed to a mental institution. This was the beginning of a few months of intensive mental manipulation, and gradually, I began to doubt my own sanity.

The reality of what my husband was up to hit me hardest when a nursing acquaintance of ours told me that when she had met Des in town recently, he had asked her what was required to get someone committed to Weskoppies, the Pretoria mental asylum. I knew then that I needed to guard my sanity. It was slowly dawning on me that it might be his goal to drive me insane, or, at the very least, to have me committed. In spite of my resolve, my health deteriorated, and things got so bad that Des almost succeeded.

His plan seemed to come together one day when the three older children were all visiting friends, and Des and I were alone with Craig. For no reason that I could identify, he flew into one of his rages. He kept yelling at me, telling me how useless I was as a wife and that I didn't deserve a husband like him. I had prevented him from becoming a doctor and that I was never going amount to anything. I had a whore for a mother, and if I wasn't one already, I soon would be. I begged him to stop. I knew I couldn't handle much more of his abuse, but my pleading fell on deaf ears, and then he said I wasn't a fit mother. That was too much! I knew I was a good mother, and he was just trying to hurt me, which he easily succeeded in doing. He said I didn't deserve Craig, and he was going to make sure that I didn't have him.

Recently he had inherited his father's Webley service revolver, a powerful handgun. Brandishing the Webley, he took Craig out of his pram, and, holding him in his arms, he walked behind the travel trailer. I was sure he was bluffing, until I heard the sound of a loud gunshot. My heart froze, and I stumbled around the back of the trailer, fully expecting to see my baby blown to pieces. Des stood there laughing triumphantly, while Craig looked at me with terrified eyes. The extent of Des' cruelty astonished me and I dread to think what effect it must have had on Craig.

Hardly able to think, I ran to the car and I found the keys in the ignition. I don't know how I managed to reverse out of the driveway, but once out of the gate, I drove as fast as I could to Patrick and Sarah's house. Once there, I couldn't speak. I was highly stressed, and I vomited before they could get me to calm down enough to tell them what had happened. Patrick then went to talk to Des, who, of course, denied everything. I am sure Patrick didn't believe him, but he knew he couldn't help someone who was not prepared to admit that he had a problem. At least he was able to calm Des down before accompanying me home.

Des later admitted that he had removed something from the engine to render the car immobile and couldn't understand how I was able to drive it. Thankfully, someone was looking out for me that day!

Following this incident, my weight dropped from 135 to 115 pounds. I couldn't eat or sleep, and I developed excruciating headaches, as well as ugly sores all over my arms and face. I needed something for the headaches, so I went to see our doctor.

Dr. Davie said he could tell just by looking at me that I wasn't eating or sleeping. In his gentlest tone of voice, he sympathized with me, and I found myself telling him a little about my husband. I asked him if he thought Des had a split personality, and he replied that, in his opinion, Des had multiple personalities, and he advised me to be careful, as he felt that my husband was capable of extreme violence. He didn't actually need to tell me what I already knew.

I had an extremely high temperature, and after looking at the sores on my arms and face, Dr. Davie asked me if I had a headache. I told him about the excruciating headaches I had been experiencing for the past few days, and he examined me carefully, searching my head for what he eventually found. A tick had buried itself in the top of my head and I had developed tick bite fever. The poison had affected my nerve endings, which caused the ugly sores to erupt. He said that I needed to rest and was pleased when I told him that we were soon to be traveling up to Zimbabwe for a holiday.

A few days later, in December of 1971, we drove up to my sister's farm in Ruwa, just outside Harare. She was shocked at my physical condition, but I didn't tell her what was causing it. We were still not very close.

Sheila and Dennis were building a house, using the clay on the farm to make their own bricks. Labor was cheap, so the cost was kept at a minimum. It was quite an experience to stay in the primitive accommodation they had to offer, but we had a great time visiting with them. The children enjoyed riding their donkeys, and playing in the pile of building sand.

There were many snakes, spiders and scorpions on the farm since this was the heart of Africa with all its many dangers. Their outside toilet was built of corrugated iron, which didn't appeal to me, but I had no option but to get used to it. I inspected it carefully each time before entering, and was fortunate enough to see only a few spiders. However, shortly after we left, Sheila told me that one day, she heard a scuffling noise and discovered there was a rat in the toilet. She ran out screaming for Dennis, who promptly came to her rescue with his shotgun and shot the toilet to pieces. I was grateful that it didn't happen while we were visiting them. Dennis often proved that he wasn't much of a handyman, and Sheila had been quick to warn me never to allow him to fix anything when they lived in South Africa.

From the mid-1960s until late in the 1970s, Zimbabwe was embroiled in the Rhodesian Bush War, a conflict that eventually led to the end of white rule in the country that was to become Zimbabwe. At the beginning of the bush war, Sheila bought a motorbike so she could spot the landmines in the dirt roads, while traveling around. I was concerned about her and tried to persuade her to move back to South Africa, but she loved her farm with a passion and told me emphatically, that this was where she wanted to live till the end of her days and that, it turned out, is exactly what she did.

Back home, while we still had a few more months of living on the farm, I received a letter from my dear friend, June, in England. She wrote that she had cashed in an insurance policy and wanted to use the money to visit me. The timing of her letter couldn't have been worse. I hadn't seen June for fifteen years, and I was terribly disappointed when I had to write back and tell her that we had no home of our own at that time and were unable to accommodate her. I couldn't bring myself to tell her about the state of my marriage and my poor health. As much as I longed to see her again, it just wasn't possible. June was her usual gracious self, and wrote back to say she completely understood. Many years would elapse before we eventually saw one another again, but her sweet letters kept coming, and our friendship grew even stronger.

One day, I was cooking in the tiny kitchen in the travel trailer. After preparing a lamb curry in my brand-new pressure cooker, I put it on high for a few minutes to reach pressure before turning it down.

Suddenly, it emitted an unusually loud hissing sound, and I discovered that the pot was swaying from side to side. The bottom of it had formed a huge bubble, and I suspected that it was about to explode. The children were playing on the other end of the trailer, so I grabbed the cooker by the handle and threw it out into the yard as fast and as far as I could. Once the heat had escaped, it slowly cooled down until I was able to open it and retrieve the contents, which I finished cooking in an ordinary saucepan. I refused the offer of a replacement, and I have never cooked in a pressure cooker since that day.

Drama seemed to follow us around like a small fox terrier, snapping at our heels, giving us a nip every now and then. A few days later, Justine ran into her father and told him that there was a large snake near the swimming pool. Grabbing his gun, he went to have a look and seeing the rolled-up hosepipe, laughed, saying it was just the garden hose. At that moment, a large puff adder shot out from between the coils of the hose and slithered between Des' legs, making for the wall of the house. I watched as Des fired a shot, and the puff adder fell dead. I was impressed, but when Des reconstructed the events, he came to the conclusion that the bullet had struck the wall and ricocheted into the snake, killing it. The lethal snake may have unnerved him but, in spite of his poor aim, at least it no longer posed a threat.

It was with considerable relief when we were able to move into the speculative house temporarily for a few months, while the second house, where we were to eventually live, was being built.

Although we weren't in the spec house for long, it was just long enough for at least one drama. Des insisted that I serve him a glass of brandy with ginger ale when he came home from work in the evenings. He usually changed out of his suit, sat down in his black leather recliner, and waited for his drink. After serving him, I then returned to my cooking.

One evening, I wasn't able to leave the cooking immediately and being too impatient to wait, he poured his own drink, sat down, and took a large gulp. He immediately spat it out all over the floor and screamed, "Are you trying to poison me?"

He was angry, and his eyes were blazing. I was bewildered. What was he talking about? Then, it dawned on me that he had taken the wrong ginger ale bottle. I had filled an empty bottle with paraffin, which I used for cleaning the floors, storing it high up on the top of the kitchen cabinet. Because Des had no sense of smell, he had unwittingly poured paraffin into his drink, instead of ginger ale. I explained to him that I never put the ginger ale on top of the cabinet and pointed to his bottle of ginger ale standing in clear view on the kitchen counter. Making Des feel foolish was not a wise thing to do, and I suffered the consequences.

A few weeks later, we were able to move into our new home and settle down. We then sold the travel trailer to some friends of Des, but they moved away and we never did receive payment from them. It was just another loss to be written off at a time when we could least afford it.

BRONBERRIK

When we built our house, Bronberrik was a pleasant residential area, mostly inhabited by younger couples with small children. Our property was part of the original farm, Zwartkop, bordering on Bronberrik, so we had the advantage of living on a few acres of land, but also having many neighbors with children for ours to play with.

Living in the speculative house for a couple of months gave Des the opportunity to spend time supervising the building of the house that was to be our new home. On three occasions, he kicked over a decorative wall just inside the front door as it wasn't built to his satisfaction. The builder, being in a high state of anxiety, told Des he had a weak heart, and that the stress of what Des was doing could cause him to have a heart attack. My husband told him emphatically that it wasn't his problem. He wanted the house built right, and it *would* be built right. Following months of conflict, we moved into 142, Pine Avenue, which was to be our home for the next nine years.

Servants were not paid well in South Africa but as unemployment was high, there was a constant stream of young women knocking on the door looking for work. One, in particular, was very persuasive, so I employed her. Des was not impressed when he came home and found

Ida working in the house. He disliked black people, saying that they were dirty and full of germs. He made it clear that she was not to touch his food unless it was going to be cooked. He never allowed a black person to have physical contact with him and insisted that the children and I should do the same. If he touched a black person, or had to handle something they had touched, he immediately washed his hands, and I was told to do likewise.

Because he refused to give me extra money for her salary, I was in no position to pay Ida more than the standard rate, which, for me, was barely affordable out of my housekeeping allowance. However, I managed to compensate her salary in other ways.

Ida and I got on well. She lived in the servant's quarters at the back of the house, going home once a month for a weekend. She soon became pregnant, and as she wasn't married, I was concerned until I learned that many of the black people in Africa believe a woman has to prove her fertility by producing a baby, before a man would be willing to marry her. When Ida left to have her baby, her mother came to work in her place for about six months. I called her Gogo, which is short for Granny, in Zulu. She was like a mother to me, and we became close. Des was far more receptive to Gogo because she was from the old school, and she treated him with the utmost respect, which suited him well.

Gogo's husband, Thomas, a kind, humble man, was a cobbler and unable to find work in Pretoria; he finally found a job in Johannesburg. Unfortunately, this posed a problem for him since, according to South African law, it was outside the area in which he was permitted to work. Gogo asked me to sign his passbook each month, to enable him to work in Johannesburg and unknown to Des, I did this for many months. I was never comfortable with the apartheid laws, and it was one small thing I could do to alleviate at least one person's hardship.

One evening, when Thomas was visiting Gogo for the weekend, I walked past their room, and noticed a flickering light that could only be from a candle. I knocked on the door and asked Thomas if the globe had blown, as I had a spare one that I could give him. He was holding his Bible in his hand and said, "No, Missus, I am reading my Bible, and it feels better for me to read it by candlelight." I was touched by such gentle humility and devotion to their traditional way of life.

When Ida stopped breastfeeding her baby, Gogo went home to take care of the child and Ida returned to work. During her absence, Ida had changed, and she was no longer the cheerful young woman I had employed. Her boyfriend refused to marry her as promised, but he still came to visit her during the week and kept her from her work. After Ida gave her boyfriend our telephone number, we received regular calls for him. I didn't mind too much, until late one night, we got a telephone call for him after we had gone to bed. Des was livid, and the next morning he told the boyfriend that our telephone was not there for his convenience and he was no longer welcome to stay in the room with Ida whenever he felt so inclined. As it was against the law, I was in no position to intervene on Ida's behalf. She became angry and left with him.

A couple of days later, Gogo brought Ida back, but one look at her face told me that it wasn't going to work, so I told them that I would be doing my own housework. Gogo was upset, but I think she understood. I was sad to see them go, but I told Gogo that Thomas could still stop by, and I would gladly sign his passbook. This gave me the opportunity to keep in contact with them.

Knowing how Des felt about having a servant, I was relieved to be doing my own housework again. It kept me busy, and I was able to save the money I had paid Ida to buy appliances, which made my days easier. During the first year, I saved for and bought an automatic washing machine, which I had installed in our bathroom as I didn't have a laundry room.

Des was able to order the washing machine through a builder friend of his, enabling us to purchase it at cost price. I appreciated the discount, but not for long. By this time, Des had joined the prestigious Zwartkops Country Club, and he invited the builder and his wife for dinner at the restaurant to show our appreciation.

There was a small dance floor on one side of the restaurant, and Des' friend asked me to dance. While dancing, he held me much too close, and I felt his body responding in an inappropriate way, so I stood still and said pointedly, "I thought you said that you wanted to dance."

He went red in the face, and accompanied me back to our table. Des asked me what was wrong, and I told him I wanted to go home. The evening was ruined, and Des blamed me for it, saying I must have flirted with the man and didn't I realize how much money he had saved us on the purchase of the washing machine? I didn't care. Saving money wasn't worth that kind of humiliation.

Because Des was seldom at home and didn't seem to enjoy spending time with his family, the children and I regularly went to the drive-in movies. We could only go to movies suitable for the children, but most of them were action movies or comedies, which I also enjoyed. I made large pots of curry and rice for our dinner, which we all enjoyed. I also put in an old blanket for the children to sit on in front of the car. If it was cold, they all sat in the car, where they constantly bickered with one another, but generally speaking, they were fun times. Quite often, when we went to the drive-in, I drove several times around a large traffic circle on the highway, which amused the children enormously.

On one of those evenings, when Des was at the club, the children said they wanted to see a movie at a drive-in theater on the other side of Pretoria. We arrived early, but because it was a popular movie, there was already a long queue stretching far down the street. It didn't look as if we had a chance of getting in, but as it was a large drive-in, we joined the queue and hoped for the best. We inched along as people paid and were admitted, but when it was almost our turn, the full sign appeared above the entrance. There, we were trapped in the line of cars, unable to turn around, so I told the children we could sit and wait for the second show. They were content to wait since we had our dinner with us and the children's playground was close by. It was the first time we had been to the second showing, which would have been fine, but it was a long movie and ended late, and we still had a long drive home.

The drive-in was packed, and it took a great deal of time for us to get out. Des usually got home at around midnight, so I knew he was bound to be worried. It was almost 1:00 am when we finally got home, and he was beside himself with worry and rage, both stewing inside him. The children went to bed crying, and I went to bed trembling, anticipating a night with little or no sleep. Des yelled at me for hours and then he told me to get out of *his* bed. It was always his bed when he was angry. When I refused, protesting that it was my bed too, he pushed me, but I didn't budge. Then he pushed harder with both his hands and feet and seeing the funny side of the situation, while at the same time feeling slightly hysterical, I giggled.

"What's so funny?" he snapped.

I must not have been thinking straight at that moment because I replied, "I'm good at making a bed, aren't I?"

My mother had taught me to make a bed hospital style, and once it was tucked in, the weight of my body wouldn't allow him to push me out. My flippant reply was all it took! He jumped out of bed, ran around to my side and pulled the covers out. He then dragged me out of bed and beat and kicked me, until I lay on the floor sobbing. Only then was he satisfied, and I remained there for the rest of the night.

The next day was a Saturday, and Des was busy moving some earth on the lot with the aid of a backhoe he had borrowed from a friend. It was hot, and he came in sweaty and irritable. He wanted something to drink, and I didn't move fast enough for his liking. With the previous evening still fresh in both our minds, it wasn't long before we were arguing again. As usual, I was useless, stupid, and a whore, just like my mother. I had another one of my crazy moments and retorted, "Yes, and what is good for the goose, is good for the gander!" Then I added, "Why shouldn't I have some fun too?"

I was tired, frustrated, and sick of being accused of things that weren't true. Des followed me into our bedroom, and losing his temper completely, he locked the door, and smashed everything he could lay his hands on, including the two bedside lamps. Then he turned on me, and I wasn't quick enough to protect my face, and it took a severe beating along with my arms and upper body. My nose started bleeding, which brought him to his senses, and as suddenly as it had begun, the fight ended, and he stormed out of the room. I heard him go to the kitchen for something to drink and then he went out of the back door, slamming it behind him.

In the bathroom, I was shocked to see the mess he had made of my face. I cleaned it up as best I could before the children came into the house. They had been playing outside, while watching their father work until he left to return the machine. The looks on the children's faces when they saw me were too much to bear, and I knew then that I couldn't go on subjecting them to this kind of life. I decided to go to the police station for help.

The policeman at the front desk was kind and while helping me fill in a report, he asked me if I wanted to lay a charge. In my stressed state, I wasn't able to think of much of anything, except that I could no longer cope with the violence at home, and I needed protection from my husband. The policeman gently asked me if there were some relatives that might be able to take us in for a while, and I told him no, since Des would know just where to look for us. A kindly detective offered us refuge for the night at their house in Pretoria, and I was so desperate, I agreed to do it. We first needed to go home to gather up some clothes.

The detective and another policeman followed us home in his Volkswagen Beetle.

When we arrived at the house, Des hadn't returned home, so the police sat in the living room while I quickly packed a suitcase. We took the bare minimum but I remembered to take my savings book with me, hoping that the contents might just be enough to cover the cost of a divorce. Before we left the house, the police asked if Des had any firearms, and fortunately, I knew where they were. To my relief, they confiscated them all.

After dropping the policeman off at the police station, we drove behind the detective's Volkswagen to his house, and his wife took us in without a moment's hesitation. They even put us up in their own bedroom and shared a large pot of soup with us. They were kind and generous, but I knew we couldn't stay more than one night. I lay awake all night wondering what to do, and the next morning, I told them that I was going to ask Aunt Joey's brother, Uncle Ross, if we could stay with them for a few days, until I could make a more permanent arrangement.

Uncle Ross and Aunt Stella graciously took us in, and Uncle Ross hid my Volkswagen Minibus in the garage and parked his own car in the carport. He said he was sure Des would check to see if my vehicle was there, and maybe if he didn't see it, he might just drive on by. His hunch proved to be right. I saw Des drive by slowly a couple of times, but since he didn't see my Minibus and the children were playing in the backyard, he must have assumed that we weren't there.

Patrick and Sarah had moved to Durban by this time, but they were the only ones I dared confide in. I called Patrick, who gave me the name of an attorney friend of his who could help me to file for divorce. I found it difficult to believe I was actually doing this, but I knew that I had to, for the children's sake. I made an appointment with the attorney for the next morning, and then spent another fitful night half expecting to hear the doorbell, with Des standing on the doorstep. The next morning, I left the children with Aunt Stella and drove into town.

The attorney was kind and understanding, and upon seeing my face, he said that he was sure I was doing the right thing. We discussed matters at length, and then I confessed that I only had my meagre savings; and asked him if it would be enough to cover the cost of the divorce. He assured me it was exactly the right amount and although I suspected he wasn't being entirely truthful, I told him to go ahead and have a summons served on Des. I walked out feeling relieved, and although I had no idea where to go, or what to do, I had taken the first step, and, at the time, it felt right.

I drove back to Aunt Stella's, trying to gather my thoughts, when suddenly, I spotted Des driving in the opposite direction. At the same moment, he saw me, did a U-turn and gave chase. The faster I drove, the faster he drove. We were driving at breakneck speed, when I took a chance and swerved into one of the suburb's side streets. He followed me as I drove dangerously fast, through the many stop signs. I changed direction several times, but I was no match for my rally driver husband, and I knew it was hopeless. I simply couldn't lose him, and I eventually drove to Ginsberg's, hoping to reach my mother before Des caught up with me. Surely, he wouldn't dare hurt me once I was inside the store.

As I reached the entrance, he grabbed my bruised arm, causing me to cry out, and several people stopped to stare. He dragged me away from the entrance and asked me where his children were. I told him that I was never going to tell him. He abruptly changed tactics and stroked my hand, saying that it would drive him crazy if he couldn't see his children. He said he knew he had treated me badly, and he was sorry.

"Please, Jakes, just let me see my children. I promise I won't hurt you or them."

I told him I wanted a divorce. He said, "I don't blame you. That is what you should do. I don't deserve any of you, but please, can I just see them?"

What could I do? He was stronger than I was. I was scared, but surely, now that I had an attorney, and the police were aware of the situation, the children and I would be safe. I confessed that we were staying with Aunt Stella. He looked surprised, obviously wondering about the whereabouts of my Minibus. He followed me to Aunt Stella's house, and we both went to the front door. I rang the doorbell, and Uncle Ross asked me if everything was all right. I told him, yes, everything was fine, and he went back inside. The children came out, and I picked Craig up. He was still little, not yet two years old. Des asked to hold him and I said no. His voice was soft and gentle as he begged me, "Please, Jakes, just let me hold him."

How could I refuse? I handed him over, and Des immediately became that other man again. He went red in the face as he snarled at me, "Thank you. You can have him back when you come home where you belong!" He then kidnapped my baby!

Before I could fully grasp what he was doing, he was in his car with Craig, who still needed the occasional bottle and a clean diaper. I called after him, begging him not to do this, but he drove off, leaving me standing there sobbing helplessly. Uncle Ross was furious! He had no idea what Des was really like and he was shocked when I told him a little of what had been going on. We called the police and told them what had happened. They were sympathetic, and after some discussion, they suggested that I go home and they would watch the house and make sure I was okay. At least I could relax a little, knowing that they still had Des' firearms.

Leaving the other children in Aunt Stella's care, I drove home. I was sick with worry about Craig, and couldn't wait to make sure he was safe. I noticed the policeman's Volkswagen Beetle parked outside my neighbor's house opposite ours, which had a good view of our living room. The police had arranged with me to try and keep Des in the living room, to enable them to watch us through binoculars.

When I arrived home, Des was there, full of apologies and promises. I managed to steer him into the living room, but it was almost as if he knew we were being watched. He may have seen the strange car parked across the street and suspected it was the police. He got down on his knees in front of me and swore never to hit me again. He was going to treat me with the love and respect he knew I deserved. Then he began to cry and said that he knew that he was sick, and promised to see a psychiatrist. Seeing Des cry had a profound effect on me. Believing that things were going to be different from then on, I agreed to give him another chance.

I bathed and fed Craig and put him to bed. We had dinner, but I had no appetite. Des was kind and gentle, and I believed that the threat of divorce had brought him to his senses, that he was now going to be the husband he promised to be. That night, he made tender love to me for the first and only time in our marriage.

The next day, I went to collect the children from Aunt Stella. I reassured her and Uncle Ross that everything was going to be okay. I don't think they were convinced, but I had to make my own decisions. I went to see the attorney again, and told him I was going to give Des another chance. He shook his head and smiled. He told me that I was a good woman. I asked him for his bill, and he promised to send me one at the end of the month. I never did receive an account, and I learned that there are some really good men in this world.

TRYING AGAIN

For a while, things were better at home. A year later, knowing that I was never going to leave Des, I finally used my meager savings to buy an electric sewing machine. Des was able to convince the police that he was a reformed man, and his guns were returned to him. He never did go to a psychiatrist for help as he had promised, but because things were better, I once again had hope.

Des could be sweet and charming but because those were such rare occasions, they remained as special memories, to be savored over and over again. Like the day he walked into the kitchen with his hand behind his back. He presented me with the stem of a rose he had taken from a neighbor's yard. He smiled ruefully, while explaining he had picked a beautiful pink rose for me, but the bloom had broken off on the way home. Because it meant so much to me, I treasured the broken stem for the longest time.

Topsy finally died of old age, and we were all sad to see her go. At more or less the same time, Mum was given a fully grown male spaniel named Prince, but after a few months, she offered him to us because he often managed to get out of their yard and wander the streets. She was concerned that he would get run over or cause an accident. We took him home, and the children changed his name to Danny. He was not as gentle as Topsy and sometimes snapped at the children, but he never bit them and he became a loyal companion to Craig, following him wherever he went.

That was the year Des bought us a television. When he brought it home, we were all astonished. He had always maintained that television was evil, and he was adamant that we would never have one in our house. Then the truth came out. Des was still an avid boxing fan, and when it was announced that Gerrie Coetzee, the South African heavyweight champion, was to fight the American, Leon Spinks, in Monte Carlo and it was to be televised, suddenly it was the perfect time to buy a TV.

The boxing match couldn't take place in South Africa due to the sports boycott caused by apartheid. Television was introduced in 1971, which was later than in most countries, but even then, with certain restrictions. It was available at the time of the match but because the fight took place on a Sunday – the sabbath – Des had to wait until one-minute past midnight to watch the local broadcast even though the fight had taken place hours earlier. The government considered it sacrilegious to allow television to be broadcast on Sundays.

The children and I didn't care that it took a boxing match for us to get a television. At the time, having one was all that mattered. We had only one government channel starting at six o'clock in the evenings; the programs were mostly boring, but not ever having owned a television, we thought they were quite marvelous.

My mother was still working at Ginsberg's, when Mr. Ginsberg employed a man a few years younger than Mum to do the bookkeeping. One evening she was sitting in her living room, with the front door standing open, when a face peered in, and Dick, the new bookkeeper, asked her if she was too tired to take a walk. Divorced, he lived alone, just across the street from Mum. She went for a walk with him; he bought her a cool drink, and they soon became inseparable. I was glad for her. She was lonely, and Dick made her laugh. Soon afterwards, Mum sold her house, and she and Ross moved in with him. A short while later, Ross fell in love, married and they moved into their own home.

I could see that Mum and Dick were serious about their relationship, so when Mum asked me to call him Dad, I obliged to please her, even though he was only seventeen years older than me. This annoyed Des, since he didn't like Dick. He said he was not providing for Mum, that he was vulgar and had terrible table manners, and I shouldn't want to call him Dad when they weren't even married. Des also objected to the children calling Dick *Goemps*, an Afrikaans endearment of Grandpa, insisting that Dick was not their grandfather.

It was not long before Mum and Dick gave up their jobs at Ginsberg's. Dick sold his house, and with the proceeds, they bought an Autovilla camper and toured around South Africa for years, returning to Pretoria now and again for a visit. Dick had sold his light fitting business some years earlier, and he had some left-over light fixtures, which they sold to various stores along the way. Mostly they were on an extended vacation, making memories, so we didn't see much of them for the next ten years. This made it much easier for me, where Des was concerned.

Since purchasing my washing machine, I carried on saving part of my allowance until I had saved enough to have carpets installed throughout the house. Along with the purchase of a vacuum cleaner, my life became a lot easier, since I no longer had wooden floors to polish. The children helped by cleaning their rooms and laying the table. They took it in turns to wash the dishes, which caused squabbles, as it always had to be to be someone else's turn, so I eventually made out a roster and decided that a dishwasher would alleviate much of the discord.

While they were growing up, Des allowed the children to have as many animals as they wanted. In fact, he encouraged this, but also made sure they took care of them. If they didn't, he offered them some physical encouragement. Larry loved reptiles, and often had a pet lizard or snake in his bedroom. Before going to school, he occasionally asked me to feed his lizard and knowing that they wouldn't eat dead flies, I had to carefully stun the fly, before taking it by a wing and offering it to the happy recipient. The children also had rabbits, hamsters, mice, chickens, and ducks, all of which had to be fed and cared for. Out of curiosity, I once attempted to work out how many pets the children had over the years. The ones I remembered amounted to over 700, not counting Larry's 1,000 silkworms.

Des rose steadily through the ranks at his company and became the National Sales Manager in charge of a team of representatives. This meant a significant increase in salary, and the first thing he did was buy an almost new Mercedes Benz. He now owned a house, a rent house, a Mercedes, a wife, four children and a few acres of land. He was a member of Zwartkops Country Club and was even friends with a Brigadier General, who lived around the corner in the original old farmhouse. Des had 'arrived!'

When I had saved up enough money for a dishwasher, I wasn't sure who enjoyed it the most, the children or me. However, our joy was short-lived when Des lost his temper in the kitchen one evening, and kicked the dishwasher's door right off its hinges. I was stunned and too shocked to say anything, which was probably a good thing. All my careful savings were gone in a moment. Even the children were silent. The repairs took care of the rest of my savings, and I decided not to save anymore. What was the point? Everything in the house was fair game for Des' unbridled temper.

His car was a different story. He was proud of his Mercedes, and I had to make sure the children kept their feet off the seats and didn't eat candy or drink anything in the car. It always had to be immaculate, and of course, it was.

Christmas came around again, and as usual, it was unpleasant. Like my stepfather, Des seemed intent on ruining my birthdays and Christmases, and this one was to be no exception. The children had decorated the six-foot tree, which stood in the living room in front of the fireplace. Most of their decorations were homemade and they had spent hours making them.

The children were up early that Christmas morning, eager to see what Father Christmas had left under the tree. They always left cookies and a cold drink or milk for him on Christmas Eve, and content to see the refreshments were gone, they sat waiting in great anticipation for Des to join us so that they could open their presents. He was painfully slow, and my heart ached for them, knowing how frustrating it was for them to wait. When he eventually came, the children eagerly tore open the gift wrapping, throwing it to one side as they did so. Des was given his presents, chosen so carefully by me and the children. Why could he not try to look pleased? I could feel the tension mounting in the room, and I knew that he was stewing about something. The children hardly had time to look at their presents, when he exploded. "Clean up this bloody mess. Look at it! Anne, get the vacuum cleaner. Larry, throw the papers away! Justine, Craig, tidy up this bloody mess! Doreen, why can't you control the children?"

I begged Des to let the children enjoy their gifts. Justine was crying. She and Anne wanted to save the gift cards and here they were being made to throw them away, along with the giftwrap. Intervening was hopeless. For whatever reason, Des was in a foul mood, and nobody was going to enjoy the day, because he couldn't! The children weren't able to clean up quickly enough for his liking, and before I could say or do anything, he stood up, picked up the Christmas tree and, holding it high above his head for a brief moment, threw it through the service hatch into the kitchen. The crash was accompanied by the tinkle of broken ornaments, and I felt as if my heart would break for the children. All their hard work, all the anticipation, all the joy was gone, destroyed in an instant. The children were all crying, and I asked Des if he was satisfied? He had ruined their Christmas! His response was to push me flying against the living room wall.

When I recovered, I ran out of the kitchen door and around to the back of the house, where I sat on the trashcan sobbing. I sat there for the longest time. Nobody came near me. The children didn't dare, and Des didn't care. Eventually, I got in my Minibus and drove down the street, turning onto the main road to Johannesburg. I drove aimlessly for quite a way, until, not knowing or caring where I went, I turned off onto a small dirt road leading into the open countryside. There, I stopped and sat quietly, wondering what to do.

I was a million miles away, when a face suddenly appeared at the window next to me, and a man was asking me if I was all right. I got a terrible fright, assured him that I was fine, and drove straight back home, as I really had nowhere else to go. Des sneered at me and said that he knew I would be back, and asked me where the hell I had been. I ignored him. The children had cleaned up the living room, and the Christmas tree lay discarded next to the trashcan. Christmas was over, but Des wasn't satisfied yet.

That night, Des told me that I could find somewhere else to sleep. He didn't want me in *his* bed. As we had no spare bed, I got into our bed anyway and begged him to let me sleep. I couldn't think when he yelled at me, and I was physically and emotionally drained. He ranted on for hours until, eventually, I could stand it no longer. I got up, took my mother's old feather eiderdown out of the closet and went to sleep on the couch in the living room. It was a small two-seater couch, which I knew was not going to allow me to sleep comfortably, but I had no choice.

I took the precaution of locking the living room door and was attempting to sleep when the kitchen light was turned on and I saw Des standing at the service hatch. He was drinking a glass of milk and asked me if I was comfortable. The triumphant look on his face should have been a warning, but I didn't heed it. I quietly said that I was, thank you. He grinned and then deftly threw his glass of milk at me. His aim was good, and it covered me, the eiderdown, the couch and the new carpet. I never would have suspected that one glass of milk could cause so much havoc. He then laughed and asked me if I was still comfortable and went back to bed. I spent most of the night cleaning up the mess.

In January of the following year, the children were attending three different schools and delivering and picking them up kept me busy, along with my housework. We sold the spec house to the renters, and with the money, Des turned the double garage into a new living room, which enabled us to turn the existing living room into a dining room. He then had a new double garage built next to the old one. He also invested some of the money in diamonds and emeralds for the girls and me, which was generous of him, but sadly, we never had the pleasure of wearing them.

The tension caused by Des' unreasonable behavior regarding the children's punishment, led to a lot of frustration and anger, which the children then vented on one another. There was a lot of sibling rivalry between the children, which was understandable, and I'm sure that none of them felt they received enough love and attention. I loved them all dearly, but I was constantly trying to survive, while protecting them from Des and one another. At the same time, I had to run the house while taking care of their many needs, so I am sure they must have felt neglected.

Our parental example of how to live was completely abnormal. Des kept me short of money and sleep, which made me tired and irritable much of the time. I was constantly worried about the finances, and all this was more than I could manage without any support. Because our home life was so dysfunctional, the children demanded more than I had to give. I wanted to make things right and always believed that, eventually, I would be able to, but this remained a foolish dream while the children were growing up.

Always terrified of the children making Des angry, I tried to manage their discipline. This led me to administer a great deal more punishment to the children than I wanted to. They always had to be clean, neat and tidy for their father, as did I. Things were much more relaxed when Des was away, but when he was in town, order had to be maintained. I dispensed discipline with my hand or a wooden spoon. Wooden spoons were used to stir the pap, the porridge made from corn meal, so we called them pap spoons, and they were plentiful in South Africa. Because they were flimsy, they didn't last too long in the Jacobs household. But I'm sure the children found them preferable to Des' sjambok. He had long since replaced seelkunde with a sjambok, and it left terrible marks on the children.

We were always on show, and when we went out, I had to make sure the children all looked perfect. Inevitably, Des got dressed and then went to sit in the car, blowing the horn impatiently, until we joined him. He then wanted to know why we were always late, never offering to help get the children ready or to lock up the house.

The house also had to be perfect, but nothing I did was ever good enough for Des. The children and I were trophies to be exhibited as a measure of his success. Although I no longer had to defend and protect my mother, I now had four children to protect and it wasn't easy. He expected the children to do well at school, but instead of encouraging them, he threatened them or told them that they were never going to amount to anything. He could never compliment them when they did well. He expected their best and their best was never good enough. His controlling nature was probably driven by the fear and anxiety of being seen as a failure in the eyes of those around him. As a consequence, he had much to lose, so his discipline was harsh, and he had many rules that had to be strictly obeyed.

It was Des' habit to whistle for the children, after which they were given a few seconds to respond and appear before him. If they took longer than he deemed necessary, they were punished. Sometimes, he did this as a test, which caused the children a lot of frustration. As long as they obeyed their father, I was the one who bore the brunt of his wrath.

Our arguments were mostly confined to the bedroom, where Des always locked the door before he beat me. Standing outside the door, the children begged him to let me go. He reassured them that everything was perfectly alright, that he and I were just talking and that they should go and play. They were not always reassured, especially when I emerged battered and bruised. Larry wanted to please his father, so he mostly kept quiet, but the girls often tried to intervene and paid a heavy price for it. Craig was still too small to understand and usually stayed out of the way. He learned early on that keeping out of the way was his best method of coping.

I seemed to spend my life saying I was sorry or begging Des not to hurt me. As a result, I had very little self-respect. I still had no identity, and was constantly accused of trying to be like one of my friends. Maybe Des was right in that regard. Because I didn't know who I was, I tried to emulate one of my friends, anyone else other than me. I was living on the edge, frightened, stressed and clinging to my sanity. He was trying to push me over the edge, while I was determined not to let him.

Being in the car with Des was always nerve-racking. He was forever chasing people in order to instruct or assist them with their driving techniques. If a car followed too closely behind him, he slammed on his brakes to give them a fright, even with his family in the car. That none of them ever ran into us was nothing short of a miracle. To Des' great satisfaction, the other driver inevitably got such a fright, that they then maintained a safe distance.

Once, out on the highway, a car dared to overtake and cut in front of us. Des always drove fast and hated for anyone to pass him at any time, and since he was a rally driver, he decided to teach the man a lesson. Seat belts were not yet in use, and with the children screaming, he sped after the car, and when he was alongside it, he proceeded to edge closer and closer to the offending driver, until my side mirror briefly touched his. The car swerved off the road in a cloud of dust, and Des proudly bragged to us that he had shown that fool who was the better driver. We drove the rest of the way in stunned silence.

I didn't often stand up to Des; the results were too painful. But occasionally, I did. One day, he lost his temper while standing in the kitchen holding a bowl of hot soup in his hands. He threw it up in the air, and it crashed to the floor, splashing soup everywhere as the bowl shattered. I don't know what came over me at that moment. I was also holding a bowl of soup, and I found myself calmly saying, "Oh, that looks like fun!"

I then threw my bowl into the air, and, not surprisingly, achieved the same result. Of course, this was a foolish idea. He grabbed me by my hair and pulled me all over the kitchen, screaming at me that I was totally crazy. I found it bizarre that it was okay for him to do things like that, but when I did it, I was accused of being crazy.

Des had a beautiful physique, and he was proud of his body. He worked out regularly at a gym in Pretoria. The owner of the gym, who was at one time Mr. South Africa, told Des that he had a perfect body and could also have been Mr. South Africa, had he trained and entered the competition. Des then set up his own gym in our garage at home, where he worked out either before or after work. This resulted in Des constantly flexing his muscles, while bragging that he was a 'body man.' Never relaxing for a moment, he strutted rather than walked and appeared to be self-consciously preening himself. It occurred to me that he should have used the strength he built up in his muscles in a boxing ring, or at some useful labor, rather than on his wife and children.

One of the many things about me that irritated Des was the click in my jaw when I chewed. I don't remember exactly when it started, but it drove him crazy. He remarked on it constantly, and I became self-conscious about it. While we were eating, he often stared at me with a look of disgust on his face. I tried everything to prevent it happening. I even tried chewing on my front teeth, but nothing helped. Des, in the meantime, developed a habit of clenching his teeth, whereupon a tiny muscle pulsated in his temple, and this was always a sure sign of his displeasure. When I saw it start up, I often lost my appetite, particularly if I felt my clicking jaw was the cause of it.

The children's table manners were carefully scrutinized and challenged. Des spent mealtimes dissecting their behavior, and anyone who was not conducting themself in what he considered a proper manner, was reprimanded, and then we were given an exaggerated demonstration of the misdemeanor to emphasize his displeasure. The clatter of knives and forks was demonstrated with great gusto, and it was fortunate our plates were sturdy, or they wouldn't have been able to withstand the onslaught. Chewing with the mouth even slightly open ensured a display of this evil, with a mouth full of food. This inevitably led to at least one of the children giggling, which made him so angry that they were sent to their room without food, to await further punishment. Elbows on the table was another crime. He demonstrated this with such force, I am surprised he didn't hurt his elbows. The children were told to chew their food twenty-seven times before swallowing, and he constantly screamed at one of them, "Chew your food!"

Mealtimes were not something we looked forward to in our house. If Des asked the children what they had done that day, they could never please him with their response. On a few occasions, he overturned the table full of food because one of us dared to defend ourselves against some accusation we felt was unfair. We eventually learned to keep quiet, so most of our meals were conducted in silence. At least, the children and I were silent.

The children suffered under their father's discipline. When he sent them to their rooms, he made them wait until he considered the time was right for them to receive their punishment. Sometimes, he made them wait for an hour or more, by which time the child was in a high state of anxiety. If I dared to question his methods, or the harshness of his punishment, his fury then turned towards me, and sometimes it made it even harder for the child.

GUN SHOTS

Late one evening, we were discussing the children, and I disagreed with something Des had said about the way we should raise them. It always had to be Des' way. He was excessively strict, and he was stifling them. I begged him to give them more freedom, and he told me that if he listened to me, the girls were sure to turn into whores and sluts and the boys into hippies. When I tried to reason with him, he hit me, and I broke down crying.

He then screamed at me that he had no option but to kill me. He said that I didn't deserve to live, and the Sunday paper headlines would read how he had shot and killed his wife and four children, and then himself. He was beside himself with rage, and nothing I said helped; in fact, I don't believe he even heard me. Then suddenly he told me to get out! He never wanted to see me again. He pushed me out of the front door and slammed it in my face. His change of tactics caught me totally off guard, and I didn't know how to react.

I scarcely remember walking through Bronberrik to the main road, and by the time I got there, it was nearly midnight. I saw a car's headlights approaching and was about to stop the car, but having no idea who it might be, I turned around and hid in the bushes at the side of the road.

Slowly, I retraced my steps until I was outside my neighbor's house, where I sat down on the curb. Not knowing what to do, and out of sheer hopelessness, I allowed my tears to flow. I don't think I had sat there more than half an hour when I heard four gunshots shatter the stillness of the night. They came from our house, and for a moment, I was paralyzed with fear. Terrified of what I might find, I could hardly move, but somehow, I managed to stumble across the road. As I reached the front door, it flew open, and Des stood there with his revolver in his hand, laughing at me. "I thought that would bring you back," was all he said.

I don't recall going to bed that night, or anything else for that matter, but I do remember waking in the morning and wishing that I hadn't. I was terrified of my husband, frightened for myself and even more frightened for my children.

Des loved the power guns gave him, and he liked using them. One evening, our neighbor, who was in the army, had a break-in, and he was chasing the thief with an assault rifle. Des was quick to grab his shotgun and join in the chase. They chased the man for quite a while, until he managed to escape.

On another occasion, late one afternoon, the children and I were waiting for Des to arrive home for dinner, when we heard his car skidding into the driveway. Next thing, he came running into the house shouting, "Where's my gun? Where's my gun?"

I told him I had no idea where he had put it. He was always hiding them in different places. By this time, he had a revolver, a gas pistol, a shotgun and the Webley. He locked the front door and ran to our bedroom. Almost immediately, another car screamed into our driveway. Des came back with his revolver just as two men ran towards the front door. Before they could reach it, he shot at them through an open window. I clung to his arm, trying to stop him firing again. He pushed me roughly away and told me to stay out of it.

The men quickly retreated and got back into their car. They then drove to our neighbor's house across the street, and seeing this, Des ran to Larry's room and demanded his cap gun. Larry had a small cap gun that looked and sounded just like a real gun. Bewildered, I followed Des into our bedroom and watched him take a match and rub the match head on the cap gun where the caps were normally placed. I couldn't imagine why he did that, but I was soon to find out.

Very shortly, the police arrived, and two officers entered the house. They questioned Des and asked him why he had fired at the men who had pursued him. Des gave them a quizzical look and laughed. Sneering, he showed the officers the cap gun and declared that that was the weapon he had fired. "If you don't believe me, smell it!" he declared triumphantly. One of them did so, and found it highly amusing that Des had tricked the men into believing he had used a real gun. My clever husband had lied to the police, persuading them that he had fired the cap gun out the window. The police left, but not before Des had convinced them that he was a law-abiding citizen and had only been trying to prevent those men from exceeding the speed limit on the highway. I could only imagine how he had done that. So convincing was his report, that shortly afterwards, he became a police reservist.

Not long after the incident, the children and I were leaving for a short trip to Durban when Craig ran into the house, telling me that I had to come and see the cat. "What cat?" I asked. The girls pulled me out onto the porch to see the cause of their excitement. There on the wall sat a beautiful fluffy ginger cat. I have always loved cats, but this one was special. We all descended on the cat, and completely unafraid, it didn't attempt to move. Craig begged, "Can we keep her, Mom? Can we keep her? Please, Mom, please."

I told him that we definitely couldn't keep the cat, as we were going away for a week. The children were disappointed, as was I, but when we arrived home a week later, we found the ginger cat sitting on the front porch, waiting for us. The children went wild with delight.

Because the cat was so pretty, we all assumed she was a female, and when one of the children turned on the radio, the popular song, 'Tammy,' was playing, and that became her name. One of the first things she did was to jump into the children's bathtub and urinate over the drain outlet. At first, I was horrified, thinking about the odor that might result from such behavior, but I had to agree with Des, who was obviously impressed, and said that he thought that the cat was very smart. We concluded that Tammy must have lived in an apartment, and the previous owner had trained her this way. I discouraged the habit and Tammy quickly learned to go outside. We later discovered that Tammy was a male, but by then, we were used to calling him by that name, so it stuck, and he became a welcome addition to our family.

Des never trusted anyone and often accused me of having an affair, and I suppose it was because he himself was not trustworthy. One evening, I went to the convenience store to buy some bread and milk, and as I drove down the street, I saw lights turn the corner and continue down the street behind me. I had a feeling it was Des. When I arrived at the store, out of the corner of my eye, I saw him park under the trees on the other side of the street. I made my purchases and put them in the car. I reversed and made as if to drive home, but then rapidly changed direction and drove right up to Des' car with my headlights on bright. I got out of my car and asked him why he was following me. He was furious and looked at me with such hatred that I was afraid that he was going to get out of his car and strangle me right there in the middle of the road. I had humiliated him! He drove off at high speed, and I went home. He returned late that night, and I paid a heavy price for what I had done. I felt bad. It had not been the right thing to do, and I regretted my actions in more ways than one.

It was around this time that Des and I had another strong disagreement. We happened to be standing in the dining room, when I dared to offer my opinion in what I felt was a reasonable manner. He didn't agree, and a side plate on the table provided him with instant ammunition. He threw it at me with such force that when it hit my shin, it cut into the bone and left me with a lasting reminder of his fiery temper. When he saw what he'd done, he attempted to come to me to assess the damage. The children were all standing behind me at the time, except Larry, who was standing behind his father. Larry pushed past Des and joined the other three children, telling his father to leave me alone and not to touch me. This was unusual, since Larry didn't readily stand up for me. At fifteen, he was at an age when he needed his father's approval. He felt a loyalty to Des, which I had always encouraged.

In spite of everything, I always tried to teach the children that they should love and respect their father, simply because he was their father. Des looked astounded at seeing the children rallying around me. It was not something he was used to dealing with, and he made it obvious that he didn't like it.

One thing I appreciated about Des was that he was a good provider when it came to a home and cars, but I discovered later that by telling the children what a good father and provider he was, to encourage their love and respect for him, it was to backfire on me. They compared Des to their friends' fathers, and what they saw didn't tally with my explanation. I reasoned that if I could encourage the children to respect their father, then surely, he would love and respect them in return. I didn't want them to become estranged, and Des was quick to write people off. If he could estrange himself from his own mother, which he had done years earlier, then I could easily imagine him doing the same with the children.

Following some exceptionally heavy rains, many of the roads around the city were flooded, which led to a catastrophe for Des. Late one afternoon, he went to drop Larry off at a friend's house, and his route took him under a railway bridge, where the road dipped steeply, and on his way there, he noticed that there was quite a lot of rainwater in the dip. While chatting to the boy's parents, the storm intensified, and Des had to stay and wait it out. By the time it had passed, it was dark and returning by the same route, he noticed that there was more water in the underpass, but sure he could make it through, he drove on, much to the amusement of a couple of young boys sitting on the wall, obviously aware of what was about to happen. Des' car died midway through the underpass in muddy water up to the windows. Climbing out through the window, he walked to a nearby house to call for help getting the car towed. His new Toyota was not yet a month old, and he was dressed in a white safari suit. His company car was ruined, as was his suit.

I now believe that my continuing to treat Des with love and respect was seen by him as a sign of weakness, and his contempt for me grew. I went to great pains to make myself look pretty for him, especially when we were going out. He usually looked me up and down and told me that my petticoat was showing, that my hair was sticking up at the back, or that he didn't approve of my dress. He could never give me a compliment.

If I asked him how his day had been, his reply was invariably that he couldn't discuss it with me, since I was too stupid to understand. At other times, he accused me of showing no interest in his job or anything that he did. Either way, I couldn't win.

One of Des' colleagues was a man he highly respected. There were not many people that he considered worthy of his respect, and it was good to hear Des speak well of this kind, gentle man. Doug was a happily married man with two daughters.

Being a responsible family man, Doug went to his general practitioner for an annual check-up, and the doctor remarked on a large mole on his upper arm, saying it could easily be removed. Doug was in his fifties at the time, and he protested that he had lived with the mole all his life and that it hadn't ever bothered him. However, the doctor persuaded him that a simple procedure was all that was needed to remove it. Sadly, upon removing the mole, the doctor discovered that it was malignant, and the cancer rapidly spread to Doug's brain, leaving him with only six weeks to live.

Des suggested that we drive over to Johannesburg to say our goodbyes and during the visit, Doug and I were left alone in the living room for a short while. As was my habit, I sat with my hands clenched together in my lap. When Doug asked me show him my hands, I immediately tucked them beneath my arms. I had always considered my hands, like my feet, to be ugly. He walked over to me and took my hands in his, and his next words changed my attitude about them forever.

He said, "Doreen, you have beautiful, hardworking, capable hands. With hands like yours, I would trust you with my life. Promise me, you will never hide them again. He gave me such confidence that I never did hide them again.

When we returned home, Des went into Larry's bedroom and closed the door, and I heard him sobbing. It was only the third time I ever heard Des cry.

PROBLEMS

When Mum and Dick returned to Pretoria for a visit, they came to stay with us. When they drove up in their Autovilla, they parked on the lawn before coming in and announcing their arrival. I was at the kitchen sink washing dishes, when suddenly, I was grabbed around the waist from behind and held tightly. Much too tightly! Not knowing who it was, my instincts kicked in, and my elbow jabbed Dick sharply in the ribs. Turning scarlet, he abruptly let me go. When I saw it was Dick, I didn't apologize. I was uncomfortable, and by not apologizing, I wanted to ensure that it never happened again. I am not sure if my instincts were correct, but he treated me with a great deal more respect after that.

Shortly after their arrival, I heard Des and Mum shouting at each other. I was in the kitchen preparing food, but I couldn't help hearing Des calling my mother a whore. He told her he knew all about her shipboard romance. She retorted that she knew all about his affairs. It was dreadful! Neither of them seemed to know or care that the children were standing there, listening to every word.

Naturally, this only stressed their already strained relationship. I think Des had long ago suspected that Mum was the one who told me he was having an affair while I was in the maternity hospital. As a result, they left and didn't visit us again for a very long time.

After they left, Des attempted to discredit Mum and Dick in the children's eyes. He told them that they were not married and were living in sin. Anne retorted that they already knew and that it didn't make any difference. She told him that her grandmother stood to lose her pension and medical insurance if she remarried, and anyway, after fourteen years, they automatically became married under common law. I am sure that helped Mum feel better, but I know that she was never completely accepting of the arrangement. She referred to herself as Dick's wife, but all her legal documents proved that she was still Mrs. Paul Welman. Many years later, the pension laws changed, but Dick never told her. For reasons of his own, it suited him to keep things as they were.

The few visits we made to Witbank were usually unpleasant. The farm was much improved, but it was never good enough for Des. I was always tense when we went to visit his family, and our arrival did nothing to make me feel more relaxed. Des drove extremely fast on the gravel road leading to the farm, and at the last moment, he pulled on his handbrake, sliding in, narrowly missing the curved stone entry walls in the process. This was meant to impress us, but the children and I always held our breath, waiting for the crash that never came. He was a good rally driver.

Most of the arguments in Witbank were about the state of the farm. Often, Des left in a huff, vowing never to return. On one of these occasions, we stayed away for months, and I had to beg him to return. I reminded him that his parents were still the children's grandparents, and it wasn't fair to deprive them in the same way that I had been deprived. He eventually relented, and when we returned, his mother ran out of the house, eager to greet us and cried while she held him in her arms. He stood in front of her, stiff and unresponsive. I quietly walked up behind him, took his arms and placed them around his mother. She was hurting, and I knew how she felt. He later reprimanded me, but I felt it had been the right thing to do.

It was about this time that Des had applied for, and was accepted as, a police reservist. He used this authority to enforce the law whenever the opportunity presented itself. If someone was speeding, he took it upon himself to chase them until he was able to force them off the road. He then proudly produced his identity card while informing the offender that he was a police reservist and that he could have him arrested. It became even more terrifying to accompany him in the car. With no safety belts, we were at his mercy. Truck drivers who weren't driving in the slow lane or who failed to come to a complete stop at a stop sign or traffic light were confronted and harassed, and many black drivers were slapped or punched if they dared to question his authority.

One day, the children and I were on our way downtown, when we stopped at a traffic light, and the children excitedly shouted, "Mama, there's Dadda!" They opened their windows and shouted, "Hello, Dadda!"

Des was driving a red sports car, accompanied by two young women. I was stunned. Who were those women, and where did he get that car? I was about to ask him when he sped off, cutting across in front of me, and up into a side road. Caught off guard, it took me only a moment to recover enough to put my foot down and follow him. He zigzagged in and out of side roads with me in hot pursuit until, eventually, we were up on the scenic drive overlooking Pretoria. He was a good driver, but he had taught me well, and I managed to keep up with him, until he suddenly disappeared. A small side street led to a look-out point with a panoramic view of Pretoria. I slowly drove in and found him with his arm around one of the women, while smiling back at the other. He obviously thought he had outsmarted me, but there I was! I got out of the car, determined to confront him, but he was not prepared for that.

In a cloud of dust and stones, he sped off, and I was compelled to give up the chase.

After finishing my business in town, we drove home. That evening when I asked him whose car he was driving and who were those two young women, he asked me what I was talking about, saying that now, he was *sure* I was crazy. I told him that I was not, and that the children had also seen him. He shook his head and walked away. I never learned who the car belonged to. Maybe one of the women, maybe Des, but with him being so devious, I would never know.

Des ate out often, telling me that they were business lunches. I had no idea if this was true, or if he was entertaining one of his girlfriends. One of those lunches led to serious consequences when he ate steak tartare. He later suffered severe abdominal pain, and a visit to our doctor revealed that he had a tapeworm. The prescribed medication to kill the tapeworm produced terrible side effects. Seeing Des writhing in agony on the bathroom floor, bathed in perspiration and gray in the face, was a terrible sight. He loved to eat exotic foods, but he learned a harsh lesson that day.

THE TUMBLEWEED TAVERN

Early in 1978, Des decided to open a restaurant in Lyttelton. I have no idea what prompted him to do so. He hired a manager to run it, while he kept his job as sales manager for the pharmaceutical company. He was always full of grand ideas but this one surprised even me. When I asked him where he was going to get the capital, I was told that it was none of my business. I had no idea how much money we had in the bank, but I knew that little of his salary was going into housekeeping. Des used our entire savings, along with the proceeds of the sale of the Mercedes, the diamonds, and the emeralds he had bought for the girls and me, and became a restaurateur.

Renting premises above a bank in Lyttelton, he called the restaurant, The Tumbleweed Tavern, but because the majority of the people in Pretoria were Afrikaans, it became known as *Die Tolbos Taverne*. That was quickly shortened by everyone to *Die Tolbos*, or The Tolbos. It took a few months to get the restaurant up and running and it was the beginning of June before we were in a position to open for business. Des employed one of our neighbors as his manager, and handed the running of the restaurant entirely over to him, which turned out to be a big mistake. Kells gave us the impression that everything was going well, when it really wasn't.

We were to find out the grim truth when, early one morning at the end of September, the doorbell rang. Des opened the door, and his manager entered with an armful of mail. He looked extremely uncomfortable as he laid the mail on the dining room table, and told us that there was no money to pay the bills. Des looked at him in amazement. Trusting Kells completely, he had not been checking the books, so he was totally unaware of the financial status of the restaurant. The mail consisted of final demands as well as several summons from the various companies who supplied the food for The Tolbos. where Des had opened accounts.

Kells had been regularly ordering supplies, but apparently, he had not paid any of the companies since the restaurant had opened four months previously. Des stared at Kells for a few moments, seemingly lost for words, then holding his breath; his face became so red, I feared that he was going to have a heart attack. The tiny muscle at his temple was dancing up and down at a terrific pace as he picked up one final demand and summons after the other, looking at each one in disbelief. The anger in Des' eyes grew when he looked at Kells, and I was sure that he was about to hit him. Instead, he picked up one of our oak dining room chairs and slammed it down on the floor with such force that it split in two. Then, through clenched teeth, he told Kells to get out quickly, because the next thing he was about to break would be his neck!

Kells was a big man, overweight and generally slow to move, but he was out of the house and down the street as fast as his legs could carry him. Des went through the check stubs and discovered that Kells had been paying his house mortgage, utility bills, his son's private school tuition and many other private accounts with Tolbos checks. He later learned that Kells often flashed a thick roll of bank notes, telling people he was making a fortune with *his* restaurant! Ironically, Des had offered him shares in the business, but only after he had earned them.

I felt sick! Everything we owned was invested in the restaurant. We had sold all there was to sell except our house. Would we have to sell that too?

Almost instantly, Des had what he considered to be the perfect solution. He calmly turned to me and said, "Jakes, you will have to go in and run the restaurant!" Flabbergasted, I told him he must be joking. I hadn't worked in seventeen years, and I had no idea how to run a restaurant, but I should have known better than to protest.

The very next day, I was a restaurateur!

As a result, I had to employ a full-time housekeeper to take care of the house and cook for the children. The first woman who came to the house looking for work got the job. Her name was Flora, and she was an older woman. Remembering dear Gogo, I thought she would be ideal, but Flora was nothing like Gogo. She wasn't clean in her appearance, didn't clean the house well, sniffed snuff all day long, and the children hated her cooking. But at the time, I had no choice but to leave my home and children in her care. As for Des, it suddenly became very convenient for us to have a fulltime servant but, at the same time, he made sure that he ate most of his meals at the restaurant, where he also worked in the evenings and on weekends.

The day after Des fired our manager, he went to a lawyer and obtained a lien on Kells' house, which he held for as long as we had the restaurant. This prevented Kells from selling it, which seems to have been his intention, judging by the 'for sale' board that appeared outside their house on the same day that he brought us the overdue bills. Holding the lien gave Des a great deal of satisfaction. I wanted him out of our lives, but Des was bent on revenge.

Leaving the children to go and work in The Tolbos was one of the hardest things I have ever done. By that time, Larry was sixteen, Anne, fifteen, Justine, eleven, and Craig, almost eight. They had never been left in anyone else's care before. None of them had even been to nursery school. Des and I had always planned on sending them to boarding school when they reached high school age, but when the time came, I couldn't bear to let them go.

When I left the children to go to work in the restaurant, there was no Mama to get them off to school or make their sandwiches. No Mama to drive them around in the afternoons. No Mama to play referee when they were having sibling fights. No Mama to cook for them or help them with their homework projects, and no Mama to hold them tight, when they needed a hug. Without my supervision, problems arose when I was at work and on one or two occasions, I had to lock up the restaurant and drive home in the afternoon to sort them out.

Transport for the children was not a big problem because Justine and Craig were able to catch the bus to school, and Anne could take another bus to the high school. Larry had a motorbike, so his transport was also taken care of. But they were used to me being there for them all the time and I couldn't imagine how they could possibly manage without me. I didn't want to leave my children, and I certainly didn't want to run a restaurant. In fact, I wasn't even sure that I could. When I said as much to Des, he told me, "Of course you can do it. Run the restaurant the way you run the house, and everything will be fine." He couldn't bring himself to say that I might be good at it, but then, I never really expected him to.

After not having worked outside the home for so many years, I lacked the confidence I needed. To make matters worse, a few days before I began work at The Tolbos, I was standing in the kitchen holding Tammy in my arms, when, at that moment, Craig came running in with Danny close on his heels, and Tammy got a fright. He twisted around in my arms, and stuck his claws in my face. One claw penetrated a vein just below my eye, resulting in a black eye that rivalled many of those which I had received from different sources, but this one was really bad timing.

The first day I went to work, I found myself ill-prepared to be a restauranteur, having few clothes that were suitable, and my hair was in dire need of a permanent. That first morning, Des drove behind me, and after unlocking the restaurant and showing me how to work the cash register, he left me to work things out on my own. I had no idea at the time that the restaurant was about to take over my life for almost three years. During the first year, I worked mostly part-time during the day, and Des took over in the evenings. We both had to work on the weekends, when the restaurant was at its busiest.

Having eaten at The Tolbos a few times, I had already met the staff. We had employed two male chefs, a helper, one waiter, as well as two women who made the salads and cleaned the restaurant. I promised them that although I knew nothing about running a restaurant, I was going to do my best, and that they should feel free to come to me with any problems they might have. I am sure they all wondered about my black eye, but I didn't feel led to explain to them how I had come by it. The customers who came in at lunchtime were another matter. I had only three tables that first day. It was a Monday, when few restaurants were open. Ours was, because we needed to build up a clientele. I had a fairly large group of men from the Lyttelton City Council and another large group from a local engineering company, plus a young couple, all who were to become regular customers. The men teased me outrageously about my black eye and my embarrassment is the thing I remember most about my first day.

Out of necessity, my practical housewifery kicked into high gear. The morning was spent supervising the cleaning and preparation for lunch. The staff knew by that time what was expected of them on a Monday, and everything went smoothly. That afternoon, I called the companies who were threatening to sue us for nonpayment; wanting to get that unpleasant task over with as soon as possible. I knew that for Des to ask for their help would be too humiliating for him, so it was left up to me to do it. I explained what had happened, and asked for a few months' grace to pay off the debts. The alternative was bankruptcy, where no one would get anything. Surprisingly, all our creditors were kind enough to agree. It was a challenge, and I surprised myself by being up to it. The debts were enormous, but as neither Des, nor I, were taking salaries, it was doable.

I worked hard at building the business, learning everything as I went along, and within four months, we were completely out of debt. The business flourished, and I became a person in my own right, not just Des' wife or the children's mother. Without realizing it, and despite my misgivings, I gained self-confidence and became a successful restaurateur. Des often bragged about how he had saved the restaurant, but I knew that it was I who had saved it, along with our investment, and although he never admitted it, I believe he knew it too.

My days were busy, arriving at the restaurant at nine in the mornings. The women arrived soon after and did the cleaning before preparing the salads for the salad bar. The chefs and waiter arrived at eleven and prepared for lunch, which generally lasted from noon until about three o'clock. The staff then went off for a couple of hours while I cashed up the lunch takings and placed the food orders on the telephone. Des usually came in and took over at about six o'clock, and I was then able to go home.

I handled my emotions well for a few months, but working seven days a week was exhausting. Constantly living with artificial lighting felt like an endless night, and I found it depressing. I longed for the sunlight and blue skies that I knew to be just outside the confinement of the restaurant walls.

Missing my children more each day, I was delighted when one day, while I was cashing up, the door opened and in walked a six-year-old schoolgirl with a book satchel on her back. She walked up to me with a confident smile and asked me if she could please have a glass of water. I was surprised. We had a large cold drink dispenser, but she asked for water! I gave her a glass of water, and she drank thirstily. Her name was Suzanne, and this was to be the beginning of a friendship that is as sweet today as it was when we first met, and Suzanne became a regular visitor to the restaurant on her way home from school. Her mother worked as a realtor, and I later learned that Suzanne needed my friendship as much as I needed hers. She never stayed long, but she sometimes brought me candy, or danced for me, and I found myself looking forward to her visits. She was completely unspoiled, and when I offered her an ice-cream or cold drink, she more often than not asked for water instead, and I found that very refreshing.

A food critic from our local city newspaper, the Pretoria News, came to review The Tolbos. Her opinion was vitally important to the future of the restaurant. Her review was in the newspaper on October 13th, 1978, and it was a great one. It was Des' birthday, and he couldn't have wished for a better gift.

That review was all we needed, and from then on, the restaurant flourished. Soon, we had people coming in from all over Pretoria, and I could hardly keep up with the orders. The income doubled, then quadrupled. I became known as Mrs. Tolbos by the adults and Auntie Tolbos by the children. Many people came to me for advice, and I became a confidante to many of our customers.

Before opening the restaurant, Des applied for a wine and malt license and was told that it would take about six months for it to be granted. When it eventually came, I found that it helped boost our income tremendously. The mark-up on wine and beer is usually one hundred percent, so it made a big difference to our profit margin.

We were fortunate to find good staff, especially our chefs. Sam, a tall, surly man, was the number one chef. I think I only saw him smile his crooked smile once in all the years I worked with him. He was brilliant at cutting meat, never wasting a scrap, and his portions were always the perfect weight. Odd pieces of meat, left over from the main cuts, were used for shish kebabs. Sam made excellent Béarnaise sauce, and his crème Brule was fabulous. He was clever, never divulging any of his recipes, which ensured his job security. Holiday was our assistant chef, and by nature, he was the opposite of Sam. Short and friendly, he was always smiling. His easygoing nature ensured that he was able to work well with Sam. Johannes, the assistant cook, was a quiet young man. He cooked the French fries, battered onion rings and dispensed the various sauces that accompanied the steaks and fish.

We employed a few college students as waitresses over the weekends, but George and Moffat became our two permanent waiters. They were both excellent, and as a result, they received great tips. In the beginning, when we were not so busy, we allowed them to take it in turns to come in for lunch, making sure we had both of them serving in the evenings. If neither one turned up for work during the day, I had to take orders and serve the food, as well as being the cashier. Those were hectic days.

Great as the staff were, we had a serious problem with the men, caused by their use of marijuana, which affected their personalities as well as their job performance. Many times, Des found them unfit for work and losing his temper, he gave them a few slaps. I was horrified, but strangely, they appeared to respect him for it.

One Sunday morning, I was alone in the restaurant and the staff were late, which made me anxious, knowing I had a lot of bookings for lunch. When they eventually arrived, Sam was very drunk, and I guessed that he had been drinking and smoking heavily. It was not long before I heard angry voices, and entering the kitchen, I was horrified to see Sam wielding his butcher knife at Holiday. I talked to him, and managed to calm him down temporarily, but I didn't dare attempt to take the knife away from him. He went back to cutting the meat and I went to the telephone and called Des. He always arrived late on Sundays as it was his habit to first read the two newspapers from cover to cover. He arrived about twenty minutes later, just in time to prevent Sam from killing Holiday. Des was fearless, and he took the knife away from Sam, beating him so badly that he was unable to return to work for two days. Des grilled the steaks that day!

Once the business was well established, I noticed that we had very few customers at lunchtime on Mondays, so I suggested to Des that we use that time to give the restaurant a thorough weekly cleaning. A restaurant can get as greasy in one week as a kitchen in a residential house gets to be in a year. The kitchen was tiled from floor to ceiling and using an industrial cleaner once a week left it sparkling clean. I was proud to show the health inspector over the restaurant whenever he came on one of his regular visits.

When meat began to disappear, we knew that someone was stealing. Taking stock was a daily chore that was necessary to prevent theft, but it worked only in theory. I kept an eye on the staff, but I couldn't spend a lot of time in the kitchen when we had customers. I was needed at reception.

One morning, Johannes walked past my desk with a small trashcan in his hands. I asked him where he was going, and he told me he was taking it downstairs to empty it. When I asked him why he didn't simply empty it in the large trashcan in the kitchen, he mumbled something unintelligible and carried on walking. I waited until he was out of the door and then quietly followed him downstairs, where, upon seeing me, he appeared reluctant to empty the can. I took it from him, and found it contained several large packages of meat and frozen hamburger patties wrapped in foil. Disgusted and disappointed, I accompanied Johannes back upstairs, where I held a staff meeting. First, I told them that hiding food in the garbage could make them sick, and then I explained that stealing from us was not going to keep the restaurant profitable, and if it wasn't, they could find themselves unemployed. I asked them for their loyalty, telling them that if they were in need, they should come to me, and if it were possible, I would try to help them.

Des also caught them stealing. He was furious, but he didn't try to reason with them. He simply beat them. Then, he devised the perfect plan to enable him to watch them at any time without their knowledge. When he was alone in the restaurant, he drilled tiny peepholes in the wall between the bar and the kitchen. By placing his eye to the hole, he was able to watch them unobserved. He then commented on things they had done when they knew he wasn't in the kitchen, and they seemed to think he had supernatural powers. Because of their superstition, he was able to take advantage of their fears.

Stealing from the restaurant was one thing. Stealing from each other, I found unforgivable. We now had three women working from nine until five. Rachel and Emily made the salads and helped with the desserts. Along with a new woman, Johanna, they shared the cleaning of the restaurant.

Rachel came to me one day and tearfully explained that someone had stolen her purse with all her money. I asked her where she had put it, and she told me she had hidden it in a dark corner next to the salad bar. We checked all around to make sure it hadn't fallen on the floor, but it was nowhere to be found. I called the staff together and had them hunt for the missing purse. When we returned to the kitchen, the purse had still not materialized. I then locked the front door and told the staff, "We have one hour before lunchtime. If Rachel's purse is not returned by then, I will call the police and they can sort out the problem. No one is allowed to leave the restaurant and, in the meantime, I suggest that whoever stole the purse, return it." I went back to my desk, and miraculously, an hour later, Rachel came to me smiling broadly. Her purse had mysteriously re-appeared, with the money intact.

We discovered that customers also took things from the restaurant mainly to keep as souvenirs. Menus, wine glasses, spoons, even knives and forks, went missing all the time until eventually, we were compelled to buy the cheapest of everything. Des wanted to impress people that ours was a high-class restaurant, so this was a continual source of irritation for him. He conveniently forgot how often he had brought home similar items from other restaurants before he became a restaurateur himself. He once stole a long carving knife by sticking it up his sleeve, while being shown the kitchen of a friend's restaurant. He bragged about it, as if it was a huge joke, but it was no longer a joke when customers stole from The Tolbos.

Breakages were also costly and we had to regularly replace the dishes. When we first opened the restaurant, we bought beautiful pottery plates in a natural terracotta color. They were expensive but the staff were not careful with them, and they soon ended up chipped and cracked. As the health inspector also inspected the crockery, we eventually replaced them with durable white china plates.

The staff was generally reliable, but their transport was not. They had to come in from the townships outside the city and this meant two train rides or a taxi, which was more expensive. Their greatest problem was with their evening transport. The men worked from eleven until two and then from five until ten at night. If they worked late on the weekends, they risked missing the last train into the city, and then they had no way of getting home. Des solved the problem by purchasing a small pickup with a canopy on the back, with which to take them into town after work at night, thus saving them the train ride from Lyttelton into Pretoria, as well as allowing them to work late, if necessary. On rare occasions, if they missed the last train from the city, he took them to their homes in the township.

After being open for about six months, we became so busy that Des insisted that I work full-time. From then on, I worked from nine in the morning until eleven or twelve at night, six days a week and from nine until five on Sundays. The restaurant flourished, but I did not. I hardly saw the children, and I longed to be home with them. Some nights while driving home, I screamed out my frustration in the car where no one could hear me. What little I did see of the children found me tired and irritable, unable to give them the love and attention they all craved.

I was nervous driving home alone on the nights when Des didn't work. It was mostly during the weeknights when he went to the club. One night, as I left the restaurant around eleven o'clock, I noticed a car following me. No matter how many times I changed direction, the headlights remained in my rear-view mirror. The roads were deserted, and I wondered if I should turn around and head for the police station, but by this time, I was almost home, and the police station was far behind me. Why hadn't I turned around sooner? I arrived at the entrance to Bronberrik and hoped I could lose him in the maze of streets.

I turned in and kept twisting and turning as fast as I dared, but he stayed close behind me. I didn't want him to see where I lived, so I drove past our house. It was in darkness, which meant that Des was already asleep. I drove into a cul-de-sac, turned left and then quickly did a U-turn at the end of the road. Almost hitting the other car, I caught a glimpse of the driver's silhouette as he passed under the street light. I now had the advantage of being in familiar territory, so I turned off my car lights and raced down Pine Avenue, quickly turning left into our side street and left again into our driveway before my pursuer emerged from the cul-de-sac. Once there, I turned off the car's engine and crouched down with my heart racing until I saw the car drive slowly past. He was looking for me, but I was safe and just as I could never tell my parents of my unpleasant encounters when I was a young girl, I never told Des. He would have undoubtedly said I must have encouraged the man, whoever he was. I did, however, appreciate the driving skills he had taught me.

The pharmaceutical company discovered that Des was spending much of his time at the restaurant and neglecting his job, so he was asked to leave. It was a bit of a shock, but by then, we were making enough money to be able to manage without his salary, so we weren't unduly worried.

The only salary I ever received was a bowl of ice cream with hot chocolate sauce, which I enjoyed every day while I worked in the restaurant. Des made it a rule that the staff, including me, were only allowed to have either a small porterhouse steak, a shish kebab or a hamburger. I stuck to that rule, but finding time to eat was always a problem, and in spite of the ice cream, I stayed pretty thin while working at The Tolbos.

Des spent more time at the restaurant after he lost his job, but he wasn't there all the time, since he still had other interests, which he was not prepared to give up. We had a lot more in common, having the restaurant to talk about, and it was good to be able to have an intelligent conversation with my husband, without him belittling me. He was still unable to compliment me, or show me any more affection than he had previously, but I felt that he had to recognize that I was now a capable businesswoman. I received many compliments from the customers, but judging by the look of displeasure on his face, he didn't appreciate the attention I received. More than anything, I longed for just one compliment from Des.

I always made a point of walking around the restaurant once or twice during the evening to make sure the customers had everything they needed. Des did the same thing, but then he often sat down uninvited and I noticed the discomfort some customers seemed to feel at the intrusion on their privacy. People liked to share the evening with their friends or family, and didn't always appreciate the owner joining them. When I pointed this out to him, Des lost his temper. His ego was such that he couldn't believe there was anyone who didn't enjoy his company.

Another thing Des did that made me uncomfortable was to record conversations when he was out to 'get evidence.' He did this on a regular basis at The Tolbos, where he invited the suspect for a meal. He kept a tiny tape recorder in his pocket at all times and recorded people saying or doing things he considered to be wrong. In this way, he was always able to stay one step ahead of other people. He often used the information that he gathered on tape as ammunition against them, should they dare to become his enemy, and through the years, he made a great many enemies.

One day, Des was criticizing me for something he was sure I had done wrong, and I surprised myself by saying that if he could do a better job, he was welcome to try. It was midafternoon, and we were alone in the restaurant. Des glared at me, and the telltale muscle in his forehead jumped up and down. I had not seen him this angry in a while, and warning bells rang in my head, but I didn't listen! I told him that he was ungrateful. I also told him that I wanted to be at home with our children, and this led to one of the worst disagreements we had ever had.

After a few moments of stony silence, I said that since I wasn't paid a salary, I was not sure if I had to give him notice, but that tomorrow, I would not be back at the restaurant, and he should find a replacement.

That afternoon, I received an exquisite arrangement of flowers. The accompanying card read:

Jakes,

I am sorry for all the nasty things I have said to you. I really don't mean what I say; I am just a miserable man. I don't like fighting with you, and it's also eating up our little ones.

We have both gone through some tough times these last two years, and not talking about it made it worse. So let's talk like adults and not fight like kids – we have a great deal to live for and to be grateful about. Together, we can make it even better. Forgive me!

I love you, Des XX

I kept the card, along with the few others he had sent to me over the years. It meant so much to read the words "forgive me" and "I love you." And so, of course, I stayed. Confessing that he was miserable, gave me hope that perhaps he was ready to get the help that he needed. I felt a compassion and love for Des that I didn't quite understand myself. That day, I caught a glimpse of a hurting little boy trapped deep within that proud exterior, and I longed to be able to help him. If only I could be sure, he meant what he said in the card. It occurred to me that he just needed me to run the restaurant, and would say anything that he thought would prevent me from leaving, but I pushed the thought aside.

Because I was not at home, Des became obsessed about Larry taking care of Anne. Larry didn't want the responsibility and resented having to take care of his sister. Anne was sixteen, and I thought she was old enough to start dating, but her father disagreed. If a young boy dared to come to the house to ask if he could take Anne out, he was interrogated about his parents, what they did, where they lived, and anything else Des felt was relevant to establish whether or not the boy's family was suitable. Inevitably, the young man stood there squirming, while looking at his shoes and more often than not, at the end of the interrogation, Des said just one word, "No!"

Anne, and later on, Justine, found this both humiliating and infuriating. Anne was pretty and popular with her peers, so she was invited to lots of parties. Des wanted a detailed report as to where she was going and who was going to be there. That would have been reasonable enough, but there were times when he drove to the house and spied on her, and at the slightest suspicion that something he didn't approve of was going on, he dragged her out of the party and took her home. Experiencing this in front of her friends was embarrassing for her, and despite my pleas, Des became totally unreasonable about her going out.

The Tolbos was now so busy that we had to rent additional space in the building for private parties. That was a big help on special occasions, particularly on Christmas Day, when we had a set menu. On busy days and weekends, especially when the staff let us down, Des allowed the children to help out. Larry had taken over my job of pouring Des' drinks at home, so it seemed only natural that his father would make him the barman. The girls became expert at waitressing and received many great tips. Craig, as young as he was, was just big enough to scrape the leftover food off the plates and stack them in the oversized dishwasher. They worked hard, and sometimes I felt bad about it, but at least we were all together.

Some of Des' friends from the city council, who frequented the restaurant at lunchtimes, came in the evenings as well. One of them brought a friend along with his son, and Des spent most of the evening sitting with them. Anne was serving tables that evening, and there was an immediate attraction between her and the man's son.

The boy owned a motorcycle, and he took Anne out on the back of his bike. When Des found out, he exploded and forbade her to ride on the back of any motorcycle. When the young man told his father, he took offense as he felt Des was implying that his son wasn't good enough for Anne. That might well have been the case, but Des was completely unreasonable when it came to Anne dating, and no one was good enough. We discovered later that Anne and the young man were meeting in secret at the home of a friend as well as at the home of the boy's uncle. I realized that just as my stepfather had influenced my life as a young girl, Des had forced Anne to become devious.

One Sunday morning, without our knowledge, Larry and Anne joined the father and son on a breakfast run to the Hartebeespoort Dam, a few miles from Pretoria. I later learned that the young man drove at speeds in excess of 100 mph with Anne on the back of his bike. He also visited Anne at our house one evening while we were at the restaurant.

When Des found out, he employed a private investigator to follow Anne, who caught her with the young man in town, bringing an abrupt end to their brief romance.

NIGHT CALLS

Our troubled lives were thrown into turmoil when we began receiving phone calls in the middle of the night. The phone rang on the hour, every hour, and when I answered, deep breathing was the only response. We had no idea who it was. I wanted to have our telephone number changed, but Des wouldn't hear of it. He was not going to be intimidated!

In those days, the phone remained engaged as long as either party kept the phone off the hook. This meant that the call was charged for, and the cost was high. Many nights, I lay the phone off the cradle after answering, which gave me the satisfaction of knowing that the caller was paying for the extended call and couldn't call again. Those nighttime calls were to continue until we moved.

The stress caused by the phone calls wore me down, but gradually, because they happened with such regularity, I was not surprised, and I often lay awake waiting for the phone to ring. However, I was totally unprepared for my first and only unpleasant experience with a customer at the restaurant.

A local pharmacist came in regularly at lunchtimes. He usually brought a client with him and often remarked on how impressed he was with the high standard of the food and service. One day, he came in with his wife and son, and they sat at the back of the restaurant at his favorite table. Their food was served, and a short while later, I heard the woman's high-pitched voice raised in anger. At first, I assumed that they were having a domestic dispute, but after a few minutes, I became concerned that whatever the problem was, they were upsetting my other customers, so I walked over to their table.

I asked the woman if there was something wrong, and she replied, "Yes, just look at the food! I cannot eat that!"

I looked down at her plate. She had a fillet steak, a baked potato, onion rings and the usual plate decoration of a lettuce leaf with a slice of tomato. I could see nothing wrong with the food, and puzzled, I asked her, "What seems to be the problem?"

She shouted at me, while pointing at her fillet, "That! I asked for a rare fillet."

I politely pointed out to her that since she hadn't yet cut the fillet, I wondered how she could tell that it wasn't rare. She then exploded, saying that she could see it wasn't rare. I offered to bring her another steak, but that only made things worse. She said she didn't have time for us to prepare another steak, because her child would be late for his horse-riding lesson. The fact that her child went horse riding was, no doubt, meant to impress me. I apologized and told her that their meal was on the house. She immediately retorted, "Well, I wouldn't dream of paying for anything so disgusting!"

The situation didn't make any sense. The pharmacist had been coming in for lunch for months now, and he had always been satisfied. I glanced at his plate, as well as that of their son and noticed that they had both eaten all their food, including the decoration.

I apologized again, and, with my cheeks burning, returned to my desk. Almost immediately, the family came to reception. The pharmacist looked highly embarrassed, the son uncomfortable, but the woman was not yet finished. She almost spat out the words, "I am going to tell all my friends how disgusting this restaurant is, and I will make you sorry."

I quietly replied, somewhat undiplomatically, "Thank you, Madam, but we have many satisfied customers, so we don't actually need you or your friends."

She took a step back as if I had slapped her and shouted at the top of her voice, "I come from Waterkloof!" Another apparent attempt to impress me with her address in an affluent neighborhood.

I replied with just one word, "Shame!"

The pharmacist and his family had barely left, when the men from the engineering company surrounded my desk and told me not to let the woman upset me. I was close to tears and they insisted that when my other customers left, I should join them for a glass of wine. I am not sure who was the most upset by the woman's behavior, the men from the engineering company or me!

The woman's plate of food was set aside in the kitchen, and I told the staff that I would investigate it later after all the customers had left. When I cut the untouched fillet open, I shuddered as I watched the blood ooze out on to the plate. It was indeed rare! Sam cut it through butterfly style, grilled it to perfection, and I ate exceptionally well that day.

When I told Des about it, he said that he had helped the husband set up his pharmacy business, and they got on well, but when he met his wife, he found her to be a thoroughly unpleasant woman.

The following week, the pharmacist came to the restaurant to apologize, and I did my best to make him feel at ease. However, after having been so horribly embarrassed, he never returned. His wife was my only unpleasant customer, and I couldn't help but feel sorry for her.

Assuming that living in Waterkloof made her superior to other people told me that she didn't enjoy a very satisfying life.

Not surprisingly, Des quickly tired of working at the restaurant, and he employed another manager to work in the evenings and weekends. He reveled in the status of being a restaurateur and liked socializing with the customers, but hated the responsibility of running the place. Besides, being tied down interfered with his own social life. The restaurant could afford it by this time, so I went back to working part-time during the week and fulltime on the weekends. After a year of working full-time, it was good to be home in the evenings again.

Eli, a gentleman with a smooth tongue and a charming manner, became our manager. It turned out that he was experienced in more than just running a restaurant, and it wasn't too long before we received complaints from the customers about that extra bottle of wine that had been 'accidentally' added to their bill. I was furious as I felt this reflected poorly on us, as the owners. Des spoke to him about it, but he convinced Des that it was easy to make mistakes when we were busy, so Des gave him the benefit of the doubt.

The final straw came when I received a beautiful arrangement of flowers from Eli for Mother's Day. At the time, I was touched by his kind gesture. This was the third Mother's Day I had spent at The Tolbos, so I knew to expect large crowds of people. We filled the restaurant more than twice over and had one of our busiest days ever. Until we owned the restaurant, I had no idea that so many people ate out on Mother's Day as we never did. On that first Mother's Day, I had been completely unprepared, and we ran out of meat, fish and baked potatoes, forcing me to turn away many of our customers. I learned well from that experience and never made the same mistake again.

After Eli left that day, I cashed up. It was after five and I was tired, but I never left the restaurant without cashing up, making sure that I balanced the income with the orders. It was my habit to add the meal slips in my head and then check them on the calculator, to make sure they were correct. That way, I kept my brain sharp and double-checked everything. I worked out my own bookkeeping system with an income and expenditure book as well as a petty cash box with its own cashbook. That day, when I checked the petty cash book, I found an entry written by Eli for one arrangement of flowers for Mrs. Jacobs. The business had paid for my flowers! The audacity of the man! When I told Des, he fired him.

Des employed another couple of managers, neither of whom worked out satisfactorily, and we discovered through experience that the only way to run a restaurant was to do it yourself. Customers enjoy the personal attention of the restauranteur, which is essential to the growth of the business.

We had had the restaurant for more than two and a half years, when Des told me that we needed to move to a larger house in a more affluent neighborhood. He always maintained that a person's address was important, and if it was a good one, it could open many doors in the business community. I also felt that we needed a larger house, but for a different reason. Justine and Craig were sharing their tiny bedroom and as Justine was now thirteen, her need for privacy was long overdue.

For more than two years, the hateful phone calls had continued to plague us on a regular basis whenever I forgot to take the phone off the hook. It was a game and the player calling never tired of it. I couldn't wait to move, knowing that it would be a while before our new phone number would be listed in the telephone directory, so the caller wouldn't be able to torment us anymore. Surely, by the time our number was listed, the caller would have tired of the game.

Aside from the phone calls, I longed to have a normal family life with Des and the children. I missed being outside during the day. There is no substitute for sunlight and I was constantly tired. One Sunday, just before we moved from Bronberrik, I returned home from The Tolbos around five o'clock. The first thing I did was to take off my shoes and walk barefoot on the lawn. Feeling the sun on my body and the grass beneath my feet was quite wonderful.

DES' DREAM HOUSE

I went house hunting in the eastern suburbs of Pretoria. I knew the house needed to be very grand to satisfy Des' taste, so I told the realtor more or less what we were looking for. She showed me a few houses, and I liked many of them, but knowing Des, I knew none of them would be acceptable. But when the realtor showed me an elegant two-story house on an acre of land in Lynnwood, I knew it was the one. It had magnificent Jacaranda trees well placed in the front yard. Overlooking a park, it had five bedrooms and three bathrooms. With a large swimming pool, a three-car garage, and servant's quarters, it was bound to be perfect for my husband. Lynnwood was one of the nicest neighborhoods in Pretoria, and the schools were among the best in the country, and I told the realtor before we even walked inside that she could show Des the other three possibilities, but this was the one he would buy. She gave me a quizzical look, but soon discovered that I was right.

The house was originally built by a prominent politician, and it had what Des considered to be the perfect address. That, of course, made it imperative that Des own it. The limestone and sandstone had been transported to Pretoria from the Lowveld area, and the beautifully cut stone added a stunning elegance to the house.

It was both big and grand, but for me, it was just a house, never a home. We bought it at the end of 1980, and it became officially ours one month later. The previous owners had to look for another house, so we had to be patient for a couple of months before taking possession. Shortly after the papers were signed, the owners changed their minds about selling, but Des was adamant. It was now his house!

Des' dream house in Pretoria, South Africa

For the first few weeks of January, I drove the three younger children over to Lynnwood every day from Bronberrik, since the school year had begun and they needed to attend their new schools. Justine and Craig loved their new school and settled in quickly. I was concerned about moving Anne for her last year in high school, but I needn't have been. When I picked her up at the end of her first day, her face glowed. She ran to the car and jumped in, declaring that the spirit at this school was fantastic, and she loved it. It was wonderful to see her enthusiasm. From then on, she did well at school, in both academics and sports.

Des had always been adamant that Larry was to study dentistry, while I was just as adamant that he should study graphic design. It took many heated discussions to convince Des that he should let Larry follow his own dream, and although he was sure that our son would turn out to be a hippy, he finally relented. Larry had his own apartment at the opposite end of the house from the other children, which was perfect because this allowed him to study in relative privacy.

Anne's large room downstairs enabled her to pursue her hobbies. In addition to sewing, she excelled in many arts and crafts, as well as photography. She went on to pass her finals at the end of the year and made us proud, after which she became a typist and went to work in the city.

My two older children were showing promise in ways that I had been unable to, and it gave me great satisfaction to observe that, in spite of everything, they were growing up to be productive human beings.

Justine shared one year with Anne in high school, and because the school had such a good reputation, Des was expecting great results from the girls. Like her father, Justine was a born leader and organizer and this caused her to clash with her teachers as well as the headmaster on several occasions. As a teenager, she was a tomboy, fearless, as well as accident-prone. I was constantly taking her to the doctor for stitches or patching her up at home. With her strong personality, she grew up knowing exactly what she wanted out of life.

Craig loved his primary school. He was also artistically talented, but it was in his love of mechanics and animals that he excelled. When he grew older, he could take anything apart and put it back together again. If he didn't have a spare part, he improvised and made one, and once, he even built himself a motorcycle from discarded parts of old motorcycles. Seeing him work with animals was pure joy. They trusted him completely and he appeared to have a sixth sense, understanding just what to do if one was hurt.

We also benefitted from having nice neighbors in the immediate neighborhood, some of who became good friends. One of my neighbors was active in the human rights movement stimulated by the Apartheid laws. When we got to know one another a little better, she asked me to join the Black Sash, a women's black rights group but I had to refuse. I knew if I got caught, that I could be arrested and then, who would take care of the children? If I didn't get caught and Des found out, I dreaded to think what his reaction might have been.

I found that the way the South African government dealt with the different races in the country was not something I could agree with. In its benevolent form, apartheid could be considered a way to allow the different cultures to live separately, without interference or influence from others, which could, in some ways, be considered a kindness. But in practice, it became a system for denying benefits to black people. And even worse, it reinforced an attitude of superiority and entitlement among the whites, which led to hostility.

It bothered me that the gulf between blacks and whites was so enormous during the apartheid years, and I questioned many things that I felt were unjust. The black people living in the rural areas built traditional mud huts with thatch roofs, and having lived that way for many years, I felt that they were content. But outside the cities where many of the black people lived to be close to work, the affordable housing the government built in the townships, was never sufficient. Those who couldn't afford them, or were ineligible for one, had to build their own homes with whatever materials they could find. Many of their shacks were built with what they could salvage from the trash dumps outside the cities. Also in the informally developed shanty towns areas, they had no sewers and no access to electricity or running water.

The relief I felt when apartheid was finally abolished was enormous, but that was still many years in the future, and there was little I could do to change the situation. Although I tried to treat people in my employ fairly, my hands were tied in many ways by other people, not the least of whom was my husband.

The children never knew how difficult it was for me to live under the apartheid regime. Telling them would only have made it harder for them, particularly since so many of our friends felt the same way as their father. Des had the advantage of his dominating personality, so I had to rely on teaching them by example, which wasn't easy.

Now that the children were older, I knew they must be aware of how dysfunctional our family life was. Des was teaching them one set of values, while I was attempting to teach them quite another. Our values were competitive, but Des had the advantage of total authority and fear. He was a proud Afrikaner, full of distain and contempt towards any other race, particularly black people, who he considered to be inferior. It was a constant struggle for me, trying to teach the children that we are all created equal in the eyes of God and that to treat people of color badly was a sin, when their father was teaching them just the opposite.

Living in a large elegant house in a beautiful suburb of Pretoria should have been the ideal setting for a harmonious family life. The children had many friends, but none of these were a substitute for a home with parents who loved them and one another, and who were unafraid to show it. The atmosphere in the house wasn't always one of strife, but it wasn't normal either.

Lynnwood lots were large with well-manicured yards. The many shrubs and trees provided an ideal habitat for birds, and we were blessed to have an abundance of them in our yard. Bright yellow Weaver Birds nested in the thorn trees, and Hadeda Ibis were frequent visitors, landing daily in the bottom of the yard and browsing in the compost for grubs. Their cries of "Ha, ha, ha-deda," earned them the name, Hadeda.

Having colorful flowering trees and shrubs, and birds of many varieties helped to make my life a lot brighter.

One day, a large bird, who walked almost like a chicken, crossed the lawn and never having seen one before, I called excitedly for Des, who also had a fondness for birds. In his bird book, we were able to identify it as a Burchel's Coucal, a member of the cuckoo family. He became one of my favorite visitors, and his lovely liquid call, echoing gently through the house, often helped to soothe my frazzled nerves.

While we were still living in Bronberrik, Wolfie developed cancer in his mouth and after having it removed, the cancer spread, and the vet had to put him down. He was sadly missed by the whole family. Soon afterward, Des bought a Rottweiler from a neighbor who was breeding them. Bowser was the biggest pup of the litter, and at only six weeks, he could hold a tennis ball in his mouth. Not only that, he growled at Des, so that had to be the one for us. Wolfie was a good watchdog, but I was even more impressed with Bowser. He grew fast, and became the largest Rottweiler I have ever seen. Although he could be gentle, he was ferocious too, which Des encouraged, and no one dared to set foot on the property without our prior permission.

Bowser and Danny loved their new home. Never having had a secure yard for them in Bronberrik, I was relieved to discover that this backyard was totally enclosed with high walls on all sides, which could only be entered through iron gates on either side of the house. The dogs had access to the house through the dining room, but the door was usually kept closed. Bowser slept in the kitchen at night, while Danny had a cozy kennel on the back porch.

One evening, the dining room door was accidentally left open, while one of Des' friends was visiting, and Bowser, hearing a strange voice, came to investigate. Upon seeing him, the friend took Bowser's large head in both hands while exclaiming, "Oh, you have a Rottweiler. I love Rottweilers."

He almost lost his nose when Bowser snapped at him. The color drained from his face, and it took him quite a while to regain his composure. Des took Bowser by the collar and led him outside, after which he told the friend that he should never look a strange dog in the eye, because it makes them feel intimidated. I was uneasy about what had happened, but I knew instinctively that with Bowser around to protect me, I was always going to be safe.

Des continued to keep me short of housekeeping money, and trying to feed a family of six, four of whom were growing teenagers, was becoming increasingly problematic. He insisted that we have a hot meal every night, because, in spite of the warm Pretoria climate, Des considered cold meats and salads to be rabbit food. I had to keep the pantry locked to ensure that the food lasted the month, and it was a constant battle trying to keep leftovers in the refrigerator for the next day. The children were always hungry, and it was impossible to explain to them how we could live in a mansion of a house, drive a Mercedes Benz and yet, food was rationed. I always bought the largest chicken I could find, because I knew it had to feed six; seven, when we had a servant. Des ate a thigh, and the children took it in turns for the other thigh and the drumsticks, causing them to argue over who ate what, the last time we had chicken. I bought everything in bulk, which ensured they had enough meat, fruit and vegetables. Luxuries like dessert, soda pop, cakes, and candy were almost unheard of and had to be bought with the children's pocket money, which is probably why they all had such excellent teeth.

When we moved to Lynnwood, the phone calls stopped. As I had anticipated, we were not yet listed in the new telephone directory, and obviously not knowing our new address, the caller couldn't get our number if he called inquiries. It was a relief to be able to go to bed without expecting middle-of-the-night calls, but my reprieve was short-lived.

Des bought himself another almost-new Mercedes. He bought me a new Volkswagen Minibus, and an Autovilla camper for the family, which we planned to use for future holidays. He wanted the best of everything, and living in King's Highway, he developed a superior attitude that I found embarrassing, especially when displayed in front of visitors.

At the same time, Des grew even more critical of me, and I couldn't do anything right in his eyes. My clothes were never good enough. My hair never looked quite right. He even told me to stop shaving my legs and then told me that he found my hairy legs disgusting. I often wondered why he wanted to stay married to me. When I mentioned this to him, he said, "I dragged you out of the gutter and made you who you are. Without me, you would have been nothing."

It didn't make sense. If he had made me who I was, why wasn't I good enough? I had, after all, saved his business and all our assets. If I dared threaten to leave him, he sneered at me, telling me I was now second-hand goods, and no one else could possibly want me. He sometimes ignored me for weeks at a time, only asking for tea, or whatever else he might want. Once, when I asked him what I had done wrong and why he wouldn't speak to me, he screamed, "Who the hell do you think you are? Why do you always think it is something you have done or said?"

He was obviously telling me that I wasn't important enough to warrant being the cause of his bad mood, but by refusing to tell me what the problem was, I was left feeling extremely frustrated. I felt Des didn't really want me in his life, but, at the same time, he didn't want anyone else to have me either.

I employed a young woman to help me with the housework. The house was large, so I was glad to have her. After Flora, Johanna was like a breath of fresh air. We got on well, but she soon fell pregnant and only worked for us for about a year before leaving to have her baby.

It was Valentine's Day, 1981, when I finally spent my last day at The Tolbos. A Saturday, the restaurant was packed. I had worked long hours that day and was relieved to be leaving it for the last time. Des had sold the restaurant but he stayed on for a few more weeks until the new owner was in a position to take over.

CULPRIT IDENTIFIED

The last night Des worked at the restaurant, the man whose son Anne had dated in Bronberrik, turned up at the restaurant with Des' friends from the city council, and they drank a few beers together. How ironic that they should turn up on that last night.

Des should have suspected something was up when they followed him into town, where he dropped off the staff at the station. They then followed him home to Lynnwood.

It was late when I heard men's voices downstairs. I was in bed reading, and I got up and stood at the top of the stairs, not recognizing the voices; I assumed they were Des' friends from the club, so I went back to bed. When the voices got louder and sounded angry, I became curious and putting on my dressing gown, I again went to stand at the top of the stairs. The one voice was much louder than the rest, and I heard him calling Des ugly names and using foul language. He said that Des thought he was better than him, and I immediately guessed that it was the father of the young man who had taken Anne out. I heard a thud, and Des shouted, "Look what you have done to my new carpet. You rubbish! Get out of my house, you bloody b..."

I was sure that they were going to exchange blows, but unobserved, I watched the three men saunter out of the front door. Des followed them, and I followed Des, just in time to see him take his gun out of his waistband and fire at the car. He was aiming at the car's tires, and I ran after him, grabbing his arm in an attempt to stop him, but he pushed me away and fired again. I begged him to stop, but he wouldn't listen. The men reversed out of the driveway and drove off up the road at high speed.

Des had had too much to drink, he was angry and our new carpet had a large whiskey stain on it. We spent most of the night arguing. I couldn't understand how Des could possibly put his family at risk, fighting with three men, who were obviously dangerous, and I knew instinctively that things were about to get much worse!

I hated it that Des carried a gun with him, but he said it was imperative when taking the staff into the city, or out to their township. I knew that it was dangerous, especially so late at night, but I was worried that it could lead to trouble. Shooting at the car, he could have accidentally killed one of the men. For someone who was so calculating about everything, it was remarkable that he seemed unable to think ahead or consider the consequences of his own ruthless actions.

The next day, I expected the police to arrive at the house, wanting to investigate the shooting. When they didn't show up, I assumed it was because the men knew they were in the wrong. I did, however, notice a car driving slowly up and down the street. The driver was looking up at our house. I watched him do this three times and I instinctively knew that it was going to lead to more trouble.

My fears were not groundless. That night, the phone rang at 2 am. It was Mr. van Niekerk! The caller now had a name and a face, but almost two years would elapse before I was able to see his face up close. Des had made a formidable enemy. Someone who was just like himself!

As in Bronberrik, the telephone was on my side of the bed. I woke with a start when it rang, and with my heart beating wildly, I said, "Hello."

This time the phone call was different. As well as heavy breathing, I heard a deep, inebriated voice say, *"Ek wil met Des praat!"* "I want to speak to Des."

Des was awake, and he snatched the phone from me. I heard him say, "You sick b...... I don't want to speak to you. Yes, you are right, I am better than you. You are rubbish! f... off!"

He handed the phone to me and told me to put it back. Two seconds later, it rang again. This time, I placed the receiver on the floor. We were back in our old routine!

Because Mr. van Niekerk now knew where we lived, it was easy for him to call telephone inquiries, give them our name and address and ask for our telephone number. The late-night phone calls came regularly, and as in the past, on the hour, every hour if I replaced the receiver. The man didn't seem to need any sleep. Des told me that he owned a factory, and I came to the conclusion he must sleep all day while his employees worked.

Often, when Des was away and van Niekerk called early in the evening, I tried to appeal to his better nature. I begged him to stop calling us, and I told him that I was the one who usually answered the phone and that I needed my sleep. I told him I was sorry if Des had offended him, but that calling us was not going to solve anything. Naturally, it didn't help, and the calls kept coming.

In May, Des arranged for a photographer to come to the house to take family pictures. To look at them, you would have thought that we were the perfect happy family who had everything. The photographer had us pose in front of our house. He took others of us smiling in front of the flowering bougainvillea creeper. Our forced smiles hid a multitude of heartache and sorrow, and when I look at the photographs now, my only reaction is one of sadness for what should have been.

When Johanna left to have her baby, I was determined to look for an older woman, and dear, gentle Nellie came into our lives. Plump and homey, with a few missing teeth, she was perfect. However, after giving her a key to the back door, I found her in the house at six every morning, and there she remained, working until seven in the evening, which I found totally unacceptable. I had to re-train her because I couldn't allow her to work such long hours. I divided the house cleaning into three parts so that Nellie could rest in the afternoons, then return at five to help prepare the vegetables and wash the dishes.

Nellie occasionally brought her daughter, Lindy, to stay with her for a couple of weeks. She was adorable, and the children and I grew to love her. When she was about four, Nellie left Lindy alone in her room for a few minutes while she came into the house to get some cornmeal to make pap for her dinner. She usually made it in the house, but this particular day, since Lindy was there, she decided to make it in her room on a kerosene stove.

As Nellie reentered the room, Lindy jumped up and knocked the pot of boiling water off the stove, spilling it all over her chest and arms. Hearing her screams, I ran to the room and arrived as Nellie came out holding Lindy wrapped in a blanket. The little girl was writhing in agony, and when Nellie opened the blanket, I saw with horror, the extent of her burns. Where the skin had been rubbed off by the friction from the blanket, pink skin revealed that her black skin was only one layer thick. We took Lindy to hospital, where it took several weeks for her body to heal, and a great deal longer for the effects of the trauma to wear off.

Des employed a man by the name of Limba to work in the yard. Des liked him because he was very respectful. Once a year, Limba went away for a couple of months, and we discovered that he liked to go home and binge drink. When Limba reappeared, he was always thoroughly drunk, unshaven, unshorn and dirty. He then cleaned and sobered himself up, returned to work, and carried on as if nothing had happened. In the meantime, Des and Larry mowed the lawn, and Craig and I took care of the swimming pool. Because he was so reliable the rest of the year and such a hard worker, Des gave Limba a beating and a lecture and took him back.

To my amazement, Des started yet another business. He partitioned off a third of the three garage spaces, and turned the front portion into an office for himself, and the back became another servant's room for Limba. Des then became a broker for a large insurance company. He employed a man to make appointments for him and to answer the telephone. Hennie had a deep, distinctive speaking voice and was perfect for the job. He had had an accident when he was young that left him handicapped, making it difficult for him to walk. Des found his slow pace irritating, but he also recognized the value of this highly intelligent man.

As a result of Des' latest venture, a company telephone was installed in the office with an extension in the house. This turned out to be a perfect solution to our nightly phone call problem. The unwanted calls usually came after ten at night, so before we went to bed, I unplugged the house phone, and we then made use of the company extension, which was in the entrance hall. We only gave the company number to Des' clients and our children, and since the phone number was listed under the company name, van Niekerk had no way of knowing what it was. I found it reassuring to know that the children could call us late at night on the office phone if they were out and needed us.

When Des was out of town, the children and I made a game out of a serious situation. When the calls came before ten, we answered it in the craziest fashion. Maybe we were the local mental asylum or the hamburger joint or the pizzeria, anything but the Jacobs residence. But when Des was at home, it was always serious. He grabbed the phone from whoever had picked it up, and the feuding began. The threats were horrible. They wanted to kill one another, and they both did their best to outsmart, out-think, and out-hate the other.

If we forgot to unplug the house phone before going to bed, and it rang, Des always snatched the telephone from me, and I could hear van Niekerk's voice threatening to kill him. Des retaliated, as only Des could, by calling him vile names and daring him to make good on his threats.

When I couldn't take it anymore, I called the police. Their response was, "We can't do anything unless the threats are carried out."

It seemed that there had to be a dead body before the police could intervene. Having received the same unhelpful response when I was a child, my belief that there was no justice in the world was once again confirmed. The rest of that year, and the whole of the next, became a blur of telephone calls, threats, and counter-threats, an unfolding drama with no possibility of a good ending.

One Saturday morning, we awoke to find that Mr. van Niekerk had paid us a visit during the night. He released the air from the tires of every vehicle parked outside the garage. This included Larry's Datsun, Anne's Mini and our Autovilla. Des had recently purchased a large truck for a bargain, which he intended to sell at a profit. It stood under the trees at the side of the property, and all six tires were flat. As Des' Mercedes and my Minibus were in the garage, they were untouched, but we were unable to get past the other cars parked in the driveway, so Des took the bus into town and bought a compressor. Craig then had the job of inflating all the tires.

The inconvenience of what van Niekerk had done was annoying, but I was far more concerned about him being on the property without our knowing it. Bowser and Danny had not sounded the alarm, which made me feel vulnerable. Ironically, we had no security fence around the front of the property, as Des was adamant that we were not going to spoil the look of the house from the street.

Living under these conditions, Des eventually became so stressed that our family doctor advised him to go away for six weeks to rest. Surprisingly, Des listened to his advice and took the camper to a friend's farm outside Warmbaths, about seventy miles from Pretoria.

With Des away, we were able to relax. I kept the telephone calls under control as best I could, but one night, I forgot to unplug the phone in our bedroom, and it rang in the middle of the night. Of course, it was van Niekerk, and I again tried reasoning with him. I told him that Des was away and he was disturbing my sleep and he must please stop. I also told him that he was stressing the children, but it all fell on deaf ears. I discovered that it is impossible to reason with a man who is blind drunk at two in the morning, so I unplugged the house phone even earlier after that.

The children were completely different with their father away, as was I. We were relaxed, laughing and joking, and generally having fun. When Des was at home, any sense of humor was stifled in the miserable atmosphere of our home. Laughter was not allowed, as life was a serious business, and we had to treat it accordingly.

Three weeks after Des went to the farm, Larry, Anne, Craig, and I were sitting at the kitchen table chatting and laughing. Justine was downstairs in her room. Suddenly, the children stopped talking, and following their gaze, I found Des standing behind me. We were all stunned because he wasn't supposed to be home for another three weeks.

Feeling guilty because we were all laughing, I knew that Des had noticed our response, or the lack of it, at his unexpected arrival. I quickly jumped up and gave him a hug, but it was too late. He just looked at us all in disgust and said it was wonderful to see how glad we were to have him home again. I tried to convince him that we were only surprised, but the damage was done. He had seen our faces. He turned around and walked down to Justine's room, surprising her also by his sudden presence. Caught off guard, she asked him what he was doing at home, and he exploded! He said that we had all made it clear he was not welcome in his own home and hurt and angry, he stormed outside.

We hadn't heard his car or his footsteps, so I guess he must have turned off his car's engine when he drove in, and then crept in the house to surprise us. He couldn't possibly understand that our lack of enthusiasm for his early return was due to our freedom to be ourselves being so abruptly cut short. If he had only been able to enjoy being with us, we would have welcomed him home. I felt deeply sorry for my husband. He had everything, and yet, he had nothing.

Occasionally, Des did something pleasantly surprising. In early September, which was supposed to be the start of the South African spring, we had an unexpected cold snap. This resulted in a light snowfall in Johannesburg, which, although only 35 miles away, is over a thousand feet higher in elevation than Pretoria. Des was there that day at his company's head office, and when he got home, there were still remnants of snow on his car. The children had never seen snow before, so he drove them over to see it. They came home excited, and it was good to catch a glimpse of the Des that I was sure was hiding beneath the stern exterior that he usually presented to his family.

Des soon became bored with the insurance business, and he bought another restaurant. I begged him not to, but his mind was made up. The Paul Kruger restaurant was well situated for lunchtime traffic, since it was on a corner of Church Square, the central square in Pretoria. Des was sure he could make it attractive enough to entice customers back into the downtown in the evenings.

The restaurant was situated on the first floor of a large old stone building. All the inside walls were covered in the original wooden paneling, and antique-style lanterns hung over the tables, giving it an old

English pub atmosphere. It had a flight of stairs leading down to a basement, which was the perfect venue for a wine cellar and small private parties. I had to admit that it had great potential. The small side street offered adequate parking at night when the parking meters were no longer in operation. Des employed a manager to run the business, but I knew it wouldn't be long before he would insist that I run it, and I simply couldn't face the prospect of working again.

In the meantime, the telephone calls continued to dominate our lives, no matter how much I tried to ignore them.

ST. LUCIA

By the end of the year, we were all ready for a holiday, except for Larry, who didn't want to go with us. By that time, he was twenty years old and enjoying his growing independence. Des arranged for us to go camping at the St. Lucia estuary, situated along the Indian Ocean in Zululand, where there was good fishing. He borrowed a travel trailer from the restaurant manager, and we packed in everything we needed for what I hoped would be a relaxing family holiday.

The night before we were to leave, the telephone rang just after dinner. Des reached the phone ahead of me, and standing next to him, I heard a loud voice say in Afrikaans, "Des, you must enjoy your holiday because it will be your last. When you come home, I am going to kill you!"

The two men exchanged harsh words, and Des slammed the phone down. How did Mr. van Niekerk know we were going on holiday? Who was keeping him informed? Whoever it was, was incredibly cruel!

We left the house in the care of the manager of The Paul Kruger. Early the next morning, I gave a huge sigh of relief, knowing that being away from telephones for a few weeks, there was a chance that we could relax and enjoy our holiday.

Upon our arrival at St. Lucia's campgrounds, Des battled to get the trailer parked to his satisfaction. After driving back and forth several times, he disturbed the two young men who were taking an afternoon nap in the next camping spot. They were friendly, and offered to help Des situate the trailer and set up the side tent. I was a bit concerned, knowing Des' views on young men, considering that we had two teenage daughters. But they were courteous and helpful, and besides, Anne had a boyfriend back in Pretoria, and Justine was considered by Des too young to be dating anyway, so surely, I was worrying needlessly.

The girls went for a walk along the beach, while Des and I sorted things out in the side tent. It was not long before I found Des watching the girls through binoculars, and when he saw that the two young men had joined them, he flew into a rage. On their return, he lectured the girls and spoiled the holiday even before it had begun. The two young men were twenty-four-year-old engineers whom Des actually grew to like, especially when he found out that they both enjoyed rugby and beer. At the time, I hoped they wouldn't be too friendly with the girls, but ironically, one of them turned out to be Anne's future husband.

Craig took along his white mouse in his cage and was content to spend endless hours building elaborate castles and tunnels for his little friend. He still needed nothing or no one to make him happy.

The rest of the family spent most of their time fishing in the shallow water, and the fish were so plentiful that you could almost grab one with your bare hands – if you were quick enough. Everyone was pulling the fish out one after the other, and they made it look so easy, I decided to give it a try. I stood there with a fishing rod for a couple of hours, unable to land even a single fish, and after a pitying look from my husband, I gave up. After that, I spent most of the time taking long, relaxing walks along the beach.

The day that Des took us for a drive along the coast, the trip ended in a family feud, and we were all ordered out of the car, and told to make our way back to the trailer camp on foot. Des seemed unable to enjoy doing anything with his family.

John, one of the engineers, despite being teased by his friend, who said something about cradle robbing, made a big impression on Anne. And it seems she made an equally big impression on him, because when we returned to Pretoria, she broke off with her boyfriend, and she and John began dating regularly.

I dreaded going home with Mr. van Niekerk's threat still hanging over Des' head. A heavy sense of foreboding filled my mind, and when we arrived, it was as if van Niekerk knew our plans down to the last detail. The calls started again immediately, and we had to unplug the telephone earlier each evening. Des again refused to allow me to have the number changed. He was not going to give in to this man. Ironically, unplugging the house telephone gave us peace, but it only frustrated van Niekerk. When he got no response to his calls, it was to lead to tragic consequences.

Wednesday, January 26th, 1983, should have been the same as any other day, but it was destined to end in tragedy. Des took me to town to help him with the new restaurant. I had seen this coming, and I felt apprehensive. He had great ambitions for it, but I wanted nothing to do with it. I begged him to give it up, as it was no life for the children or me, but Des had never listened to me before, so why should he start now?

We were attending a Baptist church in Lyttelton at the time, and while Des and I were sitting in the restaurant after lunch, our pastor happened to walk past. Des ran out and asked him if he could spare us a few minutes. The pastor put some more coins in his parking meter and then joined us at the staff table.

Des questioned him about religious matters, and then his questions became personal. He told our pastor that I didn't want him to have this restaurant and asked for his opinion. The pastor said that since we were married, we were one flesh, and Des should not go against my wishes.

He added that we should always be in agreement, especially when it came to making important family decisions. Des immediately lost his temper, and, banging his fist on the table, said in a loud voice, "I demand to know if God wants me in this restaurant or not."

The pastor shook his head, and told Des he should not make demands of God. I found it frightening that Des didn't fear God. I believe that God must have heard Des' demands that day, because he was never able to set foot in the Paul Kruger restaurant again.

A SHOT IN THE NIGHT

That evening, Des went to visit some old friends with Anne and returned home around midnight in an exceptionally good mood. His friends had given him a couple of old wagon wheels, which he wanted to use as part of the décor in the restaurant. He had had a lot to drink, but because he wasn't sleeping well, he took a sleeping pill, even though I told him it wasn't a good idea after drinking so much alcohol. The house phone was off the hook, and I was hoping for a good night's sleep, although at that late hour, I knew that it would be short.

I was awakened just before 1 a.m. by a knock at the front door. My first thought was that I must be dreaming but no, there it was again. Des was in a deep sleep, so I put on my dressing gown and went downstairs. Sleepily, I turned the latch and opened the door, forgetting the safety chain was on. It jerked closed again, giving me a fright. Thinking that it must be either Limba or Nellie needing something, I took the chain off the hook and opened the door.

Suddenly, I was wide awake. A short, stocky man stood in front of me. Something in his hand glinted in the light of the full moon. Was it a gun? I could barely make out the man's face, but I knew instinctively that it was van Niekerk. When he spoke, the voice was unmistakable. *"Ek wil met Des praat!"* "I want to speak to Des!"

I had heard him say those same words so often on the telephone, but now I was hearing them while face-to-face with the man who had made our lives so miserable for so long.

In a state of panic, I closed the door, automatically locking it as I did so. Running upstairs, I shook Des awake. I told him that van Niekerk was downstairs, but in his state of heavy sedation, he maintained afterwards, that I said there was trouble downstairs. One hour after taking the sleeping pill, in addition to the alcohol which was still in his blood stream, he was in no position to handle any situation, let alone the one that faced him.

He staggered out of bed, and clad only in his boxer shorts, went downstairs and grabbed a *knobkerrie*, (a wooden Zulu club) out of the hallstand. Flinging open the door, he stood there totally fearless, facing his assailant, not comprehending the danger he was in. I heard the man say in Afrikaans, *"Vanaand gaan ek jou vrek skit!"* "Tonight, I am going to kill you!" But the words he used were derogatory, used only when referring to the slaughter of an animal, rather than a person.

Now I was sure that it was a gun I had seen in his hand! I ran back down the stairs and reached the front door at the same time as Justine, who had been awakened by the car lights shining into her bedroom. I arrived just in time to see Des chasing the man towards the driveway, wielding his knobkerrie, when I heard what I assumed were two gun shots. Des was trying to hit van Niekerk, and missing his target; it was the wooden club striking the concrete driveway that I heard. Muffled sounds followed, which turned out to be the knobkerrie hitting van Niekerk's head. The two men ran across the street, where van Niekerk encountered the fence surrounding the park. Trapped, he then turned around and shot Des at point-blank range. The intensity of the report left no doubt in my mind that, this time, it really was a gunshot, and in that split second, all our lives were changed forever!

I saw Des fall, and ran through the shrubbery, catching my dressing gown on some branches and, snatching it loose, I reached the street. Van Niekerk had already reversed his car out of the end of our driveway, and was speeding towards the body of my husband lying in the street. He was going to drive over him, and I screamed, "No! no! no!"

At the very last moment, he drove around Des' body and, narrowly missing me, sped off into the dark. In a matter of seconds, it was all over.

I ran to Des, who was lying on his back in the street with his head on the sloped concrete curb. He looked up at me, his eyes pleading for help. "Jakes, Jakes!" was all he said.

At first glance, it looked as if nothing was wrong, until I noticed a tiny bullet hole in his chest. Strangely, there was no blood flowing from it. The children came running from the house, and I wanted to stop them, but I was unable to move in order to protect them from the terrible scene that lay before them. My voice also failed me! Everything happened so fast, and when I looked up again, I saw Craig standing next to me, looking down at his father, his small face pale and confused. I told him to go back in the house. He shouldn't have seen this. None of them should!

Two young men who lived next door, having been woken by the commotion, came running towards us. They wanted to move Des out of the street, but finding my voice, I told them they mustn't move him, since he might be bleeding internally. He was, and unknowingly, I probably saved Des' life. He had extensive internal bleeding.

I then ran into the house intending to call the police, but I couldn't think clearly, and I found myself wildly pressing numbers on the keypad until Justine plugged in the telephone and dialed the emergency number. She handled the call, allowing me to return to Des. He wasn't making much sense, but his eyes again pleaded with me to help him.

Justine brought a blanket, and we made him as comfortable as possible until the ambulance arrived.

I was told to follow the ambulance across town to the general hospital. With the siren screaming, it was a nerve-wracking drive through the red lights and stop signs of the deserted city streets, with me slowing down just enough to maintain a safe distance behind the ambulance.

Once we reached the hospital, I felt as if all the blood had been drained from my body, and it was as much as I could do to remain standing. The hospital staff whisked Des away into surgery. Then, they wanted information. While I was still in a state of shock, Justine was able to supply most of the information needed to fill in the endless forms that were required. I knew there was not much chance of Des surviving, and I found myself praying. Praying for a second chance for my husband. Praying for him to come out of this a changed man, ready to love God and his family. I had no idea when I prayed those prayers what the outcome of the shooting was going to be, or how our lives would be permanently altered by that one bullet.

Anne told the police that Mr. van Niekerk had come to the house with a gun and shot her father. The police who were on the scene were informed over their radio that van Niekerk had driven to the police station and given himself up. Because she knew him, the police took Anne to identify him. She told me later that van Niekerk was bleeding profusely from head wounds inflicted by the wooden club. Defiant, even after surrendering, he sneered at her when she identified him. The next morning, I discovered his blood splattered on the driveway along with black skid marks, where he had reversed out at high speed.

The neurosurgeon, who operated on Des had won a scholarship from the pharmaceutical company that Des worked for, when he was still a student. Ironically, it was Des who had presented the check to him, so I am sure that when he saw who it was in the operating theater, he felt an extra obligation to do whatever he could to save his life. Apparently, when he opened Des' chest, he said simply, "This man is dead!"

Des' chest cavity was full of blood. The bullet's path had severed the two main arteries in and out of his heart. It then traveled through his gall bladder and spleen before lodging in his spine. Although the situation looked hopeless, the surgeon didn't give up. He worked on Des' shattered body, mending the broken parts, but it was to be several hours before we knew whether Des was to live or die. I took Justine home and returned to the hospital later the same morning. At the time, I was so distraught, that I found myself driving through red traffic lights and stopping at green ones. It was a miracle that I arrived safely.

I spent most of the next six weeks at the hospital. In the beginning, Des was in intensive care, full of tubes and unable to speak. It was a frightening sight, and I was reluctant for the children to see him like that. Eventually, he was able to write notes, most of which were questions or instructions regarding the restaurant. He told me to fire the manager and he then asked Anne, who had been waitressing at the Paul Kruger up until that time, to run it for him, which she did for a few months. Meanwhile, I was too preoccupied with visiting Des at the hospital twice a day to keep up with anything else, and I was grateful when, due to staff problems, we finally closed the doors for good.

The phone didn't stop ringing for a few weeks. Some people genuinely cared, and some, whom I hadn't heard from in years, were just naturally curious. We didn't have answering machines in those days, and I felt that each call had to be taken. I wrote down the messages of sympathy and encouragement, and along with the cards and letters we received, I took them to Des, but he showed little or no interest in them. At least we no longer received calls from van Niekerk, but I still found it difficult to sleep at night.

Three weeks after Des was shot, the same neurosurgeon operated on Des to remove the bullet from his spine. After the surgery, I met with him, and he told me that during the removal of the bullet, he discovered that Des' spinal cord had been damaged. He said he would live, but he would never walk again. I tried to absorb his words. My brain felt numb! My legs felt numb! I was standing in the hospital corridor, and even as the shock of his words sunk in, I wondered how I was able to remain standing on legs that I couldn't feel.

February 1st was Des' worst day. He developed yellow jaundice, and looked dreadfully ill, and when I went to visit him, I found it difficult to know what to say as he only wanted to talk about the restaurant, while I just wanted it to go away.

When a fly landed on Des' leg, he screamed with pain, telling me to get rid of it. I couldn't understand how a fly could cause him pain. He told me that the nerves in his spine had been severed by the bullet, but his brain still sent messages to his lower body, and even though they had nowhere to go, the pain was excruciating. This fact was disputed and argued about during his remaining years as a paraplegic. Some doctors said he had pain, while others said he imagined it, and I could never be sure who to believe. The confusion only served to make me more apprehensive.

The physical effects of the shooting were different for each one of us. My eczema, which hadn't bothered me since childhood, returned. Larry developed terrible food allergies. Anne also developed eczema. Justine couldn't tolerate darkness and woke up often during the night. Craig became quiet and withdrawn, and for a few weeks, he looked as if he had lockjaw.

The mental effects of the shooting were even more difficult to come to terms with. In addition to the trauma of the shooting, we still had to contend with the long-term effects of Des' years of abuse that had left us damaged and searching for the ability to find acceptance of ourselves, free from his defining and negative influence.

At first, the children were reluctant to visit Des in the hospital, but as his condition improved, I encouraged them to go. One evening, I asked Craig if he wanted to go with me, but he said he preferred to stay at home and watch television. Not wanting to leave him at home alone, I asked Limba to stay with him. Craig was twelve at the time and still had a passion for mice, and the white mouse he had at this time was the same one that had accompanied us on holiday to St. Lucia. Most of the time it lived on Craig's person. A small sausage-shaped lump was often visible as it traveled around beneath his T-shirt. Now and then, a tiny pink nose and whiskers peeked out from his chin or on his arm. The two were inseparable.

I went off to the hospital, leaving Craig with Limba in the TV room. Limba was reliable and trustworthy, and I knew that I could safely leave Craig in his care. He called Craig *Klein Baasie*, which means Little Boss. Weekends usually found Craig with Limba, helping him in the yard. Limba often pushed him around in the wheelbarrow with the dogs running behind, barking and yelping with delight.

When I returned from the hospital, I found Craig crying bitterly. Limba explained that the Klein Baasie was jumping up and down on the settee, while watching something exciting on television and had accidently sat down on his beloved mouse. Craig was heartbroken and it was as much as I could do to console him. I promised to take him to the pet store the next day to buy him another mouse. Craig, unlike the girls, hadn't cried since his father was shot. He needed to cry, and I was grateful that the loss of his precious mouse had finally made it possible.

After all those years of harassment, and now the shooting, I didn't know how to regard Mr. van Niekerk as a person. I felt that I should hate him for what he had done to Des, and to all of us as a family. And yet, I could feel only pity and compassion. I found this realization surprising, but I also felt guilty, knowing that Des would not have been pleased to learn of my feelings for the man who he felt had stolen his life.

About a month after the shooting, I looked around our home and saw it through the eyes of a paraplegic. Although it was Des' dream house, I knew that it could very well become his prison. There were stairs and level changes everywhere and it was obvious that it was not wheelchair friendly. We needed to move to a house that was on one level, where he had access to a yard. While knowing that he wouldn't give up the house without a fight, I was totally unprepared for his emphatic response. Up until that point, Des had been relatively subdued and I had hoped that maybe, as a result of the shooting, he had acquired a gentler perspective on life.

I was mistaken. The next day, while visiting him at the hospital I suggested that we sell the house, and that I should look for one all on one level. He exploded. "You will not sell my house! You bitch! It's *my* house, and I will *never* give it up!"

The ward went quiet, and all eyes turned on us. Des had what we called a monkey chain above his bed. He pulled himself up by the ring, and glowered at me with such hatred in his eyes, that I cringed with fear and embarrassment. A nurse came running in to see what all the shouting was about. We tried to calm Des, but eventually, she had to administer an injection to subdue him. I knew then that it was hopeless. He was determined to stay in the house, and it was to lead to a great deal of heartache.

Des had been in the hospital for six weeks when I brought him home and asked Limba to take him upstairs in the wheelchair. Des had a drainage tube in his gall bladder, which had to be cleaned daily. He had no control over his lower extremities, and the first thing he insisted on after arriving home, was that I administer an enema. He said that he hadn't had a bowel movement during his time in the hospital. I found that impossible to believe, but he was adamant, and since I had no idea what this entailed, I did as I was told. He lowered himself out of the wheelchair down onto the bathroom floor and instructed me to insert the enema. It was a total disaster, and we both ended up in tears. That was our traumatic homecoming.

Because Des then needed to take a bath, we discovered that he couldn't even get from his wheelchair into the bathtub. Once the bathroom door was opened, it blocked access to the tub, so I had Limba remove it. Des hated that. He didn't want any changes made to the house, but in that particular case, we had no option.

I knew that a small seat lift attached to the banister of the staircase leading up to our bedroom could have made our lives so much easier, but Des said it would look hideous, so it was ruled out.

There were fewer steps leading down to the children's bedrooms, so I suggested that it might be easier to move Des down there, but there wasn't enough room to turn the wheelchair at the bottom of the stairs. The house was not wheelchair accessible, and caring for Des, under those circumstances, became a constant struggle.

One of the few changes Des allowed, was to have a monkey chain installed over our bed. He didn't want it at first, because it required an iron angle installation fastened to the wall, which then protruded over the bed, from which the monkey chain and bar could hang. Des said it was ugly, but remembering how it had helped him to turn over and pull himself upright in the hospital, he eventually accepted it. Later, he learned to use it as a weapon against his family, and he used it often.

I had received no instructions from the hospital before taking Des home. They gave us a stock of catheters and a urine receptacle and told me that Des should catheterize himself every couple of hours. We were also given a stack of linen savers, which should have told me what to expect, but never having nursed anyone before, I was totally unprepared for what was going to be required of me in the years ahead.

Under normal circumstances, Des should have gone for rehabilitation at the Spinal Unit of the rehab hospital before being sent home, but it was full at the time. As a result, he became totally dependent on me to do everything for him that he should have been able to do for himself. I didn't realize that by helping him, I prevented him from having any kind of independence, and it also ensured that I would be tied to Des every minute of the day and night.

The neurosurgeon who had performed the operations came to visit Des at home about two months after the shooting, and told him that he still had two strong arms and a good brain. This would enable him to work and lead a full and productive life. But Des was in no mood to heed his advice then, or at any time in the future.

Following the surgeon's visit, we had an excellent physical therapist come to the house, and after a careful examination, she said that, with therapy, she was sure she could have Des walking again. True to her word, with the aid of calipers and crutches, she was able to get Des walking down the stairs, into the living room, through the dining room and kitchen, and up the stairs again. It took a long time, but for me, it was a miracle. With her quiet, determined manner, she handled Des easily. He actually seemed to want to please her and I was overjoyed with his progress. The surgeon had said that Des was never going to walk again, and here she was saying he could, and she even had him doing it!

Eventually, the therapist suggested that we drive to her practice in town, because she had machines there to strengthen Des' muscles. Getting Des down the stairs in the wheelchair was a challenge. He weighed 185 pounds before the shooting, and although he had lost some weight, in the old-fashioned chrome wheelchair, he was still very heavy. When Limba was available, it was fine, but he didn't work for us every day. Nellie was terrified of Des and frequently got shouted at when she tried to hold the wheelchair steady from the front, while I steered it up and down the stairs. At the time, I was confident that I was strong enough to be able to do this on a daily basis, but I was to suffer the consequences later. Outside were more steps leading down to the driveway. Then, we had to maneuver Des into our VW Golf, and we quickly learned the best way to do that. Lastly, I had to lift the wheelchair into the back of the Golf. Getting it in wasn't so bad, but lifting it out was difficult. It was heavy, and Des was quick to warn me not to scratch his car.

Driving Des to therapy was traumatic, as he said that each bump in the road caused him pain, and I was blamed for each one of them. He screamed at me for going over a hole or a bump, even when I couldn't avoid them, due to the heavy traffic. Once there, his therapist gave him exercises to strengthen his muscles, and then she had him walk out of her driveway and down to the corner of the street. It was painfully slow going, and Des remarked that Hennie now looked like a racehorse compared to him. Understandably, he was bitter. Hennie showed Des a lot of compassion, knowing and understanding better than most of the frustration Des was experiencing. Hennie kept up with the insurance company for a while, until refusing to participate in the running of it, Des finally had to let it go.

We received a stream of visitors when Des first came home, and this continued for about six weeks, but gradually, they stopped coming. Des greeted them cheerfully enough when they arrived, but he soon became miserable, complaining bitterly about his inability to walk normally, and telling them that he was in constant pain. People eventually grew weary of his company, no matter how much pity and compassion they may have felt, and finally, only a few old friends came to visit us now and again.

Not long after the shooting, Des agreed to see a clinical psychologist who was recommended by one of the many doctors who had attended Des in the hospital. The psychologist was a capable young man, wise beyond his years. He tried his best to help Des, but after just a few sessions, he called me and asked me to drop by without my husband. He then told me that Des had many problems, but mostly, his refusal to be helped made it impossible for him to find a way forward. He warned me that Des was dangerous, and that I should be careful. He said there was a strong possibility that, in his depressed state, he would take his own life, and possibly the lives of his family as well. His words didn't surprise me, but they were not what I had hoped to hear, and I was to receive similar advice on several other occasions in the future.

It was almost as if Des had had a premonition of what was to happen, because he had taken out a disability insurance policy about six months before the shooting. He invested the money from the policy in the stock market, and we lost quite a substantial amount. After that, he allowed me to take over the finances. I knew that from then on, we had to be careful as we were facing an uncertain future, so I invested all the remaining money in a building society. The interest was much lower, but it was a great deal safer.

That was when I took over our bank account, and going through the bank statements, I was horrified to see how much money Des had been spending on his girlfriends for restaurant meals, flowers, and gifts. It hadn't been my intention to dig up the past, which I found painful, so I destroyed the statements and tried to put it behind me. After all, Des was no longer in a position to continue his old lifestyle. He was now dependent on me, and maybe, at last, we could build a reasonably good life together. I looked at the last photograph I had of Des walking, taken as he was leaving the house. He walked proud and erect, and it was

Des one month before the shooting in January 1983

tragic to think that only one month later, he would be fighting for his life, and would be told that he would never walk again.

I still wasn't sure what the true status of Des' mobility was. The surgeon had said he was never going to walk again, but the therapist had him walking. She was convinced that he would be able to get around with crutches. Once, when my sister Sheila was visiting, she said she was certain that she saw Des looking out of the window when we returned home one evening, but Des denied it. Another time, we thought that someone was trying to steal Anne's Mini, and I caught Des standing on his knees on the bed, trying to see what was going on. He said he was hanging onto the monkey chain, but he was, nevertheless, standing on his knees. Both these incidents happened within months of the shooting, before he lost the strength in his legs, and while he was still having physical therapy. Losing the strength in his legs was one thing, but it was nothing compared to his losing the will to live!

If I thought Des was difficult to live with before the shooting, I was to learn that he would be far worse afterwards. He was angry, and blamed me for his condition. I should have made it clearer that it was van Niekerk at the front door that night, then, he wouldn't have gone outside. He also blamed Anne, saying that if she had not gone out with that rubbish young man, none of this would have happened. Anne and I both had to deal with the guilt of his accusations. Des hated the body that had once been something that he was so proud of, and was now full of scars. His torso was still muscular, even more so now that he was constantly pulling himself up with the monkey chain, but his lower body lost muscle tone, and his legs became terribly thin.

One morning, after taking his bath, he stopped in front of the full-length mirror next to his bed and, looking at his naked body he said, "Look at me! I look disgusting."

His expression was one of utter repugnance. I wanted to cry for him. I put my arms around him and told him that I loved him. He pushed me away and cried, "Don't lie! How could anyone love that?" pointing to his reflection.

I quietly told him, "The outside doesn't matter to me. It's the inside that I love."

He didn't believe me, or couldn't, and when I helped him into bed, I noticed his eyes were moist. How my heart ached for him. How could I reach him? How could I convince him that I loved him, and how could I ever persuade him to have hope for the future?

In July of 1983, Des was finally admitted to the Spinal Unit hospital for rehabilitation. It was long overdue. We had struggled for months, not knowing how best to cope with an impossible situation. I was in dire need of a break, so I decided to visit our friends in KwaZulu-Natal for a few days. Our neighbor, Corrie, understanding my need for a break, kindly offered to look after Justine and Craig.

With Des in the hospital, it seemed like the perfect opportunity for me to get away, but when I went to see him and told him of my plan to fly down to Durban, he exploded and told me that I was selfish and didn't care about him. I had been taking care of him for six months, not really knowing what I was doing, since I had never had any nursing experience. Now he was accusing me of being selfish.

I explained that I needed a break, but then he accused me of having an affair and called me a whore. I begged him not to talk like that. Some of the staff and other patients were staring at us. I told him that I was sorry he couldn't trust me, but I was going anyway. He screamed at me to "f*** off", and I left in a flood of tears.

I went ahead with my plans, and found that the few days away gave me renewed strength. I came home refreshed and ready to tackle the future.

Des was in the Spinal Unit for a couple of months, during which time they taught him to take care of his personal hygiene. They also taught him how to maneuver his wheelchair, even up and down small flights of stairs and also how to wheelie. But Des was clever, and he fooled the staff. Before being allowed to go home, he had to be able to sit in his wheelchair for a certain number of hours every day. He told me that he went to sit in his wheelchair shortly before the day staff went off duty, then when the night staff came, he told them that he had spent several hours in the chair. Des was good at deception, and it worked. When he came home, he refused to walk at all anymore, and as a result, he soon became a total paraplegic. The effort it took for him to walk with the calipers and crutches was just too much for him, and even the physical therapist could no longer motivate him.

All the instruction he had received at the Spinal Unit turned out to be a waste of time, and he demanded that I take care of him exactly as I had before he was admitted. If I refused, he screamed at me, telling me I was a fraud, and obviously didn't love him. Next moment, he pleaded with me and begged me to help him, preying on my sympathetic nature. With Des' multiple personalities, I was never sure who I was dealing with. He was a manipulator, and at the time, I was easily manipulated. I didn't have the strength to refuse him, partly out of love and pity, and partly out of fear.

THE COURT CASE

Nine months after the shooting, the first day of the court case happened to be on Des' birthday. Mr. van Niekerk had entered a plea of self-defense. That morning, our lawyer called to say that the case had been postponed until the following year. After preparing ourselves for the ordeal, we were all frustrated about the delay. Then, just after lunch, the lawyer called again, and said that Anne and I had to appear in court after all.

I was questioned intensively for about two hours. The lawyer for the defense repeated the same questions over and over again, using slightly different words but, nevertheless, basically asking me the same questions. I, in turn, kept giving him the same answers. I was calm, far calmer than I expected to be under the circumstances. Seeing the man who had shot Des, I was surprised to see that he was even shorter than I remembered. Van Niekerk sat expressionless, and I wondered what he was thinking. How does a person feel when they have shot someone, taken away their livelihood, ruined their life, and their capability to walk and enjoy life's everyday pleasures?

The defense lawyer was young, and spoke quickly, with a malicious edge to his voice. At some point, he asked me how I felt about Mr. van

Niekerk. Taken off guard by his sudden change of questioning, I had no time to think, but I replied honestly, "I feel sorry for him. It must be dreadful to know that you have shot another human being, and left him wheelchair-bound for the rest of his life."

I was told to address all my answers to the judge, a much older man, but I stole a quick glance at the lawyer when I had finished answering the question. He was sneering at me. He then reverted to his original line of questioning about the night of the shooting, and I continued to give the same answers, noting that his tone of voice was becoming increasingly agitated. This seemed to go on forever, until the judge intervened. He said sharply, "You have asked Mrs. Jacobs the same questions several times, and unless you have anything further that you wish to ask her, she may step down."

I was relieved! His interrogation was wearing me down and had it gone on for much longer, I might have doubted myself.

Then, it was Anne's turn. I was told to go outside and sit in the hallway, since the court didn't allow witnesses to hear one another's testimony. We had also been told not to discuss the night of the shooting at all before the court case. That suited me since I didn't want to relive that awful night.

After I had returned home from the hospital the night of the shooting, I was distraught, and I knew that I wouldn't be able to sleep, so I had spent the remaining hours of the early morning writing down an account of everything that had happened the previous evening, while it was still fresh in my mind. It was a peculiar thing to do, but it was a lesson I had been taught by Des' example, and it stood me in good stead. Reading it before I had to testify, ensured that I had everything clearly fixed in my mind, which made it reasonably easy for me to answer the questions in court.

Anne told me that van Niekerk's son shared Des' birthday, and that this was his twenty-first birthday, always a special event in the life of a young South African. I knew that their family was suffering, just as we were from the actions of the two fathers, and I felt sure that it must have been as terrible for them as it had been for us.

With the day's proceedings over, we were told that Des and the two girls would have to return to court at the end of the month to testify again. When they did, Des' story didn't coincide with mine. I wasn't surprised, since I was sure that the alcohol and sleeping pill had to have affected his memory. When the defense attorney told him that his story differed from mine, Des said, "Then you must believe my wife, because she doesn't lie!"

I found it amazing when Des said that, and it was good to know that, at least, he believed I was honest. On December 14th, we were back in court, and the case was remanded until February of the new year. I wanted it over, but learned that we would have to be patient.

On the last day of the trial, I was sitting in court, when a strange man walked in. He walked over to van Niekerk's defense attorney, and I heard him ask, "Can you tell me what is going on here. I am replacing the prosecutor." It turned out that the chief prosecutor had been called away for military service, and this man had no idea what was going on? I could scarcely believe what I was hearing. How could this man prosecute a case he knew nothing about?

As if that weren't bad enough, at the end of the day, I walked into the elevator. I was followed by the judge. When the doors closed, he said, "Mrs. Jacobs, I know you are not going to understand this, but Mr. van Niekerk is going to get off with his plea of self-defense."

I was flabbergasted. Partly because of what he said, and partly because it was he who was telling me. Before I could respond, we arrived on the first floor, where he politely said goodbye, and walked away. My worst fears were about to be realized, and once again, I had confirmation that there is no justice here on Earth.

So now I knew the outcome before it actually happened. I didn't have the heart to tell Des. The judge was clever. He knew that with only the two of us in the elevator, even if I went to my attorney, it would be his word against mine, and it didn't take a genius to know who would be believed.

There was something extremely peculiar about the whole case. A friend suggested that the judge, the prosecutor and the defendant were all members of *Die Broederbond* "The Brotherhood," a clandestine ethnic brotherhood organization in which the members supported one another in all circumstances. Proving such a suspicion was essentially impossible, but to me, it made sense.

Could van Niekerk actually get off with his plea of self-defense? He came to our house at 1 a.m. with a gun in his hand. He had threatened to kill Des on numerous occasions on the telephone, and this had been reported to the police. That very night, he had said that he was there for just that purpose. It should not have been possible, but it was about to happen anyway. Obviously, justice was not something to be relied upon, unless you had the right connections.

The court case was hard on Des' health. He was terribly depressed, and he stopped eating altogether. He feared his assailant was going to get off, and talked about it incessantly. Des wanted revenge!

In the mornings, when I greeted him and asked him how he felt, his response was always, "Today I want to die!"

It was his vicious tone of voice that scared me the most. No amount of coaxing him to do something constructive worked. I suggested art of some kind, or even woodcarving. He was extremely talented, and could have at least kept his hands and mind busy, but he simply wasn't interested. He just wanted to die. True to his word, he didn't eat anything for almost a month, which turned out to be the first of six suicide attempts. He did, however, drink rooibos tea, a South African herbal tea, which literally kept him alive. I took him a tray of food three times a day, every day, which he refused to eat. Then suddenly, and I have no idea why, he began to eat again.

I had to have Danny put down and I found it extremely difficult to do. He was getting old, and arthritis had set in, which caused him to whimper with pain whenever he moved. It was a tough decision to make, but it would have been cruel to keep him alive any longer. I took him to the vet and returned home alone, feeling very sad.

Bowser turned out to be a marvelous watchdog, and I always felt safe, knowing that he was sleeping in the kitchen. I placed a flimsy toddler's gate at the entrance to the kitchen at night, and told him to stay. He was highly intelligent and obedient. He could have easily knocked the gate over, or even jumped over it, but he never did. Since the kitchen was next to the front door, I knew that no one could have gotten past Bowser.

I am not sure when Des agreed to see a psychiatrist, or who recommended him, but I will never forget the day when he came to our house. He arrived in an immaculate black Porsche. His fees were exorbitant, but if he could help Des, I felt it would be well worth it. He spent an hour with Des, and leaving them alone to talk; I busied myself downstairs.

At the end of the session, I offered to see the gentleman out. He stood next to his Porsche, sat down in the driver's seat and removed his shoes, which he deposited in a sack. He then placed his stockinged feet on the pedals. The carpets in his car were white, as was the leather upholstery, and it was clear to me that they were not to be soiled. The man appeared to be in need of a psychiatrist himself, and when I went up to Des' room, he exclaimed, "That man is a nut!" I had to agree, and he was not asked to return.

On March 19th 1984, we heard the results of the court case. We had lost, but there was to be a settlement. Clearly, somebody felt that van Niekerk bore some responsibility, even with an acquittal. Even so, in spite of the judge's warning, I still found it unacceptable that van Niekerk was acquitted. After the trial, Des' depression worsened, and I knew it was because he felt completely devoid of hope.

LIFE AFTER JUDGMENT

With the promise of the court settlement, Des told me that he wanted to get another Mercedes Benz. This time he wanted a station wagon with hand controls, which would enable him to drive again. Although I knew it was expensive, I didn't have the heart to discourage him; he needed something to lift his spirits. To our surprise, we discovered that a car with hand controls was, for tax purposes, considered a necessity, and, like his wheelchair, a part of his mobility. This meant that he could order one directly from the factory in Germany without having to pay the dealer's commission or customs and import duty. This reduced the price substantially. We placed the order, and it gave him something to live for, albeit briefly.

When the steel blue station wagon arrived, Des was delighted with it, and it made a tremendous difference in my life. Lifting the wheelchair into the back of the station wagon was a great deal easier than lifting it in and out of the trunk of the Golf.

Des drove the car once, but then it would be almost eighteen months before he drove it again. He just didn't have the heart to fight, or to stick with anything.

Driving home after shopping one day, I saw another Mercedes Benz just like ours, with a wheelchair perched on the roof attached to a sturdy-looking hoist above the driver's door. I was sure that it would be helpful if we had a hoist like that because then Des could drive himself around without my help. I followed the car for about five miles, and each time it turned, I hoped that it had reached its destination, but it traveled on until eventually, it came to a stop outside a primary school. I parked behind it and ran up to the car. A lady was driving, and when I approached, she opened her window. Without introducing myself, I burst out, "I thought you were never going to stop!"

She looked surprised, and then she smiled, and Irene Joubert entered my life. A kind, gentle soul, our friendship became something I treasured for many years. I stood talking to her for about a half an hour, explaining that my husband was a paraplegic, and asking her if she could please tell me where she had found the hoist. Irene was gracious and gave me all the information I needed, and also promised to visit Des sometime soon.

Irene was a quadriplegic, and her story was one of great courage. In 1971, when she was twenty-eight, she was involved in a freak motorcar accident while vacationing in Namibia. She, her husband, their two children and two friends were traveling together, when a large Kudu buck unexpectedly jumped into their path, colliding with them and landing on the roof of their car. The sudden impact, threw Irene forward, breaking her neck. Sadly, her youngest son died instantly. Her husband, who was driving, was unhurt, as well as their older son, and the passengers. Fortunately, Irene's husband was a medical doctor, and could render emergency care. They were transported to the nearest hospital, and then flown to Pretoria, where Irene spent six months rehabilitating and picking up the threads of her life, this time from a wheelchair. As a quadriplegic, she was paralyzed from the chest down.

A few years later, Irene had muscles transplanted into both of her wrists, which gave her enough movement to be able to drive, as well as the ability to write and hold things. Her kitchen was remodeled to enable her to work in it, and with the aid of a motorized wheelchair, she was able to live an active, productive life. She continued to work part-time as a secretary, and joined several committees, that promoted wheelchair-accessible facilities such as parking, toilets, and general access to public buildings. Irene was involved in the planning stage of many of the new buildings in Pretoria to ensure that they were wheelchair accessible. She also gave motivational talks, which enabled her audience to understand that inside, she was still the same person with the same needs as any other woman. Her courage and endurance were an inspiration. Spending time with Irene was a truly uplifting experience, and one that I came to look forward to during the many years of our friendship.

I was grateful when Irene offered to visit Des, but due to conflicting circumstances, she was unable to do so. I subsequently told Des about her, hoping that just by hearing the story of how she had overcome exceptional obstacles, he might be inspired to make something of his own life. His immediate response was that she obviously didn't have pain, and when I presented him with the information for the wheelchair hoist, he yelled at me that he was not going to have his car made to look ridiculous. He said that the hand controls were ugly enough, and that he would eventually have them removed.

About a year after the court case, the police called to tell us that van Niekerk had been involved in an auto accident. After purchasing the largest BMW available, he regularly drove to the Pretoria North Police Station in the middle of the night on weekends and sat outside, honking his horn, while shouting obscenities at the police. They attempted to catch him a few times, but the police vans were no match for his powerful BMW.

After a few months, the Flying Squad, a special rapid-response police unit, was called in, and when van Niekerk arrived that night, they were waiting for him. They gave chase, and on a long open stretch of road, the two cars encountered a sharp bend and van Niekerk, who was traveling much too fast, was unable to negotiate the curve. His car skidded off the road, somersaulting before hitting a tree. The top of the car was shorn off, and van Niekerk's neck was broken, killing him.

The police lieutenant following the BMW, happened to be the same man who had been the first to respond to our emergency call the night that Des was shot. He told us that van Niekerk had a younger son who was with him in the car at the time of the accident, but who miraculously survived the crash. He identified his father as the driver, and the lieutenant realized that this was the same man who had shot my husband. Justice may have ultimately been served, but if it was, it gave me no satisfaction.

WESKOPPIES

Des slept on and off through the day, and then he couldn't sleep at night. Because he took laxatives just before we went to bed, this caused his bowels to work mostly at night. I told him he should rather take them in the mornings, which just gave him the idea for one more way to manipulate me. If I arranged to go out with one of the children in the evening, he took the laxative at midday, ensuring that I couldn't leave him. He hated me going out, and used any means possible to keep me tied to his room. To keep myself busy, while sitting with Des, I took up knitting.

In August of 1985, Dr. Davie told me that I was on the verge of a nervous breakdown and should go to a nursing home for six weeks to build up my strength. I told him that I couldn't possibly leave Des for that long, so he then suggested that I visit my sister in Zimbabwe, and I agreed to go for three weeks, but I worried about leaving Des with the children. By this time, Justine was eighteen, and she assured me that they could manage, and I didn't have the strength to argue. Des had to learn to take care of himself, and he promised to try, so I booked a flight to Harare.

It did me good to spend time with Sheila. She ran two factories efficiently, and I admired her tremendously. One was a canning factory and the other made pottery, and I was impressed to see how well both were doing. She had a wonderful employer who recognized her worth and appreciated everything she did. He gave Dennis a job running errands just to keep him busy, mostly for Sheila's sake. Canning fish from Kariba Dam and asparagus grown on the farm, Sheila helped to make her employer a wealthy man.

One day, because I needed to go to the post office, I made the mistake of going with Dennis when he was running some errands. He drove much too fast on the dirt roads. I wouldn't have minded that, but when he saw black people walking along the side of the road, he honked and drove straight at them, forcing them to jump out of his way. In sharp contrast, when he saw a stray dog at the side of the road, he swerved around it, laughing gaily, while declaring that he was sure I could tell that he had his priorities right. I was disgusted and told him so. I didn't particularly like Dennis since I knew that he mistreated Sheila. He spoke to her in the same manner that Des spoke to me, and I concluded that both of us had exercised poor judgment in our choice of husbands.

Meanwhile, back in Pretoria, Des was not keeping to his word. He was injecting himself with pethidine, an alternative to morphine, for the pain and the more he used, the more he said he needed. I had left strict instructions that, under no circumstances, was Justine to give him more than the amount I had left for the three weeks. The balance was hidden away on a high shelf in my closet behind my sweaters.

After a few days, Des demanded that Justine give him more but, remembering my instructions, she told him she didn't know where it was. He told her he was sure that it was in my closet on the shelf and that she should look for it. Justine discovered where I had hidden it but told him she couldn't find it. He screamed at her to look harder and she began to cry, begging him not to make her give him more, that Mama wasn't there, and he had promised to be good. But Des had forgotten his promise, and he wanted more pethidine. When she again refused, he produced all that he had hidden under the bed covers, and wildly injected himself with one ampule after the other. This was his second suicide attempt.

Des' body suddenly went limp with the needle hanging out of his arm, and Justine ran to our neighbors, who took charge of the situation. They called Dr. Davie, who had Des admitted to the local Catholic hospital, where he was weaned off the pethidine. Des' tolerance for medication was unbelievably high. Our doctor had gone out of his way to give Des relief from his pain, but it seemed he was now beyond help. Fortunately, Des was kept in the hospital for the remainder of my time in Zimbabwe.

Doctor Davie knew about the Mercedes and how Des had refused to drive it for almost eighteen months, so he drove it to the hospital after office hours and made Des practice with the hand controls. He went far beyond the call of duty as our family doctor, and I will always be grateful for everything he did for us.

Completely unaware of all this, I returned home, somewhat refreshed at the end of the three weeks, expecting to find the children waiting to pick me up at the airport. I searched the crowd at arrivals, but they were nowhere to be seen. Then my eyes fell on a thin, gaunt man with graying hair, sitting in a wheelchair with a bouquet of flowers in his lap. It was Des, and he was alone. He looked at me, and I looked back at the man I had loved for so long, never knowing if he would ever be able to love me in return. I ran to him, and we embraced. We both cried, and when I looked up, there was hardly a dry eye among the people waiting in arrivals. I asked him, "Where are the children?" He told me that he was alone.

"How is that possible?" I asked.

"I came to fetch you, my sweet. I drove here myself," he replied.

Des had driven himself thirty miles to the airport to pick me up! I found it hard to believe, but there he was, sitting in front of me, looking gentle and kind, and unlike anyone I had seen before. Was this really my husband? I pushed my baggage trolley downstairs to the parking lot, while Des propelled himself along in his wheelchair. He parked his chair next to the driver's door. He was going to drive us home! I placed his wheelchair and my suitcase in the back, and got in next to him. He then kissed me, a soft, gentle kiss. We drove home, and with the memory of that kiss, and the fragrant aroma of the flowers in my lap, I was convinced that life was going to be wonderful from that moment on.

And it was. For two whole days, Des treated me with tenderness and respect. The second day, he asked me to lie next to him on the bed, and we talked, really talked, the whole day. We planned a bright future, and many promises were made. In the evening, he sat with me in the TV room, holding my hand, and I felt as if I was in heaven, but it was not to last.

The next day, Des woke up sick. Each time he went to hospital, he came home with a bladder infection. They usually took two to three days to develop, and this one was particularly bad. He had a high temperature and didn't want to eat. He was given one antibiotic after the other, but none of them worked, and eventually, towards the end of October, he was taken by ambulance to hospital with a massive kidney infection.

It was as if the trip to Zimbabwe had never happened!

Upon his return home, Des reverted to his old ways and became angry at the slightest provocation. Nothing I said or did could please him. Again, tensions in the house mounted, and he was constantly clanging his monkey chain or tinging the downstairs telephone, yelling at us much of the time. The children refused to go near him, and I couldn't blame them.

The night of October 28th 1985, was the culmination of months of frustration. Des totally lost control. Breaking everything he could get hold of in his room, the floor was strewn with broken china and glass. He then took his Bible and tore it into shreds, telling me I should give it to our pastor to use for toilet paper. I begged him to stop, but he went on ranting for hours. Justine was writing her finals, and she needed to study, as well as to be able to sleep, but when I mentioned this to Des, he said he didn't care, and that if he couldn't sleep, no one else would either. It was getting late, and Justine was almost in tears. "Mama, I have to study. Please make him stop," she begged.

I tried again to reason with him, and he gave me the same response. By that time, I had had enough! I walked over to my neighbor, Corrie's house and told her that Des wasn't allowing the children to study or sleep and before I even asked, Corrie offered to have the two children sleep at her house.

I ran home only to be greeted with a barrage of profanities from the top of the stairs. Des sat there in his wheelchair, shouting at the top of his voice for Limba. I helped Justine and Craig gather up their pajamas and schoolwork and accompanied them to the front door. Des was still sitting there, and he screamed, "They are not going anywhere! Justine, Craig, stay where you are! Listen to me. I am your father!"

I told him to stop it, that the children had to sleep, and he was making their lives unbearable. Suddenly, he launched his wheelchair from the top of the stairs and tumbled headlong down the stairs, landing on the floor, with the wheelchair on top of him. The children looked at me with big eyes. Amazingly, Des didn't appear to be hurt, and he then attempted to grab Justine's foot. I told the children to go to Corrie's house, and they fled.

I called Limba, and he helped me to get Des back up the stairs and into bed. That he hadn't broken any bones with the fall was a miracle. When Limba saw the state of the room, the expression on his face was one of shock and terror. While he was there, Des calmed down, and I hoped that maybe he had spent all his strength for the night and that, at last, he would be able to sleep.

That turned out to be wishful thinking. In my high state of anxiety, I was past the need for sleep, and I told Des that he could rattle his monkey chain all night and ting the telephone to his heart's content. At that moment, I simply didn't care! I took his wheelchair downstairs thinking that then, he would have to stay in bed and would fall asleep. Not so! I sat on the couch in the living room reading, trying to unwind, while Des did exactly the opposite. The screaming and shouting became louder and louder. The monkey chain rattled. The telephone tinged. He screamed for me. He screamed for Limba. This went on until about two in the morning.

At last, all was quiet, and I came to the conclusion that Des had finally fallen asleep. I turned off the light and made myself as comfortable as possible on the couch. Then, I heard muffled sounds, which gradually became louder. Des was propelling himself across the floor of our bedroom, and when he reached the top of the stairs, he snarled, "I will get you, you bitch. Tonight, I will kill you!"

I told him I didn't care, that he could do whatever he liked. I was at the end of my tether, and at that moment, I really didn't care. All the years of abuse had accumulated into one big hurt.

Des descended the stairs one at a time. He didn't wear pants at night, because his bowels were so unpredictable, and when he dragged himself across the metal seam on the floor at the entrance to our bedroom, he inadvertently scraped all the skin off his thin tailbone, leaving a trail of blood all the way down the stairs. By the time he reached the bottom of the stairs, he was raving like a madman. He grabbed hold of the hallstand in an attempt to pull it over. His rage was so great that he wanted to destroy everything within reach. I watched in the dim light as the hallstand tipped dangerously towards him, and then miraculously, it returned to its upright position. It was almost as if an invisible hand had pushed it back. Des lay there for the rest of the night, screaming and swearing at me. I sat quietly listening, praying for morning to come.

Inevitably, dawn eventually arrived, and I got Limba to help me get Des back into bed. I then called Dr. Davie and asked him if he could please come to the house to help me with Des. Thankfully, he arrived early, before going on his hospital rounds. I told him what had happened, and after seeing the state of the bedroom and examining Des, he took me aside, and told me that my husband must be admitted to Weskoppies Psychiatric Hospital. I knew this was the right decision. I had seen enough to know that Des was no longer completely sane, but I felt sick not knowing what the outcome of such a decision would be. Dr. Davie called for an ambulance, and left me to await its arrival.

As I expected, Des told the paramedics he wasn't going anywhere, and they should get out of his house. He fought so hard, that the two men couldn't hold him down to give him an injection. A second ambulance was called, and the four paramedics were then able to sedate him. The first injection proved inadequate, and it took a second one to render him unconscious. The paramedics told me that his resistance to drugs was such, that they had to administer as much tranquilizer as would be necessary to sedate a bull.

Des was taken to *Weskoppies* (West Hills), and as I had done previously when he was shot, I followed the ambulance, but this time to the mental institution. This was the same mental institution where Des had wanted to have me committed a few years earlier, and now, it was he who was going there. Dr. Davie had him committed, stating that my husband was a psychopath. In spite of everything that had happened, when I signed the papers, I felt like a traitor, and it was the hardest thing I had ever had to do.

Visiting Des in Weskoppies turned out to be a terrifying experience. He was in a large ward with many other patients, each one suffering from their own mental disability. I dreaded going there. Des told me stories of things that the other patients were doing during the night, and I was horrified to think that he had to witness them. He admitted to me that he knew he was mentally ill and begged me to let him come home, promising to see a psychiatrist. I told him he was where he needed to be to get help, and that nothing he said could convince me otherwise.

Pity now overwhelmed me for the man I had married, but I knew I could no longer help him. Des was a psychopath, and having a name for his condition made it a bitter pill to swallow. All the years of making excuses for his behavior were suddenly thrown back in my face. I had always believed that Des had a split personality and that if I loved him enough, the good side of his nature would prevail, but it turned out to be far more serious than I had thought.

The word psychopath was big, far too big for me to fully comprehend or understand, but I knew it was not something that I could handle alone. Nursing a person with a sick body is one thing, but nursing a person with a sick mind is quite another, and I wasn't equipped for either one. My heart and mind were torn between loyalty and love for my husband, and fear for the sick person that I now knew he was. Quite some time elapsed before I fully understood the situation I was facing. I just knew that I had to keep reminding myself that Des was unwell and not responsible for his actions.

Thinking back, I was able to make excuses for much of his past behavior, but that was no help in handling the present, or the future. I understood that manipulation was one of the symptoms of the illness, and knowing that, I was in a better position to deal with Des' manipulation of me. I made many promises to myself that day, but I found them far easier to make than to keep.

While Des was in Weskoppies, Justine went with some friends to their farm outside Warmbaths for a few days. When she returned, I threw all her dirty clothes on the floor of the laundry in order to sort them before putting them in the washing machine. As I did so, I noticed a movement in the pocket of her dress. I wondered what it could be, when suddenly, to my horror, a small snake emerged and rose up, ready to strike, and I recognized it as a cobra from its stance. In a flash, it slithered under the deep freeze, and I quickly grabbed the dirty laundry, stuffing some of it under the door to Larry's room, some of it under the back door and, exiting the laundry, I placed the remainder under the door from the laundry to the kitchen.

At that moment, the telephone rang. It was 10 pm, and everyone knew not to call me after nine. Almost three years of hateful phone calls had made me wary of nighttime calls. I was already shaking with fright from seeing the snake, and the phone call was the last straw.

However, it turned out to be a dear friend of mine who was on holiday in England at the time. We had a close bond, but even so, her words amazed me. "Doreen, are you okay?" she asked. "I am sorry to call so late, but I have this terrible feeling that you are in danger."

I laughed shakily and said, "Well, apart from having a baby cobra trapped in my laundry, I am perfectly fine." We chatted for a couple of minutes and then she told me to get help, and I hung up.

I called my future son-in-law, John, and when I told him about the cobra, he laughed at me and said, "I am sure it is just a yard snake, but I'll come over and take a look."

He came armed with a golf club, and after a couple of loud thuds, he emerged from the laundry wide-eyed and he told me I was right; it was indeed a baby cobra and as tiny as it was, it was as poisonous as a fully grown one, maybe even more so. I had a narrow escape that night. Had I reached in with my hand to check the pockets, things could have turned out very differently.

Des had been in Weskoppies for about three months, when I heard a vehicle stop in the driveway. Looking out the window, I saw that it was an ambulance, and two paramedics were helping Des out of it. How could this possibly be? He was a certified psychopath! I later learned that the authorities at Weskoppies had come to the conclusion that they couldn't keep Des there. They weren't equipped to deal with paraplegics in wheelchairs, so they simply sent him home!

Des was triumphant! He sneered at me, saying, "You thought you got rid of me, didn't you? Well, you didn't. Get me upstairs. Now!"

It is hard to describe how I felt at that moment. I had had three months of relative calm, enjoying the children, laughing and playing with them. I had even been able to sleep at night, and now it was over. How could this possibly happen?

I was severely tested a few days later, and I was ill-prepared for it. Des made a third attempt at suicide. He called me, and as I entered his bedroom, he said, "This is not living, and I will *not* live like this. You can't stop me this time!" Reaching beneath the bedcovers, he produced a handful of pills and threw them all in his mouth at one time, gulping them down with a glass of water. I wasn't sure where he got them, but I assumed that he had accumulated them while he was in Weskoppies, and smuggled them home. Having no idea what they were or what effect they might have, I immediately called for an ambulance, and he was rushed to the hospital, where they pumped his stomach, and kept him under observation for a few days.

As a result of what happened, I made the decision that I couldn't continue taking care of Des at home, but deciding that was one thing; telling Des was quite another.

CONSTANTIA

When I visited Des in the hospital, I told him that he couldn't come back home because it was too stressful for both me and the children, and just as I expected, he insisted that he *would* come home to *his* house! In need of advice from someone who could understand my situation, I called the matron in charge of the Spinal Unit, and she suggested that I treat Des with tough love, and stop doing everything for him. She recommended a boarding house that catered for people with disabilities and miraculously, they had a vacancy, so I booked a room for him. He fought me as I knew he would, so I told him firmly that if he stayed there and became independent, I was prepared to stand by him.

There were many nights when I thought I heard a car in the driveway, and I was fearful that it was Des. Sometimes, I even imagined that he might wheel himself the few miles from Constantia to our house in his wheelchair. That didn't happen, but one night, I received a phone call in the middle of the night. All the bad memories came flooding back as I heard someone breathing heavily on the other end of the line. It could have been Des, but I had no way of knowing whether it was or not.

When Larry finished his degree in graphic design at the Technikon, he was called into military service with the army, but he had only been gone a couple of weeks when he returned home. Because of his extreme food allergies, which made it impossible for him to finish his basic training, he was dismissed. He was then able to attend Anne's wedding before leaving for Vereeniging, where he took a job. This left Craig as my only child still at home.

With Des in Constantia, I was able to devote all my attention to Anne's wedding. After being engaged for a couple of years, she and John were to be married at the old Presbyterian Church in Pretoria on February 15th 1986.

The day of the wedding, I picked Des up from Constantia. He was to give Anne away, and there wasn't a dry eye in the church as Des wheeled himself down the aisle next to her. Seeing our eldest daughter walking down the aisle looking radiant, with her father so pale and thin in his wheelchair beside her, was bittersweet. Now and again, the wheel of his chair caught the hem of her dress, but she didn't seem fazed by it.

With Des sitting next to me in the church, tears filled my eyes, blurring the words in the hymnbook, and I found it difficult to sing. This day should have been so different. After the ceremony, I pushed Des outside into the bright sunshine. It wasn't to last long as dark clouds were building in the sky. A storm was about to break over Pretoria, while another was brewing in my husband's heart.

The reception was a huge success. Family and friends mingled, while enjoying the dancing and socializing. I felt as if I were on the outside, looking in, as I sat next to Des at the wedding table. He kept putting his arm around me, and tried to hold my hand. Feeling uncomfortable, I pulled away. It was obvious to me that he was putting on an act to show everyone that he was a loving husband. No one really knew what had been going on, and I felt sure that some of the people must have thought ill of me. I couldn't tell them what the real situation was. How do you tell people your husband is a psychopath, and had been committed to an asylum?

Des was drinking heavily and slurring his words, and I prayed that he wouldn't spoil Anne's wedding day by falling out of his chair or losing his temper. I left him for just a few minutes, while I went to speak to his mother. He refused to, so I felt I had to. When I returned, he was smoking. He hadn't smoked in twenty-five years, and I asked him what he was doing. He grinned at me and told me that tonight, he was going to sleep in his own bed in his own house. It was obvious that he was working himself up for a fight. I'm not sure how I got him out of the hotel and into the car, but somehow, I managed it. But when I pulled up outside Constantia, he exploded, screaming, "Take me home, I demand you take me home!"

I looked at him. He was blind with fury. From somewhere came the quiet words, "Des, if I take you home, I will pack my suitcase and leave, and you will never see me again. If that is what you want, just tell me, and I will take you home."

He looked shocked, but after allowing the words to sink in, he became calm and allowed me to take him to his room.

Each time I visited Des in Constantia, I came away disappointed. He wasn't keeping himself clean, and he didn't smell good. I begged him to get out of bed and start living again. He responded by saying that he wanted to take me out to dinner at my favorite restaurant. He said that he felt that I had stopped loving him, and he wanted the chance to make me love him again. Against my better judgment, I agreed. How could I refuse him, when he was living such a miserable existence.

On the arranged evening, I put on my best suit and drove to Constantia, expecting him to be dressed nicely for the occasion, but he was in his sweatsuit. No matter, it was comfortable and probably easier for him to put on unaided. He smelled good, so I knew that, at least, he had bathed. I drove us to Cynthia's restaurant, where they knew me well, since this was where I always took the children to celebrate their birthdays.

When we arrived, Des ordered a steak and a bottle of wine. Then he asked the waiter to bring him a beer, while we waited for our food. I suggested he should stick to the wine since it wasn't wise to mix his drinks, especially with the amount of medication he was taking. He laughed at me, saying he could handle his alcohol. This didn't bode well for a quiet, romantic evening.

By the time the food arrived, Des was already intoxicated, having finished the beer and a glass of red wine. In a loud voice, he told me that he was going home, and I reminded him that was not our agreement. Neither of us had touched our food. I asked him to keep his voice down as people were looking at us. He yelled, "I don't care a f*** who is looking at us. Let them look. Look people, look. Have a good f******g look!"

One of the owners came over and asked us if he could help us. He was obviously upset, and I didn't blame him. I apologized, but Des told the owner to get lost. I got up and attempted to push him out of the restaurant, but he fought me every inch of the way. Seeing me struggle, the owner took charge and pushed Des across the restaurant for me. When we reached the door, I told him I would return in a few minutes to settle the bill.

Reaching the car, I opened Des' door, but as I was trying to help him into the car, he pushed me away, telling me not to touch him. I hadn't yet applied the wheelchair brakes, so when he lifted himself forcefully into the car, the wheelchair rolled backwards, and he landed flat on his back, in the gutter.

I knew I couldn't pick him up. He was far too heavy, but I tried anyway. Then I heard a voice behind me saying, "Here, let me help you."

A young man and his wife had just arrived, and they saw Des fall. He picked Des up and helped him into the car. I closed the door and the young man then put the wheelchair into the back of the car for me. I thanked him and walked with them into the restaurant, where I paid the bill and apologized for the upset. The pitying looks I received made me feel even worse. I declined to take the untouched food home. I had no appetite, and I just wanted to get the evening over with.

When I got into the car, I could hear by Des' heavy breathing that he was still angry. A few blocks from the restaurant, he ordered me to take him home. He yelled louder and louder, and I was afraid that he might grab hold of the wheel and kill us both. After a few minutes, I could take it no more. I slammed on the brakes and pulled the car off the road. I looked at him and yelled back. "Shut up, Dessie! I told you before I am not going to take you home. If I do, I will pack my bags and leave and you can have the house to yourself. Now, what do you want me to do?"

I couldn't believe I was actually yelling at him. Was that really my voice? Des was just as flabbergasted. In stony silence, I drove him back to Constantia.

HOME AGAIN

Of course, I couldn't leave him there. My conscience wouldn't let me, and a couple of weeks later, I took him back home again. The love and pity I felt for Des kept me trapped in my own sense of responsibility and guilt. He was sick, but he was still my husband.

Des had been in Constantia for about three months when I brought him home and I had no idea what to expect, whether or not he had learned anything from his time there. The first thing I did was to get him into the bathtub and I was shocked when I saw the condition of his body. He was terribly thin, and he had an ugly bed sore on his tailbone where he had injured himself a year earlier. Two more were forming on his hips. He didn't have a monkey chain in the boarding house, and he had obviously been lying in bed most of the time. With his poor circulation and inactivity, it was inevitable that he would get bedsores. I fussed with him. How could he allow himself to get in such a terrible condition? Living in Constantia was supposed to have made him independent and now here he was, in worse shape than when he moved in.

I gently bathed him. How he tugged at my heart, and I felt it would break for this once proud man. I put him into bed with fresh sheets. He smelled good and I felt better for seeing him clean and cared for. I dressed the wound and prayed for it to heal.

It had been over three years since the shooting, and at last, we received some compensation from van Niekerk's estate. We were relieved, since our financial situation was deteriorating rapidly, due to the rise in the cost of living. The payments from the sale of The Tolbos were due to end in just over a year. The settlement helped, but without the income from the restaurant, we would again be in a shaky financial position. Something needed to be worked out before the end of the following year.

Des' bedsore didn't heal; in fact, it worsened over the next few weeks. It had been neglected for too long while he was in Constantia, and the infection had penetrated his tailbone. In the past, when he came home from the hospital with bedsores on his hips and elbows, I had always managed to get them to heal with a papaya poultice, an old-fashioned home recipe. This time, it didn't work.

In August, I took Des to Edenvale Hospital for what was commonly known as "Z" surgery. This entailed cutting flesh from his hip in the form of a "Z" and grafting it on to his tailbone, giving the grafted flesh additional flexibility. Edenvale was about forty miles from Pretoria, and I drove over to see him about three times a week during the three months he was there.

During that time, I was summoned to the hospital for a meeting with Des' physician, his surgeon, and his appointed psychiatrist. I was seated on a chair in front of the panel, while they sat at a long table making notes. They asked me many questions, which I answered as honestly as I could.

The psychiatrist asked the most questions. He told me he had concluded that Des was indeed a psychopath, who was unable to love others or feel any kind of remorse. I replied that I was well aware of the diagnosis, but I couldn't leave my husband. What was to become of him?

I explained that they had been unable to keep Des in the mental asylum, and why. He could offer no suggestion as to what I should do, other than to leave Des. He predicted that because he was so depressed, not only was he likely to end up taking his own life, but there was a strong possibility that he would attempt to take me and the children with him. I had been told all this before, and throughout my life, this had been the pattern. When I needed help, no one was able to provide any.

Almost four years of nursing Des with hardly any sleep, living with his constant depression and anger had taken their toll. We had almost no friends, and I was lonely. Our neighbor, Corrie, was the only one who came to visit us regularly.

Before bringing Des home from Edenvale, I moved into the large bedroom downstairs, where I hoped I might get a bit more sleep. Des called me by tinging the telephone, so I still had to go upstairs to help him, but at least I didn't hear the clanging of the monkey chain as loudly when he turned over, or when he clanged it in anger and frustration.

Christmas arrived, and Anne invited us all to their home in Lydenburg for dinner. We had planned the trip for weeks, but at the last moment, Des decided not to go. I told him that Anne had made a special Christmas dinner for us and pleaded with him to change his mind, but he said he didn't care, and that we should go without him. Nothing could lift him out of his deep depression, whether we went or if we stayed, so I told the children we should go and at least make Anne happy.

Nellie had asked me if she could go home for the New Year holiday, since she wanted to go to her local church for the early morning Christmas service, so she would be at the house that day. This worked out well as she was there to serve Des his lunch. Anne prepared a wonderful feast for us and we spent a delightful day with her and John, and she sent a plate of food home for Des' dinner.

On our return home, I went down to my room, and made a frightening discovery. I usually kept Des' guns hidden in the top of one of my closets under some blankets. The closet was kept locked but quite recently, I had moved them, storing them in the loft above Larry's bathroom, where I was sure Des couldn't get to them. Even though they were no longer in the closet, I had automatically locked it out of habit. The lock was broken, and it was obvious that Des had rifled through the contents of my closet. I concluded that he must have dragged himself downstairs and forced my closet door open. When I accused him, he merely denied it, asking me how on earth he could possibly have gotten all the way downstairs, when I knew he couldn't walk! By hiding the guns in Larry's bathroom loft, I had prevented Des from a fourth attempt to end his life.

In October of 1986, June, my childhood schoolfriend from England came for a visit. What a wonderful reunion that was! At the airport, she ran to me like a young teenager, and we hugged for the longest time. I had forgotten how tiny she was. The top of her head barely reached my chin, and although I was only five feet, seven, I felt tall beside her. Des was in hospital when she arrived, so I took June to visit him. She gave him a Wilbur Smith book as a gift, since I had told her that he was one of Des' favorite authors. Surprisingly, Des was actually nice to her, for which I was very grateful.

Because Des was in hospital, Anne, Craig and I were able to take June to Johannesburg for a bit of sightseeing. We then drove to Anne's house and from there, we went to visit the Kruger National Park for a few days. In just one weekend, we saw over thirty lions, including three kills. The first group of young lions that we saw were lying under a tree in the shade, obviously well-fed and feeling lazy. We parked so close to them, that if we had been foolish enough, we could have put our hands out of the open window and stroked their heads. I was excited, and could scarcely breathe for the half hour we spent with them. We also saw a pack of wild dogs and a few hyenas, both rarely seen in the park. The trip was a great success, made all the more so by seeing June again after almost thirty years. It was as if we had never been apart.

Just after June's visit, dear Nellie got sick, and I took her to the doctor, who could find nothing wrong with her. I sent her home to rest, hoping that she would get better, but a month later, her brother came to tell me that she had died. I was very sad, knowing that I was going to miss Nellie's gentle presence in my home.

I was sure that Nellie was irreplaceable, but when Maria came to the house looking for work, I liked her instantly. She was a young, confident Ndebele woman, with a pretty smile, and her open, honest face portrayed the lovely person that she was. She had one daughter, Johanna, who lived with her grandmother. Johanna's father had left Maria, and she was raising her daughter as a single mother. Over the next few years, we grew to be very fond of one another.

THE AUCTION

Des was an avid reader, and had quite a collection of books in his library, but he had re-read almost all of them since the shooting, and he was in need of some new material. Before he was shot, we had occasionally visited an auction house in Pretoria, and he suggested that I should go there and look for some books for him. I had always had a fascination with auctions since going to one in England when I was a young girl, so I was more than happy to do as he asked.

I managed to find some good books for Des, as well as a few small household items that caught my eye. Soon it became my habit to drop by almost every Saturday morning, and since Des didn't protest, I was glad for the opportunity to get out of the house and meet some new people. Pretty soon, Mum and Dick accompanied me, and then, occasionally, the children went along as well.

Many of the people who frequented the auction were regulars, and it was, as much as anything else, a social event. One day, while I was looking at something that caught my eye, a male voice behind me said, "You had better be careful, or you might end up buying that."

Turning around, I found myself face to face with a man whom I had seen several times at the auction. He was an American, but it wasn't his accent that I noticed. It was his hearty laugh. Hearing him laugh always made me smile. In response to his advice, I blushed and said I hoped not, since it wasn't something that I needed, and I quickly walked away and joined Mum and Dick. It wasn't long before the American came over and introduced himself. His name was Michael Murphy, and he was from Texas. He told us that he was working at a new Department of Landscape Architecture at the University of Pretoria.

From then on, Michael, always friendly and outgoing, greeted me, as well as whoever happened to be with me. At first, I felt shy and awkward since Des had always forbidden me to speak to other men, except, of course, at the restaurant, where I had no option. By this time, I had lost most of the self-confidence that I had gained from working in The Tolbos, but Michael was patient, and eventually, I found myself looking forward to chatting with him. Mum and Dick also enjoyed his company, and I found it a relief to be able to talk to someone who didn't know anything about our home life. As it turned out, visiting the auction was also his only social outlet since Saturdays were the only free time he had.

One day, I was alone at the auction, when Michael wandered over, and we talked. He asked me about myself, and I told him I was married, and that my husband was a paraplegic, which was why he never attended the auction with me. Michael enquired as to what had happened to him, and I said that Des had been shot in an accident. Michael was perceptive and didn't pursue the conversation further, as he could probably tell I was reluctant to talk about it.

There was another professor who was also a regular at the auction. Des had always chatted with him in the past, so when he asked me if the professor still went to the auction on Saturday mornings, I told him yes, that he was still there. I knew better than to mention that there were now two professors, as I knew that Des would never accept my friendship with Michael. His jealous nature made it almost impossible for me to have women friends.

By midyear of 1987, Des hardly ate and lay in bed all day moping, even refusing to read. In the past, he had always enjoyed watching sports on television, but now he was no longer interested in that. He became even more possessive, demanding that I stay in the room with him all the time. Whenever I went out, he wanted to know exactly where I was going, and how long I would be gone. When I returned, I had to give him a detailed account of where I had been. The only places I went to were church, Bible study, the stores, and the auction. Quite often, when I went to the stores, after I had made all my purchases, I walked around aimlessly, not needing anything in particular, but not wanting to return to the gloomy atmosphere at home.

One day, I went to the store to buy groceries, and as I entered the supermarket, I noticed a young man in a wheelchair sitting next to the entrance. He obviously had cerebral palsy, and was badly deformed. Unable to speak, he held a notice asking for donations to be placed in the tin he was holding. He was drooling long strings of saliva, and I quickly looked away. I had more than enough heartache at home and felt I couldn't handle any more. I finished my grocery shopping and averted my eyes as I left the supermarket, not wanting to see the young man again. But I had only walked a few steps, when a voice inside my head asked me how I could just walk away from him. I reluctantly turned around and walked back.

The donation I made was small, but looking at him, I felt compelled to take out a tissue and wipe his face and clothes. The crooked smile on his twisted face was a smile of thanks, but to me, at that moment, it looked more like the smile of an angel, and I felt blessed. I learned that day that there is always someone living in circumstances worse than mine, and I went home determined to persevere, no matter what.

Someone told me about a disabled psychiatrist who practiced in Johannesburg, and I begged Des to go and see him, but he refused, so I went to visit him myself to see if he could give me any advice as to how I might get Des motivated.

I was amazed at the man's courage and determination. His body was supported by a clamshell, a plastic body jacket. Due to poor circulation, he was only able to sit for short periods of time, having to stand up regularly, and move around with the aid of crutches. He listened intently, while I gave him a brief description of Des and the circumstances leading to our current situation. I finished by telling him that my husband had been diagnosed as a psychopath, and he told me that this was his specialty. I explained that Des wouldn't consider seeking his help, to which he responded that it wasn't at all surprising.

Before I left, the psychiatrist was kind enough to lend me his dissertation to take home to read. Reading the symptoms of a psychopath was like reading a description of my husband. The part that frightened me most was the acceptance rate of disablement. After the age of forty-five, Des' age, there was essentially none. Acceptance of the condition as a reality in their life became progressively less as age increased, and adaptability to being immobile was not generally a part of an older person's capability.

As before, I found myself being told by a psychiatrist that my husband was sure to end up committing suicide, and that he would probably attempt to take his family with him. He told me that I should try and find a place for Des to stay, but he also had no suggestions. He was kind, and I found reading his dissertation helpful. I was able to understand Des better and to be more tolerant, knowing he couldn't help the way he acted. It was just as much a sickness as cancer or heart disease. The psychiatrist told me that I was doing an excellent job of handling the situation, but it would be foolish of me to think that I could actually help Des. Nobody could, because he simply didn't want to be helped. He warned me that I should get out of the situation while I still could.

We struggled on, and I continued to live one dreary day at a time. One of those days, when Limba was working elsewhere, Des asked me to take him downstairs so that he could sit in the living room for a while. It happened to be Maria's afternoon off, and because there was no one to help me, I told him I wasn't able to take him down. He insisted that he and I could manage it alone and as he so seldom wanted to leave his bed, I agreed to try. It was an unfortunate decision. I managed to take him down successfully, but he was only there about an hour, when he said he had terrible pain, and insisted that I take him back to bed.

We were about halfway up the stairs, when Des leaned forward. He wanted to turn slightly and grab the banister in an effort to help me by pulling himself up, but when he tilted the chair forward, I didn't have the strength to hold him. My hand got trapped between the wheelchair's handle and the banister, and the pain was excruciating. Des fell forward, landing on the floor of the entrance hall, with the chair on top of him. Fortunately, for the second time, nothing was broken, and after wrapping a handkerchief around my bleeding hand, I managed to get him back into the chair, where we waited until Maria came home.

Visitors were rare, so I considered it a blessing when Des' cousin, Nimrod, came to Pretoria for a visit. We invited him to stay the night, and I left the two men together after dinner and went to my room. When I heard Nimrod go to his room, I went upstairs and settled Des for the night. It was late, and I fell asleep as soon as my head touched the pillow. I woke with a start when my door slowly creaked open. Startled, I sat up in bed and saw the figure of a man approaching my bed. As he came closer, I was able to see that it was Nimrod. He put his finger to his lips. "Ssh, it's only me," he said, and sat down on the side of my bed and put his arm around me.

Although his intentions were clear, I automatically asked him what he wanted. He giggled. By this time, I was shaking violently, which should have made it clear to him that his advances were unwelcome. I said, "I think you had better get out."

He replied with a great deal of amusement in his voice, "You only think so?" I nearly slapped his face. He was very arrogant, and incredibly full of himself.

"Get out!" I said, this time with a lot more feeling. I was extremely angry.

How could he do this to Des who was lying upstairs in bed, unable to walk? And how could he insult me like this? He must have assumed that I was desperate for his advances, because my husband was wheelchair-bound. He slowly got up and went back to his room. I locked my door, but it took me a long time to calm down and get back to sleep.

Early the next morning, I heard Nimrod leave quietly by the front door. When I told Des about the incident, he just gave me his usual look of contempt. I wasn't sure whether he believed me or not, and it occurred to me that it was quite possible that he had put Nimrod up to it, just to test me.

By late November, Des' depression was at its worst. He repeatedly told me how much he hated me for allowing the doctor to save his life when he was shot. He also said that he hated me for saving him every time he attempted to end his life. In short, he simply hated me! I knew that I couldn't change that. The more I tried to encourage him, the more discouraged he became. The more I tried to show him love, the more contempt he showed toward me.

One evening, when I took Des his dinner, I found him unconscious. I called for an ambulance, and discovered that he had made a fifth attempt at suicide by reversing the urine from his urine bag back into his bladder. This caused a massive collapse of his bladder. His life was spared, but his hatred for me only grew.

While visiting Des in the hospital, a strange thing happened. He was peaceful that day, almost gentle. I sat with him, not quite knowing what to say, when he looked at me as if seeing me for the first time in a long time and said, "You will probably marry again. You are still a very beautiful woman."

Overwhelmed by the kind words I had waited so long to hear so tenderly delivered, I burst into tears. "Dessie, I don't want to marry again. I want you to get well, and I want for us to be happy."

He shook his head. "I don't want to live like this, Jakes. This is not living. This body. This life is not what I want. I just want to die! Why won't you let me die?" Holding on to his withered legs, he cried, "I have pain all the time."

Words failed me for a few moments, but I wasn't ready to give up. I willed him to live, and reminded him that when he was first shot, he had been to see a specialist in Johannesburg, who had been in a car accident. He told Des that he also had a great deal of pain all the time, but that he put his pain on one side, and carried on living. He said that the busier he was, the less time he had to think about the pain, and he advised Des to do the same. It wasn't what Des wanted to hear then, and it was not what he wanted to hear now. He looked at me with renewed hatred in his eyes and said in a low, vicious tone of voice, "Doreen Wheble, I wish you pain every day of your life, for the rest of your life."

When he called me by my maiden name, he was telling me I wasn't worthy to be called Doreen Jacobs. It was not a good end to our conversation.

The next Saturday morning, my parents and I went to the auction, and Michael told us that he was returning to the United States the following month and that he was selling all his furniture. He asked if we might be interested in buying any of it. He gave us his address, and Mum bought a couple of beds, while I bought a couch, chair and lamp for my room. Because we didn't have any means of transporting it, Michael asked a friend for the use of his pick-up, and they delivered the furniture for us. Because Des was still in the hospital, Michael didn't have a chance to meet him, which was probably for the best. We were all sad to see Michael leave to go home, and I wondered if we would ever see him again.

Soon after Des returned home from the hospital, his mother called and spoke to him on the telephone. We had hardly seen the Jacobs family in the five years since he had been shot. Des was bitter about that, even though he would have nothing to do with her. He constantly complained that he knew his mother sometimes drove to Pretoria, but didn't bother to visit. I had hoped that his mother was calling to say that she was coming to see us, but almost immediately, I heard Des shouting at her. He reminded her of how she had rejected him when he was a small boy, and that it was she who had destroyed his life. He blamed her for his every failure, accusing her of one thing after another. I couldn't hear her response, but my heart went out to her. From my own experience, I knew exactly how she must be feeling. He told her that he didn't want anything more to do with her, and she was not to come to his funeral. He then slammed the phone down in her ear.

By this time, I was terribly worried about our finances. Our final payment from the sale of The Tolbos was due at the end of December, and I knew that our investment income wouldn't be enough for us to live on. Des became angry when I suggested that we sell the house and buy a small townhouse, investing the remainder of the money for additional income. He reacted in the same way as he had almost five years earlier. When I said that the only alternative was for me to go to work, not even wanting to consider that, he said there was nothing further to discuss. Frustrated, I knew the decision lay with me as to which option to pursue without Des' blessing.

A DATE TO REMEMBER

On December the 30th, 1987, Des asked me to send Craig up to his room. When I told Craig that his father wanted to speak to him, he refused to go. I understood how he felt, since Des used any means to get the children into his room and then, more often than not, he either chastised or criticized them. They could seldom please him, so they avoided going to see him. I tried several times to persuade Craig to go up, but he was adamant and wouldn't go. At the time, I couldn't possibly have understood why it was so important to Des.

That evening, after dinner, I went to Des' room to fetch his tray and asked him if there was anything he needed. He said he wanted his sleeping pills, but as it was still early, I told him I would give them to him later. He insisted that I give them to him right then because he said he wanted to have an early night, and didn't want to be disturbed. I filled his water pitcher, emptied his urine bag and settled him down for the night. Before going to bed around ten o'clock, I noticed that there was no light showing beneath his door, so I assumed he was already asleep.

The next morning at 7:00 am, I took Des' tea up to his room and found two notes lying on the floor in front of the door, one addressed to me, and the other to Craig. I knew immediately that the day I had dreaded for so long had finally arrived. It was New Year's Eve. I should have guessed!

I tried the door handle, only to discover that the door was locked. When I read Des' note on the morning of December 31st, I found it extremely sad that even in death, he was determined to destroy me. His instructions were very specific. I was to send Craig up a ladder to his bedroom window, (the only windows in the house without burglar bars.) Craig was to climb inside, where he would find the key to the bedroom door on the windowsill. He was to unlock the door for me, and after entering the room, I was to untie Des' hands and remove the adhesive tape from his head. Only then was I to call Dr. Davie and the police.

Had I done as he instructed, I would probably have been arrested either for murdering him, or assisting him to commit suicide. The note was addressed to Doreen and signed Des, noticeably without love.

My thoughts were in turmoil, but one thing I remembered clearly at that moment. Des had threatened and attempted to commit suicide many times, but he always said that it would happen on a day that I would never be able to forget. I should have guessed that New Year's Eve would be his ultimate choice.

Years previously, we had attended a New Year's Eve party at the motor club, and I noticed one of Des' friends crying while we were celebrating at midnight. Des explained that the man's twin brother had taken his life on New Year's Eve a few years earlier, and he had found it tough to celebrate since then. I said that I thought it was cruel of his brother to take his life on such a special day, because it would ruin each subsequent New Year for his family. Des must have remembered my words and decided that the 31st would be the perfect day to punish me for everything he blamed me for.

Fortunately, something told me not to do as Des' note had instructed. Instead, I called Doctor Davie, and when I told him of my suspicions, he told me to sit down and wait for him.

I went to my room and got dressed. Finding it difficult to breathe, with shaky hands, I brushed my teeth and washed my face. Dr. Davie arrived within fifteen minutes and I showed him Des' note. He then asked me if I had a spare key to the bedroom. When I said no, he walked through the house, collecting the keys from all the interior doors.

The key to Larry's door fit the lock of our bedroom, and Dr. Davie entered the room. After a couple of seconds, he came out and put his arm around me, saying, "I know this is going to be extremely hard, but I want you to see this." I believe he thought I would be able to accept and process Des' death more easily by seeing him.

I walked into the room that had been filled with so much heartache, so many harsh words, and untold chaos over the years. The scene that awaited me was unimaginable. Des was sitting up in bed with his head completely covered with adhesive tape. He looked like an Egyptian mummy. His wrists were tightly tied with electrical cord that he had taken from his bedside lamp. Having made a noose for each wrist, he had obviously pulled them tight in the last moments of his life, preventing him from removing the tape, should he have changed his mind. His hands were blue from the lack of circulation.

The room was eerily neat and tidy. Everything he had used for his sixth and final suicide attempt had been carefully put away. The scene was surreal. Was he really in there? Had he succeeded in spite of me? I had thwarted his five previous attempts, but this time, I had failed. Was this good or bad? He had hated me more each time I saved his life. God forgive me if I was wrong to do that. Was I being selfish to do it? Was it because I wanted to be able to live with myself, knowing I had saved him? I couldn't be sure. His suffering had been so great. He hated his broken body. He was in pain and didn't want to live, and who was I to interfere? He could never seem to love me, but I regret that he died hating me.

I still loved Des in spite of everything, and I felt dreadful when I realized that giving him an ultimatum about the finances may have helped to push him over the edge. He couldn't bear the idea of giving up the house he loved so much, or allowing me to go and work, so he made a third, and terrible choice.

It had always been a matter of pride, and vitally important for Des to prove to himself and his family that he was a good provider. We nearly always had a home of our own and nice cars. I admit he kept me short of money, but we never went hungry, and we always had enough clothes and other essentials.

Faced with the prospect of giving up the house in Lynnwood that he had strived for all his life, wasn't even remotely acceptable. He had life insurance and believed that by taking his life, Craig and I would be well taken care of. Ending his life not only released his body from the pain and imperfection he perceived as being so repulsive, it was his final act to show his family that even in death, he was a good provider. My heart ached for the way he must have suffered in those final moments of his life.

The police said it was the most bizarre suicide they had ever witnessed. They were shocked to read in my note that by committing suicide on New Year's Eve, Des was confident that we would all remember the anniversary of his death for the rest of our lives.

Craig's short note from Des was positive, without the hatred and bitterness he had felt for me. I was grateful that Craig hadn't gone up to see his father the day before he died, because now he has the note, a tiny memoir of all the things Des wanted to say to him. He may have forgotten some of the spoken words, but the written words will remain with him forever.

After learning that his father was dead, I heard Craig drive off on his motorbike. He told me later that he went to see our pharmacist. Apparently, a few days earlier, Des had called the pharmacist and ordered eight sleeping capsules. Unknown to me, he then sent Craig to collect them. Des was unaware that the pharmacist and I had an agreement. Having told him that my husband was constantly hoarding pills for another suicide attempt, he promised me that he would only give Des pills prescribed by our doctor.

The pharmacist was a long-time friend and business associate, and Des had used their friendship as leverage to obtain the pills. However, because of our arrangement, the pharmacist had replaced the contents of the capsules with glucose. After all his other preparations were complete, Des took all eight capsules, believing that he would go into a deep sleep, but what he actually took was harmless sugar.

In an effort to save him from himself, I may have inadvertently caused him to suffer far more than he might have otherwise. With his nose and mouth stuffed full of cotton balls and his head covered in medical tape, he suffocated without the aid of the sleeping pills. For this, I am deeply sorry.

Craig was sure that he had aided in his father's death, but the pharmacist reassured him that there was only glucose in the capsules he had given to Des. Craig suffered unnecessary guilt, and I was devastated that Des would make use of his seventeen-year-old son, knowing he would feel remorse for his role in the suicide of his father.

Watching Des' body being carried out of the house on a stretcher was the hardest thing for me. I didn't get to say goodbye to my husband of twenty-seven years, but maybe that was what he wanted.

Then, suddenly, he was gone! He was gone, but there was still more heartache to follow. I called the children and told them what had happened, and then I called Des' family. I didn't have to call many other people, as with any bad news, the word spread quickly. When I called Sheila, she offered to fly down to be with me.

Justine arrived, and we both cried, partly from grief, partly relief, and partly from exhaustion. She reassured me that we had nothing to regret, that we had all done our best under impossible circumstances. The police questioned Dr. Davie and me, taking statements. They took my note and kept it for evidence and didn't return it.

The next day, the press called! It was the Pretoria News, and I told them that I had nothing to say. The reporter told me that if I didn't give him a story, he would write his own, and it was as much as I could do to be civil. I gave him the bare facts, and the story made the inside of the newspaper, not splashed on the front page as Des had always threatened it would be.

An autopsy had to be performed, and asphyxiation was given as the cause of death. Ten days elapsed between the time of Des' death and his cremation. During that time, Des' body was first preserved in a tank of formaldehyde. I was called to identify Des' body a couple of times at the mortuary, which was highly traumatic for me. The first time I went, which I believe was the day after his death, Des' naked body was floating in a fetal position in the tank of formaldehyde. Pressed up against the glass, his face was horribly distorted, and it made him look quite grotesque. I found it difficult to believe that it was really my husband, and I was shocked to think that I had to identify him in that condition. The two images of him sitting up in bed with his head covered in adhesive tape, and the one of him in the tank at the mortuary would remain with me forever.

The day before the funeral, I was again summoned to identify Des. I had taken his favorite navy sports jacket, gray trousers, white shirt and a tie for him to be cremated in. When I looked down at him lying in the coffin, it was like looking at a stranger. He looked artificial, almost like a bad replica in a waxwork's museum. With that image added to the other two, I walked slowly away.

There were a great many people at Des' funeral, but I can scarcely remember who they were. I wore the blue suit I knew he liked best. Des had called the funeral parlor ahead of time and discussed the service with them. He had even ordered the casket he was to be cremated in. The order of service was written out in detail, and the pastor from the Afrikaans church read Psalm 31.

The pastor had been to see Des on several occasions and tried his utmost to help him, but all the promises that Des made to him were never carried out. He conducted the service with gentleness and compassion, and it was heartbreaking to hear the words of the Psalm, so typical of the anguish and pain Des himself had experienced. I struggled to keep my composure, while in my mind, I could hear Des saying the words read by the pastor. The Psalm had a positive ending, which I found encouraging.

Des was cremated on January the 11th, and it took me a while to absorb the fact that he was gone. The years of anguish and heartache were over, and I was glad that I had stayed with Des until the end. I learned that much good can come out of a terrible situation. In addition to endurance and patience, I learned tolerance and compassion, and when I was at my lowest and considered giving up, I received the strength I needed, and I was constantly reminded that wedding vows are sacred, no matter how tough things become.

When I returned home from the funeral service, my composure suddenly deserted me. I couldn't breathe, and Sheila, thinking I was becoming hysterical, attempted to slap me in my face. I managed to stop her, and fled downstairs to my room, where there was a fan. Taking deep gulps of air, the fan enabled me to breathe normally, and after a trip to my doctor the following day, I discovered that I had an underactive thyroid. This, along with the stress of the funeral, had brought on an anxiety attack.

For weeks, the phone rang almost constantly, as it had when Des was shot. Sheila took it upon herself to answer it for me. I welcomed people's concerns, but I was emotionally and physically drained, and answering the same questions over and over again was exhausting.

REVENGE

Even though Des was gone, my trials were not yet over, and the coming months proved that my husband was able to reach out to me, even from the grave. Des had told me on several occasions that after he died, I would receive a letter from him, and I was to read it carefully, because shortly thereafter, I would receive a phone call from someone who would ask me several questions concerning the letter to ensure that I had read it. Should I be unable to answer all the questions, the caller would send copies to everyone I held dear, as well as to all the leading newspapers in the country.

I had often noticed that while Des was confined to his bed, he was writing notes, which he quickly hid under the bed covers any time I entered the room. Pages of handwritten notes were kept in the cabinet of the side table next to his bed, and even though I had had many opportunities to look at them when he was in the hospital, I had not, out of respect for his privacy. I ultimately regretted not having done so, because had I known what he was writing, I could have, at least, been able to prevent some heartache for my mother and Anne.

I didn't want to believe that he would actually carry out his threat to send me a letter. What would be the point? He had been telling me how much he hated me for years. He hated me for so many reasons: for loving him, for being loyal and not leaving him, when he was sure that I would. For saving his life each time, he attempted to end it. For having friends and loving people other than him. I believe he also hated me for allowing him to treat me and the children so badly, and not standing up for myself. He had no respect for me, and I couldn't blame him. Sadly, he had spent so many years breaking me down, I was left with very little self-respect, but I could never have imagined anything as cruel as the letters he wrote.

Sheila and I were sitting chatting about a week after the funeral, when Mum called. She was completely hysterical, and unable to understand what she was saying; we quickly drove over to see her. Mum and Dick were staying with Aunt Joey at the time, since Uncle Joe had passed away, and they didn't have a home of their own. It only took a moment to discover the reason for Mum's distress. In her hand, she held a seventy-two-foolscap page letter from Des, all in his neat handwriting. Poor Mum hadn't been able to get past the first hateful page.

After calming her down, we took the letter home and sat in the yard reading it. How anyone could think up some of the things he wrote is unimaginable. It was disgusting, from beginning to end. Sheila was horrified! She had no idea that Des was so sick. No one did! I had hidden so much from so many. It took a long time to read through all the filth and libel that he had written with such viciousness and malice.

I realized that Des was bent on destroying my mother and had she read it all, he quite easily could have done so. His hatred was as venomous and deep as it was unbalanced. When we finished reading the letter, I burned it in the wheelbarrow. What had probably taken him weeks to write was reduced to ashes in a matter of minutes. I was aware that he was seriously unwell, but it didn't make the reading of it any easier.

Sheila returned to Zimbabwe soon after, leaving me to wait in trepidation for my own letter, knowing that Des would have made sure that my letter was going to be his ultimate masterpiece of destruction.

Des' brother came to visit, and took away his clothes and personal possessions. He also took the wooden bed that Des had built, as I didn't want any reminders of the many nights of heartache that I had spent in it. I was then free to move one of the single beds up from downstairs in an attempt to make the room my own, hoping to free my mind of the many hurtful memories that lingered there.

It was a spacious room with windows on both ends. The front faced out into the Jacaranda trees, the street, and the park beyond, and the back windows looked down onto the swimming pool and back yard. I had Limba put the bathroom door back on its hinges and made the room as feminine and pretty as I could, but I found that nothing could erase the nightmares of the past.

Des' letter arrived almost three months after his death, and when I went to the post box that day, it was the last thing on my mind. The shock of seeing the large white envelope with his distinctive handwriting was almost too much to bear. I walked into the house holding the last remnant of my dead husband in my hand, feeling as if he had just returned from the grave. His ashes were still in my closet, and now I held his hand-written letter. I could never have imagined just how hateful and mean it would be.

I went outside and sat in the backyard. It was a sunny autumn day, almost too perfect to be spoiled with the contents of what I knew was going to be a difficult letter to read. Seeing his handwriting made me feel as if he were alive again. The letter was long, forty-eight foolscap pages, and he didn't waste one word. It was disgusting from beginning to end, criticizing every friend and family member, his and mine, that were dear to me. My mother and Dick were to receive the brunt of his contempt. Des also said terrible things about my dead father, someone he had never even known. Surprisingly, there was not one bad word written about Stepfather, which I found strange. Friends were torn to shreds. Some of the women were accused of being lesbians. Others were accused of having abnormal relationships with animals. What he said about me, no sane person could possibly have imagined. He repeated all the mean things he had ever said to me over the years, while adding a great deal more.

The only kind thing Des said about me in the whole letter was that I was a good mother. It was such a tiny crumb, but I clung to it for many years. I placed the letter in my closet next to Des' ashes, in order to be able to answer the questions when his conspirator called me.

Anne's twenty-seven-page letter arrived in her post box on the same day as mine. Written in Afrikaans, it was dated October 19th 1987, two and a half months before his suicide. John read it first, and advised Anne not to read it, but she did anyway. It was not nearly as cruel as mine had been, but then Des said that Anne, out of all our children, had shown him the greatest kindness, and he thought that she cared for him a little. It was filled with bitterness and hatred for all the people he perceived had wronged him, along with his contempt for the world in general. My mother and Dick were referred to as whores, and, not surprisingly, were singled out for his most disgusting criticism. Mum was called scum. If anyone had any doubt about the extent of his illness, his three letters would put an end to it.

One of the things in Anne's letter that was omitted from the other two, I found hard to understand. Des fantasized about his many achievements and possessions. We found it astounding to think that he actually believed what he had written. He also said that I was always out of the house, when he kept me at home almost all the time, mostly sitting with him in his bedroom. He mentioned that he had loved me once, which gave me some small comfort. The most tender part of the letter told Anne that he was sorry that he had disappointed us all, and he signed her letter: "All my love, Dadda."

Whoever posted Des' letters was unwittingly cruel, but it showed just how charming he could be in manipulating people into doing whatever he wanted. I have a good idea who it was and can only feel sorry for that person, who obviously had no idea who they were dealing with, or what destruction they had delivered.

A WIDOW

Being a widow was an enormous adjustment for me. Suddenly, there was a peace and quiet that I was completely unaccustomed to. No more clanging of the monkey chain, no more tinging of the telephone, no more screaming and shouting, no more tension. There was simply no more Des. I wasn't used to the quiet, or the freedom to be myself and found it highly unsettling. I still didn't know who I was, and it was to take me three more years before I found my identity, and learned to love and respect myself.

I had received the promised letter from Des, but now I had to wait for the phone call, so I wasn't yet entirely free.

Apart from Craig, I no longer felt needed. The other three children were all out of the house, leading their own lives. The void Des' death left in my life was greater than I had expected, but thanks to my church, I found a satisfying way to fill it, when, during one of our Sunday services, a member of the congregation mentioned being involved with a quadriplegic home on the other side of Pretoria.

There were a dozen quadriplegics living in the home, and I felt that I could be useful to them. I volunteered three days a week, and they became like a second family to me. One by one, they found a special place in my heart, and although they constantly told me that I was a blessing to them, I knew it was really the other way around. They made me feel loved and needed, and they appreciated everything I did for them.

Because I had nursed Des for five years, I knew that, first and foremost, they wanted to be treated as ordinary, intelligent people. Often, people spoke about Des in front of him, as if he wasn't there. It was as if they assumed that because he couldn't walk, his hearing was also impaired. The quadriplegics appreciated my feeding them, reading to them and doing their shopping, but they also needed encouragement to do the few things they were still capable of doing.

Most of all, they wanted to be accepted for who they were and made to feel loved. I could relate to that. It was easy to love them, even the two grumpy ones. They were a challenge that I found irresistible, and when, after a short while, they became dear friends, I was elated. After all the years of adverse response, or no response at all from my husband, these people gave me the reward I had so long been seeking.

With Des gone, and Craig now living in Larry's apartment on the other side of the house, Bowser became even more protective of me. He still slept in the kitchen at night, ensuring our safety while I slept.

One day, while listening to Radio Jacaranda, our local radio station, I heard a request for entries for the annual South African National Song Festival competition. It was only a few days before the entries had to be in when, one morning, I woke early, at 5 am, and the words for *Africa* came to me, one verse after the other. When I went down to the laundry to put a load in the washing machine, I needed only one more verse to finish it, and when I returned to the bedroom, it was waiting to be written. I was excited about entering the competition, but I was only able to write the lyrics. I didn't have a tune in my head and besides, I couldn't write music, so I asked a local singer/songwriter, who had won the competition the previous year, to write the music for me. Together, we then asked a popular South African singer, Annelie, to record the song for us. She recorded it just before midnight on the night before entries closed for the regional competition, and with her unusually deep, rich voice, it sounded wonderful.

I was thrilled when we were told that we had won the regional competition for Radio Jacaranda, and were to go to Johannesburg to take part in the National competition. Our song was given to a well-known recording studio, where it was recorded with another popular singer, along with a back-up group. It sounded different from Annelie's version, but it was good, and we had high hopes of winning. The show was to be televised the following August, and my children all promised to be there.

In June of 1988, we made our last trip as a family to Kruger Park. Des loved the game park, so on Anne's birthday, the children and I drove down and scattered his ashes under a large thorn tree in the Skukuza Rest Camp. We held a small service for him and this helped to bring closure. Apart from the promised phone call, my long and tumultuous life with Des had finally ended.

Good things were on the horizon, and one of them was a trip to Israel, Turkey, and the Greek Islands. My dear friend Corrie suggested that I should accompany her and her husband, along with four of their friends, on the trip. At first, I refused, saying that I couldn't possibly leave Craig and my pets. When Mum heard about it, she and Dick offered to stay in the house with Craig, so then I had no excuse. Going on the trip helped to take my mind off all that had happened, and although I was single and the odd one out, I had a marvelous time. I discovered that travel is the best education and I found it stimulating as well as relaxing. I returned feeling much stronger than when I left.

I wanted to have a close relationship with Mum, but when I called and asked her if we could have a talk about my childhood, she immediately became defensive, and told me she didn't want to discuss it.

She said that she had been hurt enough in her lifetime, and I was to leave the past in the past. I was disappointed, but I didn't try to force her.

In August of 1988, I ran into Michael at the auction. It was good to see him again. I told him that Des had passed away at the beginning of the year, and he was sympathetic. He told me that he had just arrived in Pretoria for a month's stay and was working in a friend's landscape architecture firm.

The next day, the telephone rang. It was Michael. He confessed he had found my telephone number in the directory, and hoped I didn't mind him calling. He had attempted to find accommodation at the Pretoria Country club, but their cottages were all occupied. Having seen Anne's downstairs bedroom/living area when he delivered the furniture the previous year, he wondered if he could rent it for the month. After some discussion, I consented to his renting the room with the use of the downstairs bathroom. We agreed on a rental, and he moved into Anne's room with all its frills and flowers. Hopefully, his old couch and chair that I had bought from him helped to make him feel comfortable.

The morning after his arrival, I was up early, hanging some laundry on the washline, when I heard a noise behind me. I looked around to see Michael standing at the kitchen door, with Bowser standing in front of him. I asked, "Did he sniff you?" and he said, "Yes," with some apprehension.

I replied, "Good, because he either sniffs you, or he bites you." I was impressed, since Bowser didn't bite people he sensed could be trusted.

During his stay, I made traditional South African food for Michael, and he loved everything I made. As a special treat, I bought a leg of venison, and Michael said he had been told by a friend that if you marinate it in Coca-Cola, it makes it tender and tasty, so that night, I stuffed the venison with pork fat and garlic cloves and we placed it in a casserole dish, covering it with Coke. Once cooked, it tasted dreadful, and Michael was highly embarrassed. The friend had played a trick on him, and he had fallen for it. I laughed, and told him that I thought marinating in red wine would have been preferable.

Having Michael stay with us turned out to be delightful. He was easy going and friendly. Even so, not having much self-confidence, I still withdrew into my shell at the slightest provocation. It had been a long time since I had had a conversation with another man. Michael told me I was like a tortoise, and this prompted him to give me a small ivory tortoise as a gift. Craig liked Michael, and when Justine stayed at the house for a few days, they also got on well, and I began to relax. While Michael was in Pretoria, we spent our Saturday mornings at the auction, which felt just like old times.

August 20th, the night of the Song Festival, finally arrived, and Michael accompanied me to Johannesburg. Knowing it was to be recorded on television, I put a tape in the video recorder before we left home.

It was a fabulous evening. Michael and I sat at one of the tables near the stage, along with all the other competition entrants. Our song brought applause from the audience, and loud cheers and whistles from my children, who were seated in the gallery. They were proud of their mother, and it was good to experience something special that we could all share. We were able to enjoy the moment without any feelings of guilt, and our song came fifth out of the seventeen entries. The children maintained that if the back-up hadn't sung out of tune, we would have won, which made me feel good, but I felt that the winning song deserved first place, so I was content with the outcome. However, I had to admit, when I played the tape on our return home, that the children were right. The back-up group was out of tune.

On Michael's last night in Pretoria, he asked if he could take us out to dinner. I said that was kind and thanked him. The only problem was that Craig didn't want to go as he had other plans for the evening. I wasn't comfortable going out alone with Michael, but he was persuasive, and I agreed that he take me to my favorite restaurant.

When we were seated, I noticed some friends of mine sitting at another table, and I felt awkward, thinking they might assume that I was out on a date, so I asked Michael if we could please go somewhere else. Finding it amusing, he laughed, but he took me to another restaurant, where we had a lovely evening. He opened the car door and helped me to get seated at the table. I hadn't been treated like that in a long time. He was different, and I couldn't help but think of Teddy. When Michael left at the end of August, he asked if he might write to me, and I said I would like that very much.

Many people advised me not to make any major decisions for at least a year, which was good advice, but after nine months, I knew it was time to sell the house, leave all the sad memories behind, and make a fresh start.

Although I was now financially secure, having received payment from Des' life insurance, I couldn't relax in the house in Lynnwood. I still pictured Des in many of the rooms, and there were constant reminders of things he had said and done that kept the hurt alive. I was ready to move on. From a practical point of view, I had already repaired the slate roof after a bad hailstorm, and I anticipated many other repairs in the future, as is always the case with any house. I also thought it wise for us to move into a small complex where I would feel safe, so I put the house up for sale. It sold easily, and I bought a townhouse, a few miles east of Lynnwood.

I was sad to have to let Limba go, but he went to work for my brother, which worked out well. Bowser went to live with Larry, so he was also taken care of. Maria was happy to go with me, which made me feel much better about the move.

Believing property was a good investment, I also bought another small townhouse in Lynnwood for my mother and Dick to live in. They were still staying with Aunt Joey at the time, which was a temporary arrangement, so they were grateful when I offered them something more permanent.

From the sale of the house, which was fully paid for by that time, I was fortunate enough to be in a position to pay cash for both properties, so Mum and Dick had nothing to pay except the levy, which all residents paid to cover the cost of maintenance for their townhouse and yard.

Not long after Mum and Dick moved into their townhouse, Mum called me. Her speech was garbled, and she wasn't making any sense. I asked her to hand the telephone to Dick, and I told him that I was sure that Mum had had a stroke, and we needed to get her to hospital immediately. I called for an ambulance, and then rushed over. She was unable to speak, and her eyes were wild with terror. I did my best to calm her until the ambulance arrived. As it was only a mild stroke, her speech returned after a few days, and she was left with no adverse effects.

A year had passed since Des died, and it was time to burn his letter. I needed to leave all the bad memories behind when I left the house. Although the letter was hidden at the back of my closet, it was like a sore festering in my heart, and I was constantly aware of its presence. The phone call had not been forthcoming, and I realized that it was Des' final act of manipulation, forcing me to keep the letter, as I had, for all those months. I hoped that by burning it, I would be free of the past, but I was soon to discover that we can never be free of our past, and we shouldn't want to be, since for better or for worse, it is our past that makes us who we are.

We moved on December 30th, a day short of a year from when Des had died. The next day, I stayed busy, so thankfully, there was no time to brood over the first anniversary of Des' suicide.

The move to the townhouse was perfect timing for Craig, since he had just finished his final year at school. He did well, and said he wanted to study mechanical engineering. I encouraged him, and put enough money aside to cover the cost of his studies. I was sure it was the perfect decision, because he was great with his hands and working on anything mechanical came easily to him.

My townhouse was charming. It had three bedrooms and two baths. Situated on the border of a secure walled complex of fourteen units, I felt safe, until one evening, soon after I had moved in, Anne easily managed to climb over the brick wall. There were burglar bars on all the windows, and security gates on all three outside doors, but since the bars were not closely spaced, I had extra bars welded between them, after which I felt safer, but also as if I were living in a jail. Although Craig was still living with me, he had a girlfriend and was out quite often, so I felt the need for the additional security.

When I moved from the house, I gave about half of my furniture to the children. I then bought an antique oak dining room table as well as five oak dining chairs, which meant that I was one short, but I didn't mind, knowing that I had plenty of time to look for the sixth chair. I made my home feminine and homey, believing that I could live there quite happily for the rest of my life.

There was a servant's room with a bathroom at the back of the townhouse for Maria, and she was content to stay with me. The townhouse was fairly small, and since I only needed her twice a week, she found other employment for the remaining days. I suggested that if she cooked for us in the evenings, we would both be assured of a good evening meal. That way, I didn't have to rush back from the quadriplegic home to cook on the days when I volunteered. The arrangement worked out well for both of us, and I found peace and contentment in my new surroundings.

I volunteered at the quadriplegic home three days a week, and on the remaining two days, Mum spent the day with me, while Dick went to work for his son. Mum was easily bored, so I encouraged her to take up crocheting and she made doilies for every surface in her townhouse as well as mine, even making covers for my lampshades. Although I would have preferred a few less doilies, I didn't have the heart to stop her, since she enjoyed it so much. Saturdays, Mum and Dick both spent the day with me. Sunday mornings, I went to church. Sunday afternoons and evenings found me feeling a little lonesome, but I could always find something to keep me busy.

I was now fully independent. And gradually, my self-confidence returned. I loved my church family, and I regularly attended their weekly Bible study. I also joined the singles club at the church, which met once a month at Siebert's home. He was a widower and a retired policeman, who lived with his sister. We met at his house, and although he was quite reserved, he always made us feel welcome.

Mum and Dick were struggling financially, so I offered to give her a lump sum of money or, alternatively, I offered to pay her levy at the townhouse for the rest of her life. Mum chose the latter, and I assumed responsibility for her financial support until her death. This gave her independence, which I am sure was a great comfort to her. It also gave me peace of mind.

Now that I had most of my immediate responsibilities in hand, I had the time and opportunity to have my feet operated on. My bunions had become horribly painful, and I was unable to find comfortable shoes. I went to see an orthopedic surgeon, who was considered to be the best in the country. He was confident that he could ease my discomfort, and once again, I made the mistake of trusting a medical professional, but it had been almost forty years since my last surgery, and I was sure that by now, bunion surgery had been perfected.

He first operated on my left foot, and without any prior permission from me, he performed six different surgeries on it. After being told that I was just having the bunion removed and since none of this was explained to me ahead of time, I was horrified to awake from the surgery to find long steel pins sticking out of all five toes. Returning home on crutches, I knocked and bent one of the hooks as I ascended the steps, which was incredibly painful. I hobbled around on crutches for a few weeks, but at least I could still drive, which was important to me because there was no public transport nearby.

While waiting for the foot to heal, I was able to spend some of my time searching for additional pieces of antique furniture for my home, which gave me a great deal of pleasure. The sixth dining room chair proved elusive, but I wasn't ready to give up looking for it.

DREAMS DO COME TRUE

My dream of more than thirty years finally came true, when Anne accompanied me to England. June and her husband Ron picked us up at Heathrow, and we stayed with them for a few days.

On May 1st, 1989, June and I stood on the line in Greenwich that determines Mean Time. Some people say you can never really transplant yourself and settle down in another country until you have been back to the country of your birth. I found it to be true.

I visited many of the places where I had spent my childhood. 8, Farnaby Road looked much the same, except that it was covered with scaffolding. The new owners were finally re-pointing the bricks to alleviate the damp that had plagued Sheila's and my bedrooms. We asked permission to go inside, and I was shocked to see how all the rooms had shrunk! Of course, they hadn't really shrunk. It was I who had grown up, and I was now accustomed to the spaciousness of South Africa houses. This time, the lump in my throat was not one of fear, but nostalgic regrets for the many hurts I had experienced in the apartment where I had spent my childhood.

We were able to visit my remaining family members, and a few of my mother's friends while we were there. Everyone made a great fuss over us, and catching up with all the news of the intervening years was overwhelming, but also very enjoyable.

We drove to Stratford-on-Avon in Warwickshire, where I was excited to visit my schoolteacher, Miss Kerrisk. Stratford, Shakespeare's birthplace, is an elegant old town and, in my opinion, a most suitable place for such a refined lady to retire. I didn't write to tell her I was coming; I wanted it to be a surprise. We found her house and knocked on the door, but there was no answer. Her next-door neighbor heard us knocking, and came out and told us that Miss Kerrisk had just suffered a serious stroke, and was in the local hospital.

Undeterred, we found the hospital, and there was the dear lady, sitting in a wheelchair with one side of her face drooping badly. She was embarrassed for us to see her like that, but didn't allow it to overshadow her delight at our visit, and tears of joy filled her eyes. I tried to explain what an amazing impact she had made on my life and how she had saved me from making a total disaster of it. She wouldn't take the credit, but I think in her humble way, she knew I was right. Along with June, she had the naughtiest and the best-behaved pupils of the class of 1956 in her hospital room that day. Before we left, we promised to continue writing, although I knew it wouldn't be so easy for her from then on.

From there, we drove to Merthyr Vale in South Wales, where Anne and I spent a few days with my Uncle Vivian, his wife, Glenys and the family. There, I felt my deepest roots. The mountains dotted with sheep and wild ponies, and the tiny villages tucked down in the valleys of Wales held a kind of magic for me, and I felt close to my parents and grandparents and all the relatives I had never known or was too young to remember.

The family spoke incredibly fast, and all at the same time, and Anne and I struggled to understand their strong Welsh accents. We met as many of the extended family as could be crammed into the few days we were there, and I felt loved and proud to be a part of my Welsh heritage.

We then spent a few days in Northern Ireland and Scotland, where Anne's husband, John, joined us for the remainder of our trip. June and Ron picked us up in Scotland and drove us back to London. I was thrilled when they took us to Dymchurch on a freezing cold day, which brought back vivid memories of the many holidays I had spent there as a child. The final leg of our trip was a week's stay in Paris where we did all the usual sightseeing and ate lots of Chinese food as our funds were running low.

Back in London, we collected the rest of our luggage, and June and Ron drove us back to Heathrow, where we met up with our Welsh family. They had driven all the way from Wales to see us off at the airport, and I was overwhelmed with the love they showed us and left them with a heavy heart, promising to return again soon.

When I returned home from England, I found several letters from Michael waiting for me. His last letter told me that he was to return to South Africa for three months during the summer, (our South African winter,) when he was not teaching classes at Texas A&M University. That meant he would again be working at his friend's firm in Pretoria, and I was delighted to think that I would be seeing him again very soon.

Very soon turned out to be the next day, when just after 9:00 pm, my telephone rang. It was really good to hear Michael's voice, but when he asked me if I could meet him in Pretoria, I had to decline, telling him that my car had a flat tire. He didn't sound very convinced, and probably concluded that I was just being coy. But it was true, and I assured him that I would see him the next day.

About half an hour later, I heard the sound of my door buzzer from the main security gate. It was Michael! Totally flustered, I asked him what he was doing there. He replied that he had taken a taxi from town and just wanted to see me. Smiling to myself, I opened the gate for him. The taxi was still waiting outside, but he politely asked me if I could take him back into Pretoria. I reminded him about my flat tire, and then he had to believe me. I then told him that Craig was due home in an hour or two, and I was sure he wouldn't mind taking him back to the country club, where he was staying. After paying the taxi driver, he came in, and we chatted until Craig came home.

Michael became a constant visitor during his time in Pretoria. During that time, he confessed that he had watched me at the auction for three months, before he found the opportunity to speak to me. I was flattered to think that he had noticed me. He brought me flowers, and took me to nice restaurants, and we went to church together on Sundays, where he was well received by my church family. When he left for the States at the end of his visit, he made no promises, but he did say, "I know I am not the first one to say this, but I go to prepare a place for thee!" I was to remember those words a year later, when Michael called me from Texas.

At the time, I was much too nervous to ask Michael exactly what he meant, and he didn't elaborate, but his letters became more affectionate. He sent me a few classical tapes, which I played over and over again, and my love for classical music grew.

Just after Michael left, in late August, I went back to have my other foot operated on and to my horror; I woke up to discover both of my feet in plaster. The surgeon decided that his first surgery had been unsuccessful, so he did my left foot over again. Unable to drive, I had to rent a wheelchair to use at home. Along with the frustration it caused me, it brought back many unhappy memories that I was so desperately trying to forget.

At the end of it all, the surgeon had to admit that this latest surgery had also failed. He discovered, after the fact, that I had what he called sloppy joints, something he had not previously noticed, which I found quite impossible to understand when I remembered that he was supposed to be the best orthopedic surgeon in the country. He suggested performing surgery that would result in my toes being permanently stiff, but as I didn't relish the idea of walking like a duck, I declined. I went home feeling disappointed, with feet that were destined to become even more painful in the future.

Sheila became ill, and she and Dennis flew down to Pretoria. I drove her to the Sandton Clinic, outside Johannesburg, where she stayed for two months. Unfortunately, they couldn't find out what was wrong with her, and the paralysis that had started in her feet gradually spread up through her body until she became semi-paralyzed from the neck down.

During this time, Dennis stayed in my spare room, and my patience was sorely tested by his laziness. He sat outside reading books all day long, only pausing to ask for tea or to go to the bathroom. One day he called me and asked me if there wasn't any tea and I told him to get it himself! He was shocked, (as was I), but he got up and made his tea, and we had a far better understanding after that.

I drove Dennis to the clinic to see Sheila on weekdays, when I wasn't volunteering, as well as on Saturdays and Sundays. After all the weeks of spending time in so many different hospitals with Des, it was not an easy time for me. Sheila was depressed, and by the time she went home in March of the following year, it was obvious that she would no longer be able to work. Following the many years of faithful service to her employer, he showed his gratitude by continuing to pay her salary until her death.

During 1990, Justine and Larry both got married, and it was wonderful to see that both of them had made good choices. With three of my four children happily married, I felt that life was, at last, taking a turn for the better. I was shortly to find out just how much better!

DOWN THE AISLE TO HAPPINESS

One afternoon, at the end of July, my telephone rang. It was Michael calling from Texas. His first words after saying, "hello" turned my world upside down. He asked, "Doreen, will you come to College Station and be my bride?"

Without hesitating, I said, "Yes!"

The rest of our conversation was a blur, but when I put the telephone down, I suddenly realized that I had made one of the biggest decisions of my life without even praying about it, and I never made any major decisions without prayerful deliberation.

I walked around to the other side of my bed where my Bible lay. I got down on my knees and prayed, "Lord, please show me clearly in your Word if this is what you want me to do. Should I marry Michael? If it's not your will, then I won't do it."

With closed eyes, I opened my Bible, and I found myself looking at the book of John, where I read:

> Do not let your hearts be troubled. Trust in God; trust also in me. In my Father's house are many rooms; if it were not so, I would have told you. **I am going there to prepare a place for you.** And if I go and prepare a place for you, I will come back and take you to be with

me; that you may also be where I am. You know the way to the place where I am going.

John 14:1-4

I gasped as I read the passage. God was gracious, and He made His answer clear to me. I called Michael back and asked him one question. Everything depended on his answer. "Are you prepared to come to South Africa to marry me?" He immediately replied with just one word, "Yes!"

I now had my Father's blessing and needed nothing more.

When I put the telephone down, I was happy to know that not only was I going to marry the man I loved, but by marrying in South Africa, I would have the support of my family and friends at our wedding.

Ironically, I had never had any desire to go to the States. I had thought I would be living happily in my little townhouse forever. The other irony was that just that morning, before Michael called me, I had finally found and bought my sixth dining room chair. My home was finally complete, and I was settled. God must have smiled when I thought that I now had everything my heart desired.

That evening, I went to Bible study bursting with happiness, and I wanted to announce to everyone that I was now engaged to be married to Michael. My Bible study group were like family, but I wasn't sure how I was going to tell them. Siebert made it possible by asking me to attend the Policeman's Ball with him the following Saturday evening. I thanked him, but told him that I had to decline, since I had just become engaged that day. He looked disappointed, and asked me if I would have said yes, had he asked me earlier, and I replied, "Yes, I would have."

He said that he was really sorry he had waited so long to ask me out. I had no idea he was interested, although I knew he liked me. I liked him, too, but my feelings for Michael ran much deeper.

Mum, Dick and the children were shocked, but they took the news of our impending marriage quite well. Since my three older children were married and Craig was going into the Air Force to spend a year of compulsory national service, I felt the timing was perfect. At least they were grown and except for Craig, had all found their life partners.

Maria cried when I told her that I was going to marry Michael, and live in Texas. She asked me what was to become of her, and I assured her that she would be just fine. During the years that she had worked for me, I had taught her to be independent. She now had a bank account, a pension policy, and enough work with Mum and a few other people to be in good financial standing.

A few days later, I told my friends at the quadriplegic home that I was going to be married. I loved all the quads, but four of them were extra special to me, and of course, they were going to be particularly hard to say goodbye to.

In August, Sheila was still not doing well, and she spent another month in Sandton Clinic. Just as before, they were unable to help her, and she returned home in a very despondent frame of mind. I was concerned that her health hadn't improved, and disappointed that she wouldn't be well enough to attend our wedding.

There was a lot to organize before the wedding, but when I went to see my pastor at the Baptist church, I was shocked to learn that he was not able to marry us. He said that since Michael was divorced, we would be unequally yoked, and he showed me the verse in the Bible that he felt proved his point. I told him I loved Michael, and after prayerfully reading verses in my Bible, it was equally clear to me that I had my Father's blessing.

My pastor also said that if I married Michael and it didn't work out, I must know that my church family would be there for me. I was disappointed by his response, but this didn't prevent me from sending him and his wife, as well as my entire church family, an invitation to our wedding.

I also sent wedding invitations overseas to my family who, understandably, were unable to attend. Most of them had never traveled more than a few miles from home, and the airfare was expensive. I invited several of my English friends, including Miss Kerrisk. She wrote back to tell me she would have loved to come to our wedding, but she had just returned from a trip to Portugal. Judging by the photographs she sent, I could tell that she had made a full recovery from the stroke. I wrote back and promised her that I would visit her again and introduce her to Michael. Dear June flew over from England and stayed with me in my townhouse, and I was thrilled that she was able to attend.

The pastor of the Brooklyn Methodist Church said he would be more than happy to marry us, and as Michael was a Methodist, it worked out well. A week before the wedding, he flew over in time for us to attend pre-marital classes at the church. It was wonderful to see him after more than a year, and one look at his smiling face told me that I had made the right decision.

Anne made my beautiful teal wedding dress and trimmed it with lace, which we dyed in tea to make it look antique. For something old, I wore Mum's cameo that she had given to me for my fortieth birthday. It brought back pleasant memories of our frequent train trips to the East End of London. For something blue, I wore a blue garter. Anne also made my bouquet of antique cream roses as well as the table decorations. Justine made the menus for the luncheon tables. Larry proudly walked me down the aisle and gave me away, and Craig managed to get time off from the Air Force and was able to ring the church bell for us. It was wonderful to have all my children participate in our joyous day.

The ceremony was perfect. The pastor told the congregation that he had only known both of us for a couple of weeks, but seeing our obvious happiness and taking into consideration that I had been born in

England, Michael was from Texas, and that we had met in South Africa, this had to be a marriage made in heaven. He was right!

The morning service was followed by a reception in the church hall, where we served refreshments and wedding cake. My Baptist pastor was there, as well as about half of the congregation. The hall was packed with them and other close friends and family.

Michael and Doreen on their wedding day in October, 1990

Looking across the hall at June, I felt a deep appreciation for my dearest friend who had kept in contact through so many years, in spite of the five thousand miles that separated us. There was Corrie, who had been so constant and loyal, visiting Des regularly and supporting me through all those difficult times. I caught a glimpse of Suzanne, all grown up, smiling shyly at me from across the hall. Frances and her husband were there with their son, so obviously happy for me. Irene was completely surrounded by people, and I felt great admiration for this courageous woman, who had never let her disability stand in the way of her living a productive and fulfilling life. Seeing Maria looking so lovely in her pretty new dress brought a lump to my throat. We had both come a long way since that first day when she had come to work for me.

She was now comfortable to put her arm around my waist to have her picture taken with me, which was such a big step for her at that time. I was going to miss her terribly. Other friends, too numerous to mention, helped to make our wedding day perfect.

We booked a formal luncheon at a nice restaurant for our closest family and friends. The food was wonderful, although I was too excited to have much of an appetite. Michael kept looking at me as if he couldn't believe his eyes. Like me, I am sure he was finding it hard to believe that this was really happening? Speeches were made, and Chris, Michael's best man, teased him about his regular visits to the auction, and said that now he could understand why they were so frequent.

Michael responded with a great speech, thanking everyone, and I felt so proud of him. He spoke with great confidence, and he was careful not to exclude anyone.

Mum kept tearing up, and I prayed she wouldn't break down. She said that I mustn't worry about anyone other than myself, but then she kept on repeating how she was going to miss me, and didn't know how she could possibly manage without me,

My two sons-in-law had asked that we marry in the morning, because they wanted to go to the rugby match that was to take place that afternoon. It was the national playoff, and we obliged. It turned out to be perfect, as the day was barely long enough to get everything done as it was.

Because we were unable to fit fourteen wheelchairs into the small church, we drove to the quadriplegic home in the afternoon with champagne and snacks for a third reception. What a welcome they gave us. Many tears were shed when we left, as well as promises to write.

We left on our honeymoon that evening, and not wanting to drive too far at night, we booked in at the local Farm Inn, which was not far out of town. When we arrived, we found that Anne had arranged to have champagne waiting for us in the room. Michael placed a long silver

Guatemalan wedding necklace around our necks, and, kissing me gently, we toasted our future. I could never have imagined how wonderful it would be.

After a week's honeymoon in the lowveld, we returned to Pretoria, and before we knew it, it was time to leave for the United States. Mum and Dick offered to stay in our townhouse for a year, after which, we planned to return to South Africa to live. They locked up their townhouse, and moved into ours when we left. We weren't entirely sure what the future held, but with this arrangement, Maria still had a home, for which I was extremely grateful.

When the time came to leave, all four children and their spouses went with us to the airport. My heart ached. How could I leave them? Only then did the full realization of what I was doing hit me. We stood around making small talk until our departure was announced, and I knew it was time. There were hugs and tears all round, and then Michael and I mounted the escalator that was to take us to our gate to start our new life together.

This time, I was not leaving the man I loved behind. I was going with him.

PART THREE: BLESSED!

A NEW BEGINNING

On October 13th, 1990, I arrived in the United States of America, a brand-new bride. I was fifty years old, but in my happy, excited frame of mind, I felt half that age.

On our arrival at Houston airport, Michael joined the line for Americans, while I went to the one for non-citizens. After being asked a few questions by the Immigration officer, I was told that since I didn't have a visa, I would have to return to South Africa on the next flight. I was devastated because I was under the impression that with a British passport, I didn't need a visa.

I was then escorted to a back room, where I was interrogated for about an hour, and made to feel like a common criminal. I was close to tears, when suddenly Michael stormed into the room, and asked just what was going on. The official explained to him that I needed a visa to enter the country, and as I didn't have one, they were going to put me on the next plane back to South Africa. I had never seen Michael either upset or angry, so I was completely taken aback when he exploded and said, "If you do that, I will go with her, and I will never set foot in this country again!"

My interrogator immediately changed his tone of voice and asked Michael to please calm down. There was an alternative. I could enter the U.S. on the condition that I report to the Immigration Service office in San Antonio, where I should apply for a green card. Once in possession of a green card, I could then apply for citizenship, which would take another five years.

Shaken by this highly unpleasant experience, I was relieved when we were finally allowed to leave the airport. The bullying by the immigration officials had taken me completely by surprise, and my first impression of the United States was not a pleasant one.

Another unpleasant surprise awaited me as we stepped out of the air-conditioned airport to catch the shuttle to the long-term parking lot. Michael had hoped that by mid-October, the heat and humidity of the Houston summer would have dissipated somewhat, so that the shock wouldn't be too great for me. But, on taking a step forward, I took two steps back, as I was engulfed by the hot, humid air. Astonished, I asked him, "What is this?"

Michael smiled ruefully, while explaining that this was normal for Houston. After the mild, dry heat of Pretoria, I was totally unprepared for this brutally hot climate, but I attempted a brave smile as we made our way to the car. It was midafternoon, and the car was standing in the long-term parking lot, baking in the fierce Texas sunshine.

Michael put our suitcases in the trunk. As he opened the car doors, the heat trapped inside poured out, like air from a punctured air balloon. He got in and turned the key. Nothing! The battery was completely dead! My brand-new husband, who was obviously trying his best to make a good impression, had to leave me standing next to the car, while he walked over to the pay station to find a battery charger.

Half an hour later, we were on our way home, and I fell asleep almost immediately. I had been unable to sleep on the plane; the trip had taken almost thirty hours, and I was exhausted. Michael was pleased when I fell asleep, since he wasn't anxious for me to see the unsightly billboards that lined the highway between Houston and College Station. I awoke as we entered College Station, in time to see strip shopping centers strung along the length of Texas Avenue, the main thoroughfare through town.

As we turned off the main road and entered the South Oakwood subdivision, I was struck by the lack of color in the yards. There were no Jacarandas, no flowering shrubs and very few flowers. However, after making a few turns, I was delighted when we stopped outside a charming bungalow, situated on a pretty wooded lot. This was to be our home.

Michael insisted that I stay in the car while he walked around and opened the door for me. He then opened the front door, picked me up, and carried me over the threshold. My dear, romantic husband said, "Welcome home, darling girl!" and I felt both welcome and loved. We were really home!

Upon entering the house, a vague, sickly-sweet odor greeted us. As Michael proudly showed me over the home that he had so carefully prepared, we saw that there were dead yellow jacket wasps lying everywhere. Having originally made their nest in the chimney, while the house stood vacant, they had inhabited the entire house. Discovering them the previous day, Michael's son had kindly sprayed and vacuumed them up, but they had continued to enter the house by the dozens, where they died. I wondered what else I could expect to find in this strange land!

In our excitement, not even the dead wasps could put a damper on the joy we felt at being home. Michael had gathered up odd pieces of furniture from garage sales and auctions for the living and dining rooms. We had inherited his granny's antique bedroom suite, and Michael's mother had ensured that we had a good supply of linen. We couldn't have been happier!

The small rent house had large windows and glass sliding doors on the back side, looking out onto a heavily wooded lot, but there were no drapes, and Michael was soon to learn that I was uncomfortable with this arrangement. The only room in the house where I felt private was the bathroom, and it took me quite a while to feel safe, but once I did, I relaxed and enjoyed it.

Most of the properties in College Station were unfenced, giving one the feeling of living in a large open park, which was delightful, but it made me feel quite vulnerable, having lived for so many years behind the high walls and security gates common to South African homes. I found it strange that there were no people knocking on the front door looking for work, or simply checking to see where the most vulnerable spot was for breaking in during the night. There were no people running across the streets in front of traffic. No stray dogs roamed around. For me, it was a completely new way of life.

However, my biggest adjustment was being Michael's wife. In his eyes, I could do no wrong. He loved me totally and unconditionally, telling me often, and I knew he really meant it. He had many affectionate names for me and never called me Doreen. I am still mostly called my darling girl, even in the company of others, and I quickly learned to respond with, my darling boy. I received constant love and affection and thrived on it. Michael taught me to look into his eyes, something I had never done with anyone before and at first, I found it awkward to do. It felt so intimate; but gradually, I got used to it, and I felt my eyes shine in response to the love in his.

For quite a while, I found that old habits and memories seemed determined to interfere with our happiness. I half expected Michael to get angry and lose his temper, but he never did, and gradually, I learned to relax and enjoy being in the moment. When I was lost in thought, Michael didn't demand to know what I was thinking and then reprimanded me if my thoughts were not what he wanted to hear. He gently asked, "Car 54, where are you?" No longer having to be fearful about my thoughts was a completely new experience for me.

Shortly after our arrival, Michael's friend, Chris, flew in from South Africa and came to our house for lunch. The previous day I had rearranged the furniture and tried to make our home look as attractive as possible. There were no flowers in the yard but discovering a bush covered with pretty red berries, I cut a few sprays and arranged them in an oriental vase that I found in the kitchen cabinet. I carefully placed the vase on the black steamer trunk that served as our living room coffee table.

When Michael came home from work, I was excited to show him the house, but when he saw the berries, his face fell, and he said, "Oh, you cut the yaupon. You mustn't cut the yaupon, darling girl! They take years to grow."

One look at his stricken face told me I had done wrong, and I burst into tears. He lifted his arm to put it around my shoulder, and instinctively, I ducked. He gently took hold of me, and with his voice full of astonishment and compassion, he said, "Did you really think I was going to hit you?"

Then, it was my turn to reassure him, explaining that it was simply a reflex action. After years of being slapped or punched at the slightest provocation, I simply couldn't help myself. Michael held me for a long time, until, gradually, peace and calm were restored. I knew then that I had nothing to fear from this gentle man and it was a wonderful feeling. After years of being hurt and rejected, Michael was patient and kind to a fault. At long last, I had a husband who loved me and wanted to take care of me.

Michael's friends made me feel welcome, and we received many invitations to share a meal, so that I could get to know everyone. Wherever we went, he proudly introduced me as his new bride, and I was constantly blushing. He made me feel special, but it took me a while to adjust to life in America. Naturally, I felt homesick and missed my children very much.

After a while, I confessed to Michael that apart from feeling homesick, I found College Station to be quite unlovely. I hesitated to say it was ugly, but Michael had to admit that, compared to Pretoria, it was not a pretty town. The clay soil, summer drought, and hot, humid climate made it difficult for anything to grow successfully, and the proliferation of billboards and the dozens of unsightly fast-food restaurants on the main streets did little to enhance the appearance of the community.

The surrounding countryside was quite pleasant, and while on a short trip one weekend, we found ourselves in the tiny town of Rising Star. A sign outside a house told us that there were antiques and collectibles for sale. Michael bought me a small ceramic Dutch milkmaid. She was missing her milk pails and was on sale for one dollar. At the time, we could barely afford it but she is still one of my most precious possessions. A few months later, we found a copper kettle without a lid for ten dollars, which became the start of my kettle collection. Small things gave us both so much joy!

Turning our house into a home was such a pleasure. We didn't have much, and our financial situation made it impossible for us to buy anything new for quite some time. No matter, we were content, and I discovered that garage sales and local thrift stores offered an abundance of bargains. Discount coupons were also a big help when buying groceries, and as I had always lived frugally, we managed nicely. We were like two teenagers starting off in marriage, with nothing but our love for one another, and I learned, once again, that money, a fine house and a fancy motorcar are not necessary for true happiness. I had had them all, and I had been utterly miserable.

Michael appreciated and thanked me for everything I did. Meals received compliments such as, "That was wonderful," even when I felt sure they were quite ordinary. Little things made life special, like being greeted each morning with a smile and tender words. While darning Michael's socks or ironing his shirts, I noticed him watching me with a wistful smile on his face, and he thanked me for doing things that many husbands seem to take for granted. His manners were impeccable, and mutual respect came easily.

Having lived for so long with criticism, while receiving only negative feedback for everything I did, I had to learn to change my attitude and way of thinking. Michael was even helpful with that. Whenever I complained or said something negative, he smiled and said, "My darling girl, you'd complain if you were hung with a new rope."

The result was that I became acutely aware of my thoughts and words. With Michael's help, I was able to overcome my negative thoughts, and it quickly became unnecessary for Michael to mention the new rope.

Many people might find it strange when I say that I had to learn how to relax and enjoy my new life. But after having lived a lifetime with fear, abuse and criticism, that was how it was for me. Michael taught me to feel alive, how to think for myself, how to see things in a positive light, how to grieve freely and openly and how to love wholeheartedly. Michael's example of a whole person who needed no confirmation or approval from anybody was perfect for me. His self-esteem was high, he had loads of self-confidence, and his sense of integrity and high moral values made it easy for him to be who he was.

Gradually, by being treated with love and respect, I realized that I was not stupid, as Des had always led me to believe. Michael was a well-respected university professor, so it made sense that I should believe him when he told me I was highly intelligent. I knew that he meant it, and didn't say it just to make me feel good. It was encouraging to experience his respect and admiration, and I quickly felt worthy of both.

I was introduced to campus life at Texas A&M University, and never having attended college myself, it was a great experience. Formal functions and banquets gave me the opportunity to meet other faculty members, as well as many of Michael's students. We attended regular seasonal entertainment, presented by the Opera and Performing Arts Society that staged a variety of ballets and Broadway shows. We also went to concerts presented by the Brazos Valley Symphony, which were always quite wonderful.

Following my unfortunate introduction to the United States, we had to make several trips to San Antonio for my green card application. I found San Antonio to be very interesting, with an authentic Mexican flavor, and visits to the River Walk, the Mexican market, and the Alamo ensured that it quickly became my favorite big city in Texas.

A few months later, I was finally in a position to obtain my green card, but I first had to be interviewed. After my experience at the airport, I was extremely nervous. While waiting for my number to be called at the immigration office, Michael had to leave the room to replenish our parking meter. At that moment, my number was called, and terrified, I explained that my husband had just gone to put some coins in the parking meter. The official replied, "We don't want your husband; we want you!"

He reminded me of the Uncle Sam army poster so famous in America during the war years. My mouth went dry as I followed the official to the interview room. He looked at me long and hard before asking me just one simple question. "Did you marry for love?"

I blushed before replying simply, "Why, yes, of course!"

He smiled and said, "That's what they wrote on the report from the airport." I was flabbergasted. After all my nervous anticipation, that was it? One question? And such a peculiar question at that. I was granted my green card, even though I had no desire to go to work. Michael preferred having me at home taking care of the housekeeping and I was happy to do just that. I now had to wait five years before I could become an American citizen. In the meantime, as stated prominently on my new driver's license, I was classified as a resident alien, which I did not find at all flattering.

Ironically, it was to take me seventeen years to become an American citizen, due to the fact that I was nearly always in South Africa or somewhere else overseas, when the five years were up. Because I was out of the country each time, I then had to start the process all over again.

As American as apple pie. A citizen at last!

Our first Thanksgiving was something I was unaccustomed to, as it isn't observed in England or South Africa. When we were invited to Dallas to celebrate the day with Michael's sister, I was apprehensive. It was there that I was to meet Michael's mother for the first time. His father had died a few years earlier, so regrettably, I never got to meet him. Mama, as I was to call her, and I liked each other instantly, and I was quickly made to feel a part of the family.

A trip to a Dallas restaurant taught me that there were language differences that I needed to familiarize myself with. I accidentally dropped my napkin on the floor and asked the waiter for a clean serviette. The waiter looked puzzled until Michael explained that I needed a new napkin. I said, "No, that's what you put on a baby," and Michael told me that a napkin is called a diaper in America.

It was all so confusing. I also had to learn that our car had a trunk, a hood, and a glove compartment, not a boot, a bonnet, and a cubbyhole. It was almost like a foreign language.

December brought with it Christmas parties for both faculty and students, all of which were great fun. We then drove up to Dalhart in the Texas panhandle to spend Christmas with Michael's mother. It was an all-day trip of eleven hours, and I learned just how large the state of Texas really is. Mama made us a traditional turkey dinner, something I had not been used to in South Africa. We were blessed with a white Christmas, which was special for me after the many hot summer Christmases I had been accustomed to. Meeting Mama's many friends, while in Dalhart, was like being introduced to extended family members, as she was much beloved by everyone.

By this time, I had settled into my new life with Michael. We spent a year in College Station before returning to South Africa for a year, where Michael worked again in Chris' office. From then on, life constantly took us from one side of the world to the other, while we tried to decide where we should settle permanently. Understandably, we were torn between the two countries; loving both of them and having families in both made for a difficult decision.

Back in Texas, after renting an apartment for a couple of years, we bought a small two-bedroomed fixer-upper on the other side of the campus in North Oakwood, Bryan, and moved in at the end of August, 1994. I was soon to discover that the damp, humid climate in Bryan didn't agree with me, and arthritis that had started in my right thumb just before I married Michael, spread quickly to various joints in my body. Back pain had me confined to my bed for several days at a time. Having always been quite healthy, apart from stress-related illnesses, I was distraught to think that Michael must now discover that his wife was not in such good shape. When I mentioned this to him, his only remark was that he should have checked my teeth! Then he got serious and said, "My darling girl, you don't marry someone because they are healthy. You marry them because you want to be with them, even when they are not."

FAMILY MATTERS

Dennis died suddenly of a heart attack, leaving Sheila alone on the farm in Zimbabwe. Shortly after his death, I made a trip to South Africa, and while I was there, I flew up to see Sheila, and found that she was still confined to her bed due to her ongoing paralysis. She was understandably lonely and depressed. Always having been busy running the two factories, and working with the staff, she couldn't accept her current situation, and I was saddened to find that she had lost the will to live.

We discussed our childhood at length, and I was shocked to discover how much she had suffered at the hands of Stepfather, just as I had. Growing up, we had never confided in one another and, stupidly, both of us blamed ourselves for everything that had happened.

Sheila also confided in me with regard to her marriage. Like me, she had to endure Dennis' many affairs and constant brutality. Like Des, Dennis was an unhappy man with a bad temper, who didn't have the capacity to love and respect my sister. I told her she was still relatively young and that if she came to the States, we could surely get her well, and she could start a new life with a chance of happiness. She shook her head vehemently, and told me it was too late for that. She simply wanted to die on her farm with her two dogs, and I must please not ask her again.

Convinced that she didn't have long to live, Sheila asked me to help sort through her personal possessions. We spent many hours going through boxes of documents, letters and photographs. She told me things about my mother that upset me. Being so much older than me, Sheila remembered a lot that I didn't. She said she couldn't forgive Mum, and never wanted to see her again. I told her that we had to forgive Mum because she had been young and foolish, and with the war on, people often did things they may not have otherwise done, but Sheila was so contemptuous of Mum, that she refused to hear what I had to say.

In the midst of the sorting, we came across two photographs of Teddy with his wife and little girl, which Sheila gave to me. Seeing Teddy's smiling face after all those years made my heart skip a beat. Sheila told me that he had visited her in England several times after I broke off with him, enquiring about me. She then corresponded with him for a few years, after she and Dennis moved to Zambia. It turned out that Teddy had waited faithfully for me for over three years, and only after Sheila told him that I had married Des, did he find a new girlfriend who, Sheila said, looked quite a lot like me. The happy photographs convinced me that Teddy had found happiness in spite of me, and I was at last able to lay aside my guilt.

Sheila was almost sixty-one years old when she died, and sadly, she never received the letter and birthday card I mailed to her. As I had promised her six months earlier, I reluctantly complied with her request, and didn't fly back to Zimbabwe to attend her funeral. I will always treasure the memory of that week that we shared together.

We moved back to South Africa in 1998 and stayed there for two years while Michael simultaneously worked at Pretoria University and studied for his PhD. During that time, Mum and Dick went to Durban for a holiday, and while they were there, Dick fell and broke his hip. Infection set in, and he was taken to hospital, where he died at the age of seventy-five. Dick and Mum had spent twenty-five years together, and I knew that she was going to be lost without him.

Mum suddenly looked old and tired, and she became increasingly depressed. Never having been content with her own company, she was lonely and bitter, and it showed. She had previously taken great care of her appearance, but living alone, she lost interest in everything and let herself go. When I dropped by to visit, she often opened the front door and didn't even bother to say hello, before complaining about the weather as well as anything and everything else in general.

From then on, Mum told me exactly how much time, in hours, I spent with her on my many visits to South Africa, and it was never enough. No matter how much money I gave her, or how many clothes I bought for her, they were also never enough. When I was in Texas, I called Mum each weekend, only to hear a string of complaints about her health and everything else that was wrong with her life. Nothing I did was ever right and one day, totally frustrated, I told her so. She immediately said how much she appreciated what I did for her, but it was too little, too late. She always knew how to hurt my feelings or make me feel guilty, and I could never please her.

No longer happy living alone, Mum moved out of her townhouse and went to live with my brother, Ross, in Durban, but after a few months, she returned to Pretoria, where Anne managed to find her an apartment in a pleasant retirement village. Mum seemed to be content, but suggestions that she take advantage of the many activities offered there fell on deaf ears. Anne and one of Mum's old friends took care of her, visiting her regularly, for which I was very grateful.

During the years that Michael was teaching at Texas A&M, we were fortunate to spend several semesters in Tuscany, Italy, while accompanying Michael's students on their study abroad program.

Those trips enabled me to fulfil my lifelong ambition to paint, which I enjoyed tremendously. Traveling all over Italy with the students, I received the best education anyone could wish for, and my regret at having had no university education no longer seemed to hold any significance.

We finally decided that we would retire in the United States and spent two summers touring around New Mexico, looking for the perfect location. Taking into consideration my need for a dry climate, which seemed beneficial for my arthritis, we thought New Mexico would be suitable. Unfortunately, we found it to be so dry and dusty that Michael sneezed a lot, and I found it difficult to breathe.

However, each time on our way to New Mexico, we traveled through a small town in the central Texas hill country, and we both agreed that Mason was where we wanted to retire. We found the perfect fixer-upper, which turned out to be affordable, but it was to take many years of renovating it over the summers before we were able to move in.

In June of 2001, Michael and I flew to Singapore, where Michael attended a conference. I was thrilled, because the trip afforded me the opportunity to visit my father's grave. Singapore was stifling hot, and the humidity was even worse than in Houston. We took a train to the Kranji War Memorial and Cemetery on the far side of the Island. The Memorial was beautifully maintained with immaculate lawns, each grave embellished with its own individual flowering shrub. My father's grave had a shrub with tiny yellow flowers on it, and I carefully picked a couple of them to press for a keepsake. It was midday when we arrived, and by that time, the sun was fierce. Even under the shade of my umbrella, within minutes, I was drenched in perspiration.

Michael left me to spend some time alone at the graveside. I found myself speaking softly to my father, telling him how sad I was not to have known him, and how sorry I was that he had suffered so terribly at the hands of the Japanese. I said that I was blessed to be able to forgive his captors. I then spoke about my childhood and subsequent marriage to Des, which led to my telling him about his grandchildren. I sobbed as I whispered the words, until I got to the present and was able to share the happiness that I now enjoyed with Michael. I felt my father's presence and peace, and at last, I found the closure I had so long sought for.

I had not long returned from one of my annual trips to South Africa, when I received word that Mum had an aneurism. I spoke to her doctor on the telephone, and he told me she probably wouldn't live more than a few days or weeks, so I hurriedly flew back. I stayed with Mum for three weeks, sleeping on a cot in her apartment at the retirement village.

We talked a lot, but not about the things that I so badly needed to discuss with her. Had she been willing, I could have told her that all was forgiven. But, as before, she refused to speak of the past.

While I was there, I sorted through her personal things, as I had for Sheila. Photographs and letters were either given to the people who she felt might want them or discarded. She made a new will for the little that was left, which gave her great peace of mind. Nursing Mum made me realize how vulnerable we are, and how fragile our lives become as we age. I like to believe that my visit had a positive effect on her, because by the time I left, Mum was looking much better.

A year later, on my next trip to South Africa, I discovered that Mum wasn't doing well. She told me that she didn't think she would live much longer, and after thanking me for all I had done for her over the years, like my sister, Sheila, she said I shouldn't return for her funeral.

I think I was the only one who saw how deep Mum's depression had become. In the past, when she complained that she didn't see much of my children, I had told her frankly on several occasions that no one wants to be around someone who continually complains. My children lightheartedly referred to her as the Old Moan Pot, and I couldn't blame them, but I believe that towards the end of her life, Mum realized that I was right, because she made an effort to put on a more cheerful face for them. Somehow, she never felt the necessity to do the same for me. She showed no interest in going anywhere, and even her favorite soaps on TV didn't appeal to her anymore. Thankfully, I was able to feel love and compassion for Mum, which I never quite understood, but for which I was grateful.

Back in Texas, I called Mum as often as I could, but once she moved out of her apartment into Glenhaven's Frail Care Center, I was only able to speak to her on Anne's cell phone, when she was there for a visit.

The last time I called, Anne told me that Mum was dying. She held her phone to Mum's ear, and I told her I loved her. Mum's speech was barely audible, but Anne told me that it sounded as if she was saying, "Love you," over and over again. Mum took her last breath at 5 p.m. South African time on January 24th 2004, barely five weeks after my return home. Anne said Mum looked peaceful at the end. She had reached the age of ninety when, as she put it, 'she climbed the golden staircase.'

I will always regret not being able to talk to my mother about my traumatic childhood, for her sake as much as mine, but I understand her reluctance to dig up the past, and I have forgiven her for everything. I just wish I could give her a hug and tell her I love her one more time.

HEALTHY SOLUTIONS

With Mum gone, Michael insisted that if he couldn't go with me, he would prefer that I not go alone to South Africa. He said he was concerned that the trips were both mentally and physically exhausting. My worsening back pain made it difficult for me to sit, and the two long plane rides were becoming increasingly painful, requiring weeks for me to recuperate. At the time, an MRI showed that I had three herniated discs. Surgery was recommended, but a successful outcome could not be guaranteed, so I declined. I was told to avoid bending and lifting heavy things, which is difficult for a homemaker.

As my health declined, I suffered a couple of anxiety attacks. Eventually, I was diagnosed with PTSD, and I went to see a psychologist. She told me that talking about the past was part of the healing process, but that it would take some time. She said that I was very fortunate to have married someone who was not anything like my stepfather or former husband. Apparently, it is rare, once established in that pattern as I had been throughout my life, that a woman is able to break the cycle of abuse. Most women who have been abused by their fathers as children, end up marrying the same type of man, and the pattern typically continues, even into second or third marriages. After breaking the pattern, I was able to discover many ways to help the healing process along.

I went for weekly visits with the psychologist for almost a year and found her advice to be helpful. She taught me how to replace negative thoughts with positive ones, which helped to form new pathways in my thinking patterns, and once it became a habit, the new paths made it easier to have positive thoughts. She was kind and gentle, and a good listener, which was just what I needed.

I found that caring for others through volunteer work enabled me to look outside myself and my own personal needs, which was important for staving off self-pity and depression. Gentle exercise, such as walking or bicycling, and a healthy diet were also helpful. I also found classical music to be a great comfort, even up to the present day.

Friendships have been a vital contribution to my healing, and as I look back over the years, I appreciate all my dear friends, too numerous to mention, who have supported me through both the good times and bad. Some have passed away, while others are still present in my life. Even as I write, I know I can call on those still present anytime and they will be there for me. Friends are one of life's greatest gifts, and my long-standing friendship of almost seventy years with my dear, gentle schoolfriend, June, will always stand out as the greatest example of a true friend. She has remained faithful to me throughout my life, and I will always be grateful for her unconditional love and loyal friendship.

There are many types of therapy available now, and it is worth investigating which is best for you as we are all different and what may help for one person may not help for another. I have also found that my needs have changed over the years but by listening to my body and my physician, I have been able to discover which is the most beneficial for me at the time.

Doreen with her school friend, June, during a visit to Italy in 2007

MAMA AND MICHAEL

One early spring morning, Michael went out to mow the lawn, and after about ten minutes, he came in looking gray, and he was completely out of breath. Admittedly, it was the first time he had mowed in several months as the lawn had been dormant throughout the winter, but Michael had always been fit and tiring so quickly was highly unusual. I told him to let the lawn go, but after a few minutes, he felt better and resumed mowing. Ten minutes later, the same thing happened, and I insisted that he stop. Something was seriously wrong!

A call to Michael's doctor the next day, led to his seeing a heart specialist, who scheduled a stress test for the end of the week. After returning to the cardiologist for more tests, they discovered that Michael was in urgent need of bypass surgery.

We were due to fly to England the following week, and Michael asked the heart surgeon if he could postpone the surgery until after our planned trip. The surgeon smiled, and told him he wasn't even going home, let alone to England. Michael was kept in hospital overnight, and the surgery was performed early the next morning.

Seeing Michael in intensive care was frightening for me. He was full of tubes and unable to speak. I held his hand, and he gripped mine so hard, that I winced in pain. He looked at me with a wild look in his eyes, pleading with me, while trying to tell me something, but I had no idea what it was. It turned out that the air tube in his mouth made him want to cough, but he wasn't able to tell me. Everything I suggested that might be the problem only made him more frustrated. His wrists were tied to the sides of the gurney to prevent him from pulling the tubes out while he was sedated. This meant that he couldn't even write a note to tell me what was wrong. Feeling utterly helpless, I was close to tears the whole time I was there. Michael obviously needed something urgently, and I wasn't able to help him.

Even calling the nurse didn't help, as she made it clear that he had been made as comfortable as possible. Later, when the tube was removed, Michael was in a position to tell the nurse that the angle of the tube in his mouth was causing him to gag. He needed his hand free to be able to hold it down to prevent it from causing the uncomfortable coughing spasms he was experiencing, which were terribly painful considering that he had just had open chest surgery.

Therapy and daily walks followed the surgery, and gradually, Michael regained his strength. A visit to the cardiologist a month after surgery showed that all was well, and the doctor gave Michael permission to return to Mason the following week, but only to supervise the carpenters. Unable to do the work himself was not easy for Michael, but he understood that he had to be careful, and he was.

After Mama broke her leg and found her eyesight to be failing, she had to accept that she could no longer live alone. Driving had become problematic, and I sympathized with her, knowing how much she valued her independence. We drove up to see her and discussed the prospect of her moving to an assisted living facility in Dallas, where her daughter lived. It was conveniently situated near hospitals and doctors, where she could receive the injections she regularly needed in her eyes.

Mama moved into an apartment in the facility, and with her positive attitude, she made friends easily. Several other family members lived close by, and as we lived only a few hours' drive away, we were able to visit her regularly. She stayed there quite happily until they had problems with the food preparation, resulting in frequent stomach illnesses among the residents. This often caused the kitchen to be closed, preventing the residents from eating together in the dining room, which Mama, being social, missed. She was sick a few times, but after taking a course of antibiotics, she quickly recovered.

In late August of 2010. Mama became ill once again, and was taken to hospital where antibiotics were administered, but she was already too weak to respond. From there, she was moved to a nursing home. We drove up to see her every weekend, and I watched her getting progressively weaker. It broke my heart to see such a feisty little lady losing her will to live. The room was dark and depressing and the last time we went, I suggested that she might like to go outside. Mama was eager to go out into the yard and brightened up considerably while she was out in the fresh air, which gave me hope.

Unable to eat the nursing home food, which was bland and unappetizing, Mama was living on vitamin protein shakes, which upset her stomach, causing her to lose weight. Because of this, I could sense her urgent need to leave the nursing home, and after discussing it with Michael, I asked Mama if she would like to move to a nursing home in Bryan. We knew of one close to our home, and I told her that if she moved in there, I would then be able to cook for her, and she would surely become strong again, and then she would be able to live with us.

Mama said that sounded wonderful, but sadly, we were denied the opportunity to make it happen. Five days later, Mama died at the age of ninety-nine. She had so much looked forward to celebrating her 100th birthday, and as she had always been in excellent health, we were sure she would easily reach her goal. But it was not to be, and I was devastated when she died.

A week later, we attended Mama's funeral in Dallas and the next morning, we drove to Brownwood for her burial service in the cemetery with Michael's father and the rest of his parents' families. I was going to miss her visits. She had become my role model, always positive, interesting, and genuinely interested in everything we did. She almost always ended our phone calls by saying, "Doreen, I love you for calling." She had the ability to make me feel special and loved, and I felt that my calls were also important to her. I was sad that Mama never got to see the Mason house finished, and I still miss her.

We were close to finishing the Mason house, and in the months that followed, Michael and I attended the fiftieth reunion of his college graduation and a few retirement parties. Nostalgia was setting in as we accepted that we were soon to leave Bryan/College Station, the University town that had been a part of Michael's life for the past fifty years. We received many farewell invitations, and the realization that we were soon to leave became a startling reality.

In June of 2011, we moved to Mason. After twenty years of moving between Pretoria and Bryan, with extended stays in Italy, we were home at last. It had taken us nine years to make the house livable. Having spent our summers in Mason, plus numerous weekends, we had grown to love the town and the community, so it wasn't a difficult transition, in spite of our having to leave many close friends and neighbors in Bryan. We had attended the local Methodist church while working on the house, so joining it was the natural thing to do, and we were delighted to become part of such a warm and welcoming church family.

We soon found that living in Mason was even better than we could have anticipated. The people were friendly, welcoming and caring towards one another and it was not long before we were both involved in volunteer work, where we discovered the many reasons for the town's reputation as a great place to live.

MY ULTIMATE HEALING

How my life has changed and improved. Now, when I awake in the mornings, I am overjoyed to be able to spend another day with Michael. We have celebrated more than thirty years of marriage, and have been blessed with an abundance of love and laughter. We have never tried to change each other. We have never had to. Michael is, for me, the perfect husband, my best friend and confidante. The laughter I heard so many years ago at the auction regularly fills our home, and I enjoy his quick wit. I love hearing his hearty laugh, which encourages me to say things that I know he will find amusing. As a result, my sense of humor that was suppressed for so long, is thriving again. After sharing our early morning thoughts, I love being told, "Okay, you lazy heifer, get your lazy bones out of this bed." It is a happy start to my day.

I also find it stimulating to live with someone who is both interesting and intelligent. Michael has every right to be proud, but he is truly humble. He is forgiving, honorable, and faithful, and I know I could trust him with my life. When a decision has to be made, we discuss it together, and because no two people think exactly alike, both of us have learned to compromise.

When I first started writing this book, I wrote in the third person. Michael read through a few pages, and pointed this out. I wondered why I had done that, until it occurred to me that by distancing myself, it was less painful to write about my past. When I re-wrote it in first person, I was in a better position to deal with my pain, as nothing is quite as raw the second time around. Michael also encouraged me to write in a conversational manner, revealing my feelings and emotions. Each time I went back and edited the manuscript, I was able to reveal more until, eventually, when everything was written down, I was released from the burden of carrying it in my heart.

While reliving my childhood, I saw a hurting, angry little girl, one who I never much liked or understood at the time, but in writing about it, I discovered a greater understanding and compassion for the little girl who was me. For years, I had literally buried her along with all the other many bad memories, but now, at last, I am able to love her!

Writing about my life as an adult has enabled me to see many things more clearly. In the beginning, I found it almost impossible to sleep as my thoughts demanded to be heard and recorded. Painful, deep-seated memories I had not allowed myself to confront for years, buried deep in my past, re-surfaced, and I was amazed to find that they were all still there. While facing one, I found many others tumbling over one another, rather like clothes falling out of a dryer when the door is opened prematurely. Sorting and folding them into some kind of order was time-consuming, but when I was finished, the result was both satisfying and rewarding.

Pain and suffering are a part of life. We should, therefore, appreciate them because they make us who we are, while at the same time making us stronger. But this is easier done in hindsight than in the moment. Through my lifetime of experience, I was given love and forgiveness, which I am now able to extend to the people who hurt me and, in the process, I have also been blessed with an abundance of empathy and tolerance for people who are different from me, and I am grateful for these gifts.

I know that our genes alone do not define our character, or who we are. Our circumstances, as well as our experiences, family, friends, environment and most importantly, our faith, are what shape us in whatever manner we allow them to. I believe I chose the right path for me, which led me to become the person I am now, someone I can love and respect.

As I reach the final weeks of this writing, my health continues to be a problem. Post-Traumatic Stress Disorder is not something that ever goes away. Some people who suffer from PTSD have earned it through life's most challenging circumstances, sometimes voluntarily, and sometimes by having it thrust upon them. Many of us don't want to admit to having it because we fear that it may be perceived as a weakness, but if we have the courage to face it, we are able to deal with it. It is my hope that understanding my own health issues and the subsequent ways of dealing with them that I describe in this book will prove useful to others. I believe it is because of everything I have been through, that I am able to appreciate what I have now, and appreciation is another of life's great gifts.

In spite of the several occasions when I was about to give up out of sheer exhaustion, I was blessed with the strength to stay in my previous marriage. I hope that anyone reading this book who is experiencing abuse, whether mental or physical, will see that if I, after living with injustice and cruelty for almost fifty years, have been able to find peace and happiness, then surely anyone can. Staying in a difficult marriage isn't always the right thing to do, but it was right for me. We each have to seek our own destiny. I was fortunate that it all came out right for me in the end.

Michael and I continue to live an idyllic life. Our wonderful marriage is built on love, trust, and mutual respect, and we have never had to work at our marriage, as some people suggest. We are never bored, and we live each day to the full, content to be together, and I still feel my eyes shine when he looks at me with so much love in his.

All those difficult years were made bearable by God's blessing of hope, which I never lost. I wish the same wonderful outcome that I have enjoyed to anyone who has suffered the injustice and heartache of physical or mental abuse.

Today I have another wisteria growing over the arbor entry to our front porch, with its perfume wafting through the house each spring, but this time, it's not there to serve as an escape route as it did when I was a child. Its branches are intertwined, much like our two lives. Michael says that although this is now the late fall of our lives, it will always be springtime in our hearts.

Michael and Doreen, the happy ending!

www.ingramcontent.com/pod-product-compliance
Lightning Source LLC
Chambersburg PA
CBHW070455120526
44590CB00013B/648